# Embattled America

# Embattled America

*The Rise of Anti-politics and America's Obsession with Religion*

JASON C. BIVINS

**OXFORD**
UNIVERSITY PRESS

Oxford University Press is a department of the University of Oxford. It furthers the University's objective of excellence in research, scholarship, and education by publishing worldwide. Oxford is a registered trade mark of Oxford University Press in the UK and certain other countries.

Published in the United States of America by Oxford University Press
198 Madison Avenue, New York, NY 10016, United States of America.

© Oxford University Press 2022

All rights reserved. No part of this publication may be reproduced, stored in a retrieval system, or transmitted, in any form or by any means, without the prior permission in writing of Oxford University Press, or as expressly permitted by law, by license, or under terms agreed with the appropriate reproduction rights organization. Inquiries concerning reproduction outside the scope of the above should be sent to the Rights Department, Oxford University Press, at the address above.

You must not circulate this work in any other form
and you must impose this same condition on any acquirer.

Library of Congress Control Number: 2021953510

ISBN 978-0-19-762350-3

DOI: 10.1093/oso/9780197623503.001.0001

1 3 5 7 9 8 6 4 2

Printed by Sheridan Books, Inc., United States of America

*For Nina, more than ever*

# Contents

*Acknowledgments*   ix

1. Changing the Subject: The Lost Opportunities of Embattled Religion   1
2. A Brief History of Persecution Complexes in America   23
3. The Whirl: Virus, Narrative, and Noise   49
4. Worrying about Scars: Glenn Beck and Authenticity   63
5. The Dropouts: Sarah Palin, Rick Perry, and the Failures of Representation   88
6. An Unattained Goal: The Tea Party and the Problems of Public Action   116
7. The Pearls and the Coral: David Barton and the Burdens of History   141
8. Law as Winning: Anti-sharia Legislation and Democratic Self-Inventory   165
9. Locked and Loaded: On Birth, Death, Guns, and Citizenship   189
10. How to Be an American: An Address to Citizens   214

*Notes*   243
*Bibliography*   295
*Index*   331

# Acknowledgments

This book has had an unusual life. I began writing it soon after the publication of *Religion of Fear* in 2008. I worked on it for two or three years. But I turned to a different project, for, despite the urgency of my concerns for American democracy, the world felt safer then. When I returned to this book after the jarring events of 2016, I had no way of knowing just how steadily and exhaustingly worse everything would get in such a short time. And yet it has. Never more so than in 2020, when this book and thousands of others got put on pause because of a pandemic.

As I watched the world burn, reworking the manuscript later that year and into the crazed first months of 2021, I reevaluated the process of my thinking during this book's life span. After Trump was elected, I reconceptualized most of what I had begun just after Obama's first election. I changed the book's tone and purpose. You will see in the pages that follow that I have written against both distraction and despair. I have needed to do that for personal reasons, to keep my heart right and not go blind with rage. For those reasons, my debts to others are unusually deep as well.

A number of invitations to write gave me the best opportunities to think through my arguments. I am grateful to Ed Blum, Finbarr Curtis, Josh Dubler, Phil Goff, Cooper Harriss, Paul Harvey, Amir Hussain, Henry Jenkins, Sarah Imhoff, Charles Lippy, Brian Pennington, Isaac Weiner, and Peter Williams. The Conversation, Religion Dispatches, Religion in American History, The Immanent Frame, and the University of Chicago's Religion and Culture Forum have graciously allowed me to explore online. I am especially grateful to Evan Derkacz and Lisa Webster at RD, and to my friend Jonathan van Antwerpen, who encouraged me to think as broadly as I'd like at TIF. Thanks also to everyone at The Great Courses, especially Walter Jacob, for the opportunity to teach, which really energized a new round of thinking about this book.

I thank the following institutions, and my faculty hosts, for inviting me to explore this research over its long gestation: Appalachian State University, Augustana College, Duke University Department of Religion and Law School, Elon University, Haverford College, Indiana University,

Northeastern University, Northwestern University, Swarthmore College, University of Colorado–Boulder, University of Colorado–Colorado Springs, University of North Carolina–Chapel Hill, University of North Carolina–Charlotte, University of North Florida, University of Rochester, University of Texas–Austin, and Yale University.

I continue to benefit immensely from the generosity and brilliance of my friends and colleagues in the academy. For asking such good questions about parts or all of what's in these pages, I am grateful to Tariq Al-Jamil, Mike Altman, Kelly J. Baker, Ann Burlein, Chip Callahan, Jay Cameron Carter, Ipsita Chatterjea, Ira Chernus, Yvonne Chireau, Brian Collins, Matt Cressler, Brandi Denison, Spencer Dew, Darren Dochuk, Seth Dowland, Tracy Fessenden, Constance Furey, Megan Goodwin, Jen Graber, Rosalind Hackett, Paul Harvey, Stewart Hoover, Beth Hurd, Jeff Isaac, Richard Jaffe, Greg Johnson, Jessica Johnson, Sylvester Johnson, Michael Lienesch, Katie Lofton, Chris Lundberg, Laurie Maffly-Kipp, Lerone Martin, Sean McCloud, Russ McCutcheon, Maurice Meilleur, John Modern, David Morgan, Kristi Nabhan-Warren, Anthony Petro, Sarah Pike, Chad Seales, Jozef Sorrett, Francis Stewart, Randall Styers, Winni Sullivan, Jenna Supp-Montgomerie, Matt Sutton, Jolyon Thomas, Tom Tweed, David Watt, Judith Weisenfeld, Tisa Wenger, Deb Whitehead, Melissa Wilcox, and Joe Winters. Last but always first is Bob Orsi, main man and dearest of friends.

My colleagues and students at North Carolina State University continue to blow me away with their smarts, energy, and conviction. As always, thanks to my extraordinary colleagues Bill Adler, Anna Bigelow, Mary Kath Cunningham, Kathy Foody, Karey Harwood, Levi McLaughlin, and Xavier Pickett. Few are as lucky as I to have such amazing folks to work with. This book in particular has benefited immensely from conversations with NCSU colleagues outside my discipline, especially with David Ambaras, Steve Ferguson, Tim Hinton, Brent Sirota, Mary Tjiattas, Ken Zagacki, and David Zonderman. Boundless thanks, too, to Joanna King, Michael Pendlebury, Ken Peters, and Ann Rives for your patience with me and for pretending to laugh at my jokes. Thanks especially to Michael for helping me to get time off to complete the work. As an early draft came together, I was lucky to have a transcendentally great group of students in my 2018 Religion and Politics seminar. Your remarkable openness, intelligence, and moral clarity through many episodes of American madness was transformative for me. I thank in particular Morgan Barbre, Nick Billman, Brooke Ramsey, and Nick Zanzot.

It is also with great satisfaction and gratitude that I reflect on my continued relationship with all the fine folks at Oxford, especially my dear friend and longtime editor Cynthia Read. As ever, I'm grateful for the support and even more so for all the lovely talks and laughs over the years.

A wounded world clarifies the value of all that we hold dear, with none of that richer than the friends and loved ones that keep us grounded. The thanks I owe to Dr. Katherine Prakken is inestimable. To all my friends in bands and on fields and from schools, especially my expansive, beautiful, brilliant Saturday Zoom crew: yeah, we got the PMA. Special shouts to my oldest and bestest pals, my trio of brothers and our unbroken bond down the years: James Bell, Ted Leventhal, and Hans Spencer. Through them and others I have understood how broad and fluid a category family is. Challenges bring clarity, some of it bruised.

And so, at last, to Nina, to whom my bruises don't matter. And whose bruises I adore. Nothing I could write here is remotely sufficient, my love, to describe what you mean to me. I would need a new language made from stars and dog licks and gummy bears, and even that would be just a start. I'm working on it.

Bull City, October 2021

# 1
# Changing the Subject

## The Lost Opportunities of Embattled Religion

> The last shall be first.
> 
> —Matthew 20:16

If you could see America from above, through contrails and clouds, what might you learn about the country's concerns? Down there is a black man in a football uniform, taking the knee in a stadium. There is a suburban mother inveighing against a supposed war on a Christian holiday. And in Washington, DC, the Capitol is breached by a fevered crowd of white people who deny the result of a legitimate election and the reality of a pandemic. All the while, Americans by the millions curate social media profiles and seek to live their "best lives," documenting their latest quarantine meal or live-streaming their rage.

There is no equivalency between these instances of rage and protest—the state-sanctioned violence that Colin Kaepernick protests is real, while the "war on Christmas" is not—the common texture of American life is a sense of being unfairly persecuted or embattled by a disproportionately powerful minority out to undermine the American way of life. This is a claim with deep historical roots, but it has grown inflamed since the 1960s, when Embattlement began to move steadily to the center of American life.

Look closer, and see what makes up this America. Things move fast, outrage at the velocity of a tweet. Amid the big squeeze—swollen corporate power, recrudescent white rage, poisoned air and water—Americans want desperately to live a life of glory and purpose, which displaces these same Americans' deep anxiety about the future. Steady work and comfort are not guaranteed, so citizens drift into dreams of making it big with a podcast or a food truck or an armed militia. The dark energy fueling this drift is the certitude offered by the outlandish: the familiar exaggerations of social media, ranging from conspiracy theories without number to the refrain that Christianity is under assault.

Legions of pundits have pointed out the unreality of claims of persecution coming from largely comfortable white conservative Christians. Scholars have glanced at such notions amid the tide of books about the "culture wars." America is mired in debates about the "character" of Trump voters, made even more urgent by the Covid-19 pandemic, the unsettling opposition to medical science, and the January 2021 insurrection. But I believe that most approaches to this subject have it backward: the much-ballyhooed Christian nationalism of our time is the product of multiple forces, but it is not the key to understanding the roots of the many problems bedeviling America, nor should it be the main vector of analysis for those concerned about American democracy. This book tells a different story about how America became so broken. Instead of asking, "Why are evangelicals this way?" this book asks, "What has happened in America to enable such fearful changes?" The decades-old echo chamber of white conservative grievance and its debunkers is, I contend, a distraction from the urgent need to reassess what it means to live in a democracy. I hope that this story about how things have gotten so dire in American politics might show a path to how things get better.

## How We Got Here

I started this book in 2009, a geologic age ago in American politics. After I decided to write a book about music, and after the world changed, I came back to this book with very different motivations. *Embattled America* is my third engagement with the religio-political discontent that has only expanded since the 1960s. Beginning in the 1990s I have been concerned about democracy's weakening legitimacy. In *The Fracture of Good Order*, I argued that political religions might be better understood by focusing on their relation to key elements of political liberalism: individualist conceptions of citizenship, a clear separation between the public and private realms, the priority of negative liberty over agonistic participation in public life, and the constraint of certain kinds of speech and action in the realm of the political.

By the mid-2000s, I had grown concerned as both citizen and scholar that something else was taking shape and that American politics was being hollowed out through the resurgence of older forms of demonization and conspiracy thinking. *Religion of Fear* documented the role of popular entertainments in cementing religio-political resentments of difference. Not only did such entertainments reflect the familiar conservative refrain that government and politics are the enemy, but they also revealed a steady march of once-marginal ideas to the political center.

The growing normalization of religious fear has shown no signs of ending. It has made for a disturbing parallel to (and energizer of) other trends in American politics: the rise of political violence, the contempt for democracy itself, and a stunning panoply of conspiracy theories, all vivid signs of the distance between Americans' visions of themselves and how they actually interact with each other. One of the most public and provocative expressions of these trends is seen in conservative complaints about religious "persecution." I am interested not only in why different groups claim to represent the majority while at the same time claiming the mantle of the persecuted, the Embattled; I also want to document, in what is effectively a prehistory of the Trump era, how outraged attention to these claims has helped lower the guardrails of American democracy.

The claims themselves are widely discussed.[1] For every indignant complaint one encounters on Fox News or the Christian Broadcasting Network or from a Freedom Caucus Republican, there is a snarky dismissal from Bill Maher, Sam Harris, or another liberal wag. The daily news cycle reveals how central this language has become to American politics, to the point of refusing to wear masks during a pandemic and armed white men (and some women) storming the Capitol, so certain are those involved that freedom faces extinction. Focus groups, *New York Times* editorials, and news broadcasts continue to ponder the unwavering support bestowed on Trump by white evangelicals.[2] At an October 2019 rally in Greenville, North Carolina, Franklin Graham reassured a crowd of supporters that the congressional impeachment inquiry was bogus and that Trump would continue to fight for them despite his many critics.[3] Vice President Mike Pence energetically stoked the Christian victimology, warning an American Legion audience in August 2019 that Obama had banned Christmas carols at VA hospitals.[4] Christian Right stalwart Ralph Reed's 2020 book, *For God and Country*, said that no right-thinking Christian should fail to support Trump.[5] Liberty University and Turning Point USA (whose mission is to expose alleged secularist bias on college campuses) recently founded a think tank intended to "play offense against the secular Left."[6] And while Trump ascended politically through complaints about his own victimhood, he also cannily shored up his support with claims like "They're not after me, they're after you."[7]

There is, of course, considerable complexity and variety in American politics, including in conservatism, progressivism, and Christianity. Why has this complexity been largely drowned out by those claiming to be persecuted for their religion on the one hand and by those who ridicule and revile them on the other? This book engages that question out of concern for American democracy itself, which is poorly served by an obsession with the fantastical claims of Embattled America. The meanings of these loud protestations of Embattlement require not only a careful diagnosis of the way different groups talk about and act on them; more than this, if Americans wish to get beyond the power of such claims, it is imperative to understand how they function, and why they are persuasive to so many.

## How We Talk

Americans have always been angry. From the excitable print cultures of the colonial era to the voluble radio shows of the early twentieth, from the nightly news to the Twitterverse, American rage has always sought a newer, louder megaphone.[8] Public life is shaped by conflicts emanating from deep in America's many pasts: debates about the reach and legitimacy of the state; anti-intellectualism and paranoia; and the interplay of race, religion, and power. Yet for several decades such considerations have been displaced by steadily louder mass-mediated emotions.[9] Apocalyptic thought, conspiracy theory, and belligerent patriotism trade molecules in a cultural context made from emotional hyperbole and "gotcha!" exposure in journalism, social media, and elections alike. Perhaps more significantly, for half a century, large numbers of politicians, popular entertainments, and religious voices have pronounced that politics is useless, voting is irrelevant, and the wreck is going down. For citizens faced with greater uncertainty about the future, living amid the steady discrediting of political norms and institutions, and overwhelmed by public animosity, Embattlement is a convenient narrative for making sense of American decline.

In an atmosphere thick with despair, moral outrage actually works to preserve the bloated carcass of American public life. Opposing viewpoints are converted into eschatological portents, historical perversions, evidence of sinister plots, or deviations from moral true north. It lingers on, this cloud of outrages, a context so enveloping that its edges cannot be seen. It echoes endlessly, its source lost amid the clangor, with shouts of anger and whispers of conspiracy seeming to come at us as from nowhere, their sonic number America's shared politics. Decades pass but the fog of enemies never dissipates, always gathering in number and intensity to rain down new panics. This growth, this continuity, is made possible not only by the succession of outrages but by repetition, volume, and the technological force of what I call the *Whirl*.

This vertiginous Whirl of information is a powerful vector for spleen and confirmation bias, because the limits of human cognition demand that we employ filters to navigate the overwhelming sea of data in which we all swim.[10] We now know that, despite the availability of all the world's information, attempts to disprove or fact-check or contextualize claims of Embattlement not only rarely work, but may be counterproductive because independent knowledge has been so thoroughly discredited. Pointing out examples of bad history or trying to shame people out of their false consciousness—strategies I call *Gotcha! Epistemology*—are interpreted as further evidence of Embattlement. What matters, then, is not whether any particular controversy lasts beyond the current election cycle or tweetstorm, but how America became a place where such eruptions are not just possible but likely.

*Embattled America* holds that the ascension of persecution and victimization claims among religious conservatives since the 1960s, and the legions of indignant detractors they generate, reveal that one of America's most recognizable expressions of grievance actually sustains the very conditions it laments. Broadly speaking, two public conversations about "religion," which share revealing groups of similarities, have made more impact than others. The largest, loudest voice is that of the group I call the "Martyrs," who frame themselves as the righteous victims of a "religious bigotry." Shaped largely by institutionally powerful, richly funded speakers—from media personalities like Glenn Beck to politicians like Mike Pence—Martyrs decry what they feel is an unjust marginalization of Christians from public life by secular liberals who oppose America's Christian legacy. The implication for public life is grave, since Martyrs often claim that simply being made aware of difference is a kind of assault. The very existence of difference leads to tangible suffering. The discourse of the Martyrs has since the 1960s moved steadily to the center of conservative politics, accruing social capital precisely through decrying the lack of it. The opposing discourse comes from those I call "Whistleblowers," whose media expressions—ranging from websites like Salon to theophobic texts by the "new atheists"—have sought to "blow the whistle" on evangelicals said to be seeking theocratic rule.[11] Whistleblowers contend, often with high-minded disdain, that the very public presence of conservative religion is a code red for America. The tone of their allegations—enraged, panicked, dismissive, snarky—has grown more strident as conservative Christianity has ascended since the Reagan era.

Both groups see themselves as an Embattled Majority, as representatives of the "real" America, unfairly victimized by zealots. Each advances their criticisms of the other in fearful rhetoric built around highly charged depictions of religion. To Martyrs, religion—which they define as a providential, politically and theologically conservative Christianity—is firmly rooted and evident in a steady march of American righteousness that spans the roughly four centuries between John Winthrop and the "war on terror."[12] A central index of patriotism and good citizenship, religion here is not only a central part of the political process but a force of cohesion, a foundation that undergirds social virtue, a barometer by which the nation's health is measured. On this account, the growth of religious and political pluralism chronicles both an unprecedented corruption of this religion's flourishing—a claim Martyrs bolster with familiar assertions about an activist judiciary, the secularization of public life, and so forth—and a call to reassert the proper power of religion by rolling back the forces of "religious bigotry."

To Whistleblowers, religion is not reliably benevolent but instead often dangerous. For them, religion is not what has been corrupted (though there is a sense that religion is okay if thoroughly privatized and/or consistently progressive) but rather what undermines the secular, rational character of American ideals and procedures.[13] Religion represents to them a dangerous return of the Enlightenment's repressed other, a puritanical pre-echo of the real American history that began with philosopher kings in Philadelphia.[14]

Both Martyrs and Whistleblowers define religion using shared images (the wall of separation or the wall of oppression), legal norms (free exercise or religious overreach), and justifications (rights or excessive burdens). Each vision is shaped by the political exhaustion and disenchantment of post-1960s American life. Both discourses insist that an undeserving minority is getting away with something, and that this creates a state of exception in American politics. Convinced of this, both rely on hyperbolic oppositional imagery depicting an America where two monolithic forces duke it out in a Boss Battle for the American soul.

This condition can't be understood by relying on the familiar dualism of conservatives and liberals, not only because these standard ideological classifications fail to capture the emotion of the claims, grounded in protestations of suffering and historical drama; the old terms are also misleading, given that they are the product of a political history whose lack of legitimacy is precisely what fuels Embattlement. It is similarly unhelpful to define Martyrs by the fact that most are evangelicals.[15] My analysis has less to do with evangelicalism itself than with focusing on the combustibility of "religion" in order to understand larger transformations in American public life. The ongoing investment of outrage in white evangelical persecution complexes impedes our adjustment to those same transformations. Embattlement is thus crucially important, but not for the reasons Martyrs or Whistleblowers think.

In constructing this narrative around a duality, I am not seeking to mimic "culture wars" analysis. But the shared sense among different Americans that this *is* a truthful formula merits further scrutiny, not because it reveals independent value-sets that are irrevocably conflictual; rather, Embattlement's controversies are carefully produced and managed to distract from more productive political activity. What we see, then, is that in conceding the centrality of religion to contemporary acrimony we are getting in our own way politically.

I think we should try a different approach, and try ignoring this particular genre of grievance in favor of talking more about these other categories and problems. It may seem strange or even self-defeating for a scholar of religion to argue that talking about religion is unproductive. But I make this claim only with regard to Embattlement claims, not about religious petitions for human rights, debates about justice, or acts of mercy. Self-righteous critique of Embattlement only gives life to Embattlement's narrative, which already occupies too much real estate in American life; we would be better off tabling this entire conversation as a practical matter of removing oxygen from a conflagration. Without this narrative of convenience, Americans might be able to turn to the issues necessary for democracy's survival. So, in an especially dark moment of American life, *Embattled America* is a story of bruised hope that in the lost opportunities that have led us to the Trump era, we might yet find a path forward.

## The Burden of Being American

Let me explain a bit more about why I take this approach. The distressed state of American life is obvious. The fractious final year of the Trump presidency revealed only some of the most obvious and enduring contours of this condition. I remain unconvinced, however, by most readings of the religio-political antagonism that sits at the heart of it all. Embattlement is not merely about demographic shifts, or fealty to "tradition" (the basis for James Davison Hunter's well-known work on "culture wars").[16] More than any of this, Americans are feeling the squeeze of a political architecture that was already under strain from the rapid growth of nineteenth-century mass democracy; with the pressures of postindustrial informational "democracy" and the corporatization of public life, Americans are caught between the recognition that the fractures are features rather than bugs of our politics, and the refusal to begin difficult systemic change.[17]

As fury ratchets up, as new norms are trampled daily, as racial and religious atavisms are exhumed, it is fair to wonder in the face of wheezing democracy if this is all a great political beta-test designed by an otiose god. There is no right relation to religion that will be our way out of this moment. To focus only on conservatives who protest against "religious bigotry," or even to hope with good reason for the amplification of other religious voices, is to misconstrue the condition: we have not come to grips with our ambivalent attachments to democracy itself. Martyrs speak the language of gaining seats at the table, of injecting conservative religious voices into the conversation, of wanting the right to participate or strut, maskless, in public space. Yet they reproduce in their petitions the vulnerability and instability built into democratic politics. Whistleblowers claim to channel a Madisonian fear of public enthusiasm, of rabid minoritarianism (which professes majoritarianism), in the name of order and rationality. Yet they reproduce in their opposition to conservative religion the exclusions of narrowly construed liberal democratic politics. They portray religion as both too powerful *and* too vulnerable for public life, and thus doubly inauthentic. The condition sustained by such claims is exacerbated by America's abundance of rage and therapeutic discourse alike, which work together to deflect the fear that our lives lack significance and that America has failed at democracy.[18] Embattlement may liven up a narrative, but it directs us away from deeper sources of political discontent.

Of course, democracy depends on complaint, on repeated petitions for the expansion of publics and rights. But the hypertrophy of anger and offense marks something different, for they do not engage the commons in order to reshape it, but rather spew bile in the face of those who think and live differently. This nonprincipled refusal to accept our fellow citizens' difference is an awfully big arterial block in the body politic. More than this, the very idea that public life might demand accommodations from us, that our self-interest must be constrained, is perhaps what many Americans find most vexing of all.

There is a very real sense in which nothing can now be heard in American life unless it speaks the language of outrage. Martyrs and Whistleblowers are master practitioners of this language, and have used it to rewire the way Americans think about religion and politics. Terms like "culture wars" explain away the complexity of this rewiring. Such images or formulations do the thinking for us. To focus only on the religion that Embattled Americans *tell us* is central is not only to ignore the makings of our moment, but to accept the conceptual givens of public discourse rather than try to recast them. I find more useful explanations in the American love for sensation and spectacle, the seductions of conspiracy theory, and the addiction to technologies of self-creation, which collectively work to displace more politically productive reflection and practice. What is striking, though, is that Embattlement lives not only in the margins or the sub-Reddits of crackpottery but expresses itself also through the star-spangled desire to *make it*.[19] Embattlement gives you cred.

None of this simply arrived on the doorstep in 2016 or 2020. Trump and Embattled religion are the natural products of a corporatist politics whose chief product is a restlessness that sends us, raging, to the action movie of our collective imagining. The very desire to bring the system down—the institutional system and the imaginal system—is often a byproduct of the hypercapitalism that masks itself as American democracy, where our hunger for the continual new, for the upgrade, distracts our attention from the foundational elements that protect democracies. The January 2021 insurrection was inevitable, with its apoplectic whiteness, "Don't Tread on Me" merch, and AR-15s, screeching about taxation and tyranny. Beyond this rage, the superfluity of technology and social media so binds us to the apocalyptic/therapeutic—the inescapable ☹/☺—that to abandon this mode of self-definition is perhaps to abandon the self. So Embattlement is felt to be a necessary mode of outrage, even as it confirms the triumph of anti-politics.

I am interested, then, in the conceptual tectonic plates moving behind Embattlement.

To map this out, I have harvested from the Obama and Trump eras, the time of peak Whirl and peak Embattlement, a series of instructional episodes revealing the expectations that Americans have of elements central to democratic life: through Glenn Beck's controversial emotionality we find a desire that *authenticity* be unencumbered by other persons; examining evangelical presidential candidates like Sarah Palin, we see that Americans often mistake mimicry for political *representation*; in David Barton's pseudohistory is a larger assumption that *history* tells people their own story and mutes others'; in the story of the Tea Party, we discover that many Americans expect *public life* to be an arena for antistatist lament, rather than the crafting of inclusive civic identities; in examining proposals for legislation outlawing sharia law, we find that collective assumptions that law is meant for communitarian ends propel *law's circularity regarding religion* rather than resolving it; and in sensational claims about Barack Obama's birth certificate and religion, we find that Americans have been conditioned to avoid rethinking *what American citizens are entitled to*.

The furious assertion of Martyr religion in each case was met with an equally furious Whistleblower backlash. Because these are fantasies that assuage feelings of fragility and insignificance, it is not hard to reason that Embattlement is a distraction from the structural forces producing these feelings. I am not suggesting that Americans no longer employ recognizable political first principles in our public speech. But terms like individual liberty, fairness, and freedom of religion, in all of their colossal vagueness, are often invoked to exempt ourselves from the responsibilities of citizenship, from care for the poor to social distancing. With the Whirl and a jobless future and all those other people who intrude on the digital worlds we make to distract ourselves from the dehumanizing morass we have made, the mere declamation of political ideals cannot change the fact that in America today, showy emotionalism holds greater appeal than the purposive action many claim to want.

At a moment when Americans should be reassessing norms and foundations, America has obsessed about religion, often understood as simultaneously special and outrageous, to sustain a condition defined by acrimony and by the lure of harmony without cost.[20] This preoccupation with religion has deep historical roots, flowing from a national self-consciousness that at times borders on solipsism, so dependent is America's self-image on the narrative of, variably, the lively experiment of religious pluralism or the ongoing sacred history begun providentially at Plymouth. Yet this obsession, investing eagerly in manufactured outrage, rarely considers the constancy of religious violence in American history, from repeated attempts to extinguish whole groups of persons to the episodic use of power (legal and otherwise) to constrain religious otherness or to suppress the galvanizing force of religious protests.²¹

In a culture bloated by self-congratulation and inattentive to its own historical makings, it is perhaps little surprise that principled critique is regularly framed as antithetical to the good order. American suspicion of institutional power collapses instead into total apathy or apocalyptic fright. While many Americans use prophetic language to spur collective action, it has proven far more seductive for many others to cosplay some cinematically brave freedom fighter, waiting for signs of government tyranny that must be resisted. Stock your basement with canned goods. Wait for the jackbooted thugs to come for the modified AR-15s in your gun closet. Convert your savings to cash, so as to outlast the collapse of the paperless economy. Strap a bazooka to your back to protest masks during a pandemic.²² But by no means should you rethink yourself or your country.

## Victims and Killers

The enthusiasm we invest in these flare-ups reveals the degree to which we have lost confidence in other kinds of political communication. Instead of the hard work of self-limiting politics, we have doubled-down on what I call *Life as Action Movie* (LAAM). Such cinematic imaginings of American life trade heavily in the tropes of victimhood and violence. These assume imaginative power for citizens accustomed to thinking about religion as a vector of Embattlement and convinced that politics is for suckers. At a moment when many Americans see citizenship as a waste of time, when they are busy fighting over the future's table scraps, the appeal of togetherness and the ideal of inclusivity are less convincing than the notion that we are unfairly being left out. And if the social justice movements of 2020 revealed traces of solidarity, there is also the dispiriting spectacle of crowd-sourced entitlement and rage in the January 2021 insurrection. Hope alone is insufficient without fundamental reassessment of norms and institutions.

Consider some political implications of this condition, both conceptual and practical. The flourishing of Embattlement in a liberal democracy raises questions about some of the fundaments of democratic culture. "Bigotry" only makes sense if there is a background expectation that citizens are entitled to "respect."²³ These are the terms bequeathed to modern societies, which orient them both politically and philosophically. And they connect with related expectations that religious and political pluralism depend on "tolerance" for the Other.[24] It is common to note how this formulation smuggles in a hierarchy placing the "tolerant" One in a position of privilege, entitlement, or superiority with respect to the Many or the Other, locating a discrepant arrangement of power within the very origins of liberalism. Liberal constitutionalism may be ill-equipped to settle conflicts (at least more than provisionally), because it cannot shake this baseline hierarchy where white Protestants "tolerate" Others.[25] Beyond simply registering the shortcomings of "tolerance" as a category, though, perhaps this system actually requires conflict for its legitimacy. I am not gesturing historically toward liberalism's prioritization of individual rights as a way to avoid conflicts like the Wars of Religion.[26] It is worth exploring whether the ascendance of Embattlement represents the apotheosis of political liberalism rather than its exhaustion.

Many theorists—Edmund Burke, Sigmund Freud, and René Girard, among only the most obvious exemplars—have held that violence is foundational to societies, even those which (as is the case with liberal constitutional polities) insist on the priority of order over a flourishing public life.[27] This is not simply a rephrasing of Hegel's dictum that absolute freedom could be experienced as terror, or Freud's contention that it represents Thanatos unbound; because what defines us as humans is not only our conditioned nature but our awareness of these limits, this radical freedom represents a formal impossibility (since humans cannot be absolutely free) that might be experienced as something very much like nothingness, the void.[28] And yet modern persons are—consciously or not—committed to the idea that their selves are born unbounded and autonomous. This is one plank of liberal democracy's conception of citizenship. Through this freedom, and the institutions and principles enshrining it, emerges an expectation that we are entitled to non-encroachment from other persons or institutions except under strict conditions. Today, though, Americans often unconsciously shear from this expectation the self-limiting politics a pluralistic society requires, leaving the unconscious assumption that freedom is either total or trampled.

Conceptually, unencumbered freedom cannot be realized in societies populated by citizens with competing ends and grounded in the rule of law. In America, this also plays out institutionally; the "American dream" of self-improvement is everywhere undermined by corporate personhood, racial injustice, and other structural imbalances of power. So why does the promise of unbounded selfhood not lead to correction? I submit that this fantastic freedom has actually acquired more power even as it recedes even farther from people's grasp. The big squeeze of post-1960s America—where the broad recognition of institutional corruption, economic constraint, and apathy is not reflected in the weary civic pieties that still shape public discourse—has only further obscured conceptions of citizenship that involve compromises, of history that is not owned by just one group, of public voices that understand their own limits. So the fractures remain while Americans are sold the dream of being left alone to pursue our personal glory. Both fractures and dreams have grown in power because for at least fifty years Americans have been taught deep distrust of shared politics and the common good. This sustained lesson, which serves to further disempower citizens, I call the *Long Con of Anti-politics*.

Make no mistake: I am not pining here for some sentimental past that never actually existed, nor indulging in the cranky white theorist's lament over identity politics (Todd Gitlin and Christopher Lasch in the 1990s, Mark Lilla more recently).[29] But the absolute fractiousness of our time can only be understood via its conceptual underpinnings, as well as more broadly known historical factors. Of course American citizens mostly do not think about such matters. And it would be foolish to pin one's hopes for the future on the possibility that all Americans would download *The Federalist Papers* during quarantine. Nonetheless, the link between a politics promising radical freedom and the construction of radical Others is strengthened by our inattention to it. Such construction gives citizens a language for thinking past the constraints, losses, and difficulties that come with the former. Blame and scapegoating are not, from this perspective, deviations from liberal democracy or wrenches thrown into its works; they are recognizable parts of it, like liberty's shadow.

Embattled religion continually enacts the power this politics has over us. It disempowers us by promising a glorious overcoming of conditions, and people, that cannot be overcome. Beyond law, coherence, proof, or debate lies an avowed experience of suffering that becomes a vehicle for demanding rights of recognition and an exemption from the responsibilities of citizenship alike. These same rights, if conferred on those we regard as undeserving opponents, are converted into evidence that our personhood is being violated or that violence has been done to us. It is this thinking that led fevered throngs to the steps of the Capitol.

This mindset is where Embattlement links up to the American fascination with trauma and victimhood. As Didier Fassin and Richard Rechtman explain, the cultural evolution of trauma from a category of suspicion to one of legitimacy parallels the expansion of individual rights in some ways.[30] Trauma emerged as a human rights category in the mid-twentieth century, owing largely to the emergence of victims' rights groups and documentary films.[31] For Fassin and Rechtman, trauma presents itself as biological evidence—the body violated, manipulated, detained—and also as a species of narrative memory. Typically, victims articulate their trauma and document it so as not to be submerged in their oppressors' version of the past. Commonly cited examples of historical trauma in the United States include the systemic misogyny exposed by Betty Friedan and the poverty Michael Harrington wrote about in *The Other America*.[32] Similar to the role of authenticity in constructing modern political identities, here a shared experience of trauma leads to the consolidation of a group's self-understanding.

Because of the peculiar status of religion in American life—the assumption that it requires special protections but is simultaneously understood to be interior and shielded from scrutiny—the moral element common to all recognitions of trauma is linked not to accepting the truth of another's suffering but to suspicion, because of the murkiness of interiority, and outrage that it is not we who are angling for sympathy or perhaps "special treatment." Embattlement thus begets Embattlement in an America bereft of confidence in anything but oneself. In these ways, Embattled Religion actively avoids political fundaments so that, paraphrasing Friedrich Nietzsche, those who perceive themselves as "victims" use this status to become aggressors and "killers" themselves.[33]

The power to make such moves comes in no small measure through control over language. This means more than just rhetorical constructions of opponents that gain power through volume and repetition. The Embattled use performative language to "produce a culturally meaningful *environment* as opposed to simply communicating ideas or attitudes."[34] With the discrediting of larger, shared political projects and the fetishization of victim narratives (even by those who appear to be privileged), Americans have been taught to accept that these are the rules of the game, and that the route to flourishing is through a cosplay of performed grievance. Clearly, religion is not the only topic in American life that fuels acrimony and complaint, nor are religions inconsistent with democracy. But the zero-sum stakes at the heart of Embattled Religion feeds the broader sense that politics must be about victory, and that to accept anything else is to welcome a boot on your neck.

All of this leaves us yearning for other ways of being Americans. This is where I have found the unexpected significance of the figures I write about in this book. They may fade from memory in time (though each has proven surprisingly durable, demonstrating that Embattlement is a powerful brand). Their significance lies not only in the political influence they have been able to achieve but in how they exemplify a condition that characterizes American politics more broadly. The energies that elevated these figures, and the antagonisms they have provoked, show few signs of fading.

Acrimony defines other national imaginaries, of course: think of Brexit, of the global rise of authoritarianism and far-right racial movements.[35] But in America such impulses combine with obsessions with religion, personal branding, and action movies to create an intoxicating sense of purpose that is pointed precisely away from the possibilities of multiracial democracy. Embattlement is a glue holding these obsessions together, by selling the false promise of escape and providing the resources for rage when escape proves, inevitably, impossible.

There are public, political matters with respect to religions that need to be addressed in American life, including, most obviously, the plight of minority religions that suffer actual legal or political persecution.[36] The ground game of various religious and social movements has always remained strong, as have varied strains of community activism.[37] The exhaustion and the rage, however, have taken up far more space, as has been evident since the far-right freakout intensified after Barack Obama's 2008 election. It is evident is that there are powerful forces in American life benefiting from the sensationalism and hyperbole of Embattlement; making it central to our discourse has proven an effective distraction from oligarchical politics. The Long Con has protected such a politics by cultivating the assumption that the market is all that matters, at the expense of basic social goods. The terms of the game have been defined by those whose comfort and privilege are so unquestioned that they refuse to see it, and their plans are often advanced via the juridical and cultural specialness of religion. This is never more effective than if they can claim they are being persecuted. And thus, prospects for change will remain dim as long as Embattlement assures us that an Action Movie makes our lifestyle *worth it*. Here to be oppressed is to be the victor, which means that when one can boast of suffering more than someone else, the reward is to deny their pain entirely, to deny their very identity. What is to be done?

## Changing the Subject

To overcome the politics that Embattled Religion helps create, we must stop talking about Embattled Religion. Making this move can enable clearer vision about historical change in American political discourse. I mean not simply the shift of outlandish thinking from the margin to the center, nor the sharp ideological change that has pushed all politics farther rightward since the 1980s.[38] What is more significant is how, beginning with Ronald Reagan's endorsement of and by conservative evangelicals, the link between personal religion and politics was cemented firmly in ways that now bedevil us.[39] In a time of shrinking public resources and uncertain futures, political charisma was embraced by many Americans who hoped that its warmth would sustain them where the state no longer would. Indeed, throughout the 1980s and the 1990s, these associations were steadily made more central to American politics. While Democrats ran farther to the right, generations of Americans lapped up the notion that politics were irreversibly corporatist and thus good for nothing. Television and film depicted conspiracies in the deepest recesses of the government, cheered on heroic characters who needed only a huge gun to solve their problems, and embraced an "irony" that laughed off political principle or idealism as naive.

It is not hard to see how contempt for the idea that institutions are worth defending, and for the idea that other people's needs might sometimes require our assistance, was woven into the nation's DNA. This was the Long Con at work: teach people apathy, play to their selfishness, and throw them in the ring like pit bulls, blood-mad about "religious liberty" or "death panels" or KILLARY or Antifa. And as Facebook likes became tweets became Instagram posts, Americans came to care more energetically about participating in the fantasy of Life as Action Movie than in purposeful reform, about announcing outrage than in finding ways out of it.

Finding ways out of this condition depends on a particular kind of language and analysis. Paramount for both is my scholarly conviction that I have a responsibility to name things accurately. Because of the urgency of this political moment, there is an even greater need to avoid scholarly obfuscation. This is why I rely on social criticism, rather than dispassionate analysis, to commend a changing of the subject. Since the 1990s I have watched the slow entrenchment of antidemocratic tendencies in public life, by which I mean American citizens' disregard for the norms and practices of lived democracy, and the shocking ease with which a failed businessman and reality TV star took the system to the edge of collapse.

Pundits and scholars meditate on "populism" or "tribalism" to make sense of this furor. There has been a near-limitless outpouring of commentary on Trump and evangelicals, as if this was the relationship that could unlock the key to our democratic future.[40] Elsewhere we find loose talk about pluralism or constitutionalism, where the uneasy center cannot quite welcome the new. Much of this work is the political equivalent of empty calories: insufficient to sustain the actual work of politics itself. I am tired of scholarship and politics that tell us—once more, with feeling—we should be less judgmental or more concerned about civic discourse, yet do so without a sufficiently rigorous diagnosis or even a cursory road map. Instead of telling yet again the tale about how America overcame anti-Catholicism and lived through the civil rights era, this book diagnoses things differently. America is getting worse, and we are all implicated in it. Things will not get better simply by reiterating the therapeutic mantra that we have to be more accepting of other people. We can only get better if we think new ways to expand rights and institutionalize democracy fully.

It is bad scholarship to parrot the journalistic reliance on "culture wars" as an explanation for religious acrimony. It is even worse politics. Though this book examines two groups of citizens (and styles of discourse) who imagine themselves locked into cosmic struggle, my aim is to cast suspicion on the simplistic dualisms Americans often uncritically rely on to navigate public life. If we continue to assume that the real conflicts in American politics pit tradition against progress, religion against secularism, or cosmopolitanism against *Duck Dynasty*, nothing will change. For the "Two Americas" narrative quite simply *is* the status quo, and reiterating it reduces politics to a zero-sum game that allows us to enjoy the luxury of avoiding self-reflection.

The academic imperative to get inside the worldview and the feelings of the people we study is vital as a pathway to understanding, but it is no sure template for the political. My own analysis is guided by George Orwell, whose 1946 essay "Politics and the English Language" retains its power to warn of the political complicity that often follows the evasion of moral clarity. Orwell observed that "political language . . . is designed to make lies sound truthful and murder respectable, and to give an air of solidity to pure wind."[41] Those who speak and write responsibly about their world must recognize that "the present political chaos is connected with the decay of language," and that fuzziness about meaning can be manipulated by others and used "as a pretext for advocating a kind of political quietism."[42] My interest is in understanding how religious discontent with the political, and the backlash against this discontent, quite simply disempower citizens from reassessing democracy's foundations. To explore this is necessarily to explore how things like egalitarianism and human rights and justice have been weakened in contemporary America. When these things are manifestly true, I do not refrain from saying so, occasionally with what I hope is authorial force. I have no interest in writing a Religious Studies version of *Strangers in Their Own Land* or *Hillbilly Elegy*.[43] Empathy remains a fundamental democratic virtue, and I am not standing in opposition to it. But if we as citizens and scholars want to move the conversation, I submit that when we make it about the self-understandings of those who claim to be victimized by multicultural curricula, like it or not we are contributing to the sense that religious citizenship is exempt from some of the other demands *of* citizenship.

Dealing with the problems of religion in public life will not occur without discomfort. To privilege a kind of academic writing that avoids discomfort is not only intellectually narrow; it does a disservice to politics, by possibly mimicking America's cultural orientation to religion as so juridically and politically special that we treat religion with kid gloves. But to treat politics *as politics* is not to tell people that their concerns about salvation are misplaced; it is only to remind each other that what counts in public life cannot be shaped in the service of a single viewpoint simply because it happens to be religious (as if other religious people would always and everywhere be in accord, for that matter). Of course not all Christians, and not even all conservatives, speak the language of Embattlement. This is not a book about those others, though they likely have some role to play in remaking American politics. And of course not all critics of the Martyrs are irreligious or antireligious; the sloppy association of all criticism with the theophobic broadsides of Sam Harris, Christopher Hitchens, and Richard Dawkins is also part of the problem. But know this: I have no interest in misdiagnosing the condition of American politics simply because *some* evangelicals have questions about whether they are working to advance the American imperium, or because *some* secularists acknowledge the political legitimacy of religions.

Other books, with different methods and aims, would tell a different story than I do, as in Christian Smith's well-known documentation of evangelical self-understandings and feelings of marginalization.[44] Yet while I employ history and cultural theory in the pages ahead, this is a work of critique whose aim is to explore the possibility of creating a politics different from what either Martyrs or Whistleblowers are capable of imagining. In other words, my writing makes no pretense of avoiding judgment. Now is not the time to avoid critical assessment of American life, and mindless tolerance of repugnant viewpoints is partly responsible for the sorry condition of our politics. Though I share many of the grievances of the Whistleblowers, and though I am personally and professionally compelled by religious activism, I give credence to neither of the cultural conversations herein, because their focus is misdirected.

I encourage changing the conversation because we are running out of time to fix what needs fixing. This requires restoring confidence in politics as such, against the idea that you can be both Embattled *and* in the majority. There is little use in chest-beating about how outrageous it might seem for a wealthy white man to claim he is Embattled. Instead, we ought to think harder about how such claims were carefully manufactured to disempower and depoliticize us. Beyond structural changes necessary to reorient American religion and civic life, perceptual changes are required too. *Embattled America* gambles that new ways of describing, and asking different questions about, American political religions can shift (however subtly) our sense of the possible.

Each chapter will conclude with my reassessment of a foundational political category, and in the book's conclusion, I take up the possibilities of new political languages and identities, and through them a renewed sense of mutual obligation and self-limitation in our democracy. One of the most important elements of self-limiting politics, though, is its grounding in human rights and political rights that cannot be displaced for the sake of a particular moral or religious perspective. These are complex arguments that I pursue in more detail ahead. But what this means is recognizing the necessity of insisting that certain political positions are simply wrong. This is not an antireligious argument. Indeed, there are strong religious reasons for supporting such a shift in focus. There are, after all, abundant religious resources (conceptually and historically) for self-limitation, coalition-building, pluralistic democracy, and more. Of course religious freedom is among the political rights possessed by citizens in a democracy, and of course religious people can be marginalized and belittled by insensitive secular conceptions of politics. But the kingdom of sentiment that gives birth to Embattlement is clearly of a different order than harassment, juridical constraint, or institutional prohibitions.

What is more, democracy does not hang on enabling discriminatory viewpoints or practices because they are "sincerely held." Democracy, rather, is for citizens who begin their public life with the understanding that none of us is more deserving than others. And if America is to live up to the myths we tell ourselves (and I take it for granted that there are good arguments for abandoning these myths), then we must together accept that a single religious or political narrative that asks all others to conform to it is the antithesis of democracy. The refusal to say these things forcefully is part of why we are here. The profession that we must listen to the soul cry of the white nationalist not only reeks of noblesse oblige; it punts the actual political fight against intolerance down the road. For too long, cultural conversations about conservative religion have felt close to the way biologists talk about a misunderstood species. The old conversations have not worked.

I am not calling for religious people to stop talking religiously in public life; that is a nonstarter, both theoretically and practically. Freezing religion out of the process obviously feeds the very wellspring of Embattlement. Indeed, aggressive calls for privatization or anticlericalism are part of the larger condition that requires change. Such calls can be strident and simplistic and misconstrue what democracy requires just as grossly as do Martyrs' claims about "religious bigotry." In politics, we must listen to religious people just as we listen to other citizens: because listening is part of good democratic practice, not because a scholar of religion reminds us that we should only use words that they would recognize and affirm. Political speech, then, must be treated as political speech. Because only politics can save us from what politics has become.

The way forward is to reconceive of politics as a space not where victories are achieved and foes vanquished but as the principled conciliation of reasonable differences with regard to matters of public life. Every word of that is contestable, I am well aware. But this book looks hard at the unmovable negativity of American politics and embraces instead a defiant optimism. We must make the distinction between reasonable and unreasonable differences central to our politics. We must learn what matters are genuinely of and for the public, and what we can do to make a more just public. We must navigate difference affirmatively so that better outcomes can be achieved on the basis of shared principles. In these projects, if different groups of religious citizens cannot make themselves intelligible on nonexclusive grounds, shared by different groups of citizens, then their claims are likely to have little success in public life. And if the nonreligious cannot make their claims intelligible to the religious and offer compelling visions of the principles grounding political life, their claims are also likely to falter. Throughout, I will argue that such shared grounds can be located in universal human rights and shared standards of public democratic practice.

Doing so will, I hope, expose the entire conversation about Embattlement as contingent (it is the product of historical and institutional forces that can be undone, albeit with great work) and misplaced (keeping us focused on the wrong things). Despite all that has happened in recent years in America, and despite the darkness of 2020 and early 2021 in particular, I will not relinquish optimism, nor even some measure of confidence in my fellow citizens. That might sound bizarre at this juncture of history. But in order to open up the possibility of change, we must begin to think and perceive and practice a new politics on a different scale, working toward a comprehensive overhaul of American institutions. We start by sustaining those values we think are worth sustaining, and seeking out new ways of realizing them with other humans. This is crucial for reassessing our civic practice, our political priorities, and our relationship to our sisters and brothers in the human family.

I do not think that these efforts will magically overcome political stasis, or help QAnon devotees see the light of rationality. But radical incommensurability and extremes can be filtered out in ways that promote practical, local, revisable problem-solving based on reassessment of transparent procedures and first principles. The "problem" of Embattled religion is thus not a thing to be solved—by injecting the right quotient of morality into the polis, or by erasing religion from public life—so much as an area of continued acrimony which reveals some of what continually (and in large degree unconsciously) vexes American democracy: anxieties and uncertainties about the fundaments of democratic politics are the deep geologic forces beneath Embattlement. If our focus is there, we might starve Embattlement of its oxygen.

My arguments are thus both strategic and theoretical. Whistleblowers sometimes manage to produce principled arguments; they also are not always disdainful of religion, and are often interested in preserving fairness and transparency. But they too often, and too eagerly, play the lead role in a narrative that gives comfort to Martyrs. It is clear that most Martyrs do emphatically believe their religion is at risk. But if we seek to undermine the politics accompanying this belief by focusing on, say, the religiousness of David Barton's history curricula or Mike Pence's homophobia, we give them power. The lesson that their ideas and public power teach is that we should challenge their views not because they are religious but because they are grounded in bad understandings of citizenship.

America is a tangle of things. America is made of greed and racism and war and sanctimony. But America is also made of other stuff, weirder stuff that might not seem political on the surface but which underscores the creative, improvisatory vitality that as yet has not been crushed out in this country and whose dogged refusal to submit might make for bright moments in our future together. This is the America of the Port Huron Statement and of Charles Mingus's undaunted musical exultation in the face of white supremacy. This is the America where Jayne Cortez asks, "Do you really think time speaks English in the men's room?" This is the America of Henry McNeal Turner's coruscating speech to the 1868 Georgia House of Representatives, and the America of Emerson's naked eyeball opening to the Oversoul. America gives us these ways of being in the world, too: an entire topography of political resistance and artistic subcultures, self-determining and dreaming new human existence into being, conduits for experiencing the flash-heat of life in ways that forever recalibrate your connection to the human family, which can rewire your politics, justice replicating on new strands of cultural DNA.

Whether or not any of these instances clicks for you, my point is that America contains abundant resources for thinking and acting toward creative transformation. Despite the absolute horror-show of America's past and present, America also gives us possibility, in a shifting constellation of influences and openings that demand our response. Why not go big at this fragile moment, and seize control of the resources that are there to inspire new movements and new politics? Wreck the sound system that is pumping out the music driving us all mad, and play something new together. This book embraces the idea of a cultural remix, led by new political emcees, a redescription that places theory and history on a par with art installations and basement shows. This book looks at the down-hearted death-trip that punctuates American history—the 1890s, 1970s, and 2010s—and reminds us that for every spasm of nihilistic rage that produces Charles Manson or QAnon, there is an instrument made from a hubcap, a squat turned into a performance space, kids making machines talk, producing blasted art from the refuse America dumps on them.

The rubble of politics and culture lies at our feet. Fill your heart with rage but also purpose, and ask with me, what can we make with it?

# 2
# A Brief History of Persecution Complexes in America

> Nothing stands still for us. This is our natural state and yet the state most contrary to our inclinations. We burn with desire to find a firm footing, an ultimate lasting base on which to build a tower rising up to infinity, but our whole foundation cracks and the earth opens up into the depths of the abyss.
> —Pascal, *Pensées*

> I think you've had it backwards all this time. You wanted to enter history. Wrong approach, Leon. What you really want is out.
> —Don DeLillo, *Libra*

Polls consistently show that white evangelicals in America believe themselves to be the "most persecuted group in the world."[1] Before his election-rigging debacle, North Carolina's Mark Harris warned of the imminent criminalization of Christianity, adding to a long history of such conspiratorial complainers.[2] Iowa's Steve King claimed, after being publicly chastised for a career of racist remarks, to "have better insight into what [Jesus] went through for us."[3] Other white Americans, concerned about the ascent of intolerance characteristic of the Trump era, concluded that "the culture war over religious morality" had faded, birthing a "secular, more ferociously national and racial culture war."[4] Certainly, the 2020 protests in the wake of the murder of George Floyd provide evidence of a sharpened engagement with white supremacy; but in response to such engagement, Martyrs have passed laws banning "critical race theory" in schools, complained about masks during a pandemic, and exulted in the cosplay fantasy of a stolen election.

This is how public discourse about religion goes most visibly in America. To be sure, there is all manner of laudable religious activism outside the big pileup of conventional politics: charity and sanctuary on the southern border, Moral Mondays in North Carolina, and the bright sustain of interfaith activity surrounding Black Lives Matter. Nonetheless, you can always seem them coming, freeze-framed just before the collision: liberal pundits telling us that conservative religion is finally going away, and conservatives who inveigh against the "war on religion."

Persecution, religious and otherwise, is real in America. From the Puritans' wars against or forced conversions of those who lived and prayed differently to the Alien and Sedition Acts of 1798, from the Indian Removal Act to ongoing legal and political violence against African Americans, from the harassment of Catholics and other religious minorities to the Palmer raids and the internment of Japanese Americans, from the FBI and COINTELPRO blacklisting of dissidents to post-9/11 profiling, American history is home to many millions of Americans whose daily lives have been rooted in Embattlement.[5] The struggle to vote, to get decent schooling, to avoid intimidation by those who would be your neighbor, or to find safe spaces to worship remain challenges for many.

Yet American airwaves and broadband are choked with white American Christians protesting that they are being treated like minorities, the subjects of discrimination. No one should profess to understand this too easily. While I am suspicious of these claims on plainly factual grounds, there are nonetheless complex and uneven relations among religious and civic identities. After all, juridical and administrative power in the United States can be tone-deaf to religion—what it is, what it feels like, how it shapes practitioners' understanding of political and legal authority. And in courts as well as in religious communities, Americans regularly debate the trade-offs between different— and sometimes competing—sets of norms and obligations. We just don't hear much about these slow, deliberative, provisional reckonings because Americans favor the splash of outrage.

Hence, the Action Movie that is the "culture wars." Initially popularized as a warning intoned by former Nixon speechwriter Pat Buchanan, who in the early 1990s sounded the alarm that multiculturalism and economic globalization put nothing less than "the soul of the nation" at stake, the term has been endlessly recirculated by public intellectuals like James Davison Hunter, whose widely read 1992 text framed cultural conflict as a contest between traditionalists and modernists.[6] I think this way of understanding our public life obscures the fact that America's obsession with "religion" endlessly reproduces the same language, the same complaints, the same exhaustion for all participants. Though the rhetoric surrounding these "wars" may sound ominous and disruptive, it actually produces the same politics that drives complaint in the first place. The culture war is a hamster wheel.

On it goes, regularly bandying words like martyrdom, persecution, and embattlement, that conjure up whole histories, replete with lurid images of bodies straining against torment, archaic torture instruments, jeering crowds.[7] The fascination with persecution, and with valorous heroes who overcome it, is ancient. We can locate themes of persecution in Euripides's *Bacchae* and in Dionysian myths. Dionysius's destiny is bound up in a persecution that, as Mircea Eliade wrote, "dramatically expresses the resistance against the god's mode of being and his religious message."[8] Vengeful kings persecute dissidents in every historical era, and such tales are converted into post hoc accounts of the triumph of free will and liberty. In Embattled America, though, the idolization of martyrdom isn't focused on the performance of virtue and sacrifice; it is, more often, a way to command attention and demand special treatment because of one's special torment.[9] In this, it is curiously all-American.

## Righteousness and Faction

In his *Second Treatise on Government*, John Locke wrote, "In the beginning, all the world was America."[10] America itself, of course, was no tabula rasa. Long before the "discovery" of the "new world," America was home to hundreds of Native American cultures that were seen by Spain, France, and England as impediments to the realization of their economic and religious visions. Certainly the English Puritans who began arriving in New England in 1620 often thought of themselves in the idiom of martyrdom. Despite their zeal for practicing persecution—banishing Anne Hutchinson and Roger Williams, executing the Quaker Mary Dyer, quarantining "praying Indians" in "praying towns," going to war with the Pequot in 1636, and of course in the Salem Witch Trials—Puritans regularly depicted themselves as God's suffering servants. In an unforgiving place, overrun with "savages" and the godless, Puritans would seek the lofty heights Americans associate with the familiar rhetoric of the "city upon a hill," authored by Governor John Winthrop in 1630.

As historian Adrian Chastain Weimer notes, the intellectual culture of early modern England—replete with antinomian movements and expressed in texts like John Foxe's *Acts and Monuments*, a popular compendium of martyrdoms—shaped the Puritans' fusion of glorious suffering with institutional ambition.[11] Suggestively, however, it was Quakers, Baptists, and other dissidents, targets of the Puritans' righteous ire, who developed the familiar impulse to use tales of persecution "as an amplifier" for their own claims to moral superiority.[12]

The regularity of these two different modes of claiming public virtue by claims to persecution shaped the thinking of the American Framers, whose ambivalence about democracy loomed large in their reckoning with the role of religion in public life. The Madisonian vision that was ultimately enshrined in American political architecture held that "men who possess the most attractive merit" would, along with the separation of powers and restrictions on franchise, limit or eradicate any "unjust and interested majority" out for anything but a common good.[13] Anxiety about faction, political party, and majoritarianism were common among the Framers' generation, especially in documents like *The Federalist Papers*. But a popular press that we would today call viral was an equally important component of early American culture, often giving voice to grievances and demonology as overwrought as those of the present. Mockery of the well-heeled and the educated long predated cable television. Seeing political disagreement as a sign of the Constitution's doom or the extinction of real religion is also old hat. Early American democracy was thus as much a regime of feelings as an experiment in institutional architecture and political representation.[14]

Popular democracy conjured crisis after crisis, but in a way that only prolonged familiar debates rather than resolving them: visions of rugged individualism competed with genuflections to the will of the people; Thomas Jefferson cautioned against being trapped by tradition, even as early America sought to construct a past glorious enough to sanctify its self-regard; confidence in public opinion and a free press were celebrated, even as the sheer multiplicity of popular outlets fragmented and polarized the citizenry. Long before the internet, belief that information was transparent was undermined by a glut of opinions on these and other matters. Early Americans often reacted to this abundance of information with a retreat into "common sense."[15]

So the factional passion the Framers so feared became central to how Americans defined themselves. Far from the deliberative salons dreamed of by democratic theorists, American citizenry became as much about bonding together in the face of authority as about representation, fairness, or peaceable pluralism. While contemporary Americans often rely on the maxim "speaking your truth" as if it were an insight new to Oprah's America, it was common two centuries ago for "average Americans . . . to see it as a patriotic duty to begin speaking their own minds."[16] Democracy's fantasy of a collective public was, in practice, overrun with panic, anger, and defiant religion in equal measure. Whether in the new classes of politicians appearing in American cities, the associational networks springing up in civil society, or in the religious revivals galvanizing Americans, the ability to declare that an opinion was commonsensical, and that its "plain truth" was for/of the people, and to do so in a way that demonstrated the intensity of the conviction, mattered as much as the substance of the thing being declared.

The imperative of self-expression, and the conviction that this is what democracy exists for, thus made it easier to convert fellow citizens into rivals, competitors, or even evildoers. Something more than the Puritans' lust for righteousness was at work here. R. Laurence Moore describes how religious groups ranging from the Millerites to the young Mormons gained authenticity and street cred from their harassment or denunciation: "Condemnation provided a collective ego boost to a new movement. It was a sign that it was taken seriously. Sensational 'exposés' functioned as a backhanded aid to religious proselytizing."[17] Catholics, Masons, and Mormons all fell under suspicion because of the threat of bloc-voting, among other potential panics.[18] But reputational or physical harm not only promoted social cohesion among the maligned religions; they were understood, consciously or not, as confirmation of a righteousness pure enough for the world to hate.

It is a long way from burning down convents or the US military laying siege to Mormons to the comfortable suburbs of America's Embattled Majorities. But this history produced some of Embattlement's conceptual DNA. The unquestioned American belief in individual self-governance has always been about bucking authority as much as about classical liberalism's rational selves. That belief has fueled Americans' resentment of anything smacking of federalism, and a desire to get all freedom-trampling government out of our lives. Michael Kazin rightly notes that the baseline understanding that developed in the nineteenth century was such that "any other path would violate the belief in free will, the 'self-sovereignty' that was a gift from God."[19]

Most traditions, of course, did not retreat into intentional communities or enclaves for these reasons. And it is common to narrate American history as structured by a steady push-pull of pluralistic and antipluralistic forces. But what may be more important than attitudinal (and sometimes legal) shifts in the embrace of religious diversity is a shift in attitudes toward the political, now seen as a contest over which institutions the state could control and which could be overseen only by religious authorities. Such a shift made it easier to smuggle into politics the sense that legitimacy was being denied if government established its own authority. This sense was amplified by conservatives who, long accustomed to calling for the moral reform of American life, began to shift from making largely theological arguments to inveighing against the big sociopolitical Other that was the leviathan state. The cultural conflicts most associate with the 1960s were clearly evident no later than the 1920s, when a specifically (and self-consciously) conservative form of "civics" was deployed against both science curricula and "Progressivism" more broadly.[20] In the 1920s and 1930s, this fueled conservative critiques of Darwinian social science as well as natural science, and contrasting them with reverence for the Constitution and nationalism.

The steady refrain was that the Constitution was being trampled. Religion was being targeted. America itself was at risk. This resonant language, framing issues to appeal to anxiety and patriotism simultaneously, was facilitated by far-reaching media and the establishment of counterinstitutions. Conservative Protestants, especially, began to see the state in ways that reflected nervousness about the New Deal and its suspected connections to global communism.[21] This bred an unexamined belief that the existence of government as such constituted an offense.

## Tarnished Gold

In the so-called golden age of post–World War II America, dark imaginings throve beneath a veneer of contentedness. Consider that, as historian Kevin Schultz notes, as moderate a publication as the *Christian Century* worried about the "national menace" of unchecked pluralism, whose "instability" it feared would topple "the traditional American way of life."[22] A particular form of religious public privilege was at stake in this way of life, one that could even be threatened, Schultz shows, by the ascendance of a generic cultural "religion" meant to contrast with godless communism. Even as early as 1952, Will Herberg noted that mainline Protestantism saw itself as "threatened on all sides" by Catholics, Jews, and other newcomers to the "mainstream."[23] History and culture were the stakes, not merely theological particulars. It is here that we see the Martyrs' restlessness converted to action.

Brylcreemed anti-communist warrior Billy James Hargis, renowned for sponsoring flights to airdrop Bibles over communist countries in the 1950s, helped craft a species of "real" patriotism around this notion of cultural decline, one that contemporary readers will recognize.[24] Hargis and others thought President Dwight Eisenhower was a closet liberal, insufficiently militant in his defense of traditional America as they understood it. In this, Hargis found an ally in Major General Edwin Walker, an ardent member of the John Birch Society, and a close friend of founder Robert Welch. For Hargis, Walker, and their sympathizers, the subsequent election of John F. Kennedy to the presidency in 1960 set off a current of alarm not unlike that of Barack Obama's in 2008. JFK, they protested, was an out-of-touch liberal elite, a practitioner of a shadowy religion, the Machiavellian architect of an anti-American agenda of activist courts and enforced school integration.[25]

Hargis habitually opened his speeches by quoting Ephesians on "the full armor of God," a text recently revived as a rallying cry at "Liberate Michigan" rallies and the US Capitol siege. Hargis asserted, "The thing that's wrong with America today is the spirit of anti-Christ in the fields of religion, education, politics . . . the sophisticated professors in the State Department . . . full of traitors."[26] For his part, Walker thought that the very existence of the United Nations foretold the end of American sovereignty. He issued a call to action: "We have been pushed around by the anti-Christ Supreme Court. It's time to rise."[27] New laws or government agencies were taken as evidence of a dictatorship in the making. Today, such claims would be the equivalent of memes about the deep state or the Clintons eating babies. Hargis and Walker created a 4Chan of the Holy Spirit, God's own hyperpatriotic sub-Reddit.

Convinced that they stood for a silent majority, in 1963 Hargis and Walker undertook Operation Midnight Ride, bringing antistatist conspiracy theories to the masses. The Operation claimed to have moles inside the NAACP, who could confirm that it was a communist organization. In turn, both the FBI and the NAACP monitored the tour to see if sponsor groups were fronts for the KKK. It is a fascinating episode from the beginning of America's long decline, a forerunner of QAnon and related conspiracies. But what makes it distinctive in the history of Embattlement is the way Hargis and Walker thrived on protests against them, feeding off their counterenergy. Opposition was confirmation of the taken path.

Robert Alan Goldberg documents the cognitive habits embedded in this way of thinking. Even in the eighteenth and nineteenth centuries, he shows, conspiracy theory relied on "frequent repetition, sensationalism, and the status of advocates."[28] Long before Twitter and the Whirl, each virtuoso of conspiracy "transform[ed] allegations into facts and buil[t] a database that contained only self-reinforcing information."[29] Mainstream politicians dismissed Welch and his supporters in the 1960s. But somehow his rants about the un-Americanness of the New Deal, about Supreme Court justices secretly advancing Marxism, and about business as the chief engine of democracy have all become boilerplate for conservative politicians.

Elected officials and high-ranking members of the Trump administration daily traded in conspiracy theory. Large groups of citizens gobble up outré worldviews ranging from QAnon to antivaccination theories to an unpredictable resurgence of flat-earth belief. Such thinking was endemic to Hargis's and Walker's activism, especially in its connections with the Birchers. What unites such conspiracy theorists—whether their obsession is UFOs, George Soros, the 9/11 attacks, or the Covid-19 "hoax" to take down Trump—is the way in which they "stud[y] history for secret patterns and intrigues."[30] Seeking to overcome their unease in a world that does not sanctify their identity, conspiracists confer order and narrative form on what they haul in on their obsessive data-trawl. If they encounter the absence of evidence, it is taken as a sign that the plot they are uncovering was especially effective. If they encounter denial, it just means the deniers are in on it.

Perhaps the "master narrative" of democracy has failed more Americans than we thought, and conspiracy provides comfort. More likely, we are witnessing the runoff from decades of knowing political manipulation and disinformation. What is more important to conspiracy's appeal, though, is that conspiracy is on some level simply the inversion of the idea that "God has a plan for me" or "Everything happens for a reason." Conspiracy is what happens when you remove the smiley face from this most American of sentimental pieties. What remains is your own personal action movie.

When the sixties heated up, mainline conservatives began more frequently to convert criticism into fuel. The old minoritarian standby, which Hargis had linked to the "real" America lurking in wait, was now employed by the *National Review* and William F. Buckley, inveighing against the know-it-all liberals who sought to change the country too much and too fast.[31] Indeed, that magazine's 1955 debut had trumpeted its intention to "stand athwart history, yelling Stop!"[32] This was not new, especially not to the observer of John Calhoun or the Populists of the 1870s, of the anti-Federalists, or 1930s Southern Agrarian populists. But after their corrosive experiences with Joseph McCarthy and Barry Goldwater, whose flirtations with conspiracy the Republican Party had sought to exorcise, Republicans embraced the idiom of combat, pointing to the specter of a sometimes equally conspiratorial Left as evidence that the country was teetering far from its moral center.[33] They heaped scorn on "eggheads" or "bleeding hearts" who privileged new social rights or new identities over plain talk and authenticity.

Segregationist champion George Wallace, though disavowed by most conservatives, was a major influence on Martyrs. Wallace invoked a religious identity and moral tradition endangered "by the national state and the 'liberal elite' that dominated American society."[34] In the age of the expansion of rights in America, what Kevin Phillips famously called "The Emerging Republican Majority" lamented the "forgotten whites" who were repeatedly told that they would be passed over for promotion by undeserving recipients of affirmative action. The "Southern Strategy," the "silent majority," and the counteridentity politics of the *Roe* era drove a wedge into old Democratic constituencies through the politics of grievance and resentment.[35]

Clearly much of this was indeed about race, though increasingly expressed in other barely concealed idioms. New Right architect and Republican kingmaker Lee Atwater (close confidant of jailed Trump associates Paul Manafort and Roger Stone) infamously summed this up in a 1981 interview:

> You start out in 1954 by saying, "Nigger, nigger, nigger." By 1968 you can't say "nigger"—that hurts you, backfires. So you say stuff like, uh, forced busing, states' rights, and all that stuff, and you're getting so abstract. Now, you're talking about cutting taxes, and all these things you're talking about are totally economic things and a byproduct of them is, blacks get hurt worse than whites. . . . "We want to cut this," is much more abstract than even the busing thing, uh, and a hell of a lot more abstract than "Nigger, nigger."[36]

Instrumental in this redirection of race-talk, and equally central to cultivating the Martyr mindset, were economist James Buchanan and the University of Virginia's Warren Nutter, a longtime Goldwater supporter. Self-styled revolutionaries who understood themselves to be keeping alive the flame of the Framers' liberty, they emerged from the 1960s calling for the creation of conservative counterinstitutions in response to what they held was a compromised government and judiciary. They argued that "the crux of the desegregation problem was that 'state run' schools had become a 'monopoly,' which could be broken up by privatization."[37] Arguments for maintaining racial privilege were thus commuted into arguments about unchecked statism, and about whether big government has the solutions or whether these reside with the will of the people, expressed in private initiative and opportunity.

This substitution of terms and categories became the stock response to criticism, and they helped circulate and amplify the energies of outrage. Unsuccessful court cases were attributed to hostile judges or activist judiciaries, engaged in a war on faith. The social services of the New Deal were making a new religion of bureaucracy, manipulating the language of the commons in order to funnel your tax dollars to the undeserving.[38] The sanctity of the individual was at risk, and the personalism that was a product of the conservative myth of tax theft shaded easily into the personalism of "sincerely held" religious belief, a phrase initially coined in contrast to fraudulence but now meant to protect the murky inner realm of feeling from sources of unease.

## The Us versus Them Decade

As curricula changed in public universities, as rights expanded, and as money disappeared during the Vietnam years and became ever more precarious in the postindustrial 1970s, Martyr messaging started to take root in the idea that, in Luke O'Brien's reckoning, "they were rising up against unchecked political correctness that maligned white males. The more the liberal establishment chose to revile them, the more they embraced their role as villains."[39] None of this was arbitrary. Soon to be appointed associate justice to the Supreme Court, in summer of 1971 Lewis F. Powell Jr. penned a memorandum in which he summed up two decades of growing conservative grievances, attributing most social change of the time to "communism." "No thoughtful person," Powell wrote, "can question that the American economic system is under broad attack."[40] Restraints on corporations—as proposed by unions, or by Ralph Nader, for example—were hamstringing the American future. The American way of life, Powell urged, had to be protected by business interests.

This had the effect of galvanizing conservatives in ways that led to the formation of institutions like the Heritage Foundation, the Cato Institute, the Manhattan Institute, and the Business Roundtable. Their emphasis on corporate freedom resonated with the populist inklings of revolt against permissiveness and what Wallace had called "pinhead" ideas.⁴¹ Change was attack, and thus required defense. This idea was the gravitational force that promised to hold things together in vertiginous, rubble-strewn America.

In the Sun Belt, older Goldwater ideas were given fresh life in this reconfiguring landscape.⁴² Some of his ideas might have been out there, new conservatives began to note, but at least he said what he thought and spoke out against authority. And wasn't that what America was all about? This fevered negativity produced weird fragments of optimism, hard-as-diamond fantasy compressed from the dreary coal of public life. Ronald Reagan embodied this, telling conservatives (especially conservative religious believers) that they had been given a raw deal, that they were the real Americans, and that he would fight for them. As governor of California, Reagan had been flamboyantly suspicious of democracy. He chided protesters for being brats. When students at San Francisco State College occupied a campus building, petitioning the administration to start an ethnic studies program, Reagan sent soldiers with bayonets.⁴³ And yet Dutch promised to defend innocent taxpayers from government's rough beast, in all its expressions.

Such antistatism dates back not only to the late nineteenth-century populist movement but to the earlier valorization of the rugged individual, the cowboy, the frontiersman, and the myth of Horatio Alger. They came roaring back into American consciousness after the Days of Rage bled out into the long, frazzled haze of the 1970s. The principled youth of Students for a Democratic Society, the civil rights movement, and the Newport Folk Festival gave way to Charles Bronson, skull-beating Philadelphia mayor Frank Rizzo (who infamously urged his supporters to "vote white"), and popular televisual fantasies of detachment like *Swiss Family Robinson* and *Little House on the Prairie*. In different ways, each of these examples reflected white resentment that "other" citizens were now integrating schools and doling out "special privileges" like drink tickets. To many aggrieved conservatives, it felt like bigotry. Yet Whistleblowers saw a different danger in the misty-eyed, rearward-gazing nostalgia that was soft-pedaled in *Happy Days* and *Grease*, and grew in popularity when evoked by antigovernment, law-and-order crusaders like Reagan. The great postmodern reframing had begun: the turn against the engine of stability became the response to perceived instability. A longing to escape history was concealed with the fetishization of history.

For all this conjoined dreaming and rancor, the clear fact that American democracy had begun suffering a severe legitimation crisis was little remarked. There were many who raised questions about the ethics of war and free-market capitalism, and about the place of rights- and identity-based social movements in American society, but the energy seemed focused on restoring abundance and stability rather than understanding why they had disappeared, and why they weren't reliable to begin with.

Conservative religious activists began filling the void in public life, their narratives grounded in the assertion that a lost golden age had been disrupted by hostile "elites" and other antagonists. In these narratives, America did not require fundamental procedural and conceptual reassessments; rather, America's true citizens needed to "take back" the mantle of legitimacy, to reassert their authority and their values against those who would make them victims of illegitimate taxation, immoral legislation, and selective use of legal neutrality as cover for giving preference to undeserving others. This remains the conservative playbook. Underlying these claims is the belief that political liberalism represents not only a threat to well-meaning citizens and "people of faith" but also a perversion of the vision of the American Framers. This orientation to political history de-emphasizes shared institutions and mutual investment in the democratic process in favor of a language of persecution and righteous triumph. This is a cultural ethos kept alive in the privileged inhabitants of Embattled America's incessant claims of victimization. These defiant Martyrs told themselves that, if these were the stakes, then Goldwater was correct that "extremism in the defense of liberty is no vice."

The avatar of the 1970s is thus not a disco dancer but an angry white protester. In response to desegregation rulings, Bostonians held Whites Have Rights rallies. In response to busing and school integration efforts, new citizens' groups like Restore Our Alienated Rights protested, too.[44] The changing demographics, and the changing priorities of each successive generation, were framed as a loss of rights and liberties. To be fair, some (often white) leftist activists also found authenticity in their repression, with some even trying to goad cops into beating them in a mimesis of the Right's demonization of hippies. But it was the Right's belief that they had power beyond numbers that, in the 1970s, prevailed over the Left's notion that it had the inevitability of future demographics on its side.[45] Religion stood in for fidelity to tradition, for the way things used to be, for getting off my lawn, and for the absolutes of the new politics, defined by the glamorization of outlaws and resistance to compromise.

Richard Nixon's embrace of such sensibilities made possible the idea that the beneficiaries of society's unspoken rules could resist fairness and equality by claiming to be victims. For all the unreality of this gambit, then and now, Nixon succeeded by articulating a basic sense of disbelief and outrage that the old ways were being criticized. Rick Perlstein aptly observed that, in this, Nixon was embraced for his pugnacity, and "proved that he could *take it* . . . the cross-bearing embodiment of a Silent Majority's humiliations, humiliating their shared tormentors in return."[46] So the 1970s were about many things: themed Slurpee cups, muscle cars, socially aware sit-coms, and prog rock. But it was also the decade when America's lust for authenticity and purpose became more openly weaponized. The conservative revolt against politics described itself as embracing tradition. So, too, did the counterattack. Each side insisted it was a sleeping giant awakened by an interloper. Through contempt they would achieve a new political order.

We can thus understand why it was so effective for many conservative Christians in America to claim that, in their supposed exclusion from public life or their loss of privilege, freedom itself, choice itself, values themselves, and ultimately America itself were being threatened. Early opponents of *Roe v. Wade* did not simply denounce policy; they described themselves as "new abolitionists."[47] When, in 1976, Bob Jones University was denied tax-exempt status for failing to comply with federal desegregation law, the reaction was a now-familiar one, then being beta-tested. According to Randall Balmer, BJU administrator Elmer L. Rumminger claimed this ruling "alerted the Christian school community about what could happen with government interference."[48] The very existence of free-standing law, which already made provisions for exemptions if "unnecessary burdens" could be identified, was cited as evidence that something alarming was happening in the mere request for compliance. This, Rumminger and others claimed, was the true call to action, as if they were the Branch Davidians under siege at Waco. They would resist and it would be *epic*.

The New Right provided a coherent narrative and a coherent identity, and gave voters a motivation to stay on message while the Left was in the throes of an ongoing fragmentation. The rise of the Embattled proved that confidence in the postwar liberal compromise—rooted as it was in a producer economy that could balance competing interests through continued growth—had achieved fictional status. Now the old Marxist idiom of class antagonism exploded into general use, but spoken in the languages of conspiracy and prayer. Academics quaintly appropriated the discourse of radicalism—there would be contestation, sites, and deployment—while ceding the public to conservatives who transformed the old opposition to statism into solidarity.

As Christian Right stalwart Tim LaHaye put it, "There are millions of us—and only a handful of them."[49]

These shifts were accompanied by the hypertrophy of capitalism, the hollowing out of the labor base, the flatlining value of the dollar, and the assault on government legitimacy.[50] Such structural changes steadily convinced more and more Americans that the triumph of the market was the best we could hope for from democracy and that their only way to make it was to clamber over the broken bodies of their competitors. As Daniel T. Rodgers writes, what was "novel about the new market metaphors was their detachment from history and institutions and from questions of power."[51] The ephemerality of this new language prompted Americans to rage when they could not locate the source of their misery. While young post-Watergate representatives strove earnestly to remake the public trust, America was sliding back into a Gilded Age default of institutional failure and corruption. For all the queues to buy gas, the rubble in the South Bronx, the whip-crack new music of hip-hop and punk, the 1970s birthed a narco-dream of limitless space. The nascent internet, the rise of paperless finance, the fraying of once-grounding institutions: these were the effervescent realities that led America to double down on the imagination itself.

## Red Dawn

The Reagan era's frothy abstractions provided a language for dreaming outside this failure. Citizens were encouraged to imagine they were traveling on a heaven-sent path, whose paving would provide an emotional foundation to a nostalgic narrative but no institutional remedy for democracy's fractures. Reagan told us, "There are no constraints on the human mind, no walls around the human spirit, no barriers to our progress except those we ourselves erect."[52] Reagan's success came from his perfect marriage of antistatism with the promise of personal triumph. If Americans could just see that the state and regulations got in the way of one's own destiny, imagine the possibilities that might await! Religion, in Reagan's formulation, became the tradition Americans were told to defend as well as the dream of no limits. Such notions resonated with the steadily growing conviction, as consultants like televangelist Jim Bakker frequently warned Reagan leading up to the 1980 election, that "controls" on religion were a clear sign of impending apocalypse.[53] While the fact of limits—on our bodies and our institutions, or the inevitable tension between the goals different people seek—could not be avoided, as America truly entered the era of Embattlement facts and reason were increasingly experienced as things that got in the way of personal glory.

The 1980s were cranked up, despite a general agreement that they were merely vacuous. Televangelists emoted on American screens. New religions throve secretly while in the radiant atmosphere of the public strode harmonialists singing paeans of self-improvement. Something about the 1980s' combination of excess with imagination confirmed that American life was now being defined by a series of cultural and perceptual accelerants: the post-Watergate secrecy made manifest in Iran-Contra, and the *Field of Dreams* nostalgia now blossoming in historical theme parks and creative reenactments. These inevitably refashioned religion, which spilled beyond common assumptions about it and simultaneously staked out its (often unexpected) place in the world: it would not be private, interiorized, antimodern, or utopic; it would be juridically "special," a political force, or a danger to be excised. Religion became a vehicle for performing the celebratory, nostalgia-driven deflection from neoliberalism. It also became the medium of dissent from the reality principle, leaning into the triumphalism of Reagan/Thatcher conservatism and embraced as a vitality that citizens felt themselves increasingly to lack. This simultaneity of the performative and the acrimonious left its marks on the Embattled.

These unexpected juxtapositions were also what prompted the longing for permanence, status, and authenticity. What Ulf Hannerz called a "world of movement and mixture" became known by its information flows, and religions—seen as permanent outrage and balm alike—availed themselves of this potential while bemoaning the changes it embodied.[54] And if the 1980s had not yet fully manifested the centerless postmodern city or the Babel of competing discourses that its theorists noted with self-satisfaction, it nonetheless was clearly a moment when Americans became aware of their overwhelmedness in a world of exponentially increased possible meanings and ideas.

In this ferment, religion was also transformed by the combination of the therapeutic with hyperpatriotism. In this, perhaps, religions were the means by which people adjusted to the collapse of an expectation of plenty, the fraying of old political infrastructures, and retreat from reform. American religions responded, at least in part, by amplifying their more outlandish qualities: brashness, sanctimony, doominess. Among the steadily more influential Martyrs, one of the loudest notions held that, despite the obvious cultural power conservatives had achieved, if one was insufficiently vigilant about government overreach (the state was always both rapacious and feeble), one risked a scenario like the opening of *Red Dawn*, the 1984 John Milius film that depicted valiant high-school patriots engaged in guerrilla resistance to the invading Soviet army. The way to avoid such catastrophe was to respond forcefully to what neoconservatives like David Horowitz and Bill Kristol were telling audiences was a "crisis of values."[55] In conservative journals, on conservative radio, and from a growing number in the political class, familiar rants against the liberal media and the abuses of academic freedom were polished. So the sweet promises of harmony, fat tax portfolios, and eternal life were bound to the conflict Americans seemed to crave. The "culture wars," then, was just a resonant name given to a condition of despair, not just over the loss of stable language and institutions, but over political transformations that few seemed willing or able to identify.

## The "Dream-Life" of Embattlement

The elements that make up Embattled America were coalescing more rapidly. What Michael Rogin called the "dream-life that so often dominates American politics" was being amplified and made more real with the advent of new technologies that anticipated Twitter's outrageous imaginings.[56] The collapse of history into fantasy, and the imperviousness of self-expression, are written deep into American history. On Reagan's watch, they helped provide cover for, among other things, two recessions, the collapse of the social safety net, and the Iran-Contra scandal. As central as these episodes were to his legacy, Reagan's airbrushed optimism helped wrap Nixon's promise to fight for the "silent majority" in a made-for-TV narrative shorn of negativity or complexity. This was how Reagan and his supporters could deny the obvious racial overtones of his August 1980 campaign speech at Mississippi's Neshoba County Fair, where, mere miles from the site where three civil rights activists were assassinated, Reagan voiced his praise for states' rights.[57]

Fighting back, reclaiming past glories, and all the other rallying tropes of the ascendant Christian Right of the 1970s and 1980s are clear pre-echoes of the Trump era. Since the 1960s, white conservatives in America had complained loudly about continually being portrayed as the oppressor, as the out-of-touch Archie Bunker kvetching from the couch. Contemporary broadsides against "social justice warriors" or "cancel culture" are the offspring of these earlier protests. One way to understand the present, then, is to see how the politics of shame so central to early identity politics (which might have described this shame as an appeal to higher morality or to the best of America's democratic traditions) was being converted into Embattlement: your criticism of my insensitivity, or even your mere identification of it, is tantamount to an attack on my very person. This shift makes sense alongside the politicization of interiority during these years: in the protection of a child from the offense of curricula, or in the legal legitimation of religious views (regardless of content) if they were "sincerely held."

One of the masters of this convergence was Georgia politician Newt Gingrich. Years before his leadership in the 1994 midterm elections, Gingrich responded to early electoral loss by generating a series of basically postmodern insights into the possibility of spectacle, simulacra, and repetition.[58] Gingrich's influential memo, "Language: A Key Mechanism of Control," instructed candidates to rely on adjectives that would do people's thinking for them: Democrats would be discussed only using words like "sick, pathetic, lie, anti-flag, traitors, radical, corrupt."[59] Policy debates were no longer going to be the province of the wonks; they were going to be arenas for mortal combat. This would work, Gingrich correctly observed, because "the No. 1 fact about the news media is they love fights. . . . When you give them confrontations, you get attention; when you get attention, you can educate."[60] Gingrich was fond of quoting Mao on waging "war without blood," and sought nothing less than total ideological victory.[61]

The fight was the thing. The fantasy was the justification. The tech was the vector. Mixed among it all was a fascinating blend of ideological dismissal of state power as such, and outrage that illegitimate pols have seized control of it. Throughout the 1980s, organizations like the Moral Majority continued to achieve electoral success at the local and national levels, often railing against an "immoral minority" whose outlandish policies flouted "a consensus of the majority of Americans."[62] These organizations also learned to convert their failures into authenticity and social capital. After Pat Robertson's defeat in the 1988 presidential primary, he and Ralph Reed worked on conservative Christianity's ground game in ways that proved transformative, helping usher in the Gingrich-led class of 1994 in the House of Representatives. Using Gingrich's insights about language, members of this younger political class not only sharpened politics as a mode of attack but leaned into the now-powerful refrain that Christians were persecuted, and that any obligation to make accommodations to a pluralistic social order was an attack on

America's godly lineage. As Michael Lienesch points out, the narrative implied in such claims made much of themes like "testing and overcoming," of David and Goliath imagery that public figures like Francis Schaeffer (whose film *A Time for Anger* celebrated martyrdom and held that "truth equals confrontation") were eager to employ.[63]

In many cases, these themes had lasted because it was not only Christian Right figureheads endorsing them but hundreds of radio shows, and television programs on Robertson's Christian Broadcasting Network and elsewhere. As the cable age exploded in the 1980s, Christian programming became more available. And, much like other Christian "alternatives" to "secular" culture, CBN and related networks successfully mimicked the look and the format of familiar news shows. The audience and the appetite were there.

Fox founder Roger Ailes professed sympathy for conservative Christianity. Ailes had long been an in-demand political consultant who specialized in making candidates from Nixon to Reagan more palatable to viewers. In 1992, Ailes became smitten with combustible radio personality Rush Limbaugh and thought there might be good money (and good politics) in syndicating Limbaugh's talk show. Limbaugh's combative style and penchant for exaggeration were initially outliers, but proved a durable harbinger of the tone of Embattled America. The famously pugnacious and ambitious Ailes became president of CNBC in 1993. Three years later, Ailes started up Fox News for Rupert Murdoch.[64]

Ailes shared with the anchors on Christian news shows the desire to restore mid-1950s America, an impulse that continues to be marketable precisely because it is detached from the actual history of the 1950s. Yet though Fox blended news reports with ample commentary, aping not just Limbaugh's approach to the news but Christian TV's idea that viewers had to know the *right way* to interpret it, Ailes promoted the network with the well-known claim that it would be "Fair and Balanced." Indeed, at the network's inaugural press conference in 1996, Ailes declared that Fox News' very existence was a correction against the distortions of the "liberal media."[65] Inside the network's executive meetings, it was agreed that their other explicit goal was to help elect Republican candidates, its first major test coming with the 2000 presidential campaign. A University of California study found that Fox had successfully "convinced roughly 200,000 [citizens] to vote Republican" via its messaging.[66] That same year, Florida mistakenly identified twelve thousand citizens as former felons, and purged them from voter rolls, a pattern that would repeat itself in that state in 2004 and 2012.[67] What connects these two episodes is the Martyrs' increasing confidence that they had to game the system if God's favored were to enjoy victory.

Claims about persecution—ranging from outrage at the abandonment of prayer in schools to excoriations of the moral rot of the Clinton administration—became so thoroughly woven into news stories that warnings acquired the aura of facts that had already happened. And the more that Whistleblower critics coalesced in their criticisms of Fox for hyperbole, misstatements, and red-meat outrage, the more ratings increased. What made Embattled America, then, was this amplification of themes long central to Christian media and the backlash against them. Chief among these is the sense that even modest reductions in privilege constitute attacks on Christianity's "rightful" dominance.[68] Fox in particular amplified the daily refrain that conservative white Christians are America's real victims, with Fox being "a safe haven for all of us gun-toting Bible clingers," and a "voice of resistance" to aggressive secularists.[69] The emphasis on these themes emerged from Ailes's instinct that there was a vast audience that could be successfully drawn to a network catering to their sense of victimhood. In time this viewership became indissolubly linked to Republican voters. So Fox strengthened and gave credibility to Christian media from the outside, because it showed that a "legitimate" news network was endorsing the same claims. And it simultaneously became a mouthpiece for the Christian Right, even as it claimed to stick strictly to the facts.

The hollowing out of American politics, combined with new developments in communications media, gave Martyrs the opportunity to make real the fantastical elements that had been cemented to conservatives' self-understanding since the 1960s. After the era in which conservatives perfected the attack ad, the coming Embattled Majorities construed the entirety of public life as one big attack ad, offense, and response cycle. Agendas were advancing everywhere unseen as the Whirl enabled the triumph of conspiracy. Teletubbies, Disney, and Harry Potter were advancing a radical homosexual agenda in tandem with the liberal media's attempt to discredit Christianity, which legitimated a "stealth campaign" of oppression against Christians protected by an activist judiciary. National sovereignty, female bodies, and innocent kids were being put at risk on the slippery slope of tolerance.[70] Richard Land was even still upset about John Lennon, declaring in 2005 that the "secular anthem" "Imagine" promoted a future of "clone plantations, child sacrifice, legalized polygamy and hard-core porn."[71]

Article after article showed America trying to figure "the evangelicals" out, continually missing the opportunity to figure out what cultural lack this obsession obscured. As Joe Scarborough held his "Enough is Enough" rallies, as there appeared in greater number conferences like "Judicial War on Faith" and groups like the Judeo-Christian Council for Constitutional Restoration (JCCCR), and as more Americans grew used to charges of judicial or congressional tyranny, somehow all this talk and all this outrage crowded out ways of seeing this conflagration as one caused by forces far larger than the "problem" of public religion.

## Blogging against Theocracy

The response to Martyrs' cultural power has been threefold. Whistleblowers furiously attempt to expose the hypocrisy of privileged white evangelicals bemoaning their struggles. Academics either point to the "complexity" of evangelical identity or publish breezy studies of "the middle." And, regular as clockwork, people on the left panic and wonder if they ought to be more publicly showy in their religiosity. None of these responses has changed Embattled America, not even after a year of pandemic and movements for racial justice.

Whistleblower texts, which have become something of a cottage industry since the George W. Bush administration, habitually inveigh against an "army" of "theocrats"; they fume that conservative evangelicals who tilt against disestablishment are hypocritical, since they benefit so clearly from it; or they conclude that this is not the kind of religion the Founders foresaw.[72] Such publications continue to pour out at a furious rate, including works by Richard Dawkins, Daniel Dennett, Sam Harris, and the late Christopher Hitchens's orgy of self-importance, *The Four Horsemen: The Discussion That Sparked an Atheist Revolution*; or Andrew Seidel's *The Founding Myth: Why Christian Nationalism is Un-American*.[73] The spirit of revenge blends with snark and outrage in such volumes, easily converted into fuel by Martyrs alert to anti-Christian discourse.

As popular texts lean in on the discourse of hypocrisy, other scholars continue to insist, as Christian Smith's well-known formulation has it, that conservative religionists "feel excluded, marginalized, or discriminated against by secular institutions and elites."[74] This recapitulation of the terms of the discourse itself provides little analysis beyond the documentarian.

No one anymore needs reminding (again!) that not all Christians are politically extreme, or that some evangelicals are wary of Christian nationalism. That these things are true does not change the fact that the engine of American politics runs largely on the fuel of extremism. In a certain sense, our analysis should begin from the presumption that outrage, combat, and moral spleen are in no way exceptions to some putatively "normal" politics. To say once more that there is complexity in every identity is not only to say forcefully that water is wet but leads away from strategies that might diagnose the larger political condition appropriately. Similarly, books like Robert Putnam's *American Grace* or the litany of Trump-era books seeking understanding of our fellow citizens read like echoes not simply of early communitarian writing but of the bizarre Tocquevillean notion that beside every political opinion is a religious one, usually existing in harmony.[75]

Such measured prose either has not reached or has not altered the vast swaths of citizens who feed off the snark and disdain Whistleblowers deal out. It seeps everywhere across our screens and our feeds. *Saturday Night Live* mocked Tim Tebow's aw-shucks piety and Pat Robertson raged against discrimination.[76] When conservative evangelical Trump supporters are likened to a "deranged" "cult" or a "virus," Tucker Carlson or Laura Ingraham is there to gobble up such rhetorical fuel and castigate the "Stalinists" of the Left.[77] Hundreds of Whistleblower articles mock the tawdry cinematic bathos of *God's Not Dead* while Franklin Graham warns that only a Trump electoral victory could save America from godlessness.[78] Whistleblower articles repeatedly raise the alarm about the New Apostolic Reformation, or the evangelical secessionist fantasy, or the religious "war on science," and point out with glee that conservative idol Ayn Rand would have scorned right-wing religiosity.[79] Every time a social media "sick burn" compares right-wing Christians to al-Qaeda, an evangelical responds by likening mere mockery to Jim Crow or Stalinism.

We are all trapped in the continual feedback loop of this discourse, in much the same way as the movie *Persecuted* screened endlessly at the 2014 Conservative Political Action Conference.[80] Chronicling these developments ought to lead us to a different set of conclusions. Americans have been persuaded that we are born for glory, a life lived for the realization of our triumphal self. This gives a new valence to the old slogan "The personal is the political." Differences of the scale of administration or the particulars of policy still exist, of course, but they are debated by a political class that benefits from citizens who have traded a commitment to structural change for the distracted pleasures of outrage. Even when outrage is justifiably directed at privileged white oligarchs, the outrage itself is sucked into a narrative preserving their power. Concerned citizens should, then, pivot from reflecting on the purported dangers or necessities of religion; we should shift the conversation to democracy's fundamentals in a way that might reshape our approach to public life.

Consider that the New Left once attacked the largely successful welfare state as insufficiently democratic and inclusive.[81] Now the Embattled, left with table scraps, use the fact that the system has failed as a reason to give up on the idea that systemic change is possible. The beloved community and the administrative state both require too much of citizens who have imbibed the message of Anti-politics. Policy specifics and even ideological bromides (Small government! Freedom!) are sold to citizens as promoting self-actualization, not as particular expressions of political thinking. So citizens barbarically yawp down the other, naming the resulting invigoration as freedom. And the anxiety and despair abide at the roots.

The metastasis of Embattlement since the 1960s must be understood as a spasm of rage that the quest for personal glory is difficult, that it is a different kind of movie from what we had imagined, that others do not exist to enable our narrative; over time, the rage becomes so familiar that we mistake it for the quest itself. And so the very question of limits—scarcity on the one hand, the need for self-limitation in politics on the other—gets converted into the action movie howl that shouts down other citizens as interlopers in our freedom.

## Proud Boys

Though more Americans seem willing to interrogate whiteness than before the protests of 2020, polls continue to indicate that supporters of President Trump are overwhelmingly likely to believe that white males face more discrimination than Muslims, women, African Americans, or LGBTQ persons.[82] South Carolina senator Lindsey Graham, after the Senate confirmation hearings for Brett Kavanaugh, complained, "I'm a single white man from South Carolina and I've been told to shut up."[83] Gun-toting militia members paraded Covid-heavy streets braying "All lives matter." The infuriated white male victim will, of course, not acknowledge that white men's voices have never not been heard, free to shout down everyone else. How should we understand this in light of the above history?

If we were to choose a historical avatar for the American timeline that took Prince and Bowie into the *bardo* and left us with President Trump, that avatar would be Andrew Jackson. In an era when long unquestioned features of American life—political parties, the expansion of franchise, the ratification of centralizing institutions—were deeply contested, Jackson lambasted the smothering "mother banks" that controlled the economy. Not just an early instance of gendered antistatist discourse (sucking at the teat of the nanny state, which breeds welfare queens), Jackson imagined Americanism as made in the image of armed men who kept the ears and noses of "effeminate" "redskins" hung around their necks as trophies, men who "settled" wild territory as one would a mare.[84] Jackson's portrait loomed from the gilded wallpaper behind Trump in the Oval, woven into the law that forcibly defended the construction of Standing Rock's pipeline, rowdily championing manhood against imagined opponents in the streets of Charlottesville, or in the Proud Boys and the Boogaloo Boys getting wild in the streets.[85]

The American imaginary is, of course, constructed from images of white male heroism (just as the American reality is, much to the agony of many white males, far different). The popular exploits of lone frontiersmen, the celebration of gunfighters and vigilantes, all this makes for a suggestive backdrop to a history of white complaint. The historian Richard Slotkin noted that the emergence of the film industry following the presidency of the outsize Teddy Roosevelt consolidated the links between American war and entertainment with manly virtue.[86] This was also the moment when the polis itself was expanding and the state consolidating even more managerial power, the ongoing push-pull of American democracy leading to an equally inevitable backlash in antistatism, vigilantism, the exercise of power over women and people of color. This backlash is, as James William Gibson writes, integral to white men's America as "a coherent mythical universe."[87]

Male Americans are taught to worship the gun, to romanticize battlefield valor, and to imagine the dreary arc of life as having a narrative shape, ideally ending in some kind of triumph. Where mid-twentieth-century scholars like Joseph Campbell posited oh-so-innocently the universal qualities of the hero's tale, the reality for America's suburban everydude converts these materials into defiance, all the world's counterinformation making up the mightiest of chips for each brawny shoulder. Martyr identity since the 1960s has invoked masculinist language to denounce liberals as not just godless but also as wimps. Hippies were gender-bending queers. Real men didn't hug trees; they had huge cars and guns, and John Wayne would never wear a mask to Costco or let Antifa steal an election. To be a man in America is linked to avoiding tethering, shirking obligations to planet or fellow citizen so you can become your bad-ass self. Tacit and explicit acceptance of "traditional" gender roles and disciplinarian childrearing is seen as the necessary preparation for this total freedom that white males accept as their birthright in America.[88] These associations echo in a public rhetoric that has always been militarized in America. Journalists would not be so excited to write about the "culture quibbles," after all. But since the 1970s, the real prospect of the loss of white male privilege (any decade now!) coaxed from our collective consciousness an unbroken spate of vigilante entertainments where strapped loners save us from tyranny.[89]

What is more, since at least the 1930s Americans have equated democracy itself with unbounded consumption, whose opposite we are led to presume is just such tyranny. From FDR to the war on terror, it is not only that a particular pattern of social interaction or mode of managed economy went largely unchallenged; consumerism became so rampant that it shaped our self-understandings, our expectations for what a good society looked like. The freedom to buy or to upgrade became freedom, full stop.[90] Better this than acknowledge how fragile America is and how sorely in need of reinvention our institutions are. Whether focused on conspiracy theory, Embattlement, or the swaggering seductions of outsiderdom, Americans have been loud in their outrage but have produced too little in the way of systemic reform or conceptual overhaul.[91] From this perspective Trump and the alt-right are no deviation, no crazed exception, but the natural telos of a half-century of white male identitarian complaint.

## Real Religion

What this history shows us is that, while debates about religion (and its outrages) are ubiquitous in American history, it is unproductive and unimaginative to think of Embattlement as simply turbulence amid the long saga of pluralism. It is, I think, even less productive to try to settle an argument with the Embattled, as this would keep Americans' focus on the wrong kinds of political matters. Instead, I approach the atmosphere of Embattlement as a climatologist would: not simply observing the existence of language that everyone already knows is out there, and about which everyone has opinions that they demand you listen to, but tracing its history and delineating its shapes and implications.[92] Or perhaps it would be more accurate to say that I approach Embattlement like a crime scene, making chalk outlines of the ambivalences about democracy that Embattlement conceals.

My hope is to entice readers to become interested in the conditions for improved citizenship, deliberation, and political innovation. A particular kind of American selfhood has congealed as a consequence of the attention given to Embattlement, a selfhood whose "freedom" is, tacitly or explicitly, defined as happiness. In addition to its misplaced politics, Embattlement reveals that the happiness of whiteness depends on ignoring its complicity in the suffering of others, and shields itself from this complicity by professing its own injury. Victims become killers become victims. The elan of the Whirl livens up the narrative qualities of these assertions, allowing not only for their amplification but also, as trauma theorist Anne Rothe puts it, for suffering to become a vehicle for people to "revel in their own sentimental arousal."[93] Such reveling in the suffering of the self allows us to deny the suffering of others. What about *my* needs?

Americans live in something like the Black Friday sale of the soul, scrambling to the finish line and claiming American historical privilege, political right, good order, and reason, rarely stopping to consider how much their identities have come to depend on the crises they bewail. If the future is jobless and all politicians are terrible, best to give up on change and just make sure you get yours. To point endlessly to "polarization," then, or to debate its periodization, is to fall back on clichés and conceptual givens. This condition should not be thought of as anomalous. This fractiousness *is* America; it is constitutive, even "normal." Embattlement is the leading face of a politics without any relevant distinction between ideology, mood, and brand; and in a context of "whitelash" and economic precarity, Embattlement represents the triumph of Anti-politics in the kingdom of feeling, turning away from the work of the beloved community in favor of crowdsourced fury.

My hope is that in documenting the large shapes of cultural discourse around religion and the self-understandings of Americans, I can demonstrate their shallowness, their role in convincing us that a false choice is a real struggle. The struggle Americans need to be invested in has little to do with religion. Rather, it remains the struggle to fend off antidemocratic tendencies in American life. We need to reject the fundamental degradation of politics itself that is our shared atmosphere. For part of what fuels Embattlement is frustration with the incrementalism and messy proceduralism of democratic politics itself. High above the red, white, and blue, satellites map us into Google Earth. Down below, the algorithms of our daily frittering are compressed into "big data." What it shows is a country that resists understanding itself, opting instead for fury and self-congratulation.

# 3

# The Whirl

## Virus, Narrative, and Noise

> All this, with what preceded, and what followed, occurred with such involutions of rapidity, that past, present, and future seemed one.
> —Melville, *Benito Cereno*

> How am I going to use the internet to save the world if I keep getting distracted by the internet?
> —Samit Basu, *Turbulence*

> Save me, O Lord, from lying lips and deceitful tongues.
> —Psalms 120:2

Fantasies, when mistaken for reality, can turn quickly into surreal episodes of violence. Think of the screen-lit rooms that today breed fantasies, such as "Pizzagate." Shortly after the 2016 presidential election, a furiously retweeted lewd fantasy involving Secretary Hillary Clinton and a child pornography ring prompted a gunman from Salisbury, North Carolina, to make an action movie pilgrimage to a pizza shop in Washington, DC, armed for truth and patriotism.[1] This, as readers likely know, was merely the start of the furious churn of conspiracy theory that has marked recent American politics. Our technologies and our blasted politics now give us the means of remaking ourselves as the victims of unseen others or plots whose existence cannot be disproved because of the intensity of our felt convictions. Forecasts and signs and chyrons and tweets worm into our brains continually, each of us an intercessory in the ritual our species has brought into being. What are we enabling with our continued submission to all this data?

## The Information

From the invention of the first crude tools circa 50,000 BCE to the beginning of the Common Era, humans rapidly expanded the capacity to measure things, to organize responses to threats, to amass facts. Since then, the amount of information available to humans doubled in 1,500 years, then again in 180 years, to the point where information is now doubling very nearly daily; it is outpacing itself.[2] Where once all that is solid melted into air, the air has now caught fire, entering the atmosphere I described at the end of the previous chapter. It is fast enough for us not to see it. We still imagine ourselves in stable spaces, where the boiling elements can harden into steel, and where we expect the solidification of knowledge: facts gathering like metal filings to the magnet of opinion, layer upon layer of information forced into a stable referent.

This expectation is itself whisked away by the relentlessness of the ideas in motion. Humans once explained acrimony and injustice by pointing to how little we knew of each other, a condition that bred anxiety and suspicion. Yet now, the maximal availability of information has actually amplified difference and antagonism. Particular viewpoints have been rendered fragile, because they cannot escape their own contingency. The rage that accompanies this fragility is a response to the feeling of being overwhelmed by the daily experience of a culture that keeps us continually stimulated and continuously anxious. This may be why many citizens either consciously seek an out (a conspiracy, a movement, getting off the grid) or dive headlong into fantastical self-creations. If the whole cannot be grasped, the ability to experience personally any isolated fragment of information sustains the idea that one's feelings are a sign of some meaning that eludes the grasp, without which these same feelings might lack substance.

We live in a Whirl: of noise, of words, of images, of forward motion. Consider the prospect of a simple Google search: if one were to type in just the title of this book, without bracket quotes, who knows how many thousands of pages might pop up in an order that might seem random but which is shaped by multiple unseen algorithms? We search, we skim, we select, and are sweetly satisfied at what we briefly conclude is the resolution of our investigation, even as we sense these acts instantly receding like the edges of the Einsteinian universe, tugged by flickering impulse and a global restlessness. And so we are adrift.

But the Whirl refers also to the noise of acrimony that defines American life. We wake to this clangor, we monitor it incessantly for updates to its multitude. I call it the Whirl since this seems to capture the ceaseless, seemingly inescapable, motion of information, ideas, identities, and emotions. People use the Whirl like this: imagine a moving body of water, either an eddy or a brisk stream, and then picture yourself placing a small toy vessel or a message in a bottle into this water, watching it race along a current out of your control. This is what people do with ideas, knowing that while they cannot control where ideas end up or how they are used, they can at least facilitate their circulation. But people also use this ceaseless flow to embolden the conceit that things are *not* moving, that what people believe to be true must be true for everyone; to ignore what we call truth, in fact, makes one an enemy.

My use of metaphor to explain the Whirl is also part of what the Whirl is, endlessly mutable and self-referential. Perhaps imagine, instead, the interpreter of the Whirl as a kind of remote viewer, or a code-cracker, with huge Cold War earphones around his ears, hunched in some secret room listening to the din. We seek a pure signal in all this noise, one that sounds like us, confirms that we are free of this centerless drift. We are confronted each second with our own insignificance, the blunt fact of our voice drowned out. Embattlement at least partly funnels outrage at this condition, giving a name to the phenomenology of felt insignificance. The undeniable experience of feeling affronted and persecuted as deeply as Americans daily do is taken as confirmation of the self's inviolable authenticity. And this sustains the belief that we can escape the Whirl by finding the right information in its deepest vortices.

## My Own Private Network

America did not go crazy only after Facebook walls and tweets came into being. Observers of American culture in the 1950s often remarked on the superfluity of technology with a jaundiced, Weberian eye, worried about the automation of everyday life. By the late 1960s, though, trying to make sense of riots, bacchanalia, and the waning of utopian dreams, critics like Joan Didion and Renata Adler turned to the media as an explanatory force, with Adler calling it "that natural creator of discontinuous, lunatic constituencies."[3] This marked a shift from the critical language of Frankfurt School theorists like Theodor Adorno, for whom media could still be grasped as an ideological form, the expression of a singular power.[4] Somewhere between Marshall McLuhan's widely touted prophecies and the spleen of *Network*, new outlets for the voice were proliferating.[5] Yet they seemed increasingly untethered to a purpose beyond their own amplification.

By the 1980s, scolds like Neil Postman warned of our "descent into a vast triviality," a notion that makes some sense in light of cat memes and the Kardashians.[6] But to say that new technologies have emptied communication of its substance seems deeply ahistorical, while also confusing the lack of significance with a purported lack of content. I would not mistake Cardi B's Twitter takedowns of Trump for the kind of dialogic media that democracy may require (though it is hard to deny the resonance of a line like "I can't believe they wanna see me lose that bad" in Embattled America).[7] I would say instead that the triumph of the Whirl is not just in its ability to distract and titillate but in its ability to amplify older social and epistemological tendencies in a time when many Americans also require the Whirl to function as the lost polis for which they yearn. So while older historical or analytical models might have criticized media based on the presumption that revolutionary and reactionary forces could be clearly distinguished, information now is often too dense, fast, and decentered for such diagnosis.

This inability to locate a stable referent has, far beyond the now-trite observations of postmodern epistemology, had significant impacts on the larger political irrationality and incoherence that is visible everywhere. The discrediting of the political as such has meant that fewer and fewer cultural battles recognize the same stakes they once did: citizens think of themselves less as shareholders and more as protagonists-in-waiting, their opponents existing to be gunned down in the postapocalyptic wasteland. Embattlement is neither a system nor a social movement. But it has powerful actors and mappable complexity. We can think about it as the result of what Manuel De Landa calls "nonlinear history," with cultural moments shaped by "unintended collective consequences of human decisions" rather than by the exercise of a single distinct will or agency.[8] This conforms to the regular use Americans have made of new technologies to transform the world so that it mimics one's theories *about* it. After all, anonymous cranks existed long before comments sections or being ratioed on Twitter.

So while online trolls make for interesting data, my interest is in Embattlement as an illness, with the Whirl the climate facilitating the circulation of that illness. Evidence does little work when public claims produce their own affects and accretions, which absorb and transform all critique into part of what it means to be Embattled. The privatization of public life and the discrediting of expertise are clearly part of this story, too. The Long Con of Anti-politics has worked. A vast percentage of public life has been sucked down into the quicksand of American authoritarianism and anti-institutionalism, which enables the kind of radical subjectivity on which Embattlement depends. As the institutions and norms that ought to ground public life have been steadily targeted for decades—funds slashed here, anti-government caricatures absorbed there—Americans have used media to amplify the idea that politics is about not being hassled.

## From Mainframes to the Abyss

The American producer economy began to fray in the early 1970s, as corporations metastasized, industry cratered, and the buying power of the dollar flatlined.[9] This was also when something called electronic mail emerged from the hulking mainframes of 1960s MIT and 1970s ARPANET. From a storage device and filing system came the idea, faster and weirder than the telegraph from the previous century, of wired boxes talking to each other. Nietzsche's abyss in real time. Linked to developments led by the Defense Advanced Research Projects Agency (DARPA), the US military and NASA appropriated the new media, and networks of computers emerged—coaxial cables, satellites floating unseen in the void, paperless exchanges as our path to glory. By 1990, Switzerland's CERN beta-tested what would become the World Wide Web, building on the work of Tim Berners Lee as well as early graphics companies like CompuServe and AOL. New acronyms replicated quickly: URL, PCP/IP, MS-DOS, and HTML. Then came popular browsers like Marc Andreesen's Netscape, and with it followed money, dial-up, free porn, and personal pages hosted at sites like Geocities.[10]

It has not taken that long to evolve from the agonizingly slow load of a single web page to the bizarre hypertrophy of our moment, filled with Twitter bots, troll farms, deep fakes, and Instagram. Think of the blank, corroded expanse that lay inert behind Trump's flashy 1980s: a rusted out former steel mill in Elyria, Ohio, or an unfinished freeway ramp hanging over a potholed section of Baltimore road, or the encroachment of yet another bedroom community into the Inland Empire. This blank space and time had to be filled since citizens did not feel sure about what work, what pension, what future awaited them. With the revocation of the Fairness Doctrine in

1987, ideas ran riot on cable TV and AM radio, with an energy that would be hugely amplified on the Net. The Net soon became known for being acquisitive and exhaustive in ways that forecast the Whirl. This was a miracle. Francis Fukuyama was right. Information exploded into liberation once the Iron Curtain fell.[11]

In 1994, the North American Free Trade Agreement was ratified and the first spam message was sent over Usenet: "GLOBAL ALERT FOR ALL: JESUS IS COMING SOON."[12] Subjugated knowledge burst forth, buoyed equally by the spirit of yearning and of revenge. Black metal tape traders. Paramilitary groups. Exegesis list-servs. End Times preppers and UFO conspiracy theorists. The Whirl was made from the combination of digital ubiquity and the conspiratorial. Everyone was now a sweaty Lovecraft character, poring over the *Egyptian Book of the Dead*, the *Turner Diaries*, Area 51 files, and JFK assassination theories, all concealed from us by the "lamestream" media that denied the fix was in and that The Man really was out to get us, after all.

This is what it is like to live "post-truth." This is what makes us turn to Life as Action Movie, whose continued consolations depend not only on the promises of post-Reagan politicians who exploit it, nor even on the structural conditions I describe elsewhere, but also on how citizens allow themselves to become cognitively rewired to see themselves as Embattled. One part of this process is shaped by what I call the Epistemology of Favorites. For a great many citizens, news feeds, Spotify playlists, or Facebook filters serve to connect them only to what they have already accepted as valid. This shapes a mode of perception whereby the fundaments of knowledge and identity ("favorites") act as battlements, filters, and authorities that on the one hand engage in rigid boundary maintenance yet on the other hand generate a continual feedback loop between already settled convictions and onrushing data, all of which can only inevitably confirm what is already *felt* to be true, with feeling now understood as knowledge. *Pace* Cass Sunstein, social media and the "news" do not shield people from competing perspectives; we simply inhabit a condition in which they have no possibility of being anything but wrong.[13] Why is this so effective, though, and what purpose does it serve?

In my view, it helps users of the Whirl to navigate the tension between the need to narrate (that is, organize) all this incoming information and the surplus that leaves them paralyzed. The base experience is too-muchness, the self endlessly drifting apart, the yearning for stability always unmet, spinning like a stuck download. So the information people gather is understood as responsible for the lack that is characteristic of contemporary life, even as they need to be sustained by information's flow until they can finally figure out how to prove you wrong with that one deadly hyperlink.

While people insist that they deal only with things called facts, the experience of the Whirl is like being awash in a kind of informational plasma, awaiting only the right narrative. To explain this condition, it has become common to employ a core syntax made from terms like genes, memes, viruses, and fragments. Proud Whistleblower Richard Dawkins famously provided some of the base descriptions of memes and their "spreading power," their "infectivity."[14] We might think of Embattlement as an especially infectious meme, leaping constantly into renewed life with each new outraged consciousness. Religion is both the vector and the subject, enabling people to see patterns of meaning. The Whirl is no vast Borgesian library, a repository of all the secrets we can now finally find out; it is the cloud of our unknowing.

Even in the wake of the pernicious Russian interference in America's 2016 presidential election, which made clearer how the conceptual logic and designed addictiveness of apps and ads can be weaponized, language cannot quite keep pace with the Whirl.[15] We use antiquated terms like hack and leak—as if the immensity of it can be thought of as a single barrier breached, one body of information released—instead of accretions, swells, and dispersals. This is a moment when people can be taught what to think and feel simply by the crowd-source of ideas and intense emotional accompaniments. Distraction deepens disempowerment, to which people submit involuntarily by linking their feelings to the power of global data. Following a half-century in which the Long Con of discrediting politics has succeeded, to the benefit of the Far Right and the mega-rich, the triumph of exaggeration and incitement over evidence reproduces Embattlement internally.

To read the news is to wonder how so many things can actually be happening, and to wonder what in the world we can do, and to wonder how many people can see plain things so differently. The constancy of this unsettling experience inevitably produces and amplifies the paranoia that is elsewhere the product of direct manipulation. Embattlements are thus sticky in the sense conveyed by Sarah Ahmed, meaning that they are as much clusters of accumulated activity as they are circulating feelings.[16] When Mike Pence claims, for example, that criticisms of his homophobic policies are attacks on his faith, this becomes one of many moments when politics becomes emotionally overdetermined by the idea of religion as exempt from political scrutiny. And yet, those outraged by such episodes rarely pause to think how outrage itself preserves the condition people seek to escape: because the speed of the Whirl is intoxicating, the sense is that in order to outdo or out-tweet one's fellow citizens, it is imperative to surf ever faster, to keep up with the almost unbelievable rapidity with which events and feelings are spewed into the Whirl. Indeed, outrage is practically the algorithm of social media, whose intentionally addictive qualities keep users burrowing ever further into that of which they are already convinced. This leads to an uncritical assumption that people's capacities for citizenship depend on involvement—even if via principled renunciation—with these technologies. Twitter, of course, has a significant documentarian purpose, coming from citizens in the streets or from reporters chronicling the depredations of the Trump administration. But the potential ends of this documentation, and all this signifying, remain out of reach.

In an earlier America, Ralph Waldo Emerson wrote that "all conversation is a magnetic experiment."[17] A century later, C. Wright Mills extended the Deweyan distinction between a mass and a public into the age of mass media, in that mid-century moment when the world of advertising concentrated its efforts on selling the affluent on a mood and a lifestyle called America.[18] Now the chief products are speed and impatience: kill the pop-up, scroll past, swipe left. The hosannas of technology everywhere accompany this experience: blogging will save democracy by unleashing the voice of the average citizen; the Whirl is an expression of pure American possibility! But what the Whirl actually does is ensure that there are always enough "haters" to maintain your self-image.

Consider how this works psychologically. It is widely documented that, cognitively, humans give disproportionate influence to minority views if these conform to their identity.[19] The Whirl not only provides the raw materials for this tendency; it allows people to inhabit a consolatory dreamworld while still expecting the material comforts promised to the rights-bearing citizen of liberal democracy. The Whirl's power is deepened because of other cognitive patterns, too. Thomas Mulholland's well-known research determined, as early as 1964, that even brief exposure to televisual stimulation (a sitcom, the news) increased the human brain's production of alpha waves; these both increased viewers' receptivity and weakened their focus.[20] The interiority that allows the state and the judiciary to recognize something called "religion" is protected only by the thinnest membrane separating it from a deluge of stimuli. We are aware of it enough to be continually on guard, but not enough to resist. So the face of America™ is graphically morphed from a Framer in a powdered wig to a gun-prepper uploading QAnon conspiracies on YouTube.

It is chilling to think that this may represent the culmination of older patterns, that steady blurring of truth and story in what Nathaniel Hawthorne long ago called America's "tongue-governed democracy."[21] If people no longer trust that things are as obvious as facts, and will not admit that they are spinning stories about religion, the Whirl becomes the medium outside of which people cannot see, experience, or make judgments other than those they have already embraced as true. Citizens still regard themselves as individuals possessing rational faculties, but invest most of their energy in "alter[ing] an unpleasant reality by making it into something more pleasurable."[22] The pleasures of outrage can excite lives of cubicles and traffic and online shopping, as long as the categories *feel* clear, as long as my world is sufficiently distinct from yours.

On the conscious level, people know they are using technology to achieve their ends: knowledge acquisition, connection, self-promotion. Less consciously, technology is the dream that an idea will never die, much less the triumphal self. To accept that selfhood takes shape partly through such media, though, is to acknowledge that identities in Embattled America are shaped not just by the Epistemology of Favorites described above but through the constancy of ratings and evaluation that make up life online: a circumstantial, fragmentary, blink-quick toll that cannot help but make people feel that they, too, only matter through such ratification. This has the effect of amplifying two mental faculties. On the one hand, because people have more access to things that shore up their point of view, they become vastly more skeptical about alternate points of view. On the other hand, people are also far more confident in what they find online because of the unconscious belief that, shorn of the mediating interests of owners and bureaucrats, they can trust the Yelp review, the Rate My Professor evaluation, or the Metacritic movie rating. The people are speaking! In the continual momentum of this self-creation, the boundaries we work on so relentlessly are buffed down, always fragile and always in need of more work.

This is one of the reasons Embattlement is so effective: it explains an identity's fragility while also propelling its validation. Religion is an excitable actant amid the apathy that sometimes comes from informational gluts.[23] Through religion's outrages, self-recognition is made more likely, as is the maintenance of America's dreamworld: of an abundant economy, of perfect freedom, of holy isolation. Yet while religion is a vague enough category to serve such varied purposes, legally and politically it must be sufficiently tangible to become injured and Embattled. Embattlement is easily located, and always lacking substance, living in the inscrutable, unmovable domain of feeling. In the absence of any shared evaluative criteria for bestowing rights, for recognizing difference as legitimate, and for perceiving otherness as anything other than status threat, Americans continue to excoriate each other around this thing called religion. It is an alarming condition. No Martyrs or Whistleblowers are redlined by banks, subject to stop and frisk, to inequitable wages, or being separated from their parents at the southern border. This ongoing obsession of large groups of Americans is increasingly detached from the most urgent matters of justice, equality, and human rights.

## Suffering Religion Online

The fact of these anti-political debates clogging up public life reminds us that we live not at some bright dawn of utopic digital democracy, but at just another stage in corporatist, managed democracy. Frustrated of other ways of becoming citizens, the loud and the shocking are rewarded by the attention they receive. Politics now seems far removed from notions like evidence, suasion, accountability, and respect; public action often resembles online trolling: one engages in deliberate provocation, knowing that reprimands from authority will allow you to complain about unfair treatment from "mods."

Religion facilitates this combativeness not just because it can be inflammatory but because it is a thing about which Americans are largely incapable of surprise. Its public narrations are so tightly woven that no new "fact" can penetrate them unless it facilitates settled arguments. The Whirl both soothes and stokes anxiety about religion, like a WebMD symptom check, making it more probably that the very problems it promises to solve linger on and on. The lament is part of this condition, too. Even in the early 1960s, sociologist Richard Meier predicted that "society would face a deluge of data within fifty years," and that this would precipitate a crisis.[24] Multiple studies have anxiously documented the somatic effects of exposure to exponentially increasing data, which range from frustration to cardiovascular stress to "decreased benevolence," and (significantly) overconfidence.[25] The suffering of another is just noise, whereas ours is real. We want to avoid information's obligations, and enjoy its amusements. But we also mistake information for entertainment, and knowledge for pleasure.

Difference has been reduced to vexation. Because the Whirl is defined by no commonly accepted evaluative criteria, and indeed calls them into question, the habits of mind once distinctive of conspiracy theory are now everyone's habits of mind, those "portentous and sinister meanings" that "commingle facts and speculation."[26] This is no watered-down statement of Heisenberg's uncertainty principle or a nod to the neuroscientist's reminder that human agency relies on superimposing patterns of "meaning" onto the sense data we constantly receive. The Whirl goes beyond simple cognition and perspectivalism to provide an endless *narrative resource*, the explanatory power of data converted by the forces of credulity, conspiracy, and celebrity. The weight of disdain has taken the place of political conviction.[27] The content of a public narrative becomes a function of style, force, and density, all of it somehow understood as personal. This is how one comes to believe oneself part of an Embattled Majority.

The problem of truth and certainty is not new to the age of the mainframe and the iPhone, but it becomes ever more complicated when people listen so raptly to themselves. Screens, circuits, towers, satellites, a mesh of energy across the globe: we live as if in a Jungian collective unconscious dreamed up by science fiction author William Gibson. As media theorist Paul Kedrosky aptly described it, the ubiquity of media has made of life a combination of "cheap connections plus cheap collisions ... a way of throwing things into violent juxtapositions, with the resulting collisions reordering my thinking."[28]

The Whirl is not magic. It is made of machines, built from techniques that are publicly knowable, moving through energies that can be transcribed, producing speech and images and ideas that can be resisted. But the brash overconfidence of Embattlement compensates for the continuous disruption of this spin-cycle world. In this, Embattlement becomes a mode of attentiveness, of piety, almost like a prayer that the persecution will abide, since it provides the opportunity to declare the triumphal (and/as Embattled) self, whose feelings are the only things that cannot be falsified.

Americans rely so heavily on the opportunity for technological self-invention that we have grown comfortable with the presence of surveilling power in our quotidian activities. Citizens profess that they have nothing to hide from the surveillance state, and document their every activity on social media. This refusal to hide the mundane is thus one of the most powerful cognitive and documentary means we have of ratifying the technopower of the Whirl. The mutual energy that distractedness and self-exaltation conduct is part of the larger depoliticization that accounts for America's current condition. The violent, urgent reassertion of singularity that an Embattled Majority enacts is both a response to and symptom of this acquiescence to the power of the surveillance state, which traps us inside culture's giant pop-up ad just as surely as inside the frame of grainy government footage.[29]

## Virus, Narrative, and Noise

Mere criticism of social media will not chart a way beyond this condition. The principled excoriation of new technologies is, indeed, one of the most popular positions within a neoliberalism that offers different products for the overwhelmed, ranging from mindfulness apps to design podcasts that can help create a calmer workspace. None of these, however, alters the context in which ideas circulate so vigorously and sustain the inflammations of anti-politics.

Long before Covid-19 raced across the planet, the phrase "went viral" was regularly invoked in accounts of rumor, story, and reaction.[30] Think what it means. A virus is often characterized by its continual genetic mutation. The power and reach of these mutations—and their capacity to harm—depend on what is called their "antigenic makeup." Geneticists use this term to describe the "protein coat" of a virus, the surface characteristics which can enable its rapid spread via shedding. If the "protein coat" of Martyrs or Whistleblowers is made up in a certain way, fashioned from antiliberalism or anticlericalism, then its antigenic makeup is conducive to taking hold.

Whether a virus is at the lower level of mutability or the higher level, it is made up of many thousands of different strains. Viruses are actually clusters of diseases, making them harder to diagnose and to cure. If in the case of Glenn Beck's conspiracy theories or Donald Trump's tweets one thinks that "religion" is the key or the only thing, one is misdiagnosing the strain. The viruses of Embattlement are clusters, often masked by a singularity. Both epidemics (more localized) and pandemics (global in reach) are defined by the mutable quality of certain viral strains (presenting as clusters). Some strains are more likely to infect certain populations than others, depending on their political predispositions, online habits, and more. Yet whether we think about the fury of a Tea Party crowd or an evangelical history text, what seems interesting about viruses (and about virality) is that one cannot simply isolate the organism infected with the virus (e.g., swine), since the host is only one of several "vectors" by which the virus can be circulated (e.g., waterfowl or saliva or antistatism). There are always other vectors or cultural conduits by which ideas and viruses are circulated.[31]

What, then, what would a vaccine be? First and foremost, the patient needs diagnosis. The conventional take on the petitions of the Embattled, exposed to the contagions of the Whirl, is that they are responding to the violation of their selves' boundaries by an especially potent pathogen. But the implication of what I have written about the Whirl is that selves are actually made in networks and viral chains, even as they cling to fantasies of stability.[32] Fundamental to Embattlement is the conceit that religion is a single, stable thing. This is what law says it is: a protected class. This is what polling says it is: a preference, or a belief. This is what politics says it is: an identity, movement, or interest. This is what Embattlement says it is: either a hostile force, or the only thing protecting us.

In the chapters ahead, I scrutinize the construction of Embattlement through accretions of emotions and data that help sustain anti-politics. We can understand some of this by acknowledging how it amplifies older American furies and demonologies which, as Hawthorne observed, mark historical moments "without an idea beyond the momentary blaze."[33] No less than in contemporary America, the nation's oldest and most consistent mode of self-fashioning is, Hawthorne wrote, like a "great mass of fiction to which I gave existence, and which has vanished like cloud-shapes."[34] If older forms of communication had a narrative quality, now it is not simply that we don't know the outcome, we live always having lost our place in the story.

Americans need new stories within the Whirl. These will be political tales that require new languages for the telling, since what is at stake is not simply identity or moral principle, but a form of knowing. The reductive frame of Embattlement is shaped at the nexus of the exposé, the pileup of evidence, and affront. It has become too common to recognize religion in moments of outrage, which continually makes religion a fighting occasion. And citizens tell themselves that the sheer number of these fights, and their perceived importance, makes participating in them of world-historical importance. Worthy of a prominent scene in life's action movie, one often articulated through a commodified resistance, is a kind of cultural cosplay that transforms nothing. I call this a *Defense of the Suburbs*, to signify how Embattlement misreads the context and the stakes of its activities, because that most average of spaces (the suburbs) in no way requires the kind of heroic defense the Embattled imagine. Of course, the veracity of Embattlement claims clearly matters to Martyrs and Whistleblowers. This very insistence, though, helps reduce politics to a single thing: a name, an experience, a controversy, a category. Embattlement is the ordering of desire, mood, and identity in the Whirl, its outrage concealing its outrageous departure from the political in which it feigns investment.

The only reason to presume or hope that the Whirl won't maintain its power over us is if we also presume the kind of person and citizen that the Whirl arguably makes impossible. The remainder of this book is about digging toward that kind of citizenship by first interrogating its debasement—in several episodes of Embattlement—and then extrapolating an alternate conception. If Embattlement is what gives all this data its gravity and its narrative quality, we should change the subject, instead of living in the exhaust fumes of a half-century's relentless fantasy and rage. Continuing to obsess over Embattled religion is giving in to our own continued manipulation, imagining that standing in line for our own righteous Action Movie is politics enough.

# 4
# Worrying about Scars
## Glenn Beck and Authenticity

> The public has adjusted to incoherence.
> —Neal Postman

There once was a man who could cry on cue. His name was Glenn Beck and for many years he attracted fervent support and deep derision for his combination of conspiracy theory, pugnacious patriotism, and carefully manufactured emotional performance. Beck's public claims about religion remain loud, and it is surprising that a man who has been so consistently discredited remains so central to Martyrs' discourse. Yet to study Beck is to see that such discrediting is the path to *authenticity* in Embattled America. You are never more real than when they are coming for you.

Much of the initial talk about Beck focused on his on-air tears. Beck loved the country that much, his supporters swooned, while his many critics howled that he was a charlatan. His emotionally labile performances matched the higgledy-piggledy nature of the conspiracies he peddled on his shows. In makes sense that Beck emerged in a decade defined by disorientation—from the September 11, 2001, attacks to the Iraq War, from global capitalism's near collapse to the rage directed against President Barack Obama—given how regularly his broadcasts sprang from the feeling of being unmoored.[1] Beck gave voice to most of the Martyrs' go-to themes: a government held hostage by elites, fervidly chronicled secret plots, and promises to defend America and its religion.

While critics might dismiss Beck's charges that the thugs were coming for Christianity, what Beck was really up to was selling a species of emotional authenticity that entrenched the power of the triumphal American self: a self that is entitled to freedom from others, and from complexity, on a personal journey whose narrative destiny is America's, written as possibility into each heart's democratic vistas. Further illustrative of Embattled America's authenticity is his use of the tone of twelve-step programs and the therapeutic. Beck's style of conversion narrative required killing what is alien, even as the showy denunciation of critics along the path to glory showed how necessary those critics were to Martyrs' self-image.[2]

But is Embattled authenticity different from other models? Sincerity and authenticity are the inheritances of the inward turn (from Augustine to Montaigne) so central to modernity, and their ascent in modern rights-based political regimes gave primacy to a narrow, but durable conception of religion.[3] As Charles Taylor has written, it was following the Enlightenment that religion became seen as a *thing*, a discrete category or form of experience that was associated with the rights bestowed on citizens of democracies. Taylor describes how religion changed from a pillar of social order to an option inside what he calls "the immanent frame."[4] Secularism in the modern era is not, however, the absence of religion but rather, Taylor explains, a way of relating to it. In societies that ostensibly decouple social institutions from religious influence, different types of moral agents and citizens thus emerge: instead of faith in providence, society cultivates faith in "the honesty and competence of human actors, the accuracy of information, the wisdom of one's own investment decisions, and the efficacy of the legal and technological systems underpinning market exchange."[5] Modern selves are implicitly understood as deliberative but also as trustworthy in their self-reliance and rationality.

Lionel Trilling wrote about the emergence of "sincerity" as a "discernible moral value" in the sixteenth century.[6] This was linked not just to the emergence of character in fiction but to the emerging contractarian understanding of the person in the West, whereby giving one's word was tantamount to a legal guarantee between subjects, and also the expression of one's inviolable sovereign personhood.[7] In time, Trilling notes, "Authenticity as a concept came to triumph over sincerity," a transition that can roughly be summarized as the triumph of Kant over Shakespeare, the juridical over the confessional.[8] While this history can be described differently, the centrality of the individual, rights-bearing subject to modern conceptions of law and sovereignty is obvious. What is curious about America's Embattled Majorities, though, is that in their furor they do not so much reverse the transition as fuse the categories; for in both the legal and the colloquial sense, sincerity is now confused with authenticity, and it is this mashup that is often expected of "real" politicians and "real" religion.

Americans are often angry and confused about the "proper" place for religion, but generally assume that religion "at its best" is sincere, and deeply held, and solemn, and thereby authentic in the sense of being nonfraudulent.[9] Such presumed interiority links back up to the intellectual tradition that concerns Taylor, in which "the essential impact of good religion takes place *in foro interno*: on one hand, it generates the right moral motivation; on the other, by remaining within the mind and soul of the subject, it refrains from challenging the external order."[10] For Taylor, this has yielded not just the familiar and oft-debated demarcation of public and private spheres of activity but "a steadily increasing emphasis on a religion of personal commitment and devotion."[11] This seriousness of personal religion both emerges from and simultaneously demands inner vigilance, a self-policing of boundaries once imposed externally. This partly accounts for the emphasis on "sincere choice" or "sincerely held" belief in jurisprudence, in public culture, and in professing to be entitled to political rights on this basis. Interestingly, though, it is this very enhancement of the interior that creates what Taylor calls the "porous selfhood" so characteristic of modernity, one that "is more fragile, often evanescent, and subject to doubt."[12]

Seen from this perspective, shielding feeling from scrutiny and criticism is no recipe for overcoming public conflict, but instead can be interpreted as a license to act up. Assumptions about personal commitment in the cultivation of private religious sentiment may still exist as a background hunch; but on the ground, Embattled Americans generally fight about religion in the abstract rather than about assumptions about personhood that might be shaping their larger political ambivalences. Most citizens simply presume that they are the rational, self-determining agents recorded in historical and political memory, yet they rarely develop the dialogic or intellectual habits associated with such personhood. This failure left unguarded the cultural terrain where Beck and his followers linked triumphalist authenticity with Embattled religion.

## Birth of an Action Hero

In the early days of the Obama presidency, I became curious about Beck when I learned of his obsession with academics. Why would a talk-show host give so much airtime to professors he despised, like theologian James Cone or sociologist Frances Fox Piven? Beck often situated these figures on old-school conspiracy charts. One of the most elaborate depicted a "Tree of Revolution": Che, Saul Alinsky, and Keynes were rooted deep in the earth, alongside the long-defunct Students for a Democratic Society.[13] Further up the tree, dollars were festooned next to the acronyms ACORN and SEIU, leading to a treetop overseen by Barack Obama. Beck breathlessly led viewers through arcane flights of paranoia, with the indignation of a rebel, though one who only wanted to restore the status quo.

Raised Catholic in small-town Washington, Beck attended a Jesuit prep school. After his mother's death and his stepbrother's suicide, the adolescent Beck began a long relationship with "Dr. Jack Daniels."[14] Forgoing college, Beck relocated to Provo, Utah, where he became an avid talk radio listener. Beck was an autodidact, combining anti-institutionalism with a love of mass media. After breaking into radio, Beck's early shows like *Captain Beck and the A-Team* hewed to the model of the drive-time or "morning zoo" programs found across national markets (catering to white male boomers with jokes about golf and kids, loads of lame sexual innuendo, and a "party-time" vibe associated with day-drinking and Dad rock). Beck cycled through radio gigs, addictions, and marriages.[15] He began what he called a "spiritual quest."[16] He read books by authors as wide-ranging as Adolf Hitler, Pope John Paul II, and Carl Sagan. And in 1999, Beck converted to the Church of Jesus Christ of Latter-Day Saints (LDS).

Beck finally fetched up in Tampa, Florida, where his *Glenn Beck Program* debuted in 2000. Soon picked up by the powerful Premiere Radio Networks, Beck scored a prime-time opinion show on CNN. Following the 2008 presidential elections, he jumped to Fox News and emerged as one of the most combustible (and occasionally lachrymose) critics of the Obama administration. Beck's popularity soared over the next few years, as he fronted what he said was "a movement . . . not a TV show."[17]

Beck toured the country giving performances that combined rants, comedy, and self-help confessionalism. He rallied for the troops, for the National Rifle Association, for his church, and—fundamentally—for America. And it was here that Beck emerged as an energetic Martyr, homologizing his own triumph over substance abuse with America's need for independence from big government. Just as Beck the addict needed to surround himself with positive influences, America needed to remove bad people (like liberals and secularists) from its life so as not to bottom out. What was more, Beck's insight into his own special purpose could be yours.[18] The divine character of American possibility was expressed in the idiom of the therapeutic, much as in the bestselling book *The Secret*, by Rhonda Byrne, where the abundant universe opens up just for us; constraints or disagreements are framed as roadblocks to the divine itself. Critics were smugly dismissive, but Beck promised self-actualization through the defense of religion.

## Religion as Decoder Ring and Trojan Horse

Beck's worldview owes a debt to LDS political thinkers like Ezra Taft Benson.[19] But particularly alarming to Whistleblowers was the influence of Cold War conservative Cleon Skousen, whose texts *The Making of America* and *The Naked Capitalist* Beck considers "divinely inspired."[20] Skousen warned repeatedly about the need to defend a Constitution under siege from political dissidents, religious heretics, and deviants of all stripes.[21] Such views were influenced by Skousen's membership in the John Birch Society. Skousen championed a minimal state, not merely for libertarian reasons, but out of fear of a communist global state that might persecute nonconformists (as seen in his "The Communist Attack on the John Birch Society" and "The Communist Attack on the Mormons").[22]

Beck began embracing Skousen's ideas after the terrorist attacks of September 11, 2001. He admired what he saw as the uniquely American spirit on display after the attacks, but feared its erosion. Beck feared that Skousen's predictions were coming true. He founded the 9/12 Project in order to publicize his fears. In it, he "distilled the original 28 [Framers' principles] down to the 9 basic principles."[23] They seem less like a distillation of late eighteenth-century political theory than a litany of conservative talking points. Some are boilerplate celebrations ("America is good" or "I believe in God and He is the center of my life"); others celebrate Randian individualism ("There is no guarantee of equal results," or "Government cannot force me to be charitable"); and one declares that "my spouse and I are the ultimate authority, not the government."[24] These convictions, ostensibly harvested from the Revolutionary period, are underwritten by the 9/12 Project's 12 Values, among them reverence, hope, humility, sincerity, and gratitude.[25]

Americans love lists, and also the notion of "personal responsibility," not because it enshrines the kind of hard-won self-reliance each citizen yearns to manifest but because it resonates with antigovernment griping. Beck picked up on the Tea Party's energy and used the September 12, 2009, Taxpayer March on Washington as a cross-promotional opportunity to publicize the

9/12 Project. Beck liberally deployed generic populist claims: that Americans are taxed to fund social programs for free-riders, and that real Americans are deceived by liberal journalists and godless academics.[26] Any deviation from what Beck described as traditional America—whether by changing the tax code, supporting green energy, or defending state-administered social provisions—was likened to "redistribution," and thus Marxism.[27] It was also the recipe for Beck's bête noire: "progressivism." Progressivism, Beck intoned, sought to "destroy America as it was originally conceived."[28]

Beck was, in short, the master epistemologist for Embattled America: a spray of hyperlinks marketed as a worldview. The self that was rendered precarious by healthcare and bureaucracy could be protected with enough unmasking and exposure of the czars and imams Beck feared. Do not think that ACORN is just a community organization, George Soros just a philanthropist, or Obama just a president; they were all connected to what Beck alleged was a criminal network undermining American greatness. Tapping into LDS tropes of secrecy and domestic defense, Beck vowed to help expose the secret plots to undo true Americans' comfort and the Constitution. Even presidents like Woodrow Wilson and Franklin Delano Roosevelt were basically Nazis, he regretted to inform his viewers, because that's where regulation led.

The emphasis on hidden meanings in political thought is integral not only to Skousen's worldview but to neoconservative thought influenced by Leo Strauss.[29] These ideas appealed to Beck's conservative audience, searching for a name for their inchoate feelings of unease. They eagerly consumed his warnings about Mafia crooks, Chicago union bosses, Stalinists, and liberation theologians hiding behind the mantle of civil rights. Beck described Saul Alinsky and the Industrial Areas Foundation as if they were part of a terrorist faction or a new Leninist vanguard. He used the rhetoric of class warfare to defend trickle-down economics. Beck likened himself and his efforts to unmask progressives to Nazi hunters after World War II: "I'm going to find these people that have done this to our country and expose them. I don't care if they're in nursing homes."[30] This was Beck as Mel Gibson, stalking the countryside to root out unbelonging overlords. This was Beck as Clint Eastwood, back in town with justice on his mind and iron on his hip.

His chief target was President Obama, who was Hitler and Osama bin Laden and Heath Ledger's Joker in a tan suit. When Obama insisted that the country needed more frank conversations about race, Beck accused him of harboring "a deep-seated hatred for white people."[31] A radical like Obama,

Beck mused as if anticipating Trump's manifold election conspiracies, could only have won the election with covert activities from groups like ACORN, whom Beck accused of voter fraud in 2008.[32] Beck aired what turned out to be doctored footage of ACORN's alleged child prostitution ring, insinuating that this was the dark heart of the Left's ambitions.[33] Despite having to apologize for yet another falsehood, Beck continued his alarmist campaign. In early March 2010, Beck stared urgently out of screens across the country, his blue eyes wet with concern, and said, "I beg you, look for the words 'social justice or 'economic justice' on your church website. If you find it, run as fast as you can."[34] Anyone who insisted there was no cause for alarm was complicit in the biggest outrage of all: the distortion of real religion in the name of overbearing, tyrannical social programs. The radical Left! Antifa!

What made Beck such an interesting barometer for America's political unconscious was the scale of his ambition and the number of its vocal despisers. In both discourses, religion is endlessly combustible, never more than when it is unanalyzed. It is assumed to be entitled to maximal, unbounded influence in public life while also special enough to be exempted from the rigors of political scrutiny, granted exception from the burdens of deliberation and evidence. Beck's analysis of the "State of Religion in America" enshrined these assumptions. On July 1, 2010, Beck convened on his show a veritable supergroup of Martyrs, including Jim Garlow (of Renewing American Leadership), Richard Lee (author of *The American Patriot's Bible*), Robert George (of American Principles Project), John Hagee (author of *Can America Survive?*), the Faith and Freedom Coalition's Ralph Reed, and Martyr historian David Barton. Together, they wallowed in anxiety about American destiny being undermined by excessive state regulation and "a power grab on the part of the progressive left."[35] This could only happen because Obama sought to "marginalize and negate the Judeo-Christian influence in the public square."[36]

Against this "insidious thing called political correctness," Americans need "to return to being biblically correct and being constitutionally correct."[37] Identity politics was authentic only if it served the needs of conservative Christianity; otherwise it was part of a historic freefall from American glory. In this, Beck was crowdsourcing the ideas about American authenticity that Trump would later weaponize, with his movement's endless litany of complaints about "cancel culture." The participants in Beck's program reassured audiences that the Framers understood how the "moral law that comes from God" grounds all "common law," thus outlawing, for example, "arson and larceny and murder and theft and rape."[38] Would Progressives outlaw religion and permit rape?

The religious left's vaunted social justice, Beck spat, made them bedfellows of ogres like Father Charles Coughlin, whom Beck insisted was on the "left" because he was a Nazi sympathizer.[39] Beck's repeated invocations of Nazism and the Holocaust were denounced by organizations like Jewish Funds for Justice (JFSJ), whose Simon Greer said, in spring 2010, that "government makes our country function. To put God first is to put humankind first. To put humankind first is to put the common good first."[40] Beck insisted, contrarily, "Once you get into the common good, it's over," and such apparent disregard for individuals might even mean that "you are headed for the death camps."[41] How could American Jews not recognize this, Beck wondered? JFSJ excoriated Beck for this comment, prompting him to re-denounce them as a "George Soros-backed left wing political organization."[42] Beck even mused that Reform Judaism itself might be at fault, since "it's almost like radicalized Islam in a way where it's less about religion than it is about politics."[43]

As suggestive as the back-and-forth may be, what is ultimately revealing is how nothing changed in the overall assumption that "religion" was the issue at stake, singular enough to be threatened by malefactors or to breed theocracy, but also fluid enough to enable Embattlement's powerful advocacy of right-wing antistatism through the idea that religion is politically innocent. Embattled America's thunderous judgment thus advances its radiant promise of being untroubled by other people. The inviolable self, entitled to perfect freedom, holds together such perceptions in an America where even the protection of others can be described as oppression. Justice is only acceptable if it remains an abstract ideal not housed in any particular policy or institution. For when justice is directed toward particulars that are not one's own, then it becomes another offense against a religion whose authenticity requires the removal of all burdens except those of its latest Action Movie.

## Beck (Brave)hearts History

Beck understood the strategic opportunity of his critics' charge that he was ignorant about history. He might not choose his words as expertly as the professional eggheads, but Beck claimed to speak always in the spirit of the Framers. True politics and true religion were authentic because they were "about the principles."[44] These were the regular themes on the Beck show's

"Founding Fathers Fridays": we lost our revolutionary mojo by trading God-given personal responsibility for the nanny state's teats.[45] Beck, bespectacled, explained that it was the genius of the Framers to single out religion as a special, exalted feature of the self, deserving of special exemptions and protections. While Beck elsewhere bristled against some of the implications of this classically liberal formulation, especially the notion that religion might be reserved for particular spheres, in defending true religion against progressivism he invoked the image of boundaries that leftists seek dangerously to transgress.[46]

Beck would admit no ambiguity in the Framers' views about religion; "it is unmistakably clear."[47] Of course, to acknowledge the Framers' interest in religion is to acknowledge very little, given their widespread disagreement about its content, purposes, and location. But exploring specifics and nuance is far less exciting than the idea that you are ready for Embattlement's secret knowledge, which Beck, with Trump-like bloviation, promised was "the stuff you're never ever going to be taught in school."[48] Beck tied his every nonlinear thought to his personal mediumship of the Spirit of '76. He inveighed against the Obama administration's inclusion of contraceptives and morning-after pills in its healthcare provision. This amounted to "telling the Catholic Church to violate its principles and its teachings."[49] Hadn't the Framers fought principally to defend the rights of conscience and religious freedom, Beck wondered? In early 2012, against those who suspected him of anti-Catholicism, he wrote that "we are all Catholics now."[50]

Sympathizers sometimes gathered in public to "hold a candlelight vigil to discuss talking points" from Beck's shows, assemble into a prayer circle, or dress in Revolutionary costume. One Beck sympathizer, dressed as George Washington, even claimed to channel the first president's voice. Students of American religious history might see in this curious performance a link back not so much to the struggle against British rule as to the Shakers' performance of "Mother Ann's Work," the Spiritualists' travels via universal fluid into the lands of the dead, or channeling, mounting, and other diverse exchanges with spirits.[51] More salient is the link between such intercessions and participants' fetish for authenticity, not so much the modernist project of self-authentication through public purpose as the "authentic!" celebrated at a souvenir booth, where one might buy the tricorn hats or thirteen-star American flags these participants displayed as if they were saints' relics.[52]

Beck published *The Original Argument*, an annotated representation of arguments from *The Federalist Papers*, described by his publisher as "reworked into 'modern' English so as to be thoroughly accessible" to anyone interested in original debates about "big government."[53] Here was historical experience rendered in the strains of a summer blockbuster: one's drab modern life could be a white-knuckle ride into revolutionary times! The bluster about free-market libertarianism and the Framers' legacy may have traded in the idiom of revolution, but it also expressed something of Alexis de Tocqueville's (that most famous romanticizer of American democracy) longing for the order of the ancien régime.[54] These were not yet the crowds surging against barricades, taking over buildings, or clashing with cops that would eventually be galvanized by Trump's post-2020 election exhortations to "fight"; they were cultivators of grievance, grumbling through hyperlinks, and professing the need to genuflect before Framers and Deity alike so as to get back to the good old days. Years before Trump, few could miss the implications of the desire to "get back" during the era of the first African American president.

## Crowdsourcing Authenticity

Washington, DC's National Mall, with its federally funded wide-open spaces and monuments, is made for congregation--not only tourists or the volleyball games of locals but the 1963 March on Washington, the Spring 1993 Act Up March, the 1995 Million Man March, the 2017 Women's March, or the months of Black Lives Matter protests in 2020. Beck intuited such a moment was needed for the Embattled to truly display that they were a majority. His August 2010 rally named as its goal "Restoring Honor," invoking standard tropes from conservative declension narratives. Michael Sean Winters connected Beck's event and Jerry Falwell's 1970s "I Love America" rallies, whose "God-and-Country themes" Winters characterized as "Nixon's Silent Majority gearing up for the Reagan Revolution."[55]

For Beck, though, love for America and religion had to be experienced as a collective downer. Only by getting together to feel oppressed, and to hear so many national figures—including Sarah Palin and action hero Chuck Norris—string together laments of Martyrdom, could one be ready for transformation.[56] The speakers invoked history and first principles in ways that suggested these were designed for unabridged personal opportunity. The rally would restore history not as it really was but history as Martyrs needed it to be to conform to their feelings. Where Beck spoke ingratiatingly to all "people of faith," others denounced pluralism as "idolatry" and lamented that tolerance of such things could only pass because of a "politically correct fog" that had settled over America.[57] Such claims became incessant in Trump's America, where whiteness wields them like cudgels.

Bathed in the emotional mood of the event and Beck's own persona, was it even helpful to distinguish the religious from the political? Perhaps they were just different modes of calling attention to oneself, as if, gathered together under the conviction of world-historical purpose, each citizen could finally proclaim to the skies over America—as a young Ralph Waldo Emerson wrote in his journal—"I say to the Universe... If I owe my being, it is to a destiny greater than thine. Star by star, world by world, system by system shall be crushed,—but I shall live."[58] A homology between nation and self—each in need of religious rebirth, or ultimately permanence—is the crux of Beck's Embattled authenticity. Instead of eventually disappearing from memory, you joined history by defending your religion from Embattlement. In a move of grand summation, Beck intoned, "We cannot find any solutions from Washington. They will come from God, *through us!*"[59] God was the ultimate Washington outsider, whose ways are our own.

Invoking the tropes of addiction recovery narratives and postconversion enthusiasts alike, Beck opined to earnest agreement that America had "spent far too long worrying about scars."[60] In the very space where, as Beck and other speakers continually reminded audiences throughout the rally, the civil rights movement had its most celebrated moment, Beck told his audience to "concentrate on the good things in America."[61] Beck—whose career was made by telling millions that real harm to race relations had resulted when Obama won—seemed now to be saying that though the "scars" of race remain, America should just get over it already. By insisting that race still matters, Beck suggests, liberals continue to divide America. Here Beck, anticipating the Right's contortions in response to racial justice movements in 2020, invoked the common claim that simply to acknowledge the salience of race is to wallow in racial divisiveness. While Democrats are routinely racist according to this logic, Beck asserted that Republicans "have been the party of racial equality" by not addressing it.[62] What is more, Beck said that fruitless handwringing over problems like racism places false hope in the human and in the political: "There's nothing we can do that will solve the problems that we have and keep the peace unless we solve it through God."[63]

This disavowal of the political might seem merely cynical, or a sign of political exhaustion; but such statements employ the beaming smile of America™

to shame the cheerless liberals who would harsh America's mellow.[64] For Beck, having unnecessary conversations about race lends support to a president associated with ideas that "pitted victims against oppressors."[65] This was a suggestive invocation of one of the central dynamics of Embattled America, that inverted Nietzscheanism whereby "killers" become "victims," seeking to reclaim public authority by reversing the charge that they are oppressors. Beck located the authenticity in his audience's mood of victimhood, sensing that hostile would-be killers lurked everywhere, hiding behind masks of concern for the poor. Restoration would require more than repentance, then. Thus Beck, at Liberty University in May 2010, had exhorted his audience to "shoot to kill."[66] One might reasonably hear in this statement a trial balloon for what was eventually to come.

## Beck's Whistleblowers: Personal Foul

Whistleblowers would also give no ground to opponents whose religion was inauthentic. Even some conservatives stepped out of their lane to join the chorus of whistles. Fellow Fox pundit Shepard Smith called Beck's studio a "fear chamber."[67] Ever-pliable South Carolina senator Lindsey Graham dismissed Beck's sincerity: "Only in America can you make that much money crying."[68] Salon's Laura Miller invoked historian Richard Hofstadter, whose "paranoid style in American politics," Miller wrote, "reads like a playbook for the career of Glenn Beck, right down to the paranoid's 'quality of pedantry.'"[69]

Like other prominent Martyrs, Beck has been mocked relentlessly by elite Whistleblowers: Stephen Colbert (who constructed a "doom bunker" on the set of *The Colbert Report*), Jon Stewart (who, in addition to his 2010 counterevent Rally to Restore Sanity and/or Fear, proposed on *The Daily Show* an "11-3 Project" which added to eleven principles a bouquet of "three herbs and spices"), the *South Park* episode "Dances with Smurfs," Bill Maher (who derided Beck's rally supporters as an "army of diabetic mall-walkers"), and Current TV's *SuperNews!*, where an animated Jesus described Beck as "Sarah Palin farting into a balloon."[70]

Most Whistleblowers focused, however, on Beck's religion. In response to his diatribes against liberation theology, commentators accused Beck of anti-Catholicism (and shoddy history). In a *Huffington Post* blog post entitled "Glenn Beck to Jesus: Drop Dead," James Martin, SJ, scolded Beck for not knowing that "social justice" has been canonical since Leo XIII issued *Rerum Novarum* in 1891.[71] Joe Carter of *First Things* dismissed Beck as "too ignorant about history and religion to truly understand the implications of his statement."[72] Jim Wallis, of the evangelical Sojourners Fellowship, asserted that "Christians should no longer watch his show," which occupied "the same category as Howard Stern."[73] Even Brigham Young University's associate dean of religion, Kent P. Jackson, denounced Beck for failing to understand the social justice traditions of the LDS.[74]

To detractors, Beck's insistence on helping his viewers "think the unthinkable" mark him as inauthentic.[75] It gave cover to what one writer called—in a deep-breath hyphenation—"the libertarian-Tea Party-Christian-worldview-ahistorical-revisionist wing of American politics."[76] Joanna Brooks linked the last-days imaginings of Skousen-influenced Mormons to "disenchantment" with "secularization," where Mormon identity as a "peculiar people" is seen as an antidote to the flattening tendencies of McWorld.[77]

When Whistleblowers were not linking Beck's performances to theocratic subcultural connections or LDS peculiarism, with the full confidence that this was prima facie evidence of their danger, they often attributed them to "the spread of US culture-war tactics across the globe."[78] Much as Beck is quick to demonize his political antagonists by pointing to sinister historical roots or antecedents, anti-Beck genealogists frequently depicted him as a modern-day Father Charles Coughlin, Royal Oak, Michigan's infamous radio priest who once railed against the New Deal as a plot by Jewish bankers (led in stealth by President Franklin D. Roosevelt). Tom Tradup of Salem Radio Network wondered, "How much of this is religious revival and how much is a snake oil medicine show?"[79] For other commentators, what was noxious about Beck was that his rhetoric "bears no resemblance to the Beatitudes."[80]

Annette Powers pounced on a similar hypocrisy, noting that when Beck lumped Reform Judaism in with "radicalized Islam," Beck was "dismissing the heartfelt religious beliefs of millions of North Americans."[81] It was thus Beck who was not heartfelt. When Beck denounced President Obama as straying from "true" or "authentic" Christianity, Harold Attridge—dean of Yale's Divinity School –retorted that "this is nothing but political rhetoric" rather than "a genuine religious dialogue."[82] Anthony Stevens-Arroyo accused Beck of "shallow theology," arguing that mistaking "private revelations" for the proper stuff of public life is inconsistent with American traditions and even with "the Gospel" properly understood.[83] Commentator

Andrew Murphy judged that Beck—in whose rally "politics pervade," rather than genuine, unsullied religion—gets his history wrong.[84] Beck was not there in the heady 1960s, we read. Beck was insufficiently attuned to the complexity of the colonial period, we are told. His Christianity is thus ersatz. Russell D. Moore of Southern Baptist Theological Seminary dismissed Beck for his "vacuous talk about undefined 'revival' and 'turning America back to God.'"[85] Beck was thus situated in a lamentable trajectory whereby "American 'Christianity' . . . [is reduced to] a political agenda in search of a gospel useful enough to accommodate it."[86] What is worse, Moore concluded, is that Beck's "liberation theology of the Right" shares with its leftist cousin an identity consisting of little more than "mammon worship."[87]

For Whistleblowers, authenticity exists only when religion and conservative politics don't mix. This leaves politics not as the work of reflection or public purpose but codebreaking, with the public square reduced to a field of sermonic manipulation that the righteous must expose. Whistleblowers are prepared to accept as "real" religion only that which is self-evidently private or progressive. If religion is otherwise, it is likened to an "injection" of alien substance, as if a healthy society had been drugged against its will at a political rally, or had a virus released into its waterways by some diabolical supervillain from life's Action Movie.

Whistleblowers seem not to understand that assailing Beck's religion is exactly the kind of thing that empowers a constituency built precisely around the idea that the Left holds their religion in contempt. Beck once said of such mockery, "The first group, Jews—it happens every time. Second group, I think, conservatives."[88] It is, of course, preposterous for Beck to think this. And yet it is precisely by saying such things and drawing energy from the backlash that Beck has remained a figure in public life. So Beck is a boob, a hypocrite, the face of monolithic conservative sameness. He is disgraced, renounced, his shows canceled. He is too religious, not religious enough, weirdly religious. Pundits point out that when even other Martyrs appear to deny Beck, he must thus be headed to the street corner with a doomsday prophet's sandwich board. And yet how could we have arrived at this moment, when a failed businessman and former reality TV star became president, without the effectiveness of crowdsourcing conservative resentment as the model of authenticity in the face of antireligious leftists?

This is how all politics becomes clickbait in the Whirl.[89] I do not mean to suggest that detractors are wrong in identifying problematic elements of Beck's thinking. But mere debunking or refutation have contributed to the narrative of an Embattlement that is absolved from having to practice democratic politics.

## The Glorious Decline

From the heights of the rally, where Beck soaked up criticism as a whale draws moisture from the air, Beck fell. Nothing makes a narrative click—a conversion story, an action movie, or a salacious episode of *Behind the Music*—more than a perilous slide almost to the point of ruin. Beck's tumble began in August 2011 when he declaimed into the space of his slipping ratings that Hurricane Irene "is a blessing . . . it's God reminding you you're not in control."[90] Beck urged listeners to store food and study disaster preparation techniques. In response, many professed disgustedly that "in encouraging home stockpiling, Beck . . . is echoing Mormon church teaching."[91] Beck was now quite simply too other.

But if Embattlement teaches us anything, it is that there is power in downtroddenness. Thus, at a 2011 follow-up rally, Beck noted that "forces of darkness" were gathering around the Holy Land, again citing the presence of Soros and shadowy elites.[92] As he had with the hurricane, Beck wondered, "Will you be able to feed your family if disaster strikes?"[93] The very intensity of the question suggested that it surely could happen. The tone and the national mood were shifting away from him, though. He was called a fake populist for charging such high ticket prices on his American Revival Tour.[94] And Whistleblowers made great sport of Beck's Independence Park, which Beck envisioned as a way to preserve history for real Americans, since, in his words "we're already being erased."[95] The Park, which came across as one part secret society and one part edutainment complex, would also feature a "a facility where college students can be 'deprogrammed' during their Summer breaks."[96]

Beck responded to the decline in his fortunes by arranging pilgrimages to and rallies in the Holy Land itself, bathing himself in religious legitimacy.[97] Beck now found beauty in the sight of praying Jews, who couldn't possibly be likened to Muslims.[98] Like the generic religion of the Restoring Honor rally, Judaism was real because it was vulnerable to assault. In 2011, Beck began loudly declaring his "almost fetishistic 'support' for Israel."[99] As Yaakov Ariel and Gershom Gorenberg have shown, this is partly an expression of the conservative belief that Americans must support the modern state of Israel, which is to play a central role in the end times that these conservatives believe are nigh.[100] Speaking at John Hagee's Christians United for Israel and similar events, Beck not only endorsed US material support for Israel, but "warned of a Nazi resurgence," noting, too, that the Arab Spring was a dangerous front for "militant Islam."[101] Nazis, democratic insurgencies in Arab countries, progressive healthcare legislation, all connections emerged clearly in the sacred atmosphere of Jerusalem, held together by the Beckian insistence that "evil is growing . . . [d]arkness is coming."[102] As supporter Sheila Powers put it, "It's not about logic. It's about faith."[103]

This was at least partly a faith in the Whirl itself, in its ability to lend coherence to an identity that is itself "not about logic." To one's others, this is the stuff that manifests as nonsense, ripe for exposure and mockery. Whereas on the steps of the Lincoln Memorial, Beck sought a righteous synthesis of the 1770s and the 1960s, in Jerusalem he aimed to personify the biblical prophecies he insisted would come true in our time. His lastness in the eyes of critics entailed his firstness when framed by proper place and performance. Participation in this cosmic moment of significance is what Beck promised listeners they could also enjoy: his restored identity for your part in prophecy; his, the voice of your feelings in the Whirl. The truth of history was, to supporter Brian Mickelsen, "about . . . creat[ing] an urgency among the silent majority that they can have a voice."[104] Tapping into these reliable Nixonian and Trumpian tropes, Beck sought to make truth itself coterminous with one's simple faith, which fueled one's unstoppable journey.

Whistleblowers, naturally, delighted in Beck's stumbles. *Dissent*, the *New Yorker*, and the *New Republic* published major articles celebrating the power of grassroots activism in helping oust Beck from Fox.[105] As ever, it was easy to find examples of Beck relying on erroneous information or bad arguments. Yet the authors of these and other pieces seemed unable to recognize their role in the narrative they derided. Playing the part of "haters" is essential to the larger condition in which citizens cling to some version of authenticity as a life raft amid the drift and fragmentation of the Whirl. Unlike Hegel watching history move through the Napoleonic horde, there is no perch supporting objective vision, nor any algorithm that is convincing to those who do not already share a particular perspective or conviction. So Beck and his despisers alike helped sustain a context which speaks the language of facts and fundamentals but is defined by informational vertigo, backed up by the sense that our every thought is world-historical, authentic, unconditioned.

When the context does not change, Beck abides. He started Glenn Beck TV (its motto: "The truth lives here"), which averaged 230,000 subscribers monthly.[106] His style remained consistent, funneling new data into his ongoing performance. He continued his morbid fascination with George Soros, whom he now likened to the demon Baal ("Are you beginning to see the pattern?"). He sponsored a Bill Maher–styled show called *The B.S. of A*, and a *Sesame Street*–style show, which mocked "tenured schoolteacher[s]" for complaining that they can get fired for poor job performance. Ranging far beyond what Beck was permitted at Fox, GBTV also had a reality show called *Independence USA*, "in which we follow Pennsylvania's Belcastro family as it digs in for societal breakdown."[107]

In the Trump presidency there remained some journalistic interest in chronicling Beck's supposed decline. But somehow little damage to his brand was actually done, as he cranked out more books and more outrage. Fascinatingly, for Beck Trump's ascendance to the presidency became the perfect opportunity to refashion his authenticity, by criticizing a rival reality star with much greater traction. Beck, who made his name by being outraged on behalf of those who believed his outrageous claims, joked in 2016 that whether Clinton or Trump prevailed in the election he would probably end up in jail. This fantasy was simply another truth that had not yet happened. On his radio show, Beck concocted "a Trump presidency situation ... in which some 'patriot' might find himself called upon to 'remove [Trump] from office' in a less-than-legal way"; yet Beck also imitated Trump by putting on a wig and dunking his face into a bowl of ground-up Cheetos.[108] Life as Action Movie here morphed into Life as Farce.

Beck thus came to embody the achievement of American authenticity through the proud articulation of absurd claims—that Al Gore on climate change is as bad as Goebbels, or that Christians are going to be rounded up in camps—followed by the necessary performance of regret, confession, or even penitence after the damage is done. To walk a statement back, to clarify what you really meant, even to apologize as a way of maintaining one's voice, are all to insist on the inviolability of one's own persona: one tells the offended that you are sorry they are too weak for your words. Beck thus sharpened the distinction between authenticity and legitimacy. The former is presumed to flow from an unconscious conviction about the inviolability of the rights-bearing subject, here understood as expressed through forceful "speaking your truth," whereas the latter implies a kind of public ratification and consent.[109] Embattled America can be markedly uninterested in legitimacy, as the aftermath of the 2020 presidential election made abundantly clear.

Note that this is precisely how Donald Trump conducted his presidential campaign and his presidency. Like Trump, Beck does not succeed *despite* the fact that he is caught lying or indulging in hyperbole; he succeeds precisely because of it. For in a time when dialogue, reason, and expertise have been so thoroughly, calculatedly discredited, with the received wisdom being that all politicians are crooks and liars, a managed aura of authenticity effectively convinces people that the person who lies the most is actually the most honest, because they are open about what others are assumed to conceal. Beck and his critics strengthened the link between being true to oneself and being a "straight shooter."

Trump's supporters love above all that he "means what he says"; a Trump tweet or executive order or rally is not focus-grouped, but rather is shot from the hip: his is the gunslinger's authenticity. In his way, Trump simply ran with Beck's conflation of authenticity with the performed justification of our own most absurd claims. In this worldview, one must be outlandish in order for people to listen, and if a politician can insist that the outlandish serves some recognizable banality—freedom or greatness, say—then perhaps it can be forgiven, or even celebrated for its unorthodoxy. In its sheer abnormality the preposterous convinces us that it matters more than the nerdy grind of proof and suasion, and thus perhaps that our investment in it matters too.

And yet Beck would acknowledge no such similarities with the candidate against whom he fulminated throughout the 2016 campaign. Beck recalls of his decision to tilt against Trump, "I asked God, 'Am I done? Can I put my sword down now?' The answer was always 'No.'"[110] Quick to remind his audience that he also loathed Secretary Clinton, Beck performed his brave defense of first principles by saying solemnly that if his opposition to Trump meant Clinton's election, "so be it."[111] Of course, the principles themselves were not articulated, beyond Beck's assertion that one should always be oneself. In this, Beck's outrage confirmed that Trump had effectively seized Beck's former market share.[112] So to allow for Trump's election was to allow for a personage whose own megawatt threat eclipsed the aura of Beck's own self-regard, which is the American birthright.

Beck's persona had always ridden the wave of sensation, telling us that its flag was planted in the suburban lawn, the Constitutional Convention, the way things have always been. Now he had a new villain. While he publicly, self-indulgently invested in explaining and atoning for his past rhetorical transgressions, he also, through Trump, polished his brand. Beck even went so far as to produce trailers—as if for his own Action Movies—that depicted him as America's hero. In these trailers, Beck is hunted by his own personal rogues' gallery: Van Jones, George Soros, and others in the "liberal establishment."[113] And for all his emotionally fraught performance of Trump anxiety, Beck announced grimly in January 2017 that he was growing concerned once more, not only about the new POTUS, but about what he alleged was a shadowy conspiracy involving Soros, "radical Islam," and the Women's March on Washington.[114]

Above all, the brand must survive its own potential diminution. It was a mighty task to do this during the Trump presidency, with its oxygen-sucking scandals by the hour. But Beck remained on form, content with his smaller market share, akin to an underperforming sequel in the Action Movie franchise. As *The Blaze*'s ratings tanked in 2018, Beck tacked to embrace Trump eagerly.[115] Throughout the long slog of 2020, Beck insistently urged his audiences that freedom requires work and not masks; he'd "rather die than kill the country."[116] Beck, appalled that George Floyd has been made a "martyr" by the "radical leftists" distorting school curricula, came home to Trump's larger atmosphere of Embattlement; he even said, of the 2020 Republican National Convention, that he hadn't felt this good about America "since Reagan."[117] And perhaps predictably, Beck also encouraged overturning the results of the presidential election, and compared Twitter's eventual ban of Trump's account to Nazism.[118]

## Human, All Too Human

Why, though, should one pay attention to this man? There are an awful lot of angry white males on our screens, ranging from the disdainful Maher to the volcanically red-faced Alex Jones. What we learn from Beck and his despisers is that the journey of an Embattled self must not only be public, it must be mythic. Beck's overt employment of fantasy is greater than that of other Martyrs, more flamboyant in its contention that America is "burning down" because Black Panthers and progressives have been smuggled into the political mainstream, and that concentration camps are being secretly built in Wyoming and the Dakotas.[119] Black Lives Matter protests? Obviously the work of radical professors. Migrant crisis at the Texas border? It's because of Soros and "Chicago Marxists."[120] In a world of martyrs, victims, and targets,

Beck effuses to his audience that he will not give up "until my dying breath."[121] The world pinwheels madly around us, and none but the watchful guardian like Beck can divine the true inclinations of history: he says, "I fear that there will come a time when I cannot say things that I am currently saying," and so promises to throw his body onto the gears of the machine.[122]

What we see in Beck and his Whistleblowing antagonists is that we are headed toward, or already dwelling in, the totality of the imagination. Watchdog Beck tweets his followers and broadcasts his suspicions—perhaps Cass Sunstein *is* really an agent of evil, maybe Americorps *is* training communists—and in so doing makes real the sense of disenfranchisement that sees religion always victimized. Indeed, Beck seems intent on convincing his followers that seeing things in just this way—sensing the bootheels ready to crush your religion by stealing an election—is what makes one a true American. Though they might not wish to acknowledge it, little is changed by Whistleblowers' flat insistence on reason, transparency, and facts: in lampooning Beck's religion and pointing to conservative cabals, Whistleblowers fail to untangle the knot of authenticity, imagination, and brand. When political legitimacy has been so thoroughly discredited, and the very idea of independent norms or consensus achieves little traction, then the goals of self-improvement and branding are what remains of citizenship. This means that Embattlement depends on performative conviction in order for one's claims to hold as genuine or authentic.

If we change the subject from religion, we might better understand how America became the kind of place where Beckian Embattled authenticity thrives. Nietzsche wrote, in *Human, All Too Human*, about that mode of sainthood that performs its "lust for power" through its denunciation:

> He scourges his own self-idolatry with self-contempt and cruelty, he rejoices in the wild riot of his desires, in the sharp sting of sin, indeed in the idea that he is lost . . . and when, finally, he comes to thirst for visions, for colloquies with the dead or divine beings, it is at bottom a rare kind of voluptuousness that he desires.[123]

Beck's role in Embattled America is to perform this Nietzschean contest of desires. In this contest, we encounter impulses that fall outside standard conceptions of citizenship and agency. Implicit in the background of modern understandings of identity and recognition is the idea that individual dignity and rights form the bedrock of democracy.[124] And as I noted earlier, the priority of individual rights is linked to the authenticity of the rational subject democracy implies: morality would not require a transcendent source of authority but only to a law and social compact that depended on citizens' continued investment and dialogic reflection. So the politics of universalism grounding liberal democracy is premised on a denial of artificial distinctions, equalizing rights and entitlements according to principles of equal citizenship. But the politics of Embattlement that has grown in recent decades is rooted in an understanding of authenticity that resists compromises made in the name of shared political purpose.[125]

In Embattled America, it is the *violation* of one's authenticity that comes to matter, so much so that Americans often have difficulty experiencing authenticity in the absence of "haters" or those who would do us injury. And thus, a television host weeping out of concern for the nation is just the kind of anomaly that compels people to turn their attention away from things that might otherwise matter. My thinking about these matters turns on images of horses, as well as tears. Near the end of his life Nietzsche is said to have thrown his arms around the neck of a horse he had seen being whipped, and collapsed thereafter into madness. This anecdote, too, presents as anomalous, both because it seems outrageous and because its veracity has been disputed. Just as the horse-hugging story seems to capture something about Nietzsche whether or not it occurred as told (perhaps it represents the violence and vulnerability he had long seen in modern notions of reason and respect), Glenn Beck's tears capture something of how people talk about religion in America, unable to get to any understanding of authenticity shorn of outrage and simulacra.

The dynamics of Embattlement here prop up what Lauren Berlant calls the "culture of true feeling," whose "notion of social obligation [is] based on the citizen's capacity for suffering and trauma."[126] The tight link between sentimental cliché and Action Movie narrative structure leaves Beckian authenticity far from the Kierkegaardian notion of "becoming who one is," and further still from the Heideggerian mode of authenticity realized in the aversion to the technological.[127] Instead, to be "authentic" is to be "relevant," to keep your brand alive, and always, always to insist that we are worthy of *having* a brand, because everyone can make it in America. Not making it, or making it under nonideal conditions, is converted into evidence that the system is rigged against you, even as the system's opposition to your glorious You-ness is what validates the Action Movie in your mind. This is why for Beck authenticity is sustained by having an opinion about everything that happens, and seeing connections in their disparate multitudes, because everything is always about you in the Whirl. And the authenticity of Martyrs is inextricably linked to the power of whiteness to be unmoved by the consequences of its violence.

The volatile debates that emerge around Beck's tears and his religion largely conceal the mechanisms by which we might problematize authenticity as a political category. Embattled authenticity refuses to engage the categories of citizenship or participation. Instead of the complexity and ongoingness of drab realpolitik, we reassure ourselves that we are on "journeys" made meaningful either by historic assaults on our very being ("stop the steal!") or by the transcendent pleasures of seeing ourselves mirrored everywhere, Beck's teary face now our own. "Religion" matters, but what matters equally is that public life is shaped by the sheer volume of voices and the plethora of outrages that confirm an overwhelming desire for selves to mean something in the world-historical sense—to matter like the Framers' generation, for every rage-tweet to constitute revolution. Curiously, Georges Bataille contended that Nietzsche perhaps wept overmuch because the eternal return actually demotivated action by scrambling our motivation, desire, and ambition.[128] On my reading, this suggests that Nietzsche's injunction that you should approach every action in order to *will it* so is oppressive, actually evacuating meaning by demanding it absolutely everywhere. The very stasis the Embattled long to overcome is actually prolonged by their dreams *of* overcoming it.

Beck's wide-eyed, sweaty, lachrymose defense of "religion" is thus no exception to our politics, but its epitome. This politics is not simply the product of Beck's incessant invocation of heritage, history, and authority, stitched together with religion; nor is it simply that all politics has become "crazy," with everyone a Hitler and a Leviathan state that silences dissent (even when the dissenting voice has a cable show with millions of viewers). The very *point* is to substitute the affront-confession dynamic for reason, so that the Embattled can tune out the wheels of history that are actually turning—in Minsk, Minneapolis, or Hong Kong, for example—and pretend that outrages have occurred where there have been none.

Fundamentally, Beck is suggesting that change will occur when we feel differently about things, particularly about what he asserts is the precarity of religion. The ongoing attention to Beck shows that his rendition of the therapeutic is not simply a self-help gloss on the revivalistic tradition of Charles Finney and George Whitfield but a thoroughgoing abandonment of the political. Whistleblowers assume that exposing Beck's hypocrisy will be sufficient to restore reason and the good order. Why, then, has the needle not moved in rethinking the relationship between religion, social life, and the kind of intersubjective authenticity I think is more consistent with real democracy? To accomplish this, citizens must learn to distinguish conscience from authenticity more carefully, and also to distinguish conscience from simply speaking one's mind or blunt talk. There is nothing simple about the public defense of reasoned discourse. And only with great difficulty can one put forward the notion that there is a position from which to evaluate and adjudicate reasonably the claims of political agents. But it starts with undermining authenticity in the Beckian mode, and rethinking the category on more fundamentally democratic grounds.

My contention is that no legitimate understanding of authenticity can be divorced from some understanding of, if not social action, then the ineluctably social imbrications of authenticity, which Beck and his despisers alike abandon for sentimental heroic triumphalism. As Ian Shapiro writes, authenticity grounded in legitimate (and shared) social principle means acknowledging that we are "implicated in one another's activities."[129] This entails not only mutual responsibility and accountability in the generic sense but a material reckoning with issues of access to shared institutions, to resources and basic social goods, and to an array of egalitarian recognitions of personhood as such. Authentic existence is, as Melissa Orlie writes, necessarily coterminous with ethical living, which begins with the recognition that our social existence inevitably means that we are "trespassing against" the existence of others.[130]

The authenticity performed and thus strengthened by Beck and his detractors depends on powerful background assumptions about the freestandingness of Americans' rights, a kind of subjectivity reliant on a myth-making individualism that acts against a broader ethic of social, intersubjective authenticity. Whistleblowers and Martyrs both presume a political condition in which authenticity is an inviolable fact of individuals' existence, almost like unencumbered thought or freedom from manipulation or coercion. On this basis, we could only account for the failure of others to acknowledge our truth by pointing to, for example, their ignorance, or their role in a plot to conceal the real truth. With these familiar reductionisms, we have confused authenticity with imperviousness, like identitarian Teflon rather than a democratic norm that is responsive to power and injustice and the petitions of differing constituencies. Action Heroes have little time for the complexities of political agency, after all.

But how can we simply *claim* that authenticity must look different? From what perspective can I make any claim about democracy authoritatively? To insist on an authenticity that is focused on dialogue with others has merit not simply because, as a Whistleblower might say, Glenn Beck is a faker. Rather, authenticity must turn away from Embattlement's conceptual environment by restoring its link to the political qua political. Authenticity as a public claim—especially if focused on religion's status as a register of identity or political force—undermines itself by insisting that it cannot be compromised by the slow grind of procedure, institutional reform, careful and open-ended dialogue. This is not to suggest that what Václav Havel called "living in truth" is always conducive to the kind of personhood and citizenship that are possible in a complex democracy; nor is it to have unwarranted confidence that Truth or Reason can dispel ideological fog, since the reality of the Whirl is that Americans cannot agree on what political shared space or discourse even are.[131]

If we are to chart a path forward, we might focus on remaking authenticity as something beyond personalism, something more comfortable with ambiguity, risk, and uncertainty. Authenticity cannot be meaningfully achieved if it simply misinterprets—as the Embattled do—the interiority of the modernist conception of selfhood as a license for unencumbered emotional maximalism, an I-got-mine reality show triumphalism that refuses ways of life other than one's own. Authenticity is compromised if understood simply as inviolability or inflexibility in the face of complexity, or even as fidelity to an imagined tradition that is exclusivist.

If authenticity is to be tethered in any sense to the avoidance of fraud or falsehood, it must be linked indelibly to a sense of the permeability of identity, connectivity to others, and, importantly, to a sense of responsiveness to the political process itself: open-ended proceduralism, ongoing dialogue, provisionality, and mutual engagement with not just rights of recognition, but standards for suasion, evidence, and reason. I promote this sense of authenticity as emergent from legitimate politics not because I believe that it can avoid contradicting the self-understandings of participants. Again following Shapiro, I argue that authenticity is valid when it "militates against self-deception in [citizens'] dealings with themselves and against its cousin, ideological argument, in their dealings with others."[132] Religions are, of course, free to participate in public life, as they always have been in the United States.

But contesting their merits, their principles, or their outcomes—not only by the nonreligious but by the multiple religious agents who do not sympathize with Martyrs—cannot hope to advance very far if we assume the parameters of the Embattled. For, as we have seen, the Embattled insist either that anything that is not *our* religion is invalid; or that religion is only a mask, a front for ideology, and therefore unworthy of equal respect or legal protection.

If authenticity is to involve more than simply the invocation of internal language, and is to be freed from the antagonism of the Embattled, what is it that might serve to distinguish good from bad interpretations, sectarian from coalitional expressions? Standard arguments advancing some conception of "public reason" may seem desirable but alien. Perhaps instead we might commend a social fluidity and adaptability that resembles Aristotelian practical reason, or *phronesis*.[133] I want to find a path to this other kind of authenticity, one that connects human self-interest with a larger arena for Havel's "living in truth" and that does not come at the expense of other people's social safety and equality. But how do we convince people that there is a truth that is beyond them, without strangling them (and their self-understandings) with that very notion? Can we get people to accept that constraint and coercion are sometimes legitimate?

This is the work ahead of us, and of me in subsequent chapters. What we see behind Glenn Beck's tears or in the indignant Whistleblower tweet is in some sense our own complicity in the transformations of a politics increasingly defined by the languages of domination and humiliation, rather than principled, reasoned critique. Lost in the haggling over authenticity and simulacra surrounding Beck is the way our engagements with him have reproduced the terms "sincerity" and "authenticity" in the service of a "religion"—and a politics—that is perpetually ready for Embattlement, indeed indistinguishable from it. Beck's legacy is that he has helped cement the lesson of living in the Whirl by means of the fusion of affirmation and doom: as a heartfelt and sincere citizen whose selfhood and religion will not change for you, for time, or for any political goal that is off-brand. Is this the only kind of authenticity and politics available to us? It's enough to make you cry.

# 5

# The Dropouts

## Sarah Palin, Rick Perry, and the Failures of Representation

*If the real thing don't do the trick, you better make up something quick.*
—Heart, "Barracuda"

In the strangest places we find truths that resonate when we feel undone by the excesses of contemporary life. In *The Piazza*, one of Herman Melville's anonymous sailors says to the exotic, perplexing Marianna, "Yours are strange fancies," to which Marianna replies, "They but reflect the things."[1] It is hard to avoid the truth that we live choked by the "strange fancies" of others, and perhaps the related truth that this strangeness is no distortion but instead what is regular. Public discourse is choked with updates from other people's lives, as pictures of humans at their most humiliated or self-congratulatory are emblazoned on our screens. People identify relentlessly with updates to their social media status, in the conviction that this sharing is the connectivity that makes a life vital.

This bombardment, the weight of this accumulated information, is the medium of self-creation and self-representation. It is also, significantly, a key vector through which political and moral urgencies are experienced and regularly converted into outrage. Ours is a culture nervous about nipples but eager for the next installment of the *Saw* torture-porn horror franchise. How does one bridge the apparent distance between Melville's Marianna and Abu Ghraib photos or planes buzzing Notre Dame's graduation ceremony towing supersized photos of bloody fetuses? We might say with Marianna that these, too, "but reflect the things."

In recent election cycles, the fantastical has made steady encroachments into political campaigns, often in relation to religion. This chapter looks to electoral politics as a way of excavating our assumptions about representation and the "proper" place of religion. As before, these assumptions are most energetically at work in places we least expect, in places where outrage about religion creates a show that impedes consideration of what representation actually demands. Looking at how "religion" is mobilized by and against candidates (especially failed ones from the recent past, like Sarah Palin and Rick Perry) we discover an obsession with violations of the boundary between politics and religion that keeps America tethered to a model of political representation that ill serves democracy. An outraged critic might profess shock over Palin's religiosity, insisting that it must be checked at the door to the public sphere, like a coat. A champion of Perry might be outraged that the "liberal media" has shown blatant hostility toward religion, and thus revealed its distance from "real" Americans. Missing is a much-needed interrogation of one of the key conceptual foundations of democratic life, trust in those who represent us in political life.

When scholars of religion are asked to comment on challenging, potentially unsavory topics like the religion of electoral candidates, they often say, "It's complicated." We rightly remind our interlocutors that modest, respectable religion is far more common than the shrill caricature that titillates and terrifies Whistleblowers. In doing so, we fall back on well-worn responses and qualifications, reflexive reminders that identities are contested and traditions diverse. Yet in fretting about whether our depictions of religion conform to or vex such caricatures, I fear we have missed more politically trenchant concerns.

Instead, let us focus on America's assumptions about appropriate political speech, conduct, and belief. There are complex and often competing American traditions when it comes to what citizen-voters expect from candidates for office, especially presidential aspirants. On the one hand, voters rely on a liberal understanding of personhood as a kind of background assumption: transparency and accountability convey the classical liberal portrait of us as free-standing agents who invest our will in persons of like capacity when we elect them to represent us. On the other hand, there is a sharply communitarian strain that is sometimes quite explicit; many voters want to support candidates who share their values, who are "like us."

This muddle is often evident in assumptions about candidates' speech. Jean Bethke Elshtain observed that these assumptions often fall into the idea that "it's 'mere rhetoric'" and not to be taken too seriously, or that "we are all being manipulated" by disingenuous pols.[2] Yet since Jimmy Carter's election,

Americans have obsessed deeply about, broadly speaking, characterological issues. These encompass Carter's profession that he had sinned in his heart, the sculpted affability of Reagan, the everyman support for George W. Bush ("he might not be the brightest, but at least I could hang out with him at a barbecue"), and the fierce dismissals of Hillary Clinton ("She just doesn't get us").

Religion is at the center of these conceptual tangles. Martyr candidates allege that their critics seek to constrain their speech and policy, in a kind of electoral and cultural gag rule. Other Americans worry that narrow-minded Christians want to impose their morality on the rest of the country. Moreover, religion is often the vehicle of the characterological and conspiratorial at one and the same time. This becomes amplified by the Long Con, in which politics is discredited as little but a rigged game. The candidate then becomes a medium of aspirations, perhaps even of revenge. We can certainly find ample evidence of violent and demonological rhetoric in older campaigns (as early as the withering contest of 1800), what is significant now is not simply the mainstreaming of the apocalyptic (Trump's "American carnage"), but the way Embattlement denotes the absence of a shared public aspiration.[3]

The 2012 and 2016 Republican primaries revealed how powerful and central Martyr aggrievement had become. Much of it was fueled by outrage over President Obama's line about clinging to God and guns, and Secretary Clinton's reference to "deplorables." By 2020, Trump and his supporters were repeatedly claiming that the blandly devout Joe Biden was an enemy of religion. We have arrived at a moment when many Americans assume that political representation consists at least partly in defiance; pugnaciousness is no longer a disqualifier but rather a credential. Is it any surprise, then, that when representation itself becomes part of Life as Action Movie, we have such absurd candidates for high office? Everyday citizens are also complicit in representation that delights in stock movie characters, who might liven up a drab process, giving the electorate someone outsized enough to loathe or idealize, and to have the loathing and idealization stand in for citizenship. What matters is not the "reality" of what a candidate promises but the way the promise enables voters to locate their own feeling in one whom they believe speaks for them. More than some quaint idea of service or fulfilling the people's will, political representation now depends on catering to the postpolitical narratives Americans demand.

## Sister Sarah

It would be easy to imagine that the giant face emblazoned on the side of the sleek campaign bus belonged to an aging rock star, much like Sarah Palin's bellicose supporter Ted Nugent or Heart, whose "Barracuda" the candidate illegitimately used during the 2008 presidential race. The face was everywhere that year, as Palin became the Whirl's perfect cipher. With hair piled high, a peremptory finger scolding the libtards, and photo-ops at target practice, Palin was everyone's everything.

Central to Palin's brief ascendance was her origin story, which became her brand. Often in these mythic templates, it is because of one's "faith" that one is called to serve, lifted up by destiny from small town to national purpose. Americans learned that Palin—from a remote town in the remotest state, tucked like an afterthought just a good squint away from Russia—engaged the political with a "servant's heart."[4] This language was crafted from an assemblage of evangelical tropes, something the John McCain camp hoped would speak to a particular voting bloc. In fact, Palin achieved more publicity than the top of the ticket because of her zeal for Martyrdom.

Palin was said to be averse to "liv[ing] in a fragmented world."[5] This sentiment clearly reflects recognizable Christian impulses to make the world whole and heal it, but Palin was a creature of the Whirl, using sportscaster's zingers to score political points and toggling between multiple self-presentations, ranging from frontier survivalist to point guard to Mama Grizzly. Known for her snark, Palin also favored 1 Thessalonians 5:16–18's injunction: "Be joyful always; pray continually; give thanks in all circumstances." Know this, though: Palin's smiling affect is not discordant to her performed Embattlement; they are co-constitutive.

From the Wasilla City Council to the governor's office, Palin beamed through dustups with members of the press corps, and through public musings over secrecy and paranoia.[6] Palin attributed her success to "the power of prayer," a notion central to Pentecostal traditions.[7] She attested that all human action is part of a divine plan. In this, she exemplified the optimism of American positive thinking traditions, as well as the myth of the self-made citizen.[8] Yet hers is not just the sense that we each might be a Sinatra or an Oprah, but the fiercer conviction that one's own glorious emergence into public life is possible only if policy conforms to a particular religion. Politics must be the servant of "sincerely held" beliefs; and the criticism such conviction inevitably attracts is part of the power of the representation she promised: service through co-belligerency.

During the 2008 campaign, Palin-watchers noted what this vision entailed. As mayor, Palin had informed a Wasilla music teacher not only that "dinosaurs and humans walked the Earth at the same time," but that she had "seen pictures of human footprints inside the tracks."[9] Palin asked a Wasilla librarian if the town had a book-burning policy. Such refusal to bracket religion was precisely what led first many Alaskans and later many Americans to view her as "a woman of integrity," worthy of "trust."[10] Against accusations that she disregarded the Constitution, Palin and her followers insisted she was not just a servant of the gospel but the authentic representative of a people. As her, and their, religion was questioned, Palin also came to embody the possibility of a new, different public, one that feels it is in the majority and persecuted for it.

If such a public exists, it has rights; and if rights exist, they can be Embattled; and if they can be Embattled, this public's feelings must be "real." While snarky Whistleblowers mocked the imagery of dinosaurs in Eden, Palin kept ascending. It was not only because of her defiant religiosity, as Whistleblowers insisted, but because Palin captured long-gestating changes in politics: the elevation of gut over expertise, feelings over wonkiness. Palin was no mere riot of opposites, but the logical extension of a common American political impulse: to see one's own feelings not as contingent but as more American than yours.

One key to understanding representation for Embattled Americans is the conviction that real Americans did not hold policy positions; they expressed Truths. Despite the common awareness that social media distorts reality through trolls and deepfakes, politicians often command legitimacy by asserting that there is a single Truth, which they advance and their detractors threaten. Deliberation and wonkery must serve this Truth or be jettisoned. In Palin, policy flowed as much from personalism (balancing the sentimental and bellicose) as from ideology. About abortion, for example, Palin did not discuss healthcare, reproductive technologies, the right to privacy, or equal access to social services; she simply vowed to do "all I can to see every baby is created with a future and potential."[11] Emphasizing the future-oriented optimism of the American creed as bioethically relevant, Palin insisted that this "future and potential" do not require guilt trips or judicial partiality; one need only repeat "a simple message affirming life and reminding Americans that being open to family and life is beautiful."[12] Palin also linked support for parental notification laws or opposition to stem cell research with a "NEW feminism... telling women they are capable and strong."[13]

This kind of loose, sentimental valuation of "potential" has long fueled conservative antistatism, painting all things bureaucratic and administrative as in fundamental opposition to growth, and thus personhood, and thus potential, religious and otherwise.[14] As governor, Palin rejected "slush funds" that might keep citizens tethered to a nanny state that protected a political "machine" at the expense of regular taxpayers.[15] Palin called increased federal budgets—"they keep printing those dollars"—not only "mind-boggling" and "immoral," but a form of "generational theft."[16] For Palin, any constraint at all—whether in speech, expectation, engagement of competing ideas, policy differences—unfairly Embattled the bright, smiling dreams of future possibility. Unless, of course, the constraints were favored by Martyrs.

Palin described her encounter with Milton Friedman's economic theories as revelatory, especially his warnings about "the damage government can do when it steps in to replace the collective energy and decision making of free individuals."[17] If this is the "American way of life" and the economic arrangement best suited for each individual to maximize her God-given abilities, why is it not universally embraced? It is, according to Palin, because public officials do not "act as an effective CEO."[18] This, she judges, requires commitment to the force of law, to safeguard "future and potential." Where Whistleblowers see a hypocritical reversal of her antistatism, Palin links the "strong public safety presence" of police, prisons, and judges to the protection of personal opportunity.[19]

This link between law and order, and the sense of Embattlement, reflected themes central to Republican politicking since Nixon and which became overwhelming between the racial justice marches of summer 2020 and the Capitol insurrection of 2021. At an event she had dubbed "FBI Day" in Alaska, Palin warned of internet sex offenders, illegal immigrants, and gang members. Palin endorsed victims' rights related to those issues, but rejected strengthening hate-crimes legislation.[20] This is, perhaps unexpectedly, where Palin's version of feminism played a central role. Palin suggested that "conservative feminists" are more authentic because they understand that "limited government" and "fiscal responsibility" lead to the unleashing of "mama grizzly" power. So "safety"—from godless liberals and MS-13 alike—depends on "natural" gendered abilities that ground Palin's opposition to same-sex marriage and resistance to equal pay legislation alike.[21]

Palin ascribed to the Framers the contemporary term "culture of life," suggesting that colonial-era self-determination ought to shape attitudes on issues of gender, sexuality, reproduction, and education (including opposition to "explicit sex-ed programs").[22] "God-given," "natural" citizens and families can only thrive outside excessive government intrusion, from gun ownership (which should be unhampered) to the environment (where Palin enjoined America to "drill, baby, drill") to schools (where the "nanny state" has created "a generation of entitled little whiners").[23] Palin linked policies on such seemingly divergent issues by asserting that they are necessary to reverse the decline of godly purpose in America. Taking it as axiomatic that "people of faith" are marginalized, Palin described her defense of religion as a defense of "normal Americans," who are "reawakening to the ideas, the principles, the habits of the heart ... that made America great."[24] So the defense of generic religion is a defense of contentless "freedom," and even more abstractly of what Palin calls "the idea of America itself."[25]

Palin insisted throughout her gubernatorial tenure that she "would never support any government effort to stifle our freedom of religion."[26] Identifying proudly with those she claimed President Obama had dismissed as "bitter Americans, clinging to guns and clinging to religion," Palin professed that she prayed for "God to crush my 'self' and give me His strength and grace for that time" when freedom must be defended.[27] Interestingly, this very ontological stance—imagine live-tweeting your own kenosis—is for Palin "the essence of freedom."[28] Government and self must both be emptied, limited, minimal; yet the purpose is to become maximal, singular, destined. This is how and why the Embattled proclaim their freedoms most urgently precisely when faced with obligations—to refrain from defamatory speech, for example—to which they are not a priori committed.

Asked to account for her opinions, Palin blames the "lamestream media" and "our governing elites" for antagonizing "the mass of the American people" and creating a "cultural divide."[29] She is clearly proud to acknowledge her deep difference from her others: "The truth is that we ARE alien—to them."[30] And it is this literal and figurative alienation that is at the heart of what representation means for Martyrs. The very idea that a majority can be alienated is central to the emotional excess of our politics, nowhere more than in a presidential race, with their boilerplate promises of restoration through victory. We watch party conventions with weird fascination at their made-for-TV narratives that manipulate viewers' emotions. Still photos of glossy eyes staring futureward; treacly music and democratic vistas; hardscrabble childhoods and realpolitik determination. "I approve this message," their ads say. Palin reminded us of the proximity between these notions and the conviction with which she says, "I believe there is a plan for this world and that plan for this world is good."[31]

What unites these imaginings of the mundane and the cosmological, the present and the future, is the notion that we matter in the context of this plan. Visions of a deity intimately involved with our own projects makes disagreement all the more outrageous. The promises of overcoming are a "refuge" to Martyrs who see representation as consisting of an aura of religiosity and moral combat. Amid the blatant showiness of political candidacy, religion becomes part of a rooting interest and part of branding. The Whirl scatters truths until what counts as political representation is a name, a force, a repetition: "I am a Christian conservative Republican."[32] Understood in this sense, representation does not need to be free of scandal in order to be trustworthy; it is actually understood as more reliable if it confronts accusations and renames them as assaults on identity.

Prior to Trump's appropriation of these strategies, it was Palin who asserted that to question was to attack, and to investigate was to seek destruction. If this is the logic of political representation, the only appropriate response is to declare one's identity ever more brazenly. Public declarations about policy, principle, or history were reframed as questions about what the candidate—and by extension, her supporters—felt in the deepest recesses of her identity, which cannot be contained, as classical democratic theory might have it, by a "private" sphere safe from robust metaphysical claims or a "public" characterized by the austerities of reason. In the Whirl's odd conjunction of empiricism (we must see things ourselves) and narcissism (the only impressions that matter are ours), politics becomes the arena in which nobody should deny their own perceptions, which must be defended at all costs.

Palin was one of the first candidates to effectively weaponize Twitter in amplifying Martyr ideas. After making headlines for asking American Muslims to "refudiate" the construction of New York's proposed "Ground Zero" mosque, Palin was reviled for her support of Dr. Laura Schlessinger (who once used the word "nigger" eleven times in a single rant). Palin's response was: "Dr.Laura:don't retreat...reload! (Steps aside bc her 1st Amend. rights ceased 2exist thx 2activists trying 2silence'isn't American,not fair')." Palin followed up with: "Dr.Laura=even more powerful & effective w/out the shackles, so watch out Constitutional obstructionists. And b thankful 4 her voice,America!"[33]

Amid the garble can be discerned insights into how Martyrs pursue representation: the acute awareness of the threat of ceasing to exist prompts Palin to vow that she will defend supporters from "activists" who want to "silence" them; the contention that what is not ours is neither American nor fair; and the assumption that freedom is expressed through a "voice" without "shackles."

## "A Pentecostal Problem"

As soon as Palin joined the McCain ticket, the Whirl was choked with assessments of Palin's "Pentecostal Problem."[34] It was noted that the Wasilla Bible Church had organizational ties with Jews for Jesus. Katie Couric grilled Palin about her beliefs that homosexuals could "overcome" their impulses and become heterosexual. Whistleblowers professed alarm about a series of videos from Palin's old Wasilla congregation that showed glossolalia and exorcisms. If Palin was both a biblical literalist and also a participant in the suspicious enthusiasms seen in the videos, she clearly did not belong in public office. For Palin's despisers, everything was connected to this wrong religion. Her praise for God's plan for the Iraq War, or her support for a National Day of Prayer, were symptomatic of "frightened people looking for a quick fix for their fears and alleviation of their anxieties."[35]

Palin's positions on the Iraq War and gay rights merit criticism; but tethering criticisms to religion renders them ineffective, inevitably generating the counterclaim that liberals seek to excise the first freedom from public life.[36] Such bait-taking gave Palin and her sympathizers an opportunity to profess repeatedly that "faith" was one of the "things I will fight for."[37] Representation was thus reduced to readiness for struggle against liberal aggression. But rather than interrogating how representation had been distorted, critics simply unloaded on Palin's "perverted" views and on her simpleton followers.[38] She was charged with failing to understand what real prayer is.[39] In a broadside about the illegitimacy of public religion, one author wrote that "the private is still private unless you instrumentalize it to score political points."[40] Palin was not like us; she was a danger, because of her unbridled (and, thus, wrongheaded) religiosity. Randall Balmer dismissed the "morality-play vignettes" of Palin's *America by Heart* and judged that "her cosmos is not all that complicated."[41] He ridiculed Palin's claim that her "tribe" is "under attack" or "doing battle."[42]

As important as it is to signify that voices like Palin's do not speak for the whole of American religion, such critiques fit perfectly into the rhetorical and narrative frame that has long been Martyrs' path to power. Palin held that the "unequivocal divorce" of religion and politics played into the hands of those "intent on establishing a new religion in America—the religion of secularism."[43] Talking heads, bloggers, and radio hosts, however, leaned into their feverish concern about Palin's connections to the theocratic theology known as Dominionism. This was the ultimate "Gotcha!": an exposé that revealed Palin's religion to be a sweaty, superstitious surrogate for "real" religion, a left-leaning analogue to sharia-panic.

Palin's critics protested that her use of religion was a weapon giving cover to intellectually week positions. Many Whistleblowers could stomach a generic "faith" as part of a candidate's makeup, but feared Palin's plot "to tear down the wall between church and state."[44] Palin's religion, the heavily apocalyptic strain of Pentecostalism known as Third Wave, respected no boundaries. Even though the Assemblies of God and other Pentecostal denominations had twice condemned Third Wave as heresy, Whistleblowers made central Third Wave's belief in "an 'end-time' last-generation army that will cleanse the world of evil" and the belief that "Christians can develop the power to raise the dead."[45]

The possibility of a Third Wave incursion into politics was framed by militaristic imagery: the alleged plan to "conquer the world by conducting spiritual warfare around the globe to expel demons and transform cities."[46] Palin insisted that her religion would not bleed over into policy, but Whistleblowers seized on every reference to her reborn heart, to biblical literalism, or to cleansing American culture to link Palin to Dominionism and Reconstructionism. Palin was accused of covertly advancing the New Apostolic Reformation's Seven Mountains strategy, which seeks to purify government, arts, media, economy, education, family, and faith by wrestling with "territorial demons" in communities.[47]

As a " 'dream candidate' for the dominionist movement," Palin could not possibly be fit for public office.[48] Her alleged "stealth" candidacy and her public disavowals were cited as "evidence" of Palin's fluidity in moving between truth and lies, deception and exposure. Behind her was a more sinister force, often described in the purplest of prose: "Cell churches are promoted (of the same sort that are linked to short-term and long-term psychological damage and are among the most coercive tactics ever documented in spiritually abusive groups)."[49] Having watched *Jesus Camp* with alarm,

Whistleblowers saw training grounds for dominionist hordes in every youth group, a straight line connecting Campus Crusade for Christ to weapons training in a remote survivalist outpost.

These "armies" engaged in institutional infiltration and training programs are said to be aimed at creating a "thousand-year Reich of fundamentalist Christianity."[50] On Talk2Action, on NPR, and in the Huffington Post, alarm about charismatic Christianity, demonology, and Dominionism proliferated. One critic warned ominously that Palin's Alaskan pastor endorsed a "re-education scheme" that "may seem like totalitarianism."[51] Whistleblowers produced manifold allegations of theocratic outrages being plotted against the reasonable majority by a "prayer warfare network," "witch hunter[s]" linked to Palin, and even the Department of Homeland Security.[52] Defending "good religion" against "bad," Whistleblowers even charged that Palin's prayer warriors were bent on "Killing Mother Teresa with their prayers."[53]

Academic Whistleblowers made much of this moment. Susan Brooks Thistlethwaite judged Palin to be a hypocritical Christian.[54] Anthea Butler characterized Palin's supporters as "the [Christians] with cars on blocks in their yards, NASCAR on their televisions, and relatives in the military."[55] It was as if the entire country were beta-testing Hillary Clinton's "basket of deplorables" remark from the 2016 campaign, with like effects, since being on the receiving of such vitriol is absolutely vital to Martyrs' self-understanding.

At bottom, many Whistleblowers strive to make clear that while religious beliefs are not an issue in and of themselves, the way they might be crammed into secular policy debates is what raises hackles. This might seem a reasonable concern, one that is close to my argument for changing the subject away from Embattlement. But even this complaint plays into Embattlement's hand. It entirely misconstrues what "religion" actually is, agreeing that "values" or "beliefs" may legitimately shape opinions but should not be "applied" in any substantive way.[56] This leaves both Palin and her despisers assuming that legitimate representation depends on correctly diagnosing the relationship between a free-standing "religion" and a "secular government." They share the belief that figuring out this relationship is the key to protecting democracy, to shielding citizens from oppression and political life from distortions. But the assumption that religion should be relegated to proper "sphere" or place is precisely what Martyrs have protested for a half-century; to reassert this is no solution, but simply to give Martyrs a new shot clock for their next play.

Similar effects result from linking conservative religion with McCarthyism and Sharia. Palin's endgame "could be just the Taliban—only Christian."[57]

As in parts of Martyr culture, religious identities are fungible here, as Islam becomes Christianity, interchangeable in their desire to "use government to ... [create] theocracy."[58] Palin's policy blunders and prevarications, we heard, occur because she "let[s] religiosity cloud her thinking."[59] At the heart of this tangle of accusations and denunciations is the sense that religion is either the vehicle for or the victim of inauthenticity, deception, and distortion. This makes for an interesting inversion of Palin's own contention that "real Americans" have the deck stacked against them by just these kinds of Whistleblowing critiques. Palin herself, as a candidate, was seen as a shield against such cultured despisers and as the one who would take the pain for the greater good. Thus, attacks generally only strengthen the candidate's ability to represent religion. The Gordian knot of Embattlement only tightens when Whistleblowers go further and accuse the "lamestream" media of shielding Palin's faith from appropriate scrutiny. Dismissing what she called "Christians' Crocodile Tears," one critic fumed that Palin received only "softball questions" and that her reception is eased by "a double standard on churches."[60] Palin was no exception, then: she exemplified religion's power to suck public energy up into its own atmosphere of aggrievement.

The election year 2008 is long gone, and yet Palin is still a public presence. Her mode of representation has proved durable, as the Republican Party has become transformed in her image, via Trump and QAnon candidates like Marjorie Taylor Greene. My point is that this has happened in no small part because of the energy invested in the same stale discourses around political religions. It is not simply that the Embattled insulate themselves from failure, alternate viewpoints, or ambiguity; nor is it proof, as Whistleblowers might say, that Palin keeps hoodwinking people with bogus claims of victimhood and Embattlement.[61]

Central to the model of representation Palin embodies is her blend of personalism, trolling, and bellicosity. More than a rehash of familiar claims about the alienation of the faithful from a fallen world, Palin's assertion of the "right" to express the whole of the unconstrained self, in whatever forum one chooses, partakes of the tropes of the self-help industry ("speaking your truth") and expresses it in the idiom of constitutionalism and faithful service, the latter a surrogate for representation. Political identity is achieved not just through the invocation of religion, but through the insistence that all data, all categories, all criticisms have meaning only in the service of your triumphal narrative. Fact-checking Palin does not dissuade her supporters from seeing themselves in her; aside from the fact that Martyrs already believe that liberal snark is the first sign of religious oppression: manipulation of language and facts quite simply *is* the new representation's substance. Palin matters still because in her we see religion's ascent in the hypertrophy of imagistic politics, where outrage and defiance demonstrate how to be one of us.

## "I Am That Bright Color"

Rick Perry's face is as craggy as desert rock. He is crinkly with authenticity, that of a life spent laboring under American sunshine. He has Texan swagger. On the occasion of a 2012 primary appearance at Liberty University, Perry was revealed to have participated in a series of summits hosted by televangelist James Robison. Others attending included conservative Christian luminaries James Dobson, Tony Perkins, Richard Land, and David Barton, an assemblage that fueled conspiratorial suspicions. Robison described these meetings as "supernatural gatherings" wherein every attendee was "overwhelmed by liquid love."[62] Such dulcet phrases seemed uncharacteristic of the usually bellicose Robison, described by some as "God's hit man."[63] And indeed, Perry—the title of whose second book, *Fed Up!*, captured the tone of his campaign—had deep ties to Robison's ministries and worldview. Panic followed.

On the campaign trail, Perry frequently spoke of a dissolute early adulthood when, as a Democrat and a science major, he felt lost. He struggled with school, with the discipline the air force required, and with his faith.[64] As he later recalled at Liberty, he came to understand that God does not care about grades: "He doesn't require perfect people to execute his perfect plan."[65] The plan is what mattered; in it people recognize their imagined selves, naming impediments or complexity as enemies of their certain glory. Turning to God and the Republican Party, Perry began a "journey" on which he eschewed policy detail for what he saw as the overriding goal of politics in America: to counter evil.

Perry compared homosexuals to alcoholics and produced a litany of "harmful" things afflicting America: colleges where students are "taught that corporations are evil, religion is the opiate of the masses, and morality is relative," the "war on Christmas," and human rights commissions that serve as a "front for attacking institutions that teach traditional values."[66] America, Perry warned, faced more than simply a "culture war"; God's favored nation was on the brink of ruin, and Americans may soon be "living in a world where moral relativism reigns and individualism runs amok."[67]

It is the oldest page in the Martyrs' playbook, showing the influence of Perry's mentor James Leininger, a conservative evangelical and major corporate donor in Texas state politics through his Texas Restoration Project (TRP). Leininger sought to defeat not just Democrats but Republicans whom he judged insufficiently committed to the educational policies he advocated: supporting vouchers, allowing creationism to be taught in Texas schools, promoting abstinence-only sex education, and endorsing triumphalist history. Perry checked every box.

Throughout 2005, as he prepared for his gubernatorial campaign, Perry sponsored a series of statewide "briefings" held in local churches. TRP's David Lane claimed that the organization's "mobilization of pastors and pews" was tethered to the higher purpose of "restor[ing] Texas and America to our Judeo-Christian heritage."[68] Perry's star kept rising, and his presidential aspirations resonated with the Tea Party's emergence in 2009. On Tax Day of that year, Perry aligned himself with legendary Texan Sam Houston, who once said, "Texas has yet to learn submission to any oppression, come from what source it may!"[69] The idea that one lives under the yoke of oppression, or that the depredations of statists might be sufficiently dire to mandate secession, epitomizes LAAM's brand of historical dreaming, that longing to matter in a world of mundane McLives. Perry promised that the longing could be satisfied, ensconcing it in Reagan's rhetorical vistas, saying, "I am that bright color."[70]

It didn't matter that the claim was bizarre, and the oppression chimerical. What mattered was that Perry would be Martyrs' tough guy, fighting for those who believed his claims in the same way Trump later would. And the fight was necessary, Perry said, because "we're going through those difficult economic times for a purpose—and that's to bring us back to those biblical principles."[71] But take care, he cautioned: Americans must not ask "for Pharaoh to give everything to everybody and to take care of folks . . . [lest] we become slaves to government."[72] Such an elision between state provisions for medical care ("take care of folks") and slavery had an ominous resonance during the administration of the first black president, whose signature achievement was the Affordable Care Act. And they would, in time, become central to Trump's outsized bellowing.

Between 2009 and 2011, Perry tethered his political identity to the idea of a world in crisis and the need for "restoring America to its Christian principles," killing excessive government regulation, and distinguishing real issues (gay marriage) from bogus ones (global warming was "a contrived phony mess").[73] He described the Sixteenth and Seventeenth Amendments as "mistaken" products of "populist rage."[74] He denounced Supreme Court decisions with which he disagreed as issuing from "nine oligarchs in robes."[75] These things could only happen, Perry claimed, because of the persecution of Christians. Buoyed by the support of John Hagee (who called Catholicism a "godless theology") and Robert Jeffress (who has scorned nearly all traditions other than his own), Perry contrasted the simple freedom Christians sought with what he attacked as the Obama administration's socialist interventions into the marketplace, encouraging dependency in the form of "entitlements" like "Obamacare."[76] Texas would not have this, Perry threatened. Secession was an option, after all. But before any of that, Perry suggested to rapt crowds, perhaps Federal Reserve chairman Ben Bernanke would get his ass kicked.[77]

He told his supporters not to worry about how the liberal media was misrepresenting them; this was a badge of honor and a sign of the Left's panic in this historic moment. Perry boasted, "I'm just not sure you're a bunch of right-wing extremists. But if you are, I'm with you!"[78] True patriotism was thus proudly brandished extremism. Persecution was just the prelude to God's fight. Perry bragged regularly about the kind of firearm he wore.[79] He assured audiences, "I am in the garrison of an army that has devoted itself to the defense of the unborn."[80] He cited Ephesians 6:12, pledging to defend victims—unfairly marginalized Christians, fetuses, even a despised Christ—"against the rulers, against the authorities, against the powers of this dark world and against the spiritual forces of evil in the heavenly realms." This rhetoric, and the support Perry enjoyed from TRP's pastor members, invited fears of an unthinking army of God-besotted rubes.[81] But such panic fed Perry's brand. For every op-ed that reviled him for presiding over a Texas gay marriage ban, or for asserting that Social Security was a "Ponzi scheme" and a "monstrous lie," Perry grew in stature.[82]

In August 2011, at Houston's Reliant Dome, emotional citizens in the thousands crowded together at a rally called The Response. Perry insisted that the gridiron gathering was "apolitical." He announced that the political urgency of the moment—"the economy in trouble, communities in crisis, and people adrift in a sea of moral relativism"—required a purely spiritual response.[83] Yet in making a show of separating religion from politics, and then giving a speech filled with swipes at Obama and policy talking points, Perry was effectively challenging liberalism's distinction between public and private speech. Speaker Mike Bickle, founder of the International House of Prayer, proclaimed enthusiastically that "it's time to go public," to overcome oft-professed marginalization.[84] It is not playing politics, American Family Association founder Donald Wildmon insisted, to speak out when "we're at a crossroads"; he warned of a future in which "homosexuals will become part of an elite class" and "Christians will be second-class citizens at best."[85]

Offended? Well, Perry said at The Response, "maybe it's time for someone to have some provocative language in this country."[86] This performance of bravado, of *Gran Torino* nostalgia for a time when tough, leathery white guys constructed their own rugged lives like frontier cabins, never quailing before the social justice warriors of political correctness, was central to Perry's candidacy and how he promised to represent his supporters. In an early campaign spot, Perry asserted, "I'm not ashamed to admit that I'm a Christian ... there's something wrong with this country when gays can serve openly in the military, but our kids can't openly celebrate Christmas or pray in school."[87]

Marveling at statements like these, and the sheer spectacle of The Response—all those people with heads bowed so solemnly or arms raised so joyously—Whistleblowers expressed disbelief that so many seemingly affluent white Christians believed themselves to be Embattled. Dan Quinn of the Texas Freedom Network described the event as a "one of the most cynical displays of using faith as a political tool."[88] Barry Lynn, of Americans United for Separation of Church and State, described it as "a sectarian gathering that excludes millions of Americans."[89] Such assertions about the unprecedented abuse of religion "as a political tool" mirror rival allegations about the unprecedented "war on faith," each alleging the distortion of the right relation between "religion and politics." Some worried that candidates like Perry risked "breaching the separation of church and state."[90] Even eventual GOP nominee Mitt Romney was aghast at the "frenzied Bible-thumping of The Response."[91] Perry responded that his concerns about abortion and "sexual immorality," and his insistence that America heed Christ's teachings, flowed not from a political platform "but a salvation agenda."[92]

Whistleblowers responded to such assurances using the same imagery Martyrs use to denounce "secularists," suggesting that The Response was a front for Dominionism, aimed at "infiltrating politics and government."[93] Each discourse obsesses over conspiracy and hidden agendas, on the capacity of true knowledge to reveal clandestine intent. Whistleblowers add to this recipe their customary snark and scolding. Richard Dawkins penned a zinger-filled op-ed, "Attention Governor Perry: Evolution Is a Fact."[94] *New York Times* editor Bill Keller opined that Americans should worry over any religion that would substantively "shape" policy.[95] Keller additionally likened certain kinds of religious faith to the belief "that space aliens dwell among us."[96] Inevitably, such critiques were lapped up by Martyrs, and public figures ranging from Michael Medved to Ralph Reed assailed Keller for the comparison. The narrative continued its relentless progress, as religion enabled the Action Movie pitting one "majority's" authentic Embattlement against another's ruse.

In time, as Perry prepared to drop out of the race, Whistleblowers eagerly monitored his final weeks and campaign appearances for evidence of the governor's dalliance with outré doctrines like birtherism or Dominionism, presumably as evidence that no candidate possessing such views could possibly prevail at the national level.[97] On went the salacious investigation of intense religiosity labeled "bizarre" or "commanding," sure that exposure of this hydra-headed beast was the key to a decent politics.[98]

Then Obama won reelection. So perhaps 2012 was merely a suggestive blip on the electoral radar.

## Feel Your Pain

But 2012 was not a blip. As anyone reading this knows, themes of Embattlement were central to 2016's electoral turmoil, as they were to the Trump presidency, right up to its explosive demise in early 2021. For all the sober warnings about right-wing religion, things only got calamitously worse over those fraught years. Amid all the furious outpouring of writing since Trump was elected, many concluded that it was economic anxiety primarily that led citizens to cast their vote for the former reality television star and chief birther.[99] The xenophobia, race-baiting, Islamophobia, misogyny, all these things, one frequently heard, were part of strategic campaign signifying; they gave vent to Middle America's spleen, just as the previously irreligious Trump's visits with evangelical leaders were meant to reassure "values voters" that "pussy grabbing" was not what he really represented.[100]

What does it mean to run for public office, indeed to be interested in representing the will of a political constituency, when one's campaigns are crafted from debates about secrets and deceptions? Some scholars may see in the drama of Palin and Perry only the failure of the candidates' inflammatory discourse, or the endurance of the Republican-evangelical alliance. But what they illustrate, perhaps more importantly, is the failure of American politics to achieve clarity about what representation actually is. By thinking these candidates through together, my aim is not simply to observe how regularly political elites seek to corner a religious voting bloc. The combination of celebrity, conspiracy, and belligerency in these campaigns captures how American politicians gain electoral clout by transforming representation into the lead role in an Action Movie.

Representation thus takes on a different quality, focused more on the qualities that make celebrities than on preparedness for office. Instead of thinking of the megawatt smile of a candidate as supplementary, showiness and ostentation function here as the substance of complaint, too. Only the loudest, brashest, and most outrageous forms of Embattlement can hope to galvanize a constituency in a political atmosphere so utterly decentered. It is far more inconvenient to accept the partiality of one's own views than to embrace the notion that one is being wronged.

In this we see the duality of how Americans think about representation and religion. Whistleblowers are not alone in insisting that politicians partition identity and public duties, based on the conviction that doing so better approximates norms like fairness and impartiality. Martyrs, after all, invoke these categories regularly, usually insofar as they facilitate accusations of liberal distortions and skewed political judgment. Nor is it only the Martyrs who invoke the communitarian, value-laden self that is uneasy with such partitioning; Whistleblowers, too, profess to be swaddled in tradition and custom, usually as this facilitates charges of theocratic assault on true Americanism.

Such assertions, as we have seen, are part of a broader anxiety or ambivalence about democracy itself: America promises you a "dream," tells you that you can have it all, sells a boundless #freedom, and yet politics and public life make demands that speech, deliberation, and action be limited in the name of safety or the common good. Thus, many Americans have been convinced—during the time of the Long Con—that politics undermines individuality itself. This helps to explain why the Embattled seek out candidates who confirm this sense of being threatened, leaning into them as either avatar or malefactor. The environment might be trashed and the state unable to provide citizens with better social goods, but at least, Embattled Americans believe, there is a fight that gives them meaning.[101] To reckon with this condition after 2020, when so many Americans filled the streets fighting against the actual embattlement that African Americans face daily, only underscores the futility of ceding rhetorical ground to Martyrs, who benefit from the attention while actual injustice thrives. To do so after the insurrection, when organized militias and motley citizens were spurred to action by Martyr congressional representatives and senators as well as by Trump, only underscores that decades of focusing on the religiousness of these brands of conservative politicians has done nothing to impede the larger degeneration.

How can any of this be changed? Questions about representation cannot be answered solely, or perhaps even interestingly, by focusing on what a candidate believes or endorses, as if that was the only thing one needed to know about them. Nor can much of political substance be changed by seizing upon Governor Palin's winks or on Rick Perry's dominionist co-belligerents as if these told the whole tale. These things matter, of course, especially when candidates such as these advocate policies that are, relative to the standards of earlier periods of American political history and to those of other "advanced" nations, alarming.[102] But it is difficult to contest such policies in the name of reasonability and good citizenship when the focus is on outlandish religion.

So where do we go? Americans have been taught, at the behest of the wealthy and the powerful who benefit most from this vision, that "government is the problem" and that politics is inexorably broken and that citizens can have no impact on a system so large and remote and thus without merit. In response, Americans have tacked to personalism. My position in this chapter has been that a productive reassessment of representation, a fundamental node of democratic culture, is difficult precisely because to do so is to think about how—for decades prior to Trump's "stop the steal!" conspiracy—many citizens feel the loss of their voice and will, and their inescapable insignificance in a world of numbers so large and time so rapid. Embattled Americans unconsciously understand representation as a kind of totemic symbolism of shared faith rather than an agreement to undertake the articulation of a multilayered constituency's political will. There is a long political history shaping this representational conundrum, only partly alluded to above.

Certainly, modern understandings of representation are linked historically to the liberal understandings of autonomy and negative liberty emerging between the seventeenth and nineteenth centuries. Jürgen Habermas has claimed famously that no genuinely universal public sphere ever existed—only one shaped by the bourgeois reaction to the daunting prospect of political participation by the masses. In the salons and other arenas of critical debate, however, new ideas of political representation emerged.[103] Early democracies consistently imposed limits on the idea of the public and any emancipatory potential it might have. So perhaps Embattled America's narrow expectations for representation are the natural outcome of a historic ambivalence that has, in a time of economic scarcity and oligarchical creep, been converted into aggressive survivalism and entitlement. Perhaps, too, Embattlement is simply another way citizens bristle against the managerial aspects of statism demanded by mass democracy, whose scale and function vex inherited conceptions of representation and their wheezing institutions.

It also bears mentioning that, in the eighteenth and nineteenth centuries, representation itself was a considered a way to limit popular governance, out of fear of unfettered majoritarianism and factionalism.[104] Representative government would not only limit popular sovereignty (through mechanisms like checks and balances) but also protect civil society from political contestation or from being subsumed by the state.[105] Historically, the expectation was that civil society would allow for the expression of political will through contestation and suasion. And certainly in the proliferation of political parties, economic unions, and voluntary associations between the mid-nineteenth and mid-twentieth century one could find at least some evidence for this model.[106] Embattled America, though, is shaped more clearly by mid-twentieth-century "realist" political thought, aimed at preserving a kind of corporatist democracy through systemic stability rather than through citizens' participation.[107] Governmental legitimacy was sought not through mass participation in public life but in ratification of representatives and legislation. Democracy was understood as the institutional arrangement sustaining this transactional relation between citizens and representatives. This model focused largely on the increasingly specialized rationalization and justification of extant liberal democratic institutions, procedures, and norms, rather than expanding the power of the people. For a host of complicated reasons, it is precisely these features of liberal democracies that have weakened since the end of the Cold War.[108]

Americans still generally ratify the idea of an electorate picking representatives in open and inclusive elections, and then dispatching them to governmental institutions where they work on our behalf, but the crisis of representation embodied by the Martyrs in this chapter occurs in a period where flagrant gerrymandering, voter suppression, and Russian Twitter-bots have eroded confidence in the mechanisms, ends, and persons involved in these processes. Thus, after the most openly and rigorously scrutinized presidential election in history, tens of millions of Americans—among them, Sarah Palin—remain apparently convinced that a nefarious plot is impeding the divine destiny of a second Trump term.[109]

The investment in Embattled Religion is a sign of waning confidence in even this system that seems to require little of citizens beyond occasional voting. Politicians like those surveyed here understand this moment on some level, or at least intuit it. They have made representation about tapping into religion as the wellspring of deep feeling and conspiracy, but their outrage is intended to *console* supporters in the face of these other, graver doubts.

The Long Con has convinced many Americans that promises of accountability, transparency, and decency are part of the charade. The old confidence, from postwar American swagger to rational choice theory, that the voter-citizen "consumes" policy choices and maximizes her individual preferences has atrophied, and in its place is righteous anger.[110] The systemic faults opening up since the 1960s, a volatile global economy, and an ongoing legitimation crisis have not completely eroded the basic structural features of postwar liberalism. But the voices that have arisen in response to this moment of crisis are not those of the decades after the 1960s. Unlike movements seeking redress or representation through legislation, and unlike new social movements carving out space for localism, Embattled Americans do little to renew attention to normative categories like representation, to the meanings of democracy and political participation in a context shaped by skepticism about politics in general. This exhaustion has only been deepened by Americans' post-9/11 sense of fragility, and the deep unmooring wrought by Donald Trump's election and presidency.

The appeal—and the appealing outrage—of candidates like Palin and Perry and Trump is an index of how entirely the postwar political world has unraveled. America continues to impede the democracy it celebrates in the abstract. America continues to demonize as "communists" those few representatives—many of whom populate the classes of 2018 and 2020 in the House of Representatives—who call attention to larger structural injustices. There is little awareness even of the distinctions between liberal constitutionalism, civic republicanism, and direct democracy, interest in which can barely compete with the reality of so many millions having simply given up on politics. In its place are Gadsden flags on innumerable vehicle bumpers and candidates (even presidents) who affirm the feeling that one's enemies are using the leviathan state and wrong religion to undermine America.

This reflexive antistatism generally overlooks government's capacity to expand popular sovereignty and liberty. And it has only eased the continued triumph of market deregulation. The abstract forces of digital economy and exchange are linked to a "freedom" that Americans have been taught to deny themselves. The ballyhooed revolutionary discourse of the Embattled, whose speakers claim to experience world-historical assaults on their identity or that civil war is imminent, keeps these conditions firmly in place by looking away from fundaments to our own mass-mediated sense of personal destiny, especially if it comes through struggle. This, I think, helps explain what transpired in January 2021, when thousands of angry white people (who could afford to take time off work) used the Christian fundraising app GiveSendGo to raise thousands of dollars for body armor, plane tickets, and ammunition, all in the name of contesting an election that was upheld in over five dozen court cases.[111]

What might alternate traditions and conceptions of political representation and religion look like? To whom would we appeal, and how? The first move is to challenge the celebritarian shift in representation, which transforms politics into an arena of feeling, in which representatives' promise to embody and defend religious "values" from affront is emblematic. Such a politics concedes that representation is simply about a different class of elites, here robust personalities with Twitter accounts that vent spleen on citizens' behalf. Embattled representatives mistake defiance and inflexibility for the investment of trust, judgment, and accountability, doubling down on offense as that which it is representatives' job to avoid or exploit.

This is not to say that religion should be systematically avoided in political discourse, or as a medium for social cooperation. For as I have written elsewhere, part of the problem with American political discourse is that its reflexive absolutism in religion-talk—it is either everything or must be banished, to indulge in caricature for the sake of argument—does little more than reproduce the problems of American political discourse. My point is that Americans' habits of talking about religion have led too many to miss the larger transformation in representation, which has been yoked consistently to personalist combat politics.

Leaving aside the supposed First Amendment rights of corporations and the obvious effect that campaign finance laxness has on the nature of candidacy, Embattled representatives shed light on how American politics operates at a deficit of initiative, debate, and participation, marshaling enthusiasm and connection only when our Action Movie is vicariously embodied in public life.¹¹² Embattlement thus reveals how far we are from agreeing that political legitimacy—whether of institutions, procedures, or persons—can be secured through a shared faith in rationality, or in its freedom from domination. In the thick of the Whirl, it is a challenge to identify, much less defend, any such shared conceptions. And so personalism and offense renew their last-resort appeal.

## Beyond the "Pictures in Our Heads"

Despite how chilling this moment in American history is, there remain meanings and opportunities to be assessed. In *On Revolution*, Hannah Arendt famously distinguished between "representation as a mere substitute for direct action" and representation as "popularly controlled rule of the people over the people's representatives."¹¹³ Both models, Arendt observed, presume that representatives will be bound by "the will of their masters" and will be accountable to shared norms of reason and transparent procedures.¹¹⁴ But, she wondered, does the people's power exist outside of the act of electing officials? In the triumph of expertise and administration, Arendt noted, not only was the "revolutionary spirit" lost but so too was a broader sphere for and incentive toward public action and deliberation. Even the second of Arendt's formulations, while it gives lip service to the expression of the people's will outside mere administration, construes governance as "the privilege of the few" and risks breeding apathy or descent into "vested interests" among political classes who cycle in and out of office.¹¹⁵

We must wonder, then, whether America's vaunted experiment in republican governance was built on self-defeating concepts of representation from the start. This point is different from the earlier observation that the Framers often distrusted the people, and that the political institutions they constituted were under strain by the mid-nineteenth century. It was early America's confidence in the strength of the mediating system of checks and balances, the authority of the Constitution to enshrine the people's will via civic investment, and the endurance of the "revolutionary spirit" that ultimately atrophied. For Arendt, the great lost opportunity of the constitutional era was "the failure to incorporate the townships and the town-hall meetings, the original springs of all political activity in the country."¹¹⁶ Like Habermas on the Enlightenment, then, the problem might be not that these norms have been tried and found wanting; the problem is that they were never sufficiently institutionalized for long-haul duration and adaptability.

Early in the Trump presidency, there was a proliferation of town halls dotting the American mediascape. Yet since then, Martyr representatives have failed utterly to impede naked authoritarianism and grift. One wonders, then, about the possibility of shifting focus away from the state, and the entrenched powers of lobbies and parties, to the grassroots or otherwise small-scale initiatives that might transform the meanings of representation. John Dewey's writings are helpful in imagining alternatives, especially his insistence that authentic democracy requires full publicity, freedom of expression, and public opinion based on legitimate social inquiry. Representation, on Dewey's account, depends on not only sustained interaction and exchanges between citizens but on "the art of full and moving communication."[117] Representation, then, requires a kind of openness, even permeability that Dewey clearly linked to responsiveness, accountability to norms and standards that bind disparate constituencies to one another, and, as we will see in the next chapter, independent publics.

These things are nearly impossible to achieve in Embattled America, with its overwhelming sense that difference and disagreement must be tuned out as the noise of oppression. Fears of other citizens and their ways of living are reinforced by the overriding aversion to politics and the state that is force-fed us by the powerful. This is not to say, of course, that between these different ways of being and claims on public life there are no relevant, arguable differences. Indeed, part of what is so chilling about the descent of American public discourse into competing claims about Embattlement is that it represents in some profound way the eclipse of argumentation itself, the occlusion of even the possibility that social life can aspire to anything beyond defending one's own personal flag. As Dewey showed, the idea of freedom from limits descends quickly into naked individualism, and in the furnace of American capitalism, this has facilitated the divinization of the market and the demonization of the state.[118]

This detachment of governance from public life is what political representation and the separation of powers once promised to correct. But that was in a different political universe. Rather than representation in defense of positive freedom, open-ended proceduralism and dialogue, the Embattled seek a life as detached, nonpublic entities. This allows them to be managed more than represented. To look back to Dewey, then, is not to engage in nostalgia; it is to refresh the possibility of social diagnosis, to sustain the much-needed conviction that new descriptions or narratives might make communication politically purposive again.

What we have now is what we get by making decisions about representation (and other matters) guided almost solely by what Walter Lippmann once called the "pictures in our heads" rather than "the world outside."[119] Trump is what we get when such "pictures" make Embattlement the central religio-political trope. Despite the long gestation of these developments, it must be noted that it was in 2008 and 2012, in the face of Blackness, that Martyrs achieved previously improbable success in national campaigns. Trump subsequently validated what many feel to be true about America—that it has been hijacked by undeserving others. In this way, Trump truly does represent us all; for even Whistleblowers, feeling vindicated by all the whistleblowing that needs to be done, have contributed energetically to the idea that exposing the hypocrisy of evangelicals will set the ship aright.

To say this is emphatically not to excuse the most reckless administration in American history for being the most reckless administration in American history, nor is it to be sanguine about the policies endorsed by the Martyr candidates. It is to point out Americans' shared responsibility for sustaining an atmosphere in which it is difficult to make claims that can be heard by those who do not already agree with them. We cannot stop thinking in these categories, cannot escape their logic even when criticizing them.

Political divisiveness is nothing new. Nor did American voters disregard religion before Jimmy Carter's election. Think only of Al Smith, or the "infidel" Thomas Jefferson. It was not with Ronald Reagan that Americans first swooned for celebrity presidents. Think here of John F. Kennedy. But the shift in emphasis to religious rectitude in the period since the 1960s must be understood alongside the hypertrophy of media, and the strange radiation of narcissism and cynicism conjoined. Despite such cynicism, Americans actually expect *more* from representation now: that candidates look exactly like their supporters, utter exactly the bromides focus-tested and approved to appeal to the base, and deal out the most blistering critiques of the other on supporters' behalf. These expectations of course lead only to inevitable disappointment, the expression of profound narcissism itself, since to demand mimesis of an elected official misconstrues the relation between individual citizens and the polis, configuring the latter as the magnification of the former. More than this, it undermines the possibility of the very change they seek. By this I do not simply mean that our political reach exceeds our grasp.

Rather, we find ourselves in a period where the normal is actually defined by claims that all is unwell.

Thus representation has come to mean never questioning one's identity or expectations. The Embattled's anxiety about religion does not question its broadest assumptions about the quality of public life and discourse. Such evasions permit the Embattled to disregard those unlike them as incapable of speaking authoritatively. It is, of course, vital that critical suspicion inform our decision-making and that we hold politicians and other public figures accountable. But as Jonathan Rauch has shown, America has since Watergate allowed an otherwise valuable skepticism to sputter into a politics that "privileg[es] populism and self-expression over mediation and mutual restraint."[120] Compromise is equated with self-abnegation, with sacrificing one's deepest held values and practices to undeserving others. To accept this condition is to wait for a strongman who can overcome the corrupt, venal ways of Washington Insiders, who can pierce the veil of drabness and show how kick-ass America is. This is the bomb planted by Reagan and detonated by Trump.

Trump thus captures the two most important trends of post-1960s political representation. He embodies, in his propensity to frame every gesture, every signature, every conversation undertaken as world historical ("*never before in history*," he inevitably begins; "*like nothing you've ever seen*," he concludes), the grandiloquence of the self who, pressed in by its smallness and precarity, dreams big league. He also both expresses and validates the broader cynicism about political practice, for his supporters either embrace the conspiratorial rhetoric that is central to Trump's public persona or dismiss it as secondary to his willingness to fight for them.[121]

It is right to wonder how Trump managed to survive in office in a country that venerates an earlier president who warned about "men of factious tempers, of local prejudices, or of sinister designs" who "may, by intrigue, by corruption, or by other means, first obtain the suffrages, and then betray the interests, of the people."[122] And it is right to worry about the abridgment of human rights by elected officials inspired by inflexible religious views of limits on human freedom. But does the role of evangelicalism in Trump's ascendancy—not to mention the religious bellicosity on display on January 6, 2021—really mean that these problems might wither away if concerned citizens focused even harder on religious concern? I have been arguing throughout that the surest way to confer power on Martyrs is to amplify just this concern, since it confirms the Martyrs' idea that politics is rigged by anticlerical liberals. This is why, for strategic reasons, a better approach is to change the subject and demand of our representatives that they stand for full civil, political, and human rights, since these are the bedrock of democratic politics. What is more, developing a clear sense of our own responsibility as citizens may necessitate depriviliging religious goals or sensibilities. Martyrs would surely claim this is prima facie illegitimate. But the imperative is to challenge Martyrs to make persuasive arguments that do not depend on narratives of persecution, just as Whistleblowers must fashion persuasive arguments that do not depend on belittling, caricature, or naked antireligious sentiment.

As important as religion is the juridical and cultural "specialness" it is accorded in the United States make it difficult to fashion critical assessments about it in political life, one of which is that we may need to table discussion of it in the name of prioritizing other issues. Criticism is not assault; questions are not persecutions; compromises are not apostasies. There are competing principles at work (and at stake) in all registers of political life, and responsible representation must focus not merely on "viewpoints" of constituencies but on shared investments in public life, in collaborative initiatives, and in transparency of norms and procedures. There are practical ideas that might strengthen the bonds between these different levels of governance, from the aforementioned town halls to an option for citizens to determine where at least a portion of their tax money is spent. Additionally, following James Fishkin and Lawrence Lessig, it would be savvy if American politicians began to implement deliberative polling more consistently. This process builds in a process of deliberation based on initial results and concludes by an additional polling that builds on said deliberation. Lessig's vision of linking such polling to the broader goal of civic involvement—including regular use of "civic juries" to hold representatives accountable and possibly to establish constitutional conventions—is exactly the kind of ambitious, clear thinking that this moment requires.[123]

For these are dangerous times for American democracy. It is precisely now, though, that Americans should—in the name of refreshing our convictions about representation—kill the myth that anything short of total noncoercion is unfreedom, that concessions are to politics what snitching is to gangsters. For the flip side of Action Movie representation is the equally cynical, equally narcissistic "perfect candidate" fantasy, of the sort that leads some citizens to reject any "RINO" who does not exactly embody their policy wish list or others to reject Hillary Clinton's candidacy because it lacks the purity of Bernie Sanders's. As in sports, in elections defense matters. Americans should reflect on precisely *why* they vote, and what processes, institutions, and political cultures they imagine themselves contributing to *when* voting.

My hopes for an open-ended, quasi-Deweyan representation absolutely does not depend on the disappearance of religion as a factor in citizens' self-representation, or even necessarily in candidates' self-understandings. Nor do I believe that only a stronger Rawlsian public reason or democracy in the cloud will save us. But democracy can only improve if Americans learn to change the subject from feelings and mimetic candidates to a politics that stands against demonizing others and also stands against candidates who promise their own heroic overcoming of a system they will not work to change. In saying this, I am not merely defending some establishmentarian vision, although Americans have learned the hard way the importance of vetting policy, experience, and candidates' connections more openly and rigorously. Regardless of specific procedural adjustments we might aspire to, our own expectations must also be adjusted.

Doing so might help us remember that citizens are accountable to the shared projects of American politics. The regular enactment of this accountability might weaken the power of a representation that promises we can have what we want and vanquish anyone whose existence complicates that promise. Embattlement is, after all, an expression of disbelief that you cannot have it all, that you are not guaranteed the win. Embattlement is a comfort, because it insists that in all this multitude it is we who matter the most. Real politics and representation will not provide the comforts of this Embattlement, nor perhaps of any religion. But they might, at least, aspire to legitimacy.

# 6

# An Unattained Goal

## The Tea Party and the Problems of Public Action

I'm so bored with USA! What can I do?
—The Clash

Freedom and power have parted company.
—Hannah Arendt, *On Revolution*

A crowd exists so long as it has an unattained goal.
—Elias Canetti, *Crowds and Power*

America loves a crowd. Americans may tell themselves that their chief avatar is the Thoreauvian lone stroller, the rugged individual, the born again convert to new vistas of self-discovery. But they tack back to communitarianism and crowds, in love with the madding throng of a revival or a protest march, a tailgate, or a rock festival. In crowds, things bloom; ideas and energies pass between bodies to take on a life that seems independent of anyone's devising.

In these overpopulated atmospheres, the historical imagination is often kindled. In such collective enthusiasm, citizens dream of a "religion" and an "America" alive with historical purpose. On the other hand, crowds have long been a source of anxiety in a country suspicious of faction, majority tyranny, and the "passions" of the democratic mob. For every Tocquevillean rhapsody about the wisdom of plain Americans, there is a John Adams, who takes the long route on his way to the Continental Congress in 1777, in order to avoid the besotted masses he so distrusted.[1]

These hoary American debates—Federalists and anti-Federalists, Rawlsians and communitarians, a veritable pileup of dualisms between which to frame an unruly polis—bubble up in moments of social concern. Large groups of Americans assemble because they need something, or they reject something. At issue is not just the occasion for the gathering but the appearance of pressing up against the boundaries of what we assume is settled politics, acceptable levels of public enthusiasm, or the power of religion to excite assembled bodies.

The Tea Party's arrival provoked such considerations, greeted either like soccer hooligans befouling the neighborhood or like the Rohirrim arriving at Helm's Deep to fend off evil. They filled innumerable screens, their crowds now the news; they said things that outraged some and delighted others. Outsiders watched them—crowds of white folks, often brandishing outrageous signs or Lipton flair—and wondered at the combination of populist rage and picnic bonhomie. They proclaimed both their ordinariness and their difference from the usual politics. Why had this happened, this replication of crowds across the United States, this formless constituency which seemed to summon everyone's inner historical expert? They assembled, they told anyone who would listen, under grave circumstances. They would respond to a dire historical moment by creating a voice whose very elan collapsed the distance between the early colonies and the digital twenty-first century.

Much reckoning with the Tea Party's significance—its understandings of colonial America, its implications for public life—turned on ideas about its connections with conservative Christianity. It was about taxes, the state, "Tea-vangelicals," and more. But in the avalanche of public commentary, Embattled America squandered an opportunity to rethink majoritarianism and meaningful public participation.

## Original Intent

In early 2009, there was news that a movement had been born, one that hearkened back to the famed Boston protests against the British Crown's 1773 Tea Act. That event, often cited as the expression of a political independence that would ultimately give birth to the great American project of #freedom, was not characterized by any evident religious purpose or Lockean reflection on natural right, but at least partly on an enthusiasm for violence. It also actually reduced the price of tea.[2] Convinced by the recession of 2008–2009 that tyranny was afoot, on February 19, 2009, CNBC's Rick Santelli expressed outrage that the Obama administration was planning to bail out corporate mortgage lenders. Santelli's call for "another tea party" went viral.[3]

Initially, the result seemed like a bit of harmless cosplay. In tricornered hats and Uncle Sam coats, protesters invoked the colonial rebellion against monarchical power, directing it at contemporary policies and politicians they believed guilty of King George III–like overreach (leaving aside the inconvenient fact that they lived in a democratic society, albeit one with issues). They conjectured loosely about appropriate governmental authority, often using contemporary language and historical ideas interchangeably. Many Tea Partiers zealously invoked images of revolution, insurgency, upheaval, and the apocalyptic, often backed by decontextualized Jefferson quotes about the Tree of Liberty.

Mass protests have often turned on issues of labor or economic rights, from Müntzer's revolt to Shays's Rebellion to the Haymarket Riots.[4] But what distinguished the TP initially, more than its complaints about taxation and government, was participants' acute awareness of their representation in media, a feedback loop of energy coming from their own and others' outrage. Critics chuckled at the self-styled period dress of some participants. Others found ominous the recrudescence of nativism or populist tilting against the state's "bigness." But the gatherings themselves resisted any single interpretation. For every familiar refrain about pointy-headed elites steering the leviathan state, there were also angry slogans directed at the then-new president: "Obama's Plan: White Slavery"; "Stand Idly by While Some Kenyan Tries to Destroy America? WAP! I Don't Think So!!! HOMEY DON'T PLAY DAT!!!"; or "Obama-nomics: Monkey See, Monkey Spend." There were also images: Obama's face Photoshopped onto a stereotypical "tribal" figure, an old racist caricature now supplemented by the hammer-and-sickle grapheme, "Obamacare"; Obama as the 1980s television character Mr. T, demanding "Gimme Yo' Change"; or an image of a Klansman holding a small lynched Obama figurine hanging next to an actual teabag.[5]

Beyond such unsettling racism, one could also raise questions about the timing of the Tea Party's dismay over the American economy. After decades of ill-advised trickle-down economics and in a moment when trillions of American dollars were being spent on military ventures in Afghanistan and Iraq, why did the bigness of government or the profligacy of the American economy only now suddenly seem outrageous? American jobs and dollars had, after all, been limping along since the early 1970s.[6] So was the Tea Party actually a challenge to the postindustrial economy that had transformed the American landscape, as Occupy Wall Street was? Or was it a transparent defense of whiteness?

The political energy of the rallies—attended by conspiracy theorists, devotees of Ayn Rand, and antistatist evangelicals alike—were appropriated by hardline Republicans who repurposed TP slogans for the 2010 midterm elections.[7] Indeed, the movement had ties to FreedomWorks, Americans for Tax Reform, and the Ayn Rand Center for Individual Rights.[8] This led some to suggest that the TP was just a Republican faction or interest group, "Astroturf" rather than grassroots. Polls indicated that TP membership—at its peak, there were nearly three thousand organizations both national and local, with an aggregate membership in the tens of thousands—consisted overwhelmingly of well-educated, "debranded Republicans."[9]

Interest groups and party affiliation were integral to the TP's huge successes in the 2010 midterms, when multiple victories over incumbents prompted analysts to invoke comparisons with Barry Goldwater and his followers, especially in the focus on "ideological purity above pragmatism."[10] As one supporter put it, "I've talked to so many Tea Party members who said, 'I will never again hold my nose and vote for someone'... They will vote for the pure candidate."[11] Success in legislative terms was secondary to the politics of emotional enthusiasm. What crowds made possible, unlike televisual authenticity or mimetic representation, was a different kind of public will, one achieved through nostalgic cosplay, emotionality, and attention. Participation and public action here depended not on a fully formed theory of governance or conceptual link between identity and public life, but on *display*.

The TP's claims about bigness, oppressive taxation, and institutions gone awry were inseparable from emphases on emotional purity and majoritarianism. These, in turn, were said to flow from the apostolic authority of the eighteenth century. To get at these combined factors, it is unproductive to lean into the idea that the TP is merely a Christian Right front with a shaky understanding of history.[12] This reproduces the idea that religion is the central political element, whether it is a front for faction or the means by which "real" Americans distinguish hypocrisy from authenticity. I think what the TP and its Whistleblowers reveal is a deeper American uncertainty about what political participation and public life make possible.

## Debt and Religion

Beyond the slogans are divergent understandings of the relation between the state, the Framers, religion, and citizenship. The basic contention is that American politics and culture thrive in (and perish without) a lineage traceable to the Revolutionary era, whose stipulations about government and civic conduct are sufficient to guide any generation of American citizens. Acting from the questionable presumption that "the Framers" were unified on the topics of citizenship and government, the TP asserted that constitutional principles could be summed up in readily deployable slogans: limited government, divine intent, virtuous citizenry. Virtue would be defined against ostensibly leftist categories—like social justice, fairness, distribution—thought to saddle citizens with financial and moral debt. TP literature invoked well-worn populist demands for plain talk and common sense, tools to expose the machinations of those who would, in the name of "fairness in the tax code," usher in "legalized theft."[13] The TP often criticized social welfare programs by citing the biblical commandment "Thou shalt not steal."[14] TP understandings of the state's role in the market deny the legitimacy of "interventionist" institutions like the Federal Reserve, which some denounced as unbiblical, finding legitimate only those institutions and policies that can be attributable to the Framers' circumscribed understanding of "civil government."

In the TP's imagining of public life and citizenship, it is at the local level that real religion thrives, freely expressed outside the shackles of the state. Religion cannot do its proper work because of systematic misrepresentation by thuggish liberals who resist the flow of history. Equally complicit are "Washington insiders" who are puppets of corporate contributors (although the TP generally rejected market regulations or campaign finance rules that would alter this condition), out of touch with the "common voter" whose free religion required deregulation.

Whistleblowers could not restrain themselves from mockery. Eager to take the bait, they provided quote after quote for the TP to dump into the virtual harbor. A *New York Times* editorial thundered that the TP had "waged jihad on the American people." Pennsylvania representative Mike Doyle denounced the TP as a "small group of terrorists." Michael Lind described them as "neo-Confederate" "fanatics."[15] Former NPR executive Ron Schiller described TP supporters as "white, Middle America, gun-toting racists" in thrall to a "weird" Christianity, this last accusation prompting the *Tea Party Review* to speculate about NPR's own collusion with a "Muslim Brotherhood front group."[16]

According to Michelle Bachmann, it was the elitist Obama administration that was responsible for caricaturing TP supporters as "toothless hillbillies coming down out of the hills."[17] When MSNBC's Chris Matthews described TP protests as "lawlessness and anarchy," TP supporters pointed accusingly at the hypocrisy of a "liberal media" that failed to scrutinize Occupy Wall Street in like fashion.[18] This, TP writers regularly noted, was typical of liberals who restricted conservative free speech, especially the religious kind. TP identity was thus confirmed and emboldened when critics failed to recognize the legitimacy of religiosity. They might bust up your rally like "civility police," or—like the "children with inflated self-esteem" or Alinskyites they really were—this tone-deaf "ruling class" could not see what was really happening.[19]

## Masses, Faction, Spectacle

What was happening was a crowdsourced understanding of political will as synonymous with unchecked liberty, an effusion of will linked to 1773, any constraint of which is understood to be tyrannical. Against the alleged secrecy of the Obama administration, the TP often demanded that policy and public ventures be explained to citizens in transparent language. Complex policy-speak must, on this account, have a dark purpose, enabling allegedly socialist initiatives like "Obamacare." Contrarily, whatever is endorsed in a rightly folksy idiom—from fracking to the insistence that market deregulation is an American first principle, maximizing divinely bestowed potentialities—is recognized as fair and legitimate.

The TP thus constructs its history and identity by positing a negative public life, one that is collectivist, radical, and antireligion. This darker history was the narrative's necessary contrast to the brightly colored cords stretching back to Boston Harbor. In the TP's historical imagination all iterations of the American Left hang together as the opposite of the virtuous extremism of Goldwater, Reagan, and the Framers. Not only did the TP find the specter of Hanoi Jane and the Weathermen everywhere among its critics, they also claimed that a 2011 Michigan incident—in which Democrats created faux TP candidates—showed how the Left was out to get the movement.[20] Columnist Tom Tollison contrasted the TP's focus on "honoring God, our country and those who put the most on the line preserving it" with a Left that sees America as "a bad place," and dishonors American culture's "sacraments."[21] Against such threats, so central to the ascendance of Trump's constituency, particularly the obsession with Antifa and "cancel culture," an Embattled Majority gathers to ensure that a proper public is inoculated against sixties radicalism redux.

Whistleblowers continued playing the role of a snarky Greek chorus, rekindling the fires of indignation that are the Embattled's constant companion. Disdaining the TP's ignorance of history, railing against the Astroturf-ness of its publics, they tapped into older analytical veins— from classic sociological deprivation theory to Richard Hofstadter's paranoid style—to debunk TP publics. Anxiety about crowds loomed large. The *Orlando Sentinel* described TP rallies as "creepy," possessed of "glassy-eyed rah-rah attitude" and a "jingoistic program."[22] *Religion Dispatches* wrote of the "foot soldiers" advancing religious prejudices and panics.[23] Whistleblowers generally found in the TP a dangerous militarism, xenophobia masked as populism.[24] Its public zeal was said to conceal hidden agendas, an assumption that suggestively mirrored the TP's own. Frank Rich of the *New York Times* famously wrote of the movement's "dark side," a "political virus" or "tsunami of anger," invoking the biological and meteorological language common to discourses of fear.[25]

More common were self-satisfied observations that the TP misunderstood American history. Ben McGrath of the *New Yorker* observed that the Populist Party of the late nineteenth century favored nationalization, which made the TP hypocritical.[26] The TP was assailed for trumpeting its constitutional fundamentalism while anachronistically using contemporary slogans to articulate its claims. Such Whistleblowers were invested in Gotcha! epistemology, pulling back the curtain and showing us the *real story*, in which the TP is lumped in with any other group with "Religious Right, Neocon, free-market" commitments, no different than McCarthyites or Birchers.[27]

The impulses behind these analyses are often noble. And both journalism and public scholarship are welcome in an era when expertise is attacked, when universities are "downsized," and of course when actual mobs overrun the Capitol (about which more below). Yet in focusing on the TP's "true" historical significance or its "religiousness," many critics mistake the condition. Mark Lilla wrote in alarmist mode that the TP was not only trying to reverse the 1960s, but represented what he called "anti-political Jacobin[ism]." Yet rather than develop this association, Lilla says only that America's "credulous skeptic[s]" often cling to contradictions "in moments of crisis when things seem hopeless."[28] Chris Mooney likened TP "ideologues" to deluded leftists who defended Mao in the early 1970s.[29] Amitai Etzioni speculated that TP energies would eventually be absorbed into party politics and the more radical factional elements "will go the way of once-feared groups such as the John Birch Society and the Moral Majority."[30] Insisting that the xenophobic positions pounced on by other critics were not normative for the TP, Etzioni concurred with Kate Zernike's *Boiling Mad* that the TP was a conventional social movement, once its impurities were removed.[31]

Jill Lepore's *The Whites of Their Eyes* surveyed the TP's origins and its terminological habits, which replaced "capitalism" with the softer term "free enterprise" and replaced "slave trade" with "Atlantic triangular trade."[32] Fellow historian Thomas Kidd assailed Lepore for her "gratuitous fulminations" and her "predictable and ironic" "rant" against Tea Party practitioners. To Kidd, liberal or left academics write against a movement whose motivations they "cannot fathom" beyond boilerplate accusations of "racism and religious fanaticism."[33] As a veteran of some good scholarly dustups, I think conversations like this are worth having. Yet in wondering how best to document the TP, academics too often replicate journalistic assumptions or too quickly mistake surface effects for the larger shapes propelling the discourse. Neither impulse can compete with the Whirl's loosening of facts and narratives from the moorings of reasonability.

## "I Don't Know Exactly Why I'm Here"

One key to understanding these larger shapes is to focus on how TP crowds and religion take shape through a historical fetish that reveals a deep discomfort with actual pluralistic public life. In the TP's invocations of history, we encounter an odd (and perhaps unintended) sanctification of the present, an insistence on the world-historical or biblical significance of our moment. Each nod to the Framers performs not so much an argument as a theatrical move that strengthens the attachment to the hypermediated capitalism it longs to escape. Cosplaying the eighteenth century interestingly confirms the perceived flatness of the secular modern, as it is experienced by atomistic citizens, craving the thrill of the crowd and one's own Life as Action Movie. Perhaps the belief that there must be more to America than this is what accounts for the fervency of TP professions of Embattlement. This fervency is felt and described as religious, more performative than substantive. As scholars like Tracy Fessenden, Kathryn Lofton, and John Modern have shown, the secular's flatness is a construct, concealing the fundamental role of religion in the secular itself.[34] This interweaving accounts for the dependence of TP supporters, who understand themselves as providential vessels, on their detractors who defend the necessity of a godless public, and vice versa.

Stephen Eichler rhapsodized about the "good news" of the TP, whose "invisible Patriots" "fight against the darkness which covers America today." Against the "vile disembowelment" of the Constitution perpetrated by "Washington Pharisees," Eichler rejoiced that a new generation of patriots would use reading groups, text messaging, and social media to shape the popular will against "the false prophets of politics."[35] True patriots march forward into a future they hope will remember their glory, confident that their technologies possess the authenticity of the streets, where TP supporters carrying signs imagined their lives as having significance on a par with the civil rights movement or the Revolutionary War itself.

Paul Rahe, of *Commentary*, situated the TP in a lineage of popular power that runs from the English Revolution to William Jennings Bryan's "Cross of Gold" speech.[36] Rahe saw the TP as the final prophetic expression of a wholly American revolutionary spirit. In similar spirit, TP participants regularly punctuated their gatherings by marking their own historicity, usually with great solemnity. Invocations of the Constitution's authority were consistently accompanied by flamboyant claims about our audacious deviance from it. Consider a bizarre congressional ritual on January 6, 2011. Newly elected TP representatives read from the US Constitution for eighty-four minutes, capped off by the promise that on their watch no legislative "monstrosities" like "Obamacare" would be voted into law.[37] TP members visiting Williamsburg, Virginia, even asked a George Washington reenactor "how to topple a tyrannical government."[38]

It was almost as if members sought to return to the *illo tempore* of American politics, by summoning into the present profane the revivifying energies of the revolutionary era. As supporter Mark Lloyd told NPR, "There's a reawakening of that spirit of America ... [what] maybe a lot of people can't articulate is, 'I don't know why exactly I'm here—but I know something is not right, and I want to change that.'"[39] The fervency of this desire to shape public life reflects how deeply troubled TP members were by the actual flow of history—the expansion of social services, the changing demography of the United States, the legal and cultural depriveleging of Christianity—and how they sought to step outside of that flow by stepping into what they avowed was *real* history, in which publics were constituted by display. The outrage of the Obama era, the stentorian cries that the Constitution was being torched, signaled the desire that citizens' decisions would outlast them, saved onto history's hard drive long after death.

This desire is manifested in an activism and participatory ethos that the TP links to the idea of a voice and a constituency. But despite this idea, TP publics are weirdly static: a fixed people expressing a fixed will into a fixed space. They do not reflect the halting, limited, partial nature of democratic action so much as a sense of the suffocating wooliness of living in hypercapitalism. The energy and emotional atmosphere surrounding the idea of meaningful publics are the point; and they are the vectors by which religion emerges. For, regardless of medium or occasion, to link religion to the atmosphere of historical importance is a way of converting words into energy, and thereby to enhance the experience of affront. And when religion permits one to know one's feelings as genuine, it can also become the substance of what the TP believes is resistance.

Religion is the history and the freedom that will not be constrained—by a norm, a policy, or a critic—because it stands in for tradition, true Americanism, constitutional authority, and authentic citizenship. Insisting on the divine provenance of foundational documents, the TP rejected any limits at least on their own religious freedom: "The state cannot impose church on the people, but the people can display and say as much church in the public square as they desire."[40] Allen Hardage, the "Patriot-in-Chief" of Townhall.com, insisted that religion was too vital to respect any distinction between public and private: "I want no part of any faith that I can compartmentalize. That faith is worthless ... it's a matter of obedience to God's word."[41] Limiting religion in any way risks, in the words of Sharron Angle, making "government our God" and "a violation of the First Commandment."[42]

The TP had less positive thoughts about religious tolerance and pluralism, which they believed were commitments concealing a more sinister agenda. According to Tea Party Nation founder Judson Phillips, the Methodist Church is "little more than the first Church of Karl Marx" because of its support for healthcare reform and immigration rights.[43] Real American religion seeks a total break from the leviathan state. As Jim DeMint told the Christian Broadcasting Network, Americans are "realizing that it's the government that's hurting us . . . as the Bible says, you can't have two masters."[44] TP advocates Kris Mineau, an evangelical who runs the Massachusetts Family Institute, and Pentecostal Paul Jehle, head of the Plymouth Rock Foundation, asserted that "God gives rights; governments don't."[45] Self-determining citizenry, too, depended on Bible study more than political first principles.

Thus, when President Obama observed that the United States is not an explicitly or exclusively Christian nation, TP members were eager to fight.[46] It is an Action Movie, after all. So the tone of their religious responses were sometimes fearful, even violent. Some TP members uttered "imprecatory prayers" petitioning God to "smite" President Obama and varied groups of sinners.[47] Rallies often featured firearms imagery, violent rhetoric, and occasional participation by "anti-government extremists" like the Oath Keepers and the Friends of Liberty.[48] The urgent message was that the state is coming for the majority's religion and guns. Decrying the unfreedoms of socialism, increased taxation, and the Affordable Care Act, the TP insisted "there is a spiritual and biblical component" to the defense of freedom.[49]

The state's overreach demanded armed resistance. Gun Owners Association executive Larry Pratt claimed that Americans had been "disarmed by the civil government," and thus prevented from exercising their "obligation, as creatures of God, to protect the life that was given them."[50] The religion that propels this fiercely antistatist vision holds together apparent opposites: guns and peace, past and future, individual and community, ideological purity and disdain for politics. The limited sphere of government authority is a classically liberal trope, here used to discredit the idea of any boundary containing religious maximalism. The state is not just the enemy of religion, as a formal category; for the TP, the state is also the countersign to freedom and even to compassion.

Whistleblowers energetically engaged the religion that they believed fueled the TP's delusional politics. They did so without engaging with any substantive conceptualization of how religions relate to the idea of a public, but instead reduced TP activism to sentiments aroused by "social issues such as abortion and same-sex marriage," those time-tested "hot button" issues central to Christian Right mobilization.[51] Sociologists David E. Campbell and Robert D. Putnam wrote that the TP had "a low regard for immigrants and blacks" and a preference for "deeply religious" elected officials.[52] While it is deeply important to scrutinize the racial dimension of TP activism, explaining this by pointing to religious preferences that—in the minds of some Whistleblowers—might plant the seeds for the American Taliban simply reproduces the Embattlement narrative.

Louis D. Ruprecht concluded there was no "real evidence" that the TP is "something significant happening to the religious landscape." Rather, the TP was merely the latest expression of "something perennial," an easily manipulable populism.[53] Others, however, assumed that the TP rallies were actually fronts for dominionists or Christian Reconstructionists: bad religion to go with bad politics.[54] Some judged that the religious dimensions of the TP were "indistinguishable from the 1980s era church-based political organizing efforts of the religious right."[55] The range of these associations is, of course, a product of the Whirl. It allows the incidental to become major, the anecdotal to become central, the suspicion real. TP religion is dangerously shadowy, unless its moblike anger is in our face as the countersign to authentic freedom. "Christianists" and "values voters" are "teabaggers, townhallers, and birthers," a set of interchangeable identities that Whistleblowers used in the same way TP supporters manipulated Hitler and Joker images.[56] Whistleblowers thus commit to an understanding of religion as a kind of dangerous speech and factional practice, whose sphere must be partitioned from legitimate politics and its influence narrowed. Theirs is a history peopled by sagacious, self-limiting devout who protect authentic constitutionalism from the hollering, enraged rabble. To blow the whistle on the TP was to play into their appeal: participants and critics alike performed the role of biblical exegete and colonial historian, explaining the *real* meaning of the histories inspiring the *real* Tea Party.

As a scholar of religion, I would never trivialize exegesis or history. Nor, as a citizen, would I ever trivialize the violence that bumptious TP rallies helped authorize. But when critics assail the religion of the Embattled, they refresh the very lifeblood of the Embattled. What seems more important is the way the TP popularized the public as a kind of theater of redescription. On the one hand, the conspiratorial thinking that the TP uses and evokes from its critics is defined by its exacting attention to words: all those things we are told are really going on behind the innocent-seeming words, as well as incantations like "freedom" or "faith." On the other hand, the virality that permits the endless linkings of conspiracy also severs the connection between language and effects, as with the TP's disavowal of the linkage between its rhetoric and Jared Loughner's 2011 shooting spree.[57] While TP Martyrs and Whistleblowers alike insist loudly upon the singularity of words and events, they share a condition where ideas are simply loosed, crackling with the energy of free play, like the fevered political vision of a poststructuralist on meth. Is this not the very logic of Trumpian speech, which proceeds from blunt assertion to denial of assertion to walking back the implications to complete redescription?

Religion is privileged as the category that must be defended from a time of decentered truth, even as it is clearly the product *of* it. But the condition itself has not been unknotted through the ascendance of these structurally similar discourses. Despite what Whistleblowers insist, the "truth" of the TP's historical claims is not the entire point, nor is figuring out the exact measure of religion's influence on those claims. Amid the clamor and controversy that the TP provoked, and continues to provoke via its influence on conservatism in the Trump era, the collision of assertions forming their conception of public life reveals a lack that is culturally and politically illuminating.

## "The Prisoner Wishes to Say a Word"

But what is it that's lacking? Perhaps it is historical validation and purpose for a country still young, or at least young enough to be anxious and self-conscious about its identity. Is religion, then, part of the politics of nostalgia? A film suggests a more complicated answer. Long before viewers learned of his anti-Semitism, Mel Gibson's two Clinton-era "historical" films were co-opted into American politics. Strangely considering the subject of this chapter, though, *The Patriot* (2000) has proven far less influential to Martyr conceptions of politics than has *Braveheart* (1995).

A year after the "Gingrich revolution" of the 1994 midterm elections, a widely documented and discussed upsurge of white male masculinity emerged in (mostly) suburban America. First was the increasing popularity of war games as recreational activity, including not only Civil War reenactment or Renaissance Fair jousts but paintball, Green Beret cosplay, and prepper training at gun ranges, in the woods, or at separatist compounds, for men sharing the fear that the "tyranny" of big government could no longer be checked by the integrity and wholesome goodwill of "the people."[58] Some of these ideas are as old as America, but *Braveheart* framed them for millions of Americans who grumbled about "Hillarycare" or gangsta rap or NAFTA. Gibson's fictionalized slice of Scottish history stood in for any American viewer's felt experience of Embattlement and in time became perhaps a powerful Action Movie template.

The film focuses on Gibson's portrayal of the thirteenth-century Scottish hero William Wallace. Its opening images of kilted, brawny men laboring contentedly, attending fairs, falling for pale maidens, and engaged in manly feats is carefully manufactured for maximum sentimentality and appeal. Viewers' outrage is stoked at the sight of the Crown's armies robbing sweet Scotland of "her" freedom. After one too many village raids and the execution of his wife, Wallace and his merry men enter into a kind of protracted guerrilla warfare, whose resonance with the 1990s antistatist militia movements was as unmistakable as it was mostly unremarked. Wallace is eventually tried and executed himself. At the movie's conclusion, as Gibson grimaces and contorts on the rack of tyranny, a sniveling magistrate leans into his face and tells him he need only to say "Mercy" to be spared a grisly death. The magistrate announces, "The prisoner wishes to say a word," whereupon Wallace, defiant to the last, wails "FREEEEEDOOMMM!!!"

Any number of possible readings exist. Curtis Coats and Stewart Hoover have suggestively linked the film's popularity among evangelical viewers to its "essentialist narratives of patriarchy."[59] The 1990s, they remind us, also witnessed the resurgence of muscular Christianity, most obviously in the Promise Keepers' defense of male headship. Thus, for one pastor, the fact that Wallace has "a passion . . . something he is willing to die for," contrasts with the growing insignificance of American white male masculinity.[60]

What is more suggestive, though, is the way the film commends the entrance into national life via a navigation of the freedom/tyranny dyad. The lack of perfect, unencumbered liberty is not defended conceptually in the film, which focuses on realities that will, despite the dystopian fantasies of some Martyrs, likely never befall any American.[61] Wallace's own move from hearth to battlefield is echoed in a broader American conviction taking shape during *Braveheart*'s release. Important to the appeal of the Action Movie template is the caterwauling self-evidence of the idea of "freedom" as Gibson hollers it from his place of torture. Freedom does not require elaboration. Freedom's absence is torture. In this we detect an affective resonance with the TP as public, in its interior convictions, its collective effervescence, and its revolutionary kitsch, including the popularity of "Don't Tread on Me" merch, which shares with *Braveheart* the assumption that whatever produces the felt experience of unfreedom, even if it comes from a democratically elected and legitimated system, must be attributed to an illegitimate, occupying foreign power.

The religion of the TP here serves the dream of mattering like an Action Hero, of being recognized by authority as someone significant enough to attack. No particular content is necessary; what matters is only the sense that one's discomfort means someone is to blame. The very appeal of the fantasy is partly in its displacement of political debates: about what citizenry means, about the extent to which radical expressions of self-interest should be constrained by equal self-limitation, and about whether contestation is a defining feature of democracy itself.

Democracy is on the ropes in America, and renewed engagement with just those debates might help rebuild its foundations. Public life has been getting less consensual and more fractious for a very long time. Indeed, Trump's presidency—which partook of the energies and turmoil wrought by the TP during Obama's presidency—has revealed the fragility and volatility of American publics. It is difficult to focus on the possible sources and implications of these developments when large numbers of Americans are more invested in stoking social conflict than in curbing it, savoring its outrages for the purposes of self-definition. It is important, however, to historicize this condition.

We have seen how early democratic theorists—including James Madison, John Stuart Mill, and Alexis de Tocqueville—extolled popular governance in the abstract. Tocqueville was full of praise for religion's essential role in fostering democratic civility and political temperament.[62] Yet subsequent developments in politics would provoke questions about the strength and integrity of some of democracy's basic premises. Nineteenth-century public life, in Europe and the United States, was often acrimonious, even physically violent. Many have contented themselves with the explanation that such episodes of "contestation" can be contained by civil society and its associational networks. But it was the rise of mass democracy itself that challenged the framework dreamed up at the Constitutional Convention. Parties and mobs and voting blocs emerged from the demographic, economic, and structural changes of the mid-nineteenth century; and they spilled well over the boundaries of what Alexander Hamilton, in Federalist No. 9, understood as the "science of politics."[63] The 1890s and the 1920s and the 1960s and the 2000s witnessed similar spasms of collective energy that, in varying ways, signaled democracy's problems. For every historical attempt at securing suffrage or a legislative advance, there is protest and repression; for every assemblage of teeming thousands manifesting their will, there may be the crackdown of a police state or the undertow of apathy.

In response to democracy's instability, some theorists have pushed for more direct democracy, grounding political procedure in the associational networks of citizens, hoping that through them might emerge new openings for organized publics, political wills, and moral discourses.[64] Others have responded with Madisonian concerns for systemic stability over the enthusiasms of the citizenry, locating democracy in a set of institutions rather than encounters, crudely put. It is in the tension between these traditions that American dissatisfactions with and rhapsodies about democratic life have taken shape: a longing for an unfettered polis that at the same time cannot get started; a dependency on institutional power that cannot shake a desire for greater expression.

The TP's arrival might reasonably have demanded a resuscitation of these old debates. Yet we see in TP Embattlements no well-wrought theory of state power or justification of institutional constraint, nor even any robust understanding of political participation. What abides is its performed sense of crisis, a desire to yawp barbarically at a reality characterized simultaneously by the furious onrush of data and an increasingly stale range of political institutions. Public life thus becomes a barrage of assertions and defenses, a *j'accuse* of the suburbs, cosplaying William Wallace on the rack.

On my account, the TP was not seeking to expand the concept of democratic freedom, but to circumscribe it by asserting the priority of a particular religio-political identity—true history, authentic politics, real reason—precisely when these elements come to seem contingent. Since the 2016 presidential campaign, these elements have commonly been subsumed under the category "populism." This category, which has a very specific political history in the United States, is not the same as public action in the abstract, nor is it always self-consciously linked to the expression of a particular rather than a general will. But the fearful rise of far-right, antistatist, antipluralist political parties and citizens' movements across the North Atlantic—from Greece's Golden Dawn to the Britain First Defense Force, from France's Le Front National to the alt-right in America—certainly invites attention to the cross-cultural sense of Embattlement among white males.[65]

It is difficult to avoid the defensive whiteness that lurks within the TP's communitarian dreaming. The TP denounced "entitlements" that ostensibly "put everyone on the government plantation."[66] The critique of "handouts" from the "nanny state" has historically been code for criticism of social welfare programs whose primary beneficiaries have been African Americans. The TP consistently employed the rhetoric of color-blindness, which has long been used to table specific petitions of need or recognition. A 2011 poll found that TP supporters believe "too much has been made of race in America."[67] And when the NAACP issued a resolution demanding that the TP officially condemn the "racist elements" among its number, the TP dismissed the NAACP as a money-making front for corporate interests (more successful than any slaveholders, it was alleged), whose potentially legitimate claims were undermined by "playing the race card" and demanding "handouts" like cash and flat-screen televisions.[68] If it was not obvious during the TP's ascendancy, it was more than evident during the Trump presidency that the TP rhetoric of "taking the country back" is anything but racially innocent, partaking of a long lineage of anti-immigrant, exceptionalist discourse.

## America™

The dual meaning of calls for change—to change back, undoing change that discomfits us—epitomizes the transformations in American life since Reagan, where the new politics was marked by the triumph of the American imaginary over the real and the disgruntled refusal to adjust. The tension between the fantasy of post-Reagan America and the absolute material squeeze of this period has bred systemic distrust, deflected into performative publics that proclaim as patriotism the evasion of responsibility to larger justice.[69] Such a politics asserts its ubiquity by warning of its own endangerment. Yet in its very call to historic purpose, it signifies its attachment to the mundane condition that produces this very longing.[70] Can we not see in this showy public longing a clear desire to avoid an actual, recognizable public? The TP's call to action is a yearning to just be left alone, with the assertion that this is a right guaranteed by old America.

The movement's sense that the America they love is disappearing, that they can no longer recognize the past in the present, is meaningful. But the kind of nostalgia the TP and MAGA trade in—and which Whistleblowers sometimes echo with their own version of the proper American past, unsullied by conservative Christians—is antithetical to authentic public purpose: it overlooks the power of genuinely critical memory. The TP's fondness for Reagan-era conservatism goes to work just here, since the lasting contribution of Reagan was to sell Americans on slogan-driven nostalgia for an America that never existed, while their pensions were squeezed, their jobs outsourced, the social safety net slashed and discredited.

The TP is thus the latest in an ongoing franchise, eagerly delivering the key lines that tell us government is the problem. Thus the need to stop time, to freeze the demos in a particular moment, a particular demographic formation, a particular religiosity, lest it continue racing away from our control. History is not used diagnostically here; rather it is a device of atmosphere, reproducing the Embattled's conviction that "political disagreement [is] a symptom of moral failure."⁷¹ The power of crowds to strengthen this outlook sits in tension with the idea that public opinion can be rational when produced (and surveyed) by the right kinds of institutions.⁷² Instead, for all the clamor around TP religion, crowds actually become arenas of disinterest in what participation can do for citizens, what range of action and argumentation can be accommodated, and toward what ends such collectivities should be focused. Instead, Embattled Americans cry foul.

To see in the TP's religion only faction or postrationality is diagnostically incomplete. For there is also a deep sadness that accompanies TP gatherings, despite their exuberance. Behind it is loneliness, the sheer isolation of the lifestyle that many mistake for political purpose. TP Embattlement is not merely a petty bourgeois flirtation with the rhetoric of revolution; it captures what Lauren Berlant calls "cruel optimism": "attachment to compromised conditions of possibility whose realization is discovered either to be impossible, sheer fantasy, or too possible, and toxic."⁷³ The TP's crowdsourced religion is, in Berlant's sense, an object of longing and the vehicle for expressing that longing.

To enter the public sphere under these conditions, in this mode of performance, is to confirm that although *Braveheart*-ing the suburbs is deeply (if temporarily) intoxicating, it mistakes the sheer noise and density of the experience of Embattlement for democracy itself. In this way, the TP revealed an American public that avoids confronting the problems of public life. The lack to which I have referred is not only the lack of opportunity to register one's voice in public; it is also the felt lack of certitude about America, of the insulation citizens crave, continually pricked by the pain and hardships and desires of others, so much that we cannot tune them out. A TP public compensates for these feelings by being louder than others.⁷⁴

It is irresponsible to think about the TP outside its relation to other crowds. Occupy Wall Street. Bundy ranch separatists. Bird's-eye photographs of gray inaugurations. And the unsettling spectrum of 2020–2021 crowds, from Black Lives Matter to the MAGA insurrection. Each of these crowds bears the weight of America differently, and with very different stakes. More pointedly, each of them becomes public because of widely varying experiences of Others. So to describe the TP as simply a conservative religious movement is to overlook how its very existence as a public force is to authorize a turn away from the hardships others experience in the present. The TP relies on a backward-looking Life as Action Movie that confirms, in this backwardness, what it cannot announce: that to be an American is to suffer.

What matters about the TP's enthusiasms is not that they are religious but that they express a deep, narcissistic rage at a world in which it is not all working out for you. Instead of changing these conditions, Embattled Americans want to silence the pain of others so they can perform the brashest Action Movie. This is why the patriotism so garishly on display at TP rallies is so indebted to *Braveheart* and *The Patriot*, because they are not about #freedom so much as payback. TP publics enable participants to look away from the lack and attribute their feelings to exteriorized wrongdoing. They do not expand the public's capacity for greater participation, or its accommodation of new constituencies, or its utility in dialogue.[75] Instead, they exemplify the managed, performative democracy of America™. The loud and the outrageous are acclaimed as genuine because they attract attention; it is not suasion or moral power that compels, but spectacle and the urgent claim that an impostor king has sacked your village.

## The Lonely Crowd

Look, then, to that lonely inauguration on January 20, 2017. The gray damp of the Mall was no scene of glory. It was the scene of disappointment, of Photoshopping, and of the spirit of revenge. What does this moment mean for thinking about majoritarianism and public life? The ascendance of MAGA was the magnification of the TP's brand, whose authority and Americanism relied on the warning that a crisis has befallen "real" Americans. Out of that bleak afternoon came an alarming flicker of imagery. Inhabitants of Reddit or 4Chan, with "fashie" haircuts and hipster beards, suddenly wore Nazi armbands. Men in camouflage and wraparound shades once more strode menacingly among assembled citizens, automatic weapons ready for business. Other crowds marched, too, tens of thousands of women registering their dissent, and also a smattering of decentralized Antifa supporters. All of a sudden, a world of sober realpolitik and frustrating administrative inertia had exploded with terms like "race traitor," "blood and soil," and "America first." Except, as Black Lives Matter protesters and others reminded us correctly, none of this was actually sudden. It was just now permitted.

Despite my fury and horror in the face of these crowds, especially those in my hometown on January 6, 2021, I believe it is still possible to excavate alternate traditions of American public life and participation. And as citizens it is vital to assert that something else is possible, for if we do not we have abandoned the very idea of politics. The expansion of norms and capacities assumed to be fundamentally safe in democracies depends on the ability to imagine them and to articulate them to others, even others who need to be convinced of these ideas' worth. In this sense, the problem of public life in America remains communicational.

It is also crucial to consider the integrity of publics themselves beyond simple acknowledgment that citizens have an abstract right to gather in public space. It is not especially helpful to look, for example, at the August 2017 conflicts in the streets of Charlottesville, Virginia, and ask whether or not Nazis have the right to be Nazis outside of their Nazi homes. Nor is it politically honest to look at the increase of public white supremacists—for these are the crowds that matter now—and scold the Democratic National Committee for not understanding their economic anxiety. Nor, most of all, can the problems of America's publics be understood and addressed by focusing on the role of religion in these conflicts, isolated from the larger structural and conceptual considerations.

I believe we have arrived at this moment because too much credence has been given to the wrong kinds of presumptions about democracy. Genuine public life depends on the principled refusal of certain points of view, not on the mindless "tolerance" of views simply because people hold them sincerely. This presumption has given cover to far too many exclusionary assertions about who "real" Americans are, and what "real" religion is. If there is to be anything left of and for American politics, this must be abandoned in favor of contests over which political principles, which brands of moral suasion, and which ways of recognizing and interacting with other people might make publics less about cosplay and more about the achievement of justice.

Americans have, since the towers fell and the corporatized blaring of democracy's hosannas that ensued, entered a period of madness. There is Netflix and the cloud. There are hybrid cars and integrated, multiuse living spaces. But these same times have produced Ferguson and Charlottesville and the gig economy and QAnon. And even before the fire and fury of 2020–2021—which began with white men brandishing weapons in state houses, demanding that states "reopen" while a pandemic raged, and which continued through yet more police violence inflicted on innocent black men, and then protesters of said violence, and then militias attempting to overturn an election—America's crowds began to show many of the signs that precede civil wars around the planet, including "entrenched national polarization," "weakened institutions," and "the legitimization of violence."[76] And recent studies show that support for the very idea of democracy has slipped in the last generation: "support for 'Army rule' has increased to one in six Americans," from one in sixteen a generation before.[77] The communicational problems of public life, when they cannot navigate the problems of difference, degenerate into a collective Action Movie that we both fear and desire.

To see Nazis and white supremacist militias in the streets is to experience despair. To hear a president, and many more supporters than anyone reading this would ever have presumed to think, equivocate about their meaning and subsequently encourage them is to experience despair. To see peaceful protesters gassed by unidentified troops is to experience astonishment. Beyond the more obvious implications for race and nation and religion, that these publics have coalesced during the age of Embattlement, at a tipping point for democracies, bears further scrutiny. Not only did many of the far-right politicians associated with the Tea Party populate the Trump administration itself (think only of Pence or Secretary of State Mike Pompeo), Trump Svengali Steve Bannon has—since his exile from the White House—devoted himself to achieving a "Global Tea Party" by promoting authoritarianism across Europe.[78] So behind the arc tracing the rise of the TP to the alt-right, we see a particular constituency leveraging the forces that create Embattlement in order to remake the fundaments of politics in increasingly less democratic ways.

For Richard Spencer, one of the alt-right's key representatives, America is not about democracy; it is about "heritage" and "culture," which is white European. Spencer assembles crowds of supporters and detractors alike as a way of expressing antidemocracy. The identity he commends is premised on the notion that white people are the elite, racially and religious pure, not the herd. Conflating Max Weber and Carl Schmitt, Spencer is fond of intoning banalities like "Politics is inherently brutal. It's nonconsensual by its very nature. The state is crystallized violence."[79] Obviously, like a TP antigovernment broadside in the name of preserving religious liberty, this sentiment partakes of the thrill of rebellion, whose inversion is the thrill of Embattlement (where the inner experience of the state's violence is expressed as license, that *Braveheart*-ian yawp, that selfie of you lofting your AR-15 in the Capitol Rotunda).[80] Less obviously, Spencer's casual reduction of politics to governance (which he reads as inherently oppressive) is telling because it rejects politics as such.[81]

Behind many of these crowds is Spencer's contempt for politics "as an endless 'debate.'"[82] Violence, on the other hand, may be the force of leviathan crushing good-hearted Americans; but it is also the means by which the strong guide the weak. This vision of public life does not seek accommodation and coexistence but rather desires a monologue. By identifying the alt-right—from Identity Evropa to the Proud Boys to the Boogaloo Boys to the disturbing number of neo-Nazi and militia groups parading in Portland or Kenosha or DC—with the TP's understanding of publics, I submit that Americans must stop making excuses for groups who advance such views just because they don't openly wear Klan robes to Costco. There is now ample evidence that all too many Americans see politics as basically Schmittian in this way: the arena for refusing other points of view, brashly and theatrically.

So Charlottesville was not a drill. The Capitol siege was not a drill. Despite all of the chatter holding that the Tea Party, and exurban Trump supporters, and even the alt-right express some variant of populism, the bodies in America's streets since the November 2016 election (and November 2020's, in which *more* people voted for Trump, which can only be understood as a reaction against the summer's racial justice movement) confirm one of this chapter's epigraphs, from the band The Clash. Certain Americans enjoy the luxury of boredom, which is the phenomenological experience of the market sine qua non, since boredom keeps us yearning for the next fix, the next distraction from ourselves. But all these crowds discussed herein surely confirm that America is struggling with another Clash tune: "White Riot."

Like many people (I am sad not to be able to write "most"), I reject entirely the species of Americanism, masculinity, and citizenship touted by white nationalists. But if the rejection of this public force is to have any impact, it cannot be advanced by claims that rely on the same tropes of popular sovereignty and belonging, reducing politics to membership and the vainglory of cosplay. Behind them is the idea of racism as rebellion ("Fuck you, I won't do what you tell me") and the deployment of racial nostalgia against demographic change. Here, the mob reduces itself to singularity, to the forceful articulation of a will that makes public demands. But there, in response to Black Lives Matter, these same mobs insist that particularity is bogus, uttering the cynical deflection, *all* lives matter. How do we escape this condition?

In acting against a one-dimensional, subconsciously Hobbesian understanding of sovereignty—in which citizens are incorporated against their will into the governing mass of the state—America's Embattled are actually onto something, though they do not know it. We are in a Hobbesian moment in a less than obvious way, though. For the triumph of the Whirl has created a politics in which, precisely because of the interrelation of things and their proliferating effects on each other, "Every word and deed is potentially 'seditious,' an obstacle or threat to social and political order."[83] In linking public life and participation to the rejection of authorities external to us, Americans invest in the ephemera—the Whirl, "religion," "freedom"—that sustain antipolitics and mere enthusiasms.

As Mel Gibson is stretched eternally on the rack, and Nazis march in Jefferson's Charlottesville, and start-ups develop apps to measure the coalescence of emotion on Twitter, one must wonder: what kind of public sphere are Americans now willing to defend? Is it a public that is conducive to the interrogation of fundaments based on shared principles of egalitarianism, rational discourse, a preferential option for the least advantaged based on a system devoted to basic fairness, and a commitment to good citizenship that can be realized only with the equitable distribution of social goods? Or is it a public that promotes demotic episodes tailored to the Defense of the Suburbs and performance styles that speak in the idiom of Cold War exceptionalism, *Braveheart* victimization, and white identity politics, as if only these made up America? My aim is not simply to suggest the priority of progressive publics over conservative ones, but that the first public's orientation to collective will and suasion contrasts with the latter public's Action Movie deflection from the open-ended work of genuine democracy. Indeed, it is increasingly unclear what American conservatism is, over and above such performance styles.

The emergence and continued relevance of the TP confirms that many Americans have lost confidence in most everything besides themselves; that many Americans crave outrage rather than rethinking participation. But other crowds are possible, other un-ignorable identities and citizenries. Trump's rise, and his rallies with all their violence, were entirely consistent with the rise of TP crowds and the long-gestating politics they signaled. Even had Trump lost the 2016 election, those energies were in no danger of going anywhere, as we have fearfully seen after November 2020's election. They did, however, unleash other energies: the women's marches, the rambunctious town hall tilts between representatives and constituents, the crowds occupying political offices and chambers with songs and bodies at risk, the surge of Moral Mondays in North Carolina, the teeming masses at airports after the Trump travel ban was signed, among them doctors and pro bono lawyers refusing to ignore fellow humans, and most of all in the crowds at and in the wake of Ferguson and after George Floyd's execution, just two of the countless episodes of black bodies felled by the empowered.

If Spencer and Trump and the alt-eight represent the culmination of the TP's publics-as-cosplay, these alternate publics and their religio-political genealogies represent not simply a "left" alternative to a half-century's hard tilt to the right; they are about a democratic refusal to end debate. These reject the lure of the stasis housed in Embattlement's exclusive identities, which privileges narrow viewpoints in the name of "tradition" rather than a principled acceptance that identities are, and must be, chastened and agonistically linked to shared purpose. For this is the only possibility in actual democracies.

I want no one reading this to mistake me. I think the TP's culture of privileged white male complaint is transparent and shameful. But what the TP got wrong was not what Whistleblowers said. At bottom, what both Martyrs and Whistleblowers have failed to ask (or at best, failed to ask with sufficient urgency and vision) is: why are Americans not using the problems of public life and participation—the failure to institutionalize mechanisms and arenas for public debate, the inattention to developing robust dialogic skills, the deep anomie and dissatisfactions that revolutionary LARP-ing reveals—to call for wholly new institutions, norms, and mechanisms *of* that very public life and participation? We obsess over spectacle and the wrong outrages when we should be going normative.

This moment is an opportunity to rethink not only the power of participation but the way vital action can be more than merely anti-institutional; if our publics are protected and revisable, they can be geared to the reconfiguration and strengthening of just laws, norms, and institutions. It is an opportunity to imagine the power of bodies in streets, in celebration of each other's differences and, in that, celebrating the possibility of democracy—not as an artifact to be commodified or worn like a brand, as if it exists only to shield our feelings from interrogation, but as something that cannot be owned, and whose legitimacy comes only through citizens' willingness to submit to truth: not simply in the sense of verifiable statements but the truth of different groups of humans living and suffering and striving discrepantly because of the insistence of white and powerful and male Americans that "freedom" has no particular content other than to enable their lack of interest in, indeed contempt for, views and experiences that are not their own.

The implication is not that we should never talk about religion, never organize on the basis of religions, nor that religions should "know their place" and raise consciousness in the private sphere. But by talking more concertedly and rigorously about what we actually expect from public will-formation and participatory action, we may end up having to change the way we think about, and what we expect from, religion, whose "sincerely held" or stand-alone special protections do not guarantee anyone's right to be untroubled by difference. For the defense of such a "religion" is complicit in the suffering of other humans.

For all the self-evident good of people caring enough to gather in public, to sponsor candidates, and to convene for discussion and debate, the enthusiasms of the TP focused attention onto morality as a historical brand and away from the structural, systemic imbalances that are responsible for the degeneration of American politics in the first place. Rather than painting a garish, red-white-and-blue smile over our problems, let us see a public as an opportunity for clear-sightedness. A public can be a space where Americans revivify politics not as something given, not as a particular set of outcomes, but as a process rooted in a series of flexible norms that must always be understood as revisable (rather than simply reflecting our own self-interest). Despite the reality-show politics of our era, and the half-century con job which leaves corporations as persons and persons convinced politics is for suckers, possibility remains and democracy is not yet dead. A public can be an opportunity to confront what is genuinely dehumanizing, genuinely antidemocratic, and to do so by the sheer presence and force of bodies who assemble in the name of justice and inclusion, not in order to play-act oppression, mistaking not having it all for persecution.

Religions may or may not be part of the effort to reconceptualize real politics, community, change, and participation. They might play a crucial role in the associational networks and citizens' groups that will, I hope, continue to remake American publics. They will certainly be integral to conveying and sustaining a sense of authentic shared purpose to movements for justice and fairness, which is precisely the sort of project that Embattlement has proven unable to contend with. Democratic publics will organize and act in the service of a politics that is possible beyond the system, and in opposition to it, and to a lesser extent inside of it, but never in the service of a zero-sum politics that simply uses the *language* of democracy for narrow ends. To insist that freedom means only for us, and that any accommodation to the needs of other people is unfreedom, is not politics but nihilism. For too long, American obsessions with religion as the central category for making sense of public action have blocked our ability to think clearly about the salutary role of limits in public life. Shared norms and mutual accountability are not the bars of a prison cell; they are the very foundations of principled public life together.

# 7

# The Pearls and the Coral

## David Barton and the Burdens of History

> Fellow-citizens, we cannot escape history.
> —Abraham Lincoln

> History is bunk.
> —Henry Ford

> We can't change the present or the future. We can only change the past, and we do it all the time.[1]
> —Bob Dylan

It is no surprise that Americans wrangle over schools, given their role in the formation of character and citizenship. The old Deweyan vision of classrooms as democracies in miniature might be on life support, given the slashing of education budgets and the disrepute into which expertise has fallen; but schools are central to shared American myths about the common good, civic education, and progress. Through a tangled history stretching from unregulated state systems and Protestant common schools all the way through the challenges of Catholic parochialism, desegregation, and disestablishment, schools are the site of one of America's most Whiggish self-narrations.

Challenges to curricular content range from evolution to sex education to "critical race theory." Since the 1960s, Martyrs have energetically challenged such curricula, while also debating how religion is depicted in American history. Americans have always debated the past, of course, nowhere more so than through competing religious visions of Americanness, ranging from the Puritans' providentialism to Mormon sacred history to Cold War exceptionalist religion. In the contemporary furor over the place of religion in Embattled History, however, Americans avoid grappling with the complex inheritance of our democratic traditions and institutions. As Walter Benjamin once noted, "To articulate the past historically does not mean to recognize it 'the way it really was.' ... It means to seize hold of a memory as it flashes up at a moment of danger."[2]

## Brick by Brick

David Barton may not look the part of a revolutionary, but his Wallbuilders organization was founded in the late 1980s to combat what he and other Martyrs claim is a liberal, secularist assault on public education. Faced with the changes wrought by disestablishment and desegregation, prominent Martyrs have sought to transform curricula, focusing especially on textbook content.[3] For in their judgment, public schools champion a "diversity" that hypocritically silences the Embattled Majority of true Christians.

Barton was born in 1954 in Aledo, Texas. Raised evangelical, he attended Oral Roberts University, graduating in 1976 with a degree in religious education. Barton taught and later served as principal at Aledo Christian High School.[4] He later began consulting for other educational institutions and national educational lobbies (like the National Council on Bible Curriculum in Public Schools). This endeared him to conservative Christian elites, whose national organizations aggressively challenged public schools. In 1987, Barton asserted that both declining test scores and rising social delinquency were the result of the absence of prayer from public schools.[5] He began, in an ironic mimesis of the multicultural scholar's recovery of "forgotten voices," to explore "America's forgotten history."[6] He was influenced by the Vision Forum Ministries, Gary DeMar, Catherine Millard's texts and videos, and D. James Kennedy's Center for Reclaiming America.[7] Most compelling was Peter Marshall and David Manuel's 1977 book *The Light and the Glory*, which held that American history constituted "a divine drama."[8] This was the period during which such claims moved decisively to the center of conservative discourse. New Right activists bonded with evangelicals to undermine the old, wheezing Republican power structure via grassroots organizing designed to platform home Bible study and Christian schooling and to fill elected offices with "real Christians."[9] Any insinuation that America was not "special" or "providential" would be taken not merely as offensive but as a rejection of plain truth.

The lament that academia is covering up true history is an old conservative standby. It can be seen in Senator Joseph McCarthy's attempt to sniff out communist professors, the Reagan administration's opposition to multicultural education and certain strains of social science, the zeal among members of today's Turning Point USA to expose sinister secularists, and even in claims by members of white supremacist organizations like Identity Evropa that true Americans must "discover what your professors never taught you in school."[10] For decades Barton has been mainstreaming these notions. Since the purported radicalization of academic history in the 1970s, the culture at large has, says Barton, been undermined by a "historical revisionism."[11] Anticipating now-familiar charges from the Trump era, Barton was one of the earliest and loudest Martyrs, claiming that in the name of "political correctness," Christians were demonized in favor of less deserving religious identities. In his reckoning, this fabricated past would enable "outlandish" policy and legal entitlements. Barton sought educational reforms that would reassert the "real truth" of American history.

Barton's dozens of books, beginning with 1987's *The Myth of Separation*, allege that the "wall of separation" between church and state is a myth that obscures law's only legitimate purpose: to protect Americans' religious freedom from government and judicial overreach.[12] The wall his organization favors is not Jefferson's, but rather derives from the book of Nehemiah, where—Barton writes—"the nation of Israel rallied together in a grassroots movement to help rebuild the walls of Jerusalem and thus restore stability, safety, and a promising future to that great city."[13]

Wallbuilders sought to "educate the public" and provide "direct assistance to our elected and appointed officials."[14] Its influence grew quickly. Barton served as vice chair of the Texas Republican Party from 1997 to 2006.[15] During the 2004 presidential campaign, he became involved in the Republican Party's national outreach to evangelical voters. Barton became the go-to authority on American history for Focus on the Family, Concerned Women for America, the Christian Coalition, and related organizations, many of which describe public schools as "places of 'social depravity' and 'spiritual slaughter' for Christians."[16] Amplifying earlier claims about the "oppression" wrought by the secularization of public schools, Barton constructs a past that is neither murky nor complex; in it there is common sense, straight talk, and clear facts to guide us through the muddle.

Barton believes that God is "missing in action in American history."[17] For Barton, American culture has—through the normalization of "non-theistic" doctrines like evolution and the dilution of sacred purpose—created a "death struggle between civilizations."[18] Leftists and secularists, Barton asserts, not only defend debased policy and bad history; they do so in flagrant violation of "overwhelming majority" who side with Barton and his fellow Martyrs.[19]

## "We Are Not in the Minority"

Barton's history is advanced as no mere collection of data but as a vessel for the heartfelt sincerity of national concern. The gap between academic credential and authentic inquiry for Barton reveals how "what I got taught and what I've seen in the actual documents aren't the same thing."[20] In the Action Movie of Embattled History, little appeals more than "the untold story of our nation's history," kept from us by elites and wrongdoers.[21] Despite these efforts, Barton asserts that *"we are not in the minority*; we just think we are . . . by the tens of millions we just sit around doing nothing, and that's what *killing* us." To mistake your own majority status is to accept death. Those are the stakes. The only solution, then, is to honor America's real history by getting conservative Christians appointed to the courts; otherwise, "We'll keep getting pushed back further and further and further."[22]

Barton recommends that Congress "impeach judges whose rulings are opposed by social conservatives."[23] Indeed, he believes that the courts have not only protected dubious beliefs and practices in the guise of "religion," but also flirted with dangerously immoral decisions like the ruling that mandatory school prayer is unconstitutional. Barton supports his ideas by overwhelming audiences with quotations and anecdotes from the colonial era, which he claims liberals have distorted as part of a long campaign that will end in the criminalization of Christianity. In Barton's imagination, any decision that complicates conservative Christian hegemony is a kind of cultural waterboarding, the legal front of a postapocalyptic police state in which a triumphant Left will drag students from prayer groups, seize Bibles, and constrain innocent holiday cheer. That such alarmist claims have become standard conservative fare bemoaning "cancel culture" or the *New York Times*' 1619 Project shows how effective Barton has been.[24]

While Barton and other Martyrs love the rhetoric of outsiderdom, their base claim is that an illegitimate minority has managed—through manipulation and influence in key institutions—to pervert tradition and the true mainstream. Wallbuilders is thus grounded in a melancholic experience of the present, rather than in nuanced theology or archival rigor. Audiences are meant to respond to Barton's claims with a sense of shock and sadness that godlessness has prevailed.

Barton's historical view resonates with some of the assumptions behind constitutional originalism, as championed in the long line of Federalist Society–approved judges. What is fascinating is how Barton construes balance and "fairness" in his critiques.[25] At times, he champions fairness in the name of "allowing" religions to have a "voice" in the public sphere. Yet he also decries neutrality as "impossible," since it fits nowhere in the Framers' "plan for limited government." So if the Framers never intended that "the religious aspect" of either culture or the First Amendment be silenced by "a single dissenter," then the problem of majority tyranny so central to the constitutional era melts away.

Barton once proposed a "Religious Speech Amendment" to the Constitution, an effort that paved the way for now-familiar arguments put forward in state-level Religious Freedom Restoration Acts that religious speech as such is protected, even if it is discriminatory or demands exemptions from the rule of law. Whistleblowers see in these claims the seeds of theocracy. To Barton, though, they are commonsense interpretations of "the Framers' timeless proposals" that liberals have trampled. Barton presumes that if a religious expression is "popular," it should trump others, or that an expression of "long-standing" has privileges that others lack.

If the views of the Framers were "clearly presented," we would know that only pointy-headed PhDs believe that they disagreed among themselves, or that colonial religiosity may not map onto the present. If you are fearful of the present, Barton assures readers, the Framers' vision of piety and self-government "need not be a forgotten or disregarded page from the American epic." And who would not want to be part of an epic? Only a churl would fail to gush along with Barton that being an American is "to dream the unthinkable," just as the revolutionaries did in the late eighteenth century.

Barton has thus produced the basic historical framework for widespread Martyr understandings of law, liberty, and citizenship.[26] Whether addressing Justice Sunday events or the Republican National Committee, he successfully presents historical data and political terms as emotional categories; authority, freedom, and piety exist not as subjects of critical debate but as components of a single conception of citizenship and history. To followers, the emotionalism of Barton's history—not its factual accuracy—is what resonates with their own experience of this exclusivity.

But what of others left "outside" by history? If Barton wanted to avoid the politics of the multicultural historians he disdained, what would he say about slavery, Jim Crow, and ongoing discrimination against people of color? Barton's historical assertion that America is no longer "great," so clearly antagonistic to people of color, bears further scrutiny. For Barton helped pave the way not just for a general Republican evasion of race by sentimentalizing it (or relying on cynical assertions about the "party of Lincoln") but for the nihilism of Trump's pitch to African American voters: "What the hell do you have to lose?"

In a 2006 video, *Setting the Record Straight*, Barton claimed that "the Democratic Party of old was responsible for everything from slavery and segregation to lynchings and the birth of the Ku Klux Klan."[27] He contends that erstwhile Democrat defense of the *Dred Scott* decision is comparable to the Democratic Party's current position on reproductive rights, which Barton believes actually holds contemporary women in a kind of bondage: for Democrats, "an unborn human is really just disposable property . . . African Americans were the victims of this disposable property ideology a century and a half ago."[28] If you support reproductive rights, then, you are a white supremacist. What holds together such pinwheeling associations is the emotional atmosphere Barton conjures by convincing audiences that their feelings of being oppressed are backed up by history, which is itself an emotional experience of one's own authority.

The particulars of Barton's history have been regularly challenged. But, building on the era's general suspicion of authority and on the customized knowledge made possible in the Whirl, he has helped make room for a new kind of "expert," one whose chief purpose is to counteract "ridicule" with a new narrative.[29] The performance of historical or epistemological injury enables one to make of history a contest between scorn and valor, each sustained by emotional intensity rather than facts and independent sourcing. It is not that "true" and "false" have no meaning, that "accuracy" is simply swept away by the sheer multiplicity of possible historical narratives; rather, these terms achieve force through the emotional power and stakes of the "religion" they also claim to protect.

## "Liars for Jesus"

This is where Whistleblowers have weighed in. Some dismiss Barton as a shill, noting that his own books are assigned in the ideal Christian curriculum he circulates.[30] For most Whistleblowers, though, the way to undermine Barton was to substitute for his avalanche of words a different one.[31] Their strategy was to focus on presenting the Truth via a kind of principled mockery, awaiting each flubbed footnote or mischaracterization. In some reckonings, Barton is laughed off as a curiosity from the freak show of right-wing religion: indeed, on his regular appearances on *Comedy Central* shows, there is a palpable air of smugness among hosts and audiences, eager to play the role of the liberal elite so central to Martyr narratives. But Barton is far more often cited as a danger, a sign of not merely complaint or special privilege but a distortion of the true American vision, an undisguised attempt to concoct instead of facts a "secret sauce that endears him to the Republican Party."[32]

Barton is judged to be "not a student of history, but a manipulator of it."[33] How else could he propose "regulating homosexuality on the basis that we already regulate unhealthy things like smoking and trans fats"?[34] He is assailed for revisionism and poor method, with one critic deriding him for producing "pseudoscholarship" and another for popularizing "outright falsehoods."[35] History News Network referred to Barton's *The Jefferson Lies* as "the least credible history book in print," while the *New York Times* called Barton "a biased amateur who cherry-picks quotes from history and the Bible."[36] At bottom, he is accused of improperly "bringing religion into politics," sullying the authentic purposes of both.[37] He is said to make of "religion" itself "a political weapon against the constitutional principle of church-state separation, the bedrock of individual religious liberty."[38]

This weaponization leads, in turn, to urgent calls to action. A whistle would not need blowing if Barton were just a lone ranter on Twitter. Whistleblowers urge that not only should historians sign on for the debunking; real readers of scripture must get involved, too, blowing the whistle on Barton's claims that, for example, Jesus endorsed laissez-faire economics.[39] Barton is denounced for reading scripture anachronistically, promoting a "religious agenda" no less dire than his political and historical revisionism.[40]

Barton is thus identified as a point man in a factional movement with "an agenda that makes Newt Gingrich's Contract With America look like the Communist Manifesto."[41] Barton's "Christian army" wants "to rewrite schoolbooks to reflect a Christian version of American history, pack the nation's courts with judges who follow Old Testament law, post the Ten Commandments in every courthouse and make it a felony for gay men to have sex and women to have abortions."[42] What Barton calls a moral imperative to reclaim America for Christ is seen as robbery, usurpation, a dangerous admixture of church and state.

Some of the most compelling Whistleblowers are evangelical historians like John Fea, George Marsden, and Mark Noll, who concur that Barton "has no training as an academic historian, is recognized and honored by no other workaday historians, follows few canons of scholarship," and that his work is "suspect."[43] Whistleblowers also note that Barton is too much even for some conservatives. Interfaith Alliance's Welton Gaddy, once on staff for the Southern Baptist Convention, criticized Barton's "dangerous theology" and "extremist beliefs."[44] When even other evangelicals find you dangerous, the suggestion is, your critics must have the truth of things. Barton's tactics are linked to "a long, loud tradition of charismatic evangelicals capable of commanding legions."[45] Barton and the armies he purportedly commands are alleged to operate by stealth, "below the radar" like a splinter cell.[46] To concede an iota of history to Barton would be to unleash pastors from IRS regulations, to blend drivel with danger. The proper response, then, is to out the Martyrs. As Chris Rodda, author of *Liars for Jesus: The Religious Right's Alternate Version of American History*, confidently claimed, "The only advantage I have over Barton is that I'm telling the truth."[47] Whistleblowers have their own Action Movie, wherein they bravely sling stones at Christians who would rob America of its glorious secularism.[48]

In calling attention to these epistemological parallels, and structural similarities in Whistleblower and Martyr perceptions, my intention is not to suggest their equivalency; rather, I believe that these very parallels sustain a condition in which Americans are unable to get beyond false equivalencies. In critically and strategically assessing Barton's despisers, I am not unconcerned about the coordinated plan by Republican jurists to stack the judiciary, nor the far-right intolerance that has reached the highest level of American governance. It is *because* of my deep existential anxiety about America that I am pointing out a mode of critique that has not worked.

Well in advance of the Trump administration's cynical use of "alt facts," Whistleblowers understood that getting the texts and the evidence right was a high-stakes enterprise if democracy really did depend on transparency and good arguments. Yet pointing out Barton's sloppy history does little in the way of diagnosing the larger political condition that breathes life into Barton's campaigns. What is more, criticism only deepens the Martyrs' conviction that they are Embattled. This forces Whistleblowers to invest in the same kind of narrative as Barton's: outrage that truth itself should be Embattled by such naked manipulation.

Barton has indeed been energized by the criticisms. Since his Embattlement claims revolve around the idea that true history is being suppressed, critics' attempts to dismiss or undermine confirm for Barton and his supporters that he is right. It is a strange condition. There is in fact a vast array of evidence that Barton is stating falsehoods. The Framers did not at all believe that only proper Christians could ever hold office in the United States. But if Whistleblowers continue simply to play a role in the Martyrs' narrative, they will have at best limited success. Here is how it plays out at the local level.

## Storming the School Board

As the second-largest textbook market in the country, Texas has long been seen as a curricular bellwether. In the 1990s conservative Christians throughout the country ran in local elections, including local and county school boards, seeking greater representation in public life.[49] In Texas efforts to overhaul school boards were often confrontational. Candidates supported by national Christian Right organizations and sympathetic millionaires amplified warnings about the threats new textbooks posed to religion and American tradition.

James Leininger's Texans for Governmental Integrity (TGI) mounted a campaign to transform the state school board. TGI denounced a Democratic candidate as being in thrall to a "radical homosexual lobby," pushing its minority views onto an unsuspecting public (the righteous majority) through high school curricula. The group alleged that the candidate "wanted to push steroids and alcohol on children and advocated in-class demonstrations on 'how to masturbate and how to get an abortion!'"[50] Stocking the school boards candidate by candidate, citizens known even to other Texas conservatives as "radicals" began to press such educational panics even further. Cynthia Dunbar likened sending kids to public schools to "throwing them into the enemy's flames."[51]

After Rick Perry's gubernatorial election in 2000, the balance on the state board shifted to Martyrs who, despite their numbers, continued to insist on their unfair marginalization.[52] In 2007, Perry appointed retired dentist Don McLeroy, who had long participated in educational activism, as chair. Led by McLeroy, board members challenged prevailing history standards and narratives, insisting that they sought balance and fair representation to counteract the excesses of liberal histories. One of the chief advocates for such historical "equal time" was Bill Ames, an active militia member with ties to Phyllis Schlafly's Eagle Forum. Ames insisted that if history texts could valorize "illegal immigrant aliens" or push an "environmentalist agenda to destroy America," then in the name of fairness they should make room for "Newt Gingrich, Phyllis Schlafly and the Moral Majority."[53] Martyrs like Ames wanted more than simply to increase the number of references to conservative figures; taking their inspiration from authors like Barton, they insisted that these curricular efforts would also be contributions to their larger goal: restoring to American history its most authentic actors, and its Christian providential character.

In 2009, in response to critics of McLeroy, Perry appointed Gail Lowe as board chair, promising that Lowe would "ensure that Texans receive the educational foundation necessary to be successful."[54] Lowe had long embraced Martyr positions on public education: she supported the incorporation of creationism into science curricula; jettisoned a proposal increasing writing and critical thinking components in courses; and opposed modifications to health textbooks that addressed contraception, pregnancy, and sexually transmitted diseases. She denied the existence of climate change and supported "values-based" education. Most outrageous to observers was Lowe's decision to appoint Barton himself to a state-convened "expert panel" for a proposed revision to Texas social studies curricula.[55]

Barton insisted that since "only majorities can expand political rights in America's constitutional society," it should be only majorities (such as Barton's own aggrieved supporters) who can approve the representation of minority persons and viewpoints in historical narratives.[56] This frank declaration of paternalism was grounded in the insistence that it furthered the goal of balanced, fair exposure. This extends not only to representation of non-European Americans in history but to controversial subjects generally. With regard to teaching about climate change, Texan skeptics argued *against* majoritarianism (here, scientific consensus) to plead for the airing of nonexpert opinions so that students could "analyze and evaluate different views on the existence of global warming."[57]

That Barton exhibited such fluidity with terms like balance, fairness, and majority is unsurprising. What we see in the Texas education controversy is a case study in the way words wielded with enough force simply bring into being the reality they claim merely to describe. To accomplish this, Barton regularly summoned "experts" to state school board meetings, knowing how effective such testimony can be in establishing seemingly counterrational claims as authoritative. He had tested such an approach in Texas before. In July 2003, he invited to the state board two resident scholars from the Discovery Institute, the well-known "creationism think-tank" founded by Bruce Chapman to serve as an allegedly "nonpartisan" arbiter of often charged debates about science and religion.[58] They urged that the new curriculum reduce emphasis on evolution so students could, in their reckoning, better understand the "complexity of the cell" or learn to "analyze and evaluate the sufficiency of scientific explanations" as simply one explanatory option among many.[59] Discovery scholars observed that, according to Texas law, students must be taught "the strengths and weaknesses" of any position, including settled science. Science is thus, in Martyrs' imagination, not a realm of facts, testable data, and evidence but one more sphere of divergent opinions and perspectives.

The Discovery representatives insisted that they did not seek to include religious materials in textbooks (describing their interests as "secular"); had no interest in censoring scientific ideas (accusing those who would keep "Intelligent design theory" out of textbooks as the "real censors"); and that their policy goal was only to "inform policymakers and citizens" that "Intelligent design theory" is "an effort to empirically detect" "genuine design" even as it is avowedly "agnostic regarding the source of design."[60] Disagreement, the implication was, amounted to undermining an informed citizenry, and empirical, agnostic science.

An even greater conflagration ensued in March 2010, when the state board approved a heavily modified version of Texas's high school history standards. The panel had consulted Barton and Newt Gingrich, and praised curricula that sought to "restore America to its Bible-based foundations."[61] McLeroy explained, "We are a Christian nation founded on Christian principles. The way I evaluate history textbooks is first I see how they cover Christianity and Israel. Then I see how they treat Ronald Reagan."[62] The new curriculum required the omission of "Enlightenment ideas," specifically removing Thomas Jefferson from discussions of "the influence of Enlightenment thinkers on political revolutions"; it also required more attention to "the conservative resurgence of the 1980s," including to some members of the board itself.[63]

Supporters saw the changes as a long overdue counterbalance to the "liberal bias" that in their view had saturated public education since the radical 1960s.[64] Now, the right figures would be emphasized in the right ways, so that

Texas schools could produce the right kind of citizens. As Phyllis Schlafly put it, "Texas textbooks will now have to mention 'the importance of personal responsibility for life choices' instead of blaming society for everything and expecting government to provide remedies for all social ills."[65]

This is boilerplate conservative rhetoric, but it serves a larger purpose in the experience of Embattlement: to make sure that the conceptual reality of Martyrs is untroubled by the actual historical suffering of other Americans, even in textbooks. The new curriculum suggested, for example, that slavery did not play a major role in leading to the Civil War, which was fought primarily around the more abstract issue of states' rights (it also made Jefferson Davis's speeches to the Confederacy required reading alongside those of President Lincoln); and it omitted all language referring to "the common good" or "justice" on grounds that it was "too communistic" (an attempt to remove "equality" was unsuccessful).[66] The new curriculum also replaced the unsavory term "slave trade" with "Atlantic triangular trade."[67]

Though the changes themselves were defended by invoking the categories "balance" and "equality," substantively these terms were displaced in the new historical narrative, which alleged that the civil rights movement was unfair to African Americans since it produced "unrealistic expectations of equal outcomes."[68] The country was no longer described as "democratic" but as a "constitutional republic" unshakably rooted in "free enterprise."[69] Because schools had become the workshops of multicultural "thought police" seeking to enforce "political correctness," still more was necessary to create curricular "balance": Dolores Huerta and Cesar Chavez of the United Farm Workers were removed, the previous curriculum's assessment of hip-hop's significance was scratched, and the "positive" aspects of Senator Joseph McCarthy's career were presented.[70]

Whistleblowers fumed that the changes were "egregious," insisting that no textbook publishers would adopt materials so transparently geared toward conservative, Protestant, Euro-American triumphalism.[71] Dissenting board members were incensed that the Martyrs "pretend that this is a white America and Hispanics don't exist."[72] Others were aghast at attempts to downplay racism as a factor in Japanese American internment camps in World War II.[73] Seeming to acknowledge the fluidity of truth, McLeroy insisted that forcible insertions of alternate histories was the only way for Embattled Christians to resist the "threats of global government to individual freedom," "forced redistribution," or "global environmental initiatives."[74]

McLeroy and the board exulted in the controversy the changes provoked. The changes were justified, they held, because "the left has dominated a lot of history."[75] Striking Thurgood Marshall from a history text was posited as a reasonable response in the face of a "consensus" that sounded to them more like a conspiracy. True American history flows only from "our Founders' dependence on God," a linchpin claim meant to authorize any policy position linked to it.[76]

Insisting on the "accuracy" of its proposals, the board sought not only to deflect criticism but to insist that the new curriculum was transparent, lacking any politics.[77] Note that two separate meanings of transparency are at work here. The first, common in the age of the Whirl and its imaginings of digital democracy, suggests that "information wants to be free": the presumption is that only inconveniences like copyright and paywalls separate citizens from "the facts." The information is there, people presume, and the trick is simply bringing it into the open. Yet a second, less well-articulated sense of transparency is close to the sense of authenticity that Embattled public figures claim to represent: meaning what one says, talking straight, showing one's cards. Martyrs here performed both types of transparency in order to convince supporters that the new curriculum was achieved without duplicity or manipulation of the process. Fairness with the historical record entailed fairness of political representation on the school board.

It is easy to note that, because of the elision of the two modes of transparency, information is inseparable from the reflection of particular values. For board member Barbara Cargill, "A lot of the values would be upheld in the social studies curriculum: truthfulness, respect for oneself and others."[78] What this means for board Martyrs is the insertion and repetition of particular terms "over and over," in each level of the curriculum.[79] The refrain of "values," of "truth," and of "religion" emerges from this insistence on balance and equal treatment. This is how the Whirl makes Embattlement real.

Despite the fervency of their opposition, Whistleblowers preserved the language and the logic of the debate. One of the state board's earliest proposals was a ban on books alleged to contain a "pro-Islam, anti-Christian slant." Robert Jeffress of Dallas's First Baptist Seminary publicly supported the ban by redescribing it: "All it says is that all world religions ought to be treated equally, that you can't exalt one religion and vilify the other. Nobody who is reasonable would object to this unless they're more interested in indoctrination than in educating our students."[80] Professor Mark Chancey of Southern Methodist University countered that "this resolution isn't about fairness, it's about fear. The author of this resolution has said that he is afraid Muslims are taking over America without firing a shot, by taking control over the textbook market." Jeffress, pleased that his critic had taken the bait, responded that he favored educating students about the "atrocities" in Christian history, mentioning how Christianity had once been "perverted" in defense of slavery. In his haste to name his enemy's debasement, Chancey had given Jeffress an opportunity to perform his reasonability in the face of attack. Jeffress elaborated: "The truth is, it's fashionable to criticize Christianity and that's allowed. But we dare not point out any of the weaknesses of Islam. That is not fair."

We see here the emblematic repetition of America's exhausted politics, as if to say on the one hand, "Please don't bother me with differences of opinion" and on the other, "Please disagree so that I can avail myself of the opportunity for righteous indignation." Religion must be treated fairly, yet to treat it at all inevitably throws us back into the very blaze it generates. More than a window onto the way "truth" is the product of language, we see in the Embattled History controversies a vigorous Action Movie, where the "educrat conspiracy" against religion and goodness enables the performance of heroic defiance that livens up our quotidian lives. McLeroy seemed to confirm this: "We plan to fight back—and, when it comes to textbooks, we have the power to do it. Sometimes it boggles my mind the kind of power we have."[81]

Whistleblowers bemoaned this fearful power. People for the American Way, for example, described the board as a "faction" which had "created a mess."[82] Against the well-intentioned advice of "more than 1200 historians and social studies professors," the new standards were "brazenly partisan and political," "lifted from Wikipedia," and "just wrong."[83] The board was accused of politicizing religion, effectively "turn[ing] the teaching of religious liberty and the First Amendment on its head."[84] True history, once again, had been reversed.

In peddling "highly inaccurate information," the board members were abandoning their duties as elected officials for the sake of "powerful cheerleading."[85] Texas history faculty concurred, in an open letter characterizing the new standards as naked "ideology" rather than proper history.[86] In confusing the two, the historians suggested, the board was actively upending centuries of "constitutional protections for religious liberty that keep government out of matters of faith."[87] The National Council for History Education weighed in, lamenting the interjection of contemporary concerns into the past. According to chair Fritz Fischer, this was "not a partisan issue, [but] a good history issue."[88] Fischer specifically charged that the board got religion wrong, asserting that the Framers recognized religion as a preference best kept private. American traditions, he implied, were jeopardized when any other understanding of religion was advanced. The *San Francisco Chronicle* was blunter, publishing the column "Dear Texas: Please shut up. Sincerely, History."[89] The American Historical Association has regularly criticized the board's inattention to "diversity."[90] Unsurprisingly, this pushback only deepened the board's contempt for academic historians, whose very public scolding surely was confirmation that liberals had it in for the Martyrs. The flames of public acrimony cranked up, with everyone absolutely certain that history spoke in their own voice.

What remains, then, is history as self-exploration: a history that forms the preamble to an Embattled, and thus glorious, present. The insistence that one has superior historical sources, better emphases, and better political projects is largely powerless against a history that can amplify one's sense of being a world-historical Action Movie protagonist. The BBC got it only partly right in identifying an American propensity "to accentuate the positive and eliminate the negative."[91] Americans are indeed often smitten with the faultless victim finally prevailing over the negative forces unjustly marshaled against them. The school board thus becomes the arena for conspiracy cosplay, with alternate histories and cover-ups abounding.

These tendencies might appear simply to be echoes of what Richard Hofstadter described—in his 1948 work *The American Political Tradition*—as a "quest for the American past . . . carried on in a spirit of sentimental appreciation rather than of critical analysis."[92] Still more is revealed of the Embattled moment: there is no way to criticize the new standards without conceding some points of Embattled discourse in a way that keeps the feedback loop going. It is not surprising that "religion" emerges as a product of the "ability to deliver completely customized content" that has long been a feature of textbook production itself.[93] The customization of "content" is not merely a particularly rich metaphor; it captures the nature of the Embattled politics, shaped by the ways in which difference troubles the anxious identity. And so the boilerplate observation that history and tradition are arguments extended across time becomes pixelated, each flickering tile of data waiting to be gathered into the locus of our energy, the exertion of which is what counts as historically relevant.

No sane and honest observer would deny that something is wrong when textbook changes (such as refusal to treat Islam as a reasonable civic faith) are justified with statements like "Islam is coming and Islam means death," and countered with self-satisfied rejections of "idiocracy."[94] But to conclude from the Texas textbooks controversies only that debates about history are central to "culture wars" is to focus only on what the event *tells* us is happening rather than to question it. Equally important is an anxiety about time that is central to the dramas of Embattled history. This plays out, obviously enough, in the subject of certain curricular debates: the deep time of Darwinian biology, or the nostalgic time of Martyr history. But there is also palpable anxiety about time running out for those anxious about America: Martyrs bemoaning the erosion of good morality, and Whistleblowers prophesying the return of the Dark Ages.

I am in no way dismissing the importance of assessing religious obligations and civic order in relation to American history, particularly if this entails robust consideration of the claims of the Constitution, of political participation, and of civic education. All too often, however, public understandings of religion and American history are constituted through managed controversies designed to dramatize Embattlement. And these eruptions on the surface prevent citizens from recognizing a range of deeper confusions that continue working on our expectations for politics.

## Nietzsche in Texas

Embattled History speaks in melancholic tones, addressing a lack into which a surplus of emotion and memory is directed. To experience the strangeness and unfamiliarity of what we assumed was historically settled requires the assertion of a new narrative in which one prevails. Those who construct such narratives assert that they are merely transcribing what is historically obvious. Time and history thus become objectified, sources of manipulation in one's self-fashioning. And in order to overcome the fragility and uncertainty of the mundane present, the Embattled perform their victimhood by becoming killers of others' tales.

The customizable quality of facts, and thus religion, is partly a reflection of Embattled America's conviction—both sentimentalist and apocalyptic—that all events possess meanings that aggrandize the self. If one is special enough to be Embattled, then time and history have meaning. For both Martyrs and Whistleblowers, the murky present and its clarifying Embattlements are grounded by a stable past which "proves" their opponents to be misguided.

Americans have obsessed over historical authenticity and the legitimacy of tradition since at least the emergence of the cult of veneration of George Washington in the early nineteenth century.[95] More than this, some would see in Barton an example of Umberto Eco's observation that in America "the past must be preserved and celebrated in full-scale, authentic copy."[96] But I would pause before concluding that such efforts represent only the triumph of the fake, or merely the sanctification of the present. For whenever there emerge such obvious efforts to seal the past off from changes to symbolic order or identity, beneath them are roiling anxieties about political first principles. It is these changes that send Embattled Americans in search of static narratives.

I believe that democracy could actually benefit from an embrace of historical revisionism. By this I don't mean giving up on the existence of facts. Rather, I presume that the way facts are discussed and described, and the narratives in which they are included, and thus the communities that are produced and adjusted, are continually fluid and revisable. This is consistent with an understanding of democracy that is grounded in an organic, localist participation that may not be exciting but resists the power that static narratives manipulate for narrow political ends.

Anne Norton once suggested that such interpretive squabbles over foundational history be read in the light of Walter Benjamin's writings on authenticity and reproduction. She notes that, beyond the failure to achieve authenticity or dwell in its aura, reproduction is "an attempt to recall a context."[97] To this I would add, it is an attempt to conjure feeling, often a consolation for the troublesome relation to difference and flux seen among the Embattled. When feeling is powerful enough, society appears to us not just in institutional form (the market, the polis, civic associations), nor just in symbolic form (laws and norms), but also through the array of "signs and meanings" that is constantly changing but which provides a background giving shape to our actions and declarations.[98] This overemphasis on the stability of sign and narrative is what Embattled History reveals, in a process fluid enough to create narratives that deny their fluidity.

More than this, Barton's Embattled History uncovers a strangely recognizable reformulation of Nietzsche, who wrote in *Beyond Good and Evil*:

> Real philosophers . . . are commanders and law-givers: they say "thus it shall be!" They determine first the Whither and the Why of mankind, and thereby set aside the previous labor of all philosophical workers, and all

*subjugators of the past*—they grasp at the future with a creative hand, and whatever is and was, becomes for them thereby a means, an instrument, a hammer. Their "knowing" is creating, their creating is a law-giving, their will to truth is—will to power.[99]

Here, the idea of sovereignty is transformed from exterior political force into self-authorization. Is religion used to subdue the past and "reach for the future" whose very indeterminacy requires such exertions? Or is religion used to sound out the complexities and contradictions of our politics?[100] By collapsing religion, citizenship, and history into a single expression of civic fidelity, Embattled History produces the experience of being absolutely sure of oneself and feeling absolutely vulnerable simultaneously.

Whistleblowers are correct when they identify bad history and narrow-minded, exclusivist politics behind the "sincerely held" discourse of the Martyrs, but they have not managed to change the conversation. This is not only because they take the bait, nor because they fail to understand the emotional power of Life as Action Movie, but because of the growth in cultures of "alternate" expertise, which has seen the creation of many Martyr "think tanks" and the growing popularity of autodidacts like Barton.[101] Eager Whistleblowers pounce on the apparent lack of seriousness of, say, a Christian science PhD from the Discover Institute or the lack of factual evidence to support claims that children of gay parents are maladjusted.[102] But as Anthony Giddens writes of "expert systems," it is common for social actors to emulate experts self-chosen based on their own prior emotional commitments.[103] Instead of knowledge and suasion as abstract ideals shared by interlocutors, what passes for facts and data in the Whirl depends on the way such terms are defined, mediated, and perceived in specific social networks.

So the Martyrs' long-standing, canny discrediting of expertise emerges as a vector for the Long Con of Anti-politics: the repeated depiction of trained experts—from "educrats" to "fake news"—as hostile outsiders ensures that those denounced as "elites" do not have to be listened to. Such isolation did not spring forth magically from the brow of Facebook; it has been the substance of conservative counterinstitutional work since the early 1960s, a retreat from the commons that leaves dissenters with little critical purchase in a discourse protected by the legally special category of religion. Berating Martyrs for not knowing the facts plays into the hands of the berated. And if, in the postmodernist nightmare of a Texas School Board meeting, any "fact" can be renamed, renarrated, and reinterpreted so as to avoid realities that make one squeamish, it is not hard to see how America arrived in its bad-acid present, where Alex Jones conspiracy theories are not laughed back into the sewer that spawned them; where Breitbart "reporters" get White House press credentials; and where Barton's Christian nationalist vision of America's past (as if there is only one kind of Christianity, the intolerant kind) gets MAGA-ed into Betsy DeVos as secretary of education.

The Trump administration enshrined a vision of schools and history that would hollow out the state in the name of "choice" (i.e., privatization and vouchers). Institutionally this resonates with Martyr histories, which are natural extensions of white flight's desire to avoid other people. Do not feel guilt, this vision says, in turning away from the history of those who suffer for your whiteness. Do not feel guilt for renaming atrocities, or for despoiling the commons. For those views are not your views, and therefore they are nonviews; they are enemy views, enemy ways of living; the very idea that one should listen to their voices is named a form of oppression. This vision of the American past is the weaponization of the "again" in the Trump catchphrase "Make America Great Again"; you can almost imagine it warning, "or else."

Instead of chiding Martyrs for being bad readers, concerned citizens should be asking what it is about our politics that sustains the conditions for this history. What is in the atmosphere that allows Martyrs' "religion" to assert its privilege over others? It seems apparent to me that at least on some level it is because the anxiety behind not just Martyr identity but in the face of a shaky future is more powerful than the alternate histories shown by non-Martyrs (whether by other religious practitioners or by the nonreligious who are less dualistic and shrill than Whistleblowers).

While Barton continues his active influence—advising DeVos throughout the Trump presidency, signing on to Project Blitz, which aims to remake American institutions along Christian nationalist lines, influencing campus activist group Turning Point USA, or furiously seeking to debunk the 1619 Project (and a Bartonian spirit was central to the Trump administration's parting 1776 Project, a staggering compendium of white entitlement released to the public on Martin Luther King Jr. Day)—it would be wise to identify an American history that makes ample room for religion but not for domination.[104] This would require other Christians and other religions to speak more loudly, and other, more radically democratic politics to do likewise. If historical truth entails rejecting a priori all claims with which one already disagrees, then American history is reduced to the political experience of feeling. If evidence, transparency, and shared standards of reason have been sufficiently discredited, the only strategy is to triple down on the emotional remainders. The more critics point out one's inaccuracies, the surer a conviction becomes, since to experience affront is the affirmation an identity needs.

In betting that their version of the right historical narrative can prevail, the Embattled confirm how every story, every term, is everybody's: citizenship entails updating America's Wikipedia entry to create an emotional experience of nostalgia that the Embattled want converted into fact. This orientation to the logics of time and religion once again brings to mind the writings of Benjamin, whose "apocalyptic messianism" confronted the present with a "counterfactual" in order to "transform the present."[105] For Benjamin, to encounter the emptiness of familiar symbols and language ought to motivate us to confront the problems they obscure. By investing in reductive historical narrative, Americans misname these problems, endlessly repeating the same unwinnable arguments about whether America is definitively a conservative Christian wonderland or whether the constitutional philosopher-sages constituted a perfectly rational polis. Such arguments sell books, galvanize voting blocs, and keep the Action Movie sizzling; but they cannot ground an account of history suited for democratic politics, nor do they address why Americans yearn so insistently for a halcyon past.

As someone who teaches American religious history courses every semester, it is obvious to me that the Martyrs are engaged in atrocious history, one which serves dubious political purposes that are equally obvious. But perhaps even more obvious is that snark, indignation, and counterhistory are efficiently absorbed by the Martyr narrative. Not only have Whistleblowers failed to change the discourse; Martyrs overflowed a presidential administration, to the country's great damage. If Americans want to escape the prisonhouse of Embattlement, should we continue to debate the "proper" role of religion in American history? No, because that debate's dominance prevents us from engaging better questions and better debates. Any assessment of American history, in curricula or elsewhere, must be tethered to the idea of what democracy is. If Embattled History is only a vehicle for the Embattled to sanctify their selfhood at the expense of others, it not only serves no real pedagogical purpose; it cuts directly against what democracies require. More than this, the desire to be released from uncertainty pushes us to a hollow nostalgia or a misunderstanding of public life as an arena for weaponized historical data. This is the crisis of Embattled religious history: the very thing that makes possible the renewal and revitalization of the past also has this destructive effect on democratic life.

So what futures do Martyr and Whistleblower histories make possible? It seems no coincidence that commodified, sentimentalized, *Braveheart*-ed History is popular in an America where unions are being crippled, universities corporatized and "streamlined," pensions hacked or bargained away for more upper-crust tax cuts, and other offensives against social services justified in the name of taming the beast of big government. Is Embattled History complicit in futures when all Americans will be "postwork" and live on and through screens, endlessly entertained while water is befouled, more jobs outsourced to brown children who toil for subsistence wages on the other side of the globe, and more homeless Americans look searchingly into our cars at stoplights and on-ramps?

What does it even mean to be an American, when history becomes cosplay, which becomes another means of deflection from this future? Against the actual polyvocality of our historical traditions, questions about Americanness and belonging devolve regularly onto various singularities: you are an outsider, a heretic, a danger, because you live your life in a way that I do not. Americans of different stripes are comfortable sharing abstractions—the grand experiment in freedom, the melting pot, the world's oldest living democracy—but rage over particulars. America is a term easily used, a geography quickly recognized, a name for geopolitical hegemony, but fundamentally it is a placeholder for just the kind of riotous confusion and antagonism that Embattled History cannot absorb.

It is time to stop arguing about the religiousness of American history, because it actively prevents us from thinking seriously about an American history or identity that resists dualism and censorious finger-wagging. When religion is posited as a stand-alone category—measured for influence and weirdly detached from broader conceptions of public life, selfhood, citizenship, and law—it is harder to get at the questions that historical anxiety represses. Fundamentally, the obsession over tradition's ability to ground public order marks a profound discomfort with actual people's power. The disorder and violence in the streets during the tenure of an administration obsessed with precisely this discomfort and its fantasies should leave no one confused about the stakes. For if American history is to mean anything democratically productive, it must be something other than ossified tradition and something other than endless obfuscation which allows for tuning out other citizens and other pasts.

Americans might focus instead on reassessing just why history, rather than theme-park tradition, is important to democracy. Too many Americans feel that, in Hayden White's well-known formulation, they are "latecomers to a world in which everything worth doing had already been done."[106] To break the power of this conviction, Americans should work toward an understanding that history is meaningful only if what has actually been done in the past—whether it is loathsome or laudable—becomes the substance for meaningful, collaborative work in building a just future. Embattled America's obsession with one particular, and particularly rigid, historical conversation not only makes a caricature out of religion in all its unruly manyness, but displaces what should be the proper focus in history debates: rejecting virulent nationalism in favor of egalitarian democratic politics.

The way to defang Martyr understandings of gay marriage, slavery, or the rule of law is to convert history from an emotional scene to a political practice. I mean this in the Arendtian sense, insisting that "politics [is] a sphere of human activity peculiarly dependent upon truth."[107] Certain readers, beholden to older academic fashion, might wonder why I avoid interjecting the boilerplate Nietzschean point here that "truth is a mobile army of metaphors." My conviction is that the endless, reflexive concession to this observation has contributed to making a mush of public discourse, and has helped enable the atrophy of public rationality and disinterested politics. I am equally aware that these, too, are abstractions, and presume things about human rationality and self-interest that are contingent at best and unachievable at worst. Insisting on the bluntness of truth by itself cannot achieve traction with those who are conditioned and taught to deny it. This is why I have been arguing in this book that we need to change the subject from religion to human rights, political procedure, the conditions for legitimate public speech, and the capacities of law. For if we fail to conduct our politics, including our historical practice, on the basis that such things are achievable with the right kinds of work and imagination, then we remain part of the problem.

This will not happen quickly. It will take several generations to reverse the damage—financial, administrative, and curricular—done to public education in America, and to inculcate in students the kinds of deliberative skills that will permit such conversations to take root. But if Whistleblowers are willing to lay down their whistles, and stop wailing about the religion motivating Martyr histories, they would at least deprive the Martyr narrative of its central claim in so doing. There is no switch to be flipped in order to convince Martyrs to delve more rigorously into history's complexities, or into the subtleties of the *Federalist Papers* and Paul's epistles; but insisting on accountability to the same texts and the same facts as part of a broader resuscitation of civic education might work powerfully against the idea that any one constituency can control history.

History is meaningless if it belongs to only one group. So is democracy. And if Americans cannot agree on the above methods of argumentation and reading, then we deprive ourselves of an opportunity to undermine a Christian nationalist vision of public life. We rob ourselves of a powerful argument against those who believe Muslims, or nonwhite people, or queer people, or any nonprivileged citizens bear the burden of proof in easing white people's anxiety about their Americanness. If methods and narratives are shared, and we are all accountable to them, then this blasts open the content of history, too. If the conversation is not about one particular version of Christianity as the star (or the villain) in an Action Movie, we can more openly and productively talk about who participates, under what ground rules, and an implicit agreement that history is, like democratic politics, self-limiting too. If a vision of history can only persuade others by pointing to sinners and demons lurking at the gates, it is without merit. I commend a critique of Martyrs' politics that does not paint them as demons or yahoos but as citizens who are not living up to the rights and obligations of citizenship, and the extension of full human and political rights that democracy (and a great many other expressions of religion) quite simply requires.

Religion is everywhere in American history, of course. If Whistleblowers wish to deny the importance or the legitimacy of conservative Christianity as such, they themselves flirt with a counterdemocratic spirit. Rather, the arguments should be focused on contesting particular policies advocated, institutional boundaries overreached, or attempts to dominate the conversation. Participation does not entail exemption from criticism. Whistleblowers should accept religious participation in historical conversation, provided that advocates of public religion likewise accept that history is, like democracy, ongoing and revisable.

History is a place of discomfort. At this juncture in American history, the most compelling reason to investigate the past is to make the future better. Conservative religion and conservative readings of history are not privileged, but are, like all other expressions of identity and narrative, part of the range of American things for historical inquirers to evaluate. These evaluations should be guided not by fidelity to an ossified past but by resistance to self-aggrandizement and to the politics of domination.

Historical inquiry also demands calling things by their proper names. It means acknowledging who has and has not been persecuted in the American past, and what the consequences have been. That your child must learn about the experience of other humans in the American past is not a sign of persecution. Persecution is your body shackled during the Middle Passage, your back lashed for your defiance, your American bodies quarantined because of your Japanese ancestry, your Muslim body made a screen for the horrified stares of American bigots, your homes and sacred spaces demolished in the name of progress, your love and pleasure fearfully described as perversion.

These facts are multiple and obvious. They form the substance of the history of a nation grounded in, even if not entirely defined by, imperial ambition and the policing of nonwhite, nonmale, noncisgender, non-Christian bodies. Is it not well past time to tell the awful truths of American history, rather than indulging in the shallow dramas penned by the likes of Barton? After all, our religions actively and emphatically demand such truth-telling, such witness to injustice. A century ago, W. E. B. Du Bois warned of this moral condition in his assessments of early twentieth-century histories of Reconstruction and slavery. When the actual voices of the enslaved and their descendants were "barred from court," Du Bois observed, what results is not history but the "propaganda of history."[108] It is time to scratch up this propaganda's broken record and make a new playlist of riotous, discordant, bloodthirsty, and maybe someday glorious America.

# 8
# Law as Winning
## Anti-sharia Legislation and Democratic Self-Inventory

One with the law is a majority.

—Calvin Coolidge

Bad laws are the worst sort of tyranny.

—Edmund Burke

What is this thing called law? We refer to it as a singular thing, and we presume its clarity, consistency, and transparency. After all, law has a documentary record, the observable compendium of precedent regularly described as "settled" or "black letter." Shared and presumably egalitarian, American law has, since the Constitutional Convention of 1787, strived to realize such qualities in its treatment of religions. But despite its often supple analogical reasoning and deft comparisons, law fails in this aspiration.

Part of this failure can be attributed to law's imprecision as to what precisely "religion" is. Though the major documents of the Founding era use the term "religion" as a generic singular, even this period of American history contended with a broad range of traditions and expressions—from Native American cultures to numerous Protestant sects to folk and "magical" practices—that complicated this use of the term.[1] Little attempt was made to define religion for the purposes of legal reckoning. Depending on where or when one looked, religion might have resembled a highly developed community with robust institutions, a series of distinct ritual practices, or, as many of the Framers of the Constitution held, an interior, almost philosophical orientation. More pertinent to American politics, did religion have a "sphere" beyond the boundaries of which it should not spill? Could it do more than simply cultivate virtue in private?

These and other questions persist, despite the ever-accruing body of case law aiming to provide guidance (if not closure). The history of law in America has produced a conceptual vocabulary and a repertoire of descriptions used to establish and maintain what culturally normative religion is. Against this stands, purportedly, something called secularism, which recent scholarship shows to be markedly influenced by Protestant assumptions about religion's interiority, its key categories (like salvation as opposed to awakening or justice), and its political location.[2] By insisting on its impartiality while advancing particular interests in public order and interiority, law in America actually feeds the kinds of conflagrations about public religion that it believes it is quenching. In this chapter, Embattled Law reveals the textures of such conflagrations, which often center on bodies and religion marked as "other." While these concerns might be illuminated by focusing on conservative Christian legal organizations like the Alliance Defending Freedom, this chapter focuses on the contemporary wave of anti-sharia legislation, which is framed by the presumption that good law and good religion are threatened by an Islam defined as ideology, "wrong" religion, or contagion.

## Law Is King

To understand why Americans presume that religions must be both regulated by the law, and also exempt from it, it helps to think more broadly about law's status in American life. Law is a subject of profound ambivalence. The resentments to which we frequently give voice in the face of law's obligations ("Damn cops!") are balanced by our utter dependence on law ("There's never a cop when you need one"). Consciously ("We are a nation of laws") or not, law has an enduring power to shape our very identity and means of interaction. American culture is pervasively litigious even as it holds lawyers in particular scorn. Audiences cheer when the slick-haired corporate lawyer is brought low on TV, just as they applaud the crusading public attorney (as long as her pro bono work isn't too obviously leftist). But trials dealing with the fundaments of our politics provide fewer thrills, other than perhaps the persistence with which they allow certain Americans to feel persecuted: the endless interrogations of just how much religion is "allowed" in public life, whether corporations are persons, if healthcare violates interstate commerce law, and how hyperbolic a megaweapon is protected under the Second Amendment, among other ongoing dramas that perplex the rest of the world.

These uncertainties about the law reflect Americans' larger uncertainty about what democratic practice expects from them. For example, the law is criticized for its excessive rationality but also for its inability to be objective; for its distant remove from citizens' concerns and for its interventions therein. The implied considerations regarding religion are clear, even if no settled conclusions are. Should law insulate religion, and if so, whose and how much? Can all religions be treated equally, everywhere and forever? Is any stability or constancy possible in religion jurisprudence? Consider only a few of its most flamboyant expressions: here an outrageous Christmas display, there Judge Roy Moore insisting on Christocentric America; here a balanced treatment law placing evolutionary biology and young earth creationism on par, there a voucher case for parochial schools; here a gag rule on religious speech, there a concern to protect the integrity of a "way of life."

The sheer volume of religion jurisprudence has produced no consensus, but rather an agglomeration of barely coherent rules and standards by which to adjudicate current and future cases. Historians reinvestigate foundational documents, and theorists probe law's fundaments, hoping to locate an inclusive, firm standard for assessing what responsibilities the state has toward religion (and, less frequently, vice versa). Yet as Winnifred Fallers Sullivan and others have noted, what is most consistent in American law is its inability to settle fundamental issues and questions.[3]

A sanguine observer might conclude that the fact that Americans debate the law so vigorously is some proof that the deliberative core of democracy is thriving. I am less certain, and fear that bad debates about distorted issues occur more frequently than productive ones. When multiple voices insist, inflexibly, that law favor their own views and cast those of their opponents into the wilderness, something is amiss. Disagreements and counterassertions become the occasion for once again pronouncing one's rectitude and imperviousness from critique. Here as elsewhere, American relish their Embattlements. I say this not because I think some bland accommodationism will soothe Embattled feelings. Rather, too few Americans are asking what the law requires of citizens; it is much more satisfying to ask why the refs had it in for us.

One root cause of this condition is the failure of many citizens to understand the conceptual and practical grounding of America's legal traditions. The relationship between religions and the law has long been vexed in the United States. One of liberalism's primary aims has historically been to guarantee the rights of conscience and religious belief. It is widely believed that central to the constitutional "project" is the attempt to safeguard an inchoate religious pluralism, as enshrined in the First Amendment's injunction that "Congress shall make no law respecting the establishment of religion, nor prohibiting the free exercise thereof." Here religion, as a general category of belief (and, to a lesser extent, action), is seen as off limits to the state and to other citizens; religion is thus said to be one of many legal bulwarks against the infringement on citizens' rights. This understanding of religion embodies specifically liberal conceptions of citizens (defined as disinterested, rational individuals) and of which political order might best protect them (one which is minimalist and morally neutral). These conceptions, which have shaped American political and legal culture, have long been contested by scholars and citizens alike. Among the controversies is their implied understanding of religion as an individual phenomenon, which privileges belief over action, and which is practiced in "nonpolitical" spaces, clearly demarcated from the public realm of the state.

Questions about these conceptions of religion and politics are familiar. Indeed, the debates around them trace recognizably to the Framers' era. Citizens have often insisted on the inviolability of religion, generically speaking, out of a concern that unchecked power could threaten pluralism. At times this position has accompanied a defense of robust statism, and at others of localism. Equally consistent has been the insistence that religion not be insulated from the public realm, so as to allow a more robust influence of "people of faith" on political matters. Defenders of this position have generally denounced a rigorous public/private distinction as both antithetical to religions as they are actually lived and potentially antidemocratic. And, adding to the complexity of these debates, arguments abstractly favoring religious participation in public life do not clearly advance one particular administrative or ideological model over others.

Because these debates remain unresolved, Americans often look to law to settle them in their favor, even though productive, dialogic tensions are at the heart of what democracy requires. Clearly, what "productive" tension means is itself contested, and numerous conditions aside from abstract reason are needed to cultivate it: a judiciary that does not favor corporations while enabling voter suppression, a more organic connection between everyday citizens and judicial institutions, and term limits for judicial appointments, so as to reduce the degree to which they become ideological sport.

Currently law is yet another site where the triumph of Embattlement is visible. This helps extend the Long Con: the demonization of politics and the refrain that our viewpoint does not matter encourage apathy and cynicism. The existence of unresolved debates is then taken as "proof" that investment in politics is hopeless. These conclusions, and the naive hope that law will either look just like us or perform a cleanup duty that will satisfy everyone, are problematic precisely because they do not ask anything of citizens. They keep us atomized and fighting behind our screens, rather than striving to produce more fully wrought accounts of rights and public life, or rigorous reflection on the limits law may require of us. Legal "debates" thus too often mimic the rancor and recrimination that is everywhere in American politics.

## The Original Position

At the heart of Martyrs' relation to law is the long-standing claim that an "activist judiciary" enforces a hostile version of secularism. Critics of this perceived relentless godlessness have set about trying to "expose" the real history of the judiciary, and organizing to restore some lost era of greatness. For Martyrs, the beginning of the declension occurs not during the debates of the Framing era, or with Jefferson's letter to the Danbury Baptists in 1802, or with the mid-nineteenth-century Supreme Court's claim that said letter possessed "constitutional authority" but in the 1940s, during the very era widely touted as America's golden age. It was here, they allege, that SCOTUS recklessly began the "secularization" of public institutions.

It was *McCollum v. Board of Education's* (1948) engagement with public education (ruling that voluntary "released time" religious instruction in public schools was unconstitutional) that marked the beginning of Martyrs' judicial outrage. In this decision, and the previous year's *Everson v. Board of Education*, SCOTUS authorized a rigorously liberal language of neutrality that would haunt its assessments of what constituted religion and its "proper" place in the various spheres of public or private life.[4] This language was widely understood to reflect America's traditional self-image as a haven for the religiously oppressed, a multicultural polity where no particular view of the good was allowed to ride roughshod over others. Subsequent SCOTUS decisions affirmed this approach to public institutions, especially schools. *Engel v. Vitale* (1962) identified the separate and distinct functions of things properly belonging to the sphere of the state and those belonging to the sphere of religion, subsequently finding mandatory school prayer outside the Establishment Clause. With *Abington v. Schempp* (1963), the court ruled similarly against mandatory Bible reading as well.

Justice Clark urged that future decisions should be submitted to a two-part test. If legislation or policy could be construed as recognizably religious, it risked constituting an establishment. To be legally valid, a law or enactment must be marked by "a secular legislative purpose and a primary effect that neither advances nor inhibits religion." The test was expanded as part of the *Lemon v. Kurtzman* (1971) decision. The "Lemon test" posits that a statute must have a "secular legislative purpose"; that the principal or primary effect must neither advance nor inhibit religion; and that the state must not foster an "excessive government entanglement with religion."[5] This test shows the complicated relationship the judiciary has with "religion."

Many SCOTUS decisions in the intervening decades have satisfied Americans seeking to deprivilege a de facto Protestant establishment. But the public secularism that ostensibly is the product of these decisions has helped amplify the persistent conservative allegation of a "secular agenda." Critics say that whatever successes the "American experiment" has had in nurturing pluralism, these were achieved prior to the court's efforts to "secularize" public space. These critics advocate a benevolent Protestantism that paternalistically allows other religions their space, provided they do not overstep implicit boundaries. To Martyrs, the transformation of American law is not only offensive in principle—because it cuts against what they consider the grain of American social history and political principles—but it bears ill fruit. The most noxious consequence is the purported bullying of religion from its central place, which is said to have helped pave the way for decisions like *Roe v. Wade* (1973), ushering in moral permissiveness and a general social decline.

Religion jurisprudence is, if anything, even more slippery in free exercise cases, which are more central to America's Embattled. The narrative is well known, and plays into generic American pluralist self-understandings. The low point, for maximal free expressionists, came in *Reynolds v. United States* (1878), which held that the then-common Mormon practice of polygyny was not a constitutionally permissible exception to the general law criminalizing plural marriage. In subsequent decades the Court appeared more receptive to recognizing the country's demographic diversity and to acknowledging the limits that law sometimes placed on free exercise. In prominent cases between the 1930s and 1970s, the Court signaled a willingness to permit legal exemptions for free exercise, outside of exceptional circumstances. SCOTUS sought to strike a balance between laws for which there is a "compelling government interest" in adherence and those which impose an "unnecessary burden" on religious expression.[6]

Much has changed since 1990's controversial *Employment Division v. Smith*, in which a narrow majority distinguished between laws whose primary purpose would be to coerce free exercise (clearly unconstitutional under the *Lemon* test) and laws whose secondary, unintended effect may be to regulate religions. What accelerated the rise of Embattled religions was the subsequent hard tack in the opposite direction. At first this appeared unlikely, when Congress in 1993 passed the Religious Freedom Restoration Act, declaring that the government's default position would be to favor the religious unless burdening free exercise is the "least restrictive means of furthering [a] compelling governmental interest."[7] With 1997's *Boerne v. Flores*, however, the Supreme Court judged that while Congress maintained the power to pass legislation like RFRA, it could not instruct states as to how it might be implemented. In the context of the post-Reagan liberal order, this move bred fear among Martyrs that the state no longer had a designated interest in safeguarding America's Christian character. It also opened up opportunities for states to craft RFRAs of their own.

In the following decade, organizations like the Constitution Party, the Judeo-Christian Council for Constitutional Restoration, and the National Alliance Against Christian Discrimination; conferences like the War on Christians Conference or Justice Sunday; proposed legislation like the House of Worship Free Speech Restoration Act or the First Amendment Restoration Act; and conservative media called on states to preserve the religious liberty supposedly ignored at the federal level. As Elizabeth Castelli shows, these outlets collectively asserted that American religion is being threatened by excessive tolerance of non-Christian religions (and indeed, of nonreligion), or that an "activist judiciary" is undermining Christian free exercise. They alleged that government agencies function like "gestapos," that the courts have erected a "wall of religious oppression," and that judicial decisions deprivileging Christian expression, however minimally, amount to acts of hostility.[8]

The rhetoric and content are recognizable to observers of the dense paraculture of conservative Christianity in America, ranging from radio and television to think tanks, law centers, and lobbies. Since the 1980s, numerous "Christian legal societies" have been founded to challenge "official" judicial discourse. Among these are Advocates International, the Christian

Legal Society, and the American Center for Law and Justice.[9] The ACLJ was founded by Christian Right figurehead Pat Robertson as an explicit challenge (almost down to the acronym) to the American Civil Liberties Union. Its mission statement and public rhetoric trade in banalities: "Religious freedom and freedom of speech are inalienable, God-given rights for all people. The ACLJ engages legal, legislative, and cultural issues by implementing an effective strategy of advocacy, education, and litigation."[10] The ACLJ's longtime lead council is Jay Sekulow, who was closely allied with the Trump administration, and has written often about the dangers of "jihadists," activist judges, and secularists.

As prominent as the ACLJ and these other institutions have been, the themes of Embattlement are also recognizable in a moral campaign devoted to policing specific kinds of religion. In response to widespread Islamophobic anxieties in the post-9/11 period, Martyr politicians and lawyers seek to quarantine Islam by vexing its status as a religion and also by strengthening the very public/private distinction they elsewhere contest. Both tangles strengthen Embattlement.

## Relative to Terrorism

A specter still hangs over America. After September 11, 2001, ash settled in drifts across the boroughs of New York City. Clouds of matter billowed ominously over the site of what had been the World Trade Center. In time the clouds dispersed and the ash faded. But the remaining anxiety still chokes the atmosphere. The lasting pall was a renewed nervousness about law, pluralism, and minority religious traditions. Americans had been forcibly awakened to the realities of non-state-sponsored terrorism, and many were stunned to discover that America's own Muslim population was so large and of such long standing. One of the most powerful responses to this awareness was a persistent, distorted engagement with the "threat" of sharia law. In local and national moral campaigns, simply to utter the word "sharia" was to set off a blaring alarm, amplified through powerful news media, influential politicians, and well-funded citizens' groups. This fear was continually contested, by lawyers, other politicians, academics, and diverse religious organizations. In these exchanges we find evidence of how American law has come to focus on the distinction between "real" and "false" religion.

It is worth noting that Americans did not begin panicking about Islam only after September 11, 2001. Islamophobia has a long history in the United States, one that helps make sense of these legislative efforts. They are rooted in and sustained by ideas that Islam is not a "real" religion, and that it is somehow essentially violent. Critics have regularly asserted that Islam is the opposite of both Christianity and democratic reason. Historians Thomas Kidd and Timothy Marr show that one abiding strategy for justifying political plans as rational and righteous is to contrast them with the unthinking, despotic "Mohammedan."[11] Many of the most powerful of these accounts emerged in colonial America.

This lineage includes captivity narratives like William Oakley's *Eben-Ezer or a Small Monument to a Great Mercy*; theological critiques, like Francis Brooks's *Barbarian Cruelty*; newspaper pieces contrasting America's freedoms with the supposed primitivism of Muslim societies; and missionary literature describing Christians' fearful encounters with swarthy, bearded, scimitar-swinging Muslims. Since the Iranian Revolution of 1979, and especially since 2001, there has been an avalanche of alarmist American commentary denouncing Islam as a murderous ideology, a primitive myth, and more.[12] Usually these epithets are founded on little or no research, or at best cherry-picked data from sometimes questionable sources. The allegations assume that there exists a monolithic "Muslim world" that encourages violence by tapping into a primal, atavistic essence. Tales from Islam's first decades are plucked from their sociohistorical context and used to argue that Islam is premodern when compared to other traditions. Countless television shows and movies dramatize life in the age of terrorism, showing sophisticated and intrepid Western agents thwarting the Paradise-besotted Muslim Other.[13] In this imaginary, Islam is the opposite of the West, of whiteness, of democracy, ignoring the fact that the Middle East is a region of multiple traditions, that not all Muslims are Arabs (and not all Arabs are Muslim), and that Islam has often explicitly celebrated democracy as consistent with its universalism and egalitarianism.

This fearful imaginary propelled multiple state initiatives during Obama's first term as president, many fueled by ludicrous assertions about Obama's relationship with Islam. In 2010, Tennessee considered Senate Bill 1028, an act designed to amend previous legislation "relative to terrorism."[14] The bill alleged that "Tennessee in particular" is under threat of terrorism, because of the growing power of "a legal-political-military doctrine and system" that the document named as "sharia."[15] Superficially acknowledging the distinction between *fiqh* (human understanding of law) and *sharia* (the body of divine law superseding the human), the document alleged that sharia contains the "war doctrine" of jihad and "requires all its adherents to actively and passively support the replacement of America's constitutional republic."[16] SB1028 concluded that there was an "imminent likelihood" of terrorism in Tennessee.[17] A feeling had become an inevitability, which was cited in order to prosecute "wrong" religion (though the bill criminalized "only the knowing provision of material support or resources, as defined in § 39-13-803, to designated sharia organizations, as defined in § 39-13-904, or to known sharia-jihad organizations with the intent of furthering their criminal behavior").[18]

Tennessee was far from alone. Oklahoma temporarily approved an amendment declaring fealty to the state and federal constitutions, to common law, "and if necessary the law of another state of the United States provided the law of the other state does not include Sharia Law." The amendment passed in the general election, but was held from going into effect by a federal suit. Wyoming's HJR8 asserted that "courts shall not consider the legal precepts of . . . international law and Sharia law." Texas's HJR 57 more broadly forbade "any religious or cultural law." South Dakota's HJR 1004 abjured "any foreign religious or moral code." Arizona's HB 2582 focused on "Foreign Decisions," seeking to constrain not just sharia but "canon law, halacha and karma." And Arizona's SCR 1010 ordered that courts "shall not look to the legal precepts of other nations or cultures." For a time there was even a petition to force Congress to pass H.R. 973, "ban[ning] the use of foreign law in our United States court system," in order to defend "moderate religions" from the "'Islamization' of America."[19]

Similar proposals proliferated in Alaska, Arkansas, Indiana, Mississippi, Nebraska, Oklahoma, South Carolina, South Dakota, and Texas. Occasionally, some representatives (like Georgia's Mike Jacobs) professed understanding that sharia in the United States pertained almost exclusively to the adjudication of domestic matters like divorce. More commonly, one encountered sentiments like those of Wyoming's Gerald Gay, who argued for a "pre-emptive strike" against judges who would consult sharia "in cases involving, for example, arranged marriages, 'honor killings' or usury cases."[20] The hyperbolic language, the sensational hypotheticals, and the claim that the Constitution is being trampled are all exemplary of Embattled Law.[21]

At the heart of these proposed bills was the ominous suggestion that sharia exists in some fundamental relationship to a terrorism that has not yet happened yet is always *just about* to happen. These laws reflect and contribute to a broader cultural animus that deepened dangerously after Donald Trump's ascendancy as a political force, with his (and the bulk of his devotees') well-documented Islamophobia. Sikhs are attacked as Muslims. Mosques are defaced and arsons attempted.[22] Women in headscarves are lampooned and sometimes assaulted, Qur'ans are burned, and more. Crimes against Muslims have gone up over 50 percent during this period, with attacks on mosques reported in multiple states.[23] Much of this is directly attributable to a fear that is carefully manufactured.

Key to the production of this fear are the writings and activities of a range of self-styled "experts" on Islamic culture. The central figures of American Islamophobia have deep organizational roots in conservative culture, long predating 9/11. The five most-cited "experts" are Steven Emerson (the Investigative Project on Terrorism), Frank Gaffney (the Center for Security Policy), Daniel Pipes (the Middle East Forum), Robert Spencer (Jihad Watch and Stop Islamization of America), and David Yerushalmi (of the bizarrely named Society of Americans for National Existence).[24] Islamophobic "experts" regularly rely on cherry-picked Middle Easterners and Muslims like Nonie Darwish, Tawfik Hamid, Zuhdi Jasser, Walid Phares, and Walid Shoebat. This network is heavily funded by, among others, Donors Capital Fund, Becker Foundations, Lynde and Harry Bradley Foundation, Richard Mellon Scaife foundations, the Russell Berrie Foundation, the Fairybrook Foundation, and Anchorage Foundation/William Rosenwald Family Fund.

These critics hold that Islam is "the only religion in the world that has a developed doctrine, theology and legal system that mandates violence against unbelievers and mandates that Muslims must wage war in order to establish the hegemony of the Islamic social order all over the world."[25] Their connections to American political institutions make it impossible to dismiss such claims as rants from the fringe. Gaffney has ties to the Reagan administration and prominent neoconservatives like Richard Perle. The CSP has funded figures like David Gaubatz (a former State Department and air force employee who routinely described President Barack Obama as "our Muslim leader") and Paul Sperry, author of *Infiltration: How Muslim Spies and Subversives Have Penetrated Washington*.[26] The staples of conspiracy culture are all here: secret agents, fifth columns, and criminal thugs. Despite the lack of tangible evidence of America becoming "Islamized," such claims were widely publicized in conservative talk media and on websites like WorldNetDaily and Breitbart. They also received their largest megaphone in the reality star who would, improbably, become president.

Pipes wrote, in his 2003 *Militant Islam Reaches America*, that "all immigrants bring exotic customs and attitudes, but Muslim customs are more troublesome than most."[27] Pipes has denounced moderate Muslim organizations like the Council on American-Islamic Relations as deceptive fronts for a "Wahhabi Lobby."[28] He endorses racial profiling of Muslims and people from the Middle East. He was also one of the earliest to suggest (on his website The Legal Project) that it was through sharia that "Islamist lawfare" would undermine American life: "by (1) exploiting Western legal systems and traditions and (2) recruiting state actors and international organizations such as the United Nations."[29]

Spencer's website Jihad Watch (sponsored by the David Horowitz Freedom Center) has tapped into and stoked post-9/11 anxiety about Islam. Like some far-right Stephen King, Spencer contends that things we believe are innocuous—schools, languages, laws—actually conceal monstrous realities like madrassas, invading cultures, and violent customs. The very integrity of "Western culture" (as the Center puts it) depends on exposing these fearful developments. In response to accusations that they doctor facts and produce falsehoods, the critics respond that they are simply cutting through the liberal lies that teach tolerance of those who would destroy the West.[30] Gaffney, for example, consistently refers to mosques as "Trojan horses" rather than places of worship, contending that their aims of "sedition" render them ineligible for constitutional rights and protections.[31]

Most influential in advancing such claims is Yerushalmi, general counsel for Gaffney's CSP and chief author of its report "Shariah: The Threat to America." He is also legal adviser to Spencer's and Pamela Geller's groups.[32] Yerushalmi has no training in Islamic studies (much less Muslim law), yet his "American Law for American Courts" served as the model for much of the proposed legislation. Its basic presumption is not that "sharia takeover" is institutionally occurring at present, but simply that it *could*, if we fail to fear it viscerally enough.[33] Citizens are asked to wonder what they might have unleashed in their commitments to pluralism. Yerushalmi's "war on Islam" is about what he claims is terrifyingly real but also about what people can imagine. Law and religion, in this worldview, should instill in "responsible" citizens the kind of anxiety one gets from cruising WebMD, certain that one has every symptom of some horrible disease.

The views of former Trump national security advisor Michael Flynn, longtime Republican representative Newt Gingrich, Trump administration advisor Stephen Miller, and former CIA director James Woolsey can be traced back to Yerushalmi's reading of Islam as "totalitarian," and his echo of the George W. Bush administration's logic of preemption. As Guy Rodgers of ACT for America (an organization promoting the passage of sharia bans) says, "Before the train gets too far down the tracks, it's time to put up the blocks."[34] This invocation of a classic Western movie image underscores the role of Action Movie metaphor in claims to Embattlement, even in the ostensibly value-neutral sphere of law. Despite his claims to neutrality, Yerushalmi admits that the real purpose of the proposed legislation was to create "friction."[35] Provocation and staging matter as much as fact or likelihood. Friction is thus necessary for pointing to issues of concern and for sustaining the mood of Embattlement, even among critics of Yerushalmi and his supporters.[36]

The collective ideas and assertions produced by this network are appropriated as "truth" and recirculated by prominent religious figures like Franklin Graham, John Hagee, and Pat Robertson; congressional representatives like Matt Gaetz and Peter King; conservative talking heads Tucker Carlson, Sean Hannity, and Laura Ingraham; and dispersed ever outward, to what Michel Foucault would call the capillary level of power/knowledge, where feelings and ideas exist indistinguishably.[37] It is here that public opinion is shaped, with millions of Americans believing that Muslims are not fit for citizenship or legal protection. The Conservative Political Action Conference has regularly addressed such topics, on panels like "The Shari'ah Challenge to the West." Institutions ranging from Liberty University's Youth for Western Civilization to the Eagle Forum have made public pronouncements about the grave dangers of Wahhabism in America, the Muslim Brotherhood's purported influence on Barack Obama, or madrassas brainwashing Muslim American kids.[38]

Undergirding the whole topography of Martyr panic is the conviction that Christianity itself is Embattled by Islam, no longer necessarily the rival religion or empire of the Crusades but an "ideology" that is thus not protected by the First Amendment. Martyrs do not distinguish between foreign faiths, eroding national autonomy, and the dissolution of law's power. They warn that liberals in government and academia contribute to the endangerment of America's real majority, which may be rendered minor by a nonreligion falsely portrayed as a religion. As James Lafferty put it, "We are being outgunned by them, literally and figuratively," in "a spiritual war."[39]

This may seem an odd characterization if Islam is a nonreligion. But this exaggeration, that a mere "ideology" is out to capture the spirit, using law as cover, is at the heart of Martyr anxiety. Brigitte Gabriel noted firmly that a "practicing Muslim who believes in the teaching of the Quran cannot be a loyal citizen to the United States of America."[40] Gabriel's organization, ACT!, which boasted of its "direct line" to the Trump administration, echoes Yerushalmi's claims that "Islam was born in violence; it will die that way" and Gaffney's insistence that practicing Islam should be "punishable by 20 years."[41] ACT! also sponsors seminars to "train" concerned citizens, relying heavily on a PowerPoint presentation showing that Muslims want to "conquer America" and "spread Sharia."[42] The grizzled Gingrich regularly spans two eras of anxiety, likening sharia to communism: "a mortal threat to the survival of freedom in the United States."[43]

Pat Robertson blamed "political correctness" for America's vulnerability to the dangers of foreign law: "Why can't we speak out against an institution that is intent on dominating us and imposing Sharia law and making us part of a universal Caliphate?"[44] Robertson has also compared Muslims to Nazis, and their critics to the resistance.[45] Islam is thus simultaneously a frightening religious minority and an imperial cultural Other "at war with Judeo-Christian civilization."[46] Moderate and progressive Muslims, of course, have spoken out repeatedly against such caricatures, as have other American religious communities and a bevy of experts. Yet such efforts are routinely interpreted as part of the conspiracy. Geller and others even believe that sharia must be "creeping" inexorably when even blue chip food companies like Campbell's Soups offer halal products.[47]

The effects of the discourse are clearer than ever in the era of Trump, Miller, and the varied efforts to limit Muslim immigration and work visas and to recirculate suspicions about foreign others generally. As seemingly ever in post-1960s America, claims that many assumed were rooted safely on the fringe made their way steadily into the political mainstream, to the point that a sitting president of the United States could urge that Muslim congressional representatives be "sent back" to other countries.[48] It is not simply that repetition in the Whirl numbs citizens to outrage; it is a vivid reminder that America has been characterized by deep racial and religious intolerance since its inception. This is the context in which old American xenophobia was made new again, as with FOX personality Laura Ingraham's anti-immigrant broadside in August 2018: "The America we know and love doesn't exist anymore."[49] It also hangs over the disturbing July 2019 Trump rally in Greenville, North Carolina, where the president's supporters collectively called to send Representative Ilhan Omar "back" to Somalia.[50] And in the furor of Trump's final months in office, Spencer and others rather predictably asserted that Black Lives Matter protesters and Antifa were part of a shadowy plot to impose sharia law.[51]

Some Martyrs go beyond the Embattled equation of disagreement with threat; they actually contend that Islamophobia does not exist. *Commentary's* Jonathan Tobin mocked what he called the "backlash myth."[52] Citing the incontrovertible fact that the US Muslim population is growing, Tobin wondered disbelievingly how a purported backlash can coexist with a population increase. Yet while other commentators and critics protest with the aid of alternate statistics and sources, wondering why conservatives cannot acknowledge the difficulties American Muslims have faced, they are also (as sad as it may be to admit it) missing the point: it is precisely *because* of the exposure to the pain of others that critics of Islam defend their cultural privilege by denying that pain.[53]

## The Beginning of a Crusade

Whistleblowers understand themselves to be the correctors of bogus facts. They are the shamers of the ignorant. They assume, broadly speaking, that law is a transparently secular vehicle to be defended from religious distortions. In this spirit, early responses to anti-sharia legislation came with defenses of "real" Islam. Websites like Beliefnet and Defending Religious Freedom (DRF), academics like Omid Safi, and left-wing pundits by the score took to screens to pour out different words, produce different links, and intone a different set of warnings.[54]

Against contentions that sharia is a military ideology or a form of totalitarianism, Whistleblowers document the practices of moderate and liberal Muslims, map the complexities of religion, and note Islam's consistency with pluralism and religious freedom. DRF explained in its publications that penal laws make up only a small percentage of the Qur'an and that sharia deals overwhelmingly with "marriage, inheritance, and business transactions."[55] Against such mundaneness, Martyrs are quick to cite the alleged ubiquity of "taqiyya," understood as "concealing one's faith out of fear of death."[56] Islamic studies specialists point to the complexity and detail of the tradition, and assert correctly that sharia is no monolith, but changes from time to time and place to place. These are important projects, of course, fueled by good intentions and often leading to laudable outcomes. Yet they have not worked. Not only do such moves play into the Martyrs' suspicions that sharia is stealthy and fluid enough to conceal its true ambitions, they do not question the assumption that the problems of law can be resolved by arriving at the proper explanations of "real" religion.

And so it is common for editorialists and talking heads to profess snarky disbelief that any rational person could imagine, for example, that "everybody in Oklahoma would be forced to submit to Allah."[57] A US district court was similarly impatient when ruling against the Oklahoma law, judging that sponsors "do not identify any actual problem" or "even a single instance where an Oklahoma court had applied Sharia law."[58] Yet as soon as this decision was announced, it was interpreted as evidence of the court's barely concealed collusion with "radical Islam."[59] Impatient Whistleblowers often respond to such retrenchment with open mockery, as when bloggers suggested that Tennessee practices, and should consider banning, "redneck law."[60] Standing beside high-minded dismissal is Whistleblowers' more common insistence that "Christianists" represent the *real* danger to American democracy, for their willingness to waste resources on a new "Crusade."[61] Whistleblowers are eager to define which religion counts in public life, and to announce their own status as the Embattled Majority, bravely defending the Framers and the Constitution against medieval yokels. If religion will not play nice in the ways liberals expect, it must be quarantined in the name of good order.

Just as Martyrs homologize and conflate leftist academics, activist judges, and fifth-column sharia zealots, Whistleblowers similarly envision fundamentalists, neocon war hawks, and economic libertarians all working in concert toward an exclusive fusion of law and religion no less dire than sharia.[62] Indeed, it was common in the 2012 and 2016 presidential campaigns to allege that Republicans had become an "American Taliban."[63] In saying this, I am not shrugging off the cultural politics of the Islamophobes, who are uncomfortable with the pluralism of the very Constitution they celebrate in the abstract. But panicky op-eds about the dangers of "God's law" offer no robust engagement with how categories like religion are constructed (which is no mere academic matter) or how inclusive civic identities are protected. When conservative religion is simply met with a "creeping theocracy" meme for every utterance of "creeping sharia," this keeps things exactly where they are, to our political and religious discredit.

Each side accuses the other of purveying "myths," of fabricating or misappropriating texts in order to substantiate a feeling, and even of mirroring the practice of *taqiyya*. These are all issues to be concerned about, and, having written extensively about the role of fear and sensationalism in American politics, I do not need convincing about the fallout from such imagery. Yet principled outrage or dismissal of conservative religion's seriousness has not produced a different politics. Accepting that Whistleblowing is counterproductive when it comes to shifting America's largest conversation about religion might seem a bitter pill to swallow while America deals with the wreckage left in the aftermath of Trump's presidency. But though their concerns for Muslims' safety and for pluralist politics are laudable, Whistleblowers reproduce dualistic thinking and, in attacking Martyr religion, undermine themselves strategically. That is no less true here, in the case of law.

## Creeping Secularism

Law in Embattled America is assumed to protect religion: from nonreligion, from wrong religion, and mostly from citizens who do not live and think as we do. Each mode of complaint—and it is complaint and alarm rather than argumentation that we see here—shares a similar style and a range of pliable categories like freedom and citizenship designed to elicit support (who opposes freedom, after all?) and others to inspire revulsion (who digs a caliphate?). In legal panics surrounding real and false religion, real and false America, law not only shapes our recognition of good and bad religion, but also grounds an assumption that law is linked to citizens' self-authentication. Despite stated convictions that law is, and should remain, free-standing, Americans generally will not budge on the assumption that they have a national birthright to existential fulfillment, or at least to using law to silence one's critics.

Denunciations of "false" faiths have occurred often in American life, often using the trumpet of law to amplify their urgency. Yet while law has often sought to correct this impulse, by recognizing the legitimacy of religious exemptions, for example, it is not the language of exemption that compels Embattled America. No inflammatory documentaries are produced to expose the grave danger of the Amish taking their children out of public schools, after all. Rather, sharia and non-Christian religion prompt the language of exception and threat, which animate and amplify demands for new laws and new regulations on bodies. The unconscious assumption that religion is about belief lends this language urgency. For, as Kirstie McClure shows, early modern states employed this privileging of belief in order to regulate those citizens whom they suspected of intending to generate "worldly harm."[64]

Interestingly, law itself is conspicuously fluid in key parts of these conversations. Court precedent holds that separate bodies of law may be invoked to settle particular disputes. As Rafia Zakaria notes, the "neutral principles doctrine" took shape in the 1970s, conferring upon "religious bodies the freedom from having their doctrines and beliefs judged or defined by civil courts."[65] In the name of "neutrality," cases like *Avitzur v. Avitzur* (1983) held that courts could sometimes apply "religious law" "provided that the clauses in question do not require the court to engage in religious or doctrinal interpretation."[66] Purportedly allowing itself greater flexibility in adjudication, the judiciary has limited its own power in order to preserve the special status afforded to (some) religion. Whether overly zealous or overly solicitous, law has not settled the riot of claims surrounding sharia and religious otherness. In this, law has not hampered the ability of the Embattled to posit religion as simultaneously social boon and cultural threat, both beneficiary and target of law's power.

Law in this vision is less an idiom of rational deliberation than a vehicle for taming or reshaping religion. This is consistent with what Sullivan describes as "a shift in what religion is understood to be. . . . As [religion] is being naturalized it is becoming an accepted part of the domain of government."[67] Public discourse, including Embattlement, still assumes that secularism's separate domains are what is at stake, whether understood positively or negatively. This, Sullivan rightly notes, conceals the naturalization of religion as "internal, chosen, and believed."[68] Not only are religions deeply interwoven with ostensibly secular laws and institutions, but these secular presences are often recognizable only by the very murkiness that generates outrage. The impassioned attempts to clarify secularism's muddles end up remuddling it, in its dependence on the same limits and categories, particularly the conception of a free-standing religion as a protected entity.

This feedback loop—institutions and feelings, tacit acceptance and volcanic resistance—preserves Americans' ambivalence about law and religion. The enforcement of secular law, or criticism of its uses and interpretations, is felt by Martyrs to be a Trojan Horse for sharia itself. The laxity of law with regard to religious speech in public is felt by Whistleblowers to be the start of a new era of witch-burning. My intention is not to come across as indifferent to the actual violence against Muslim Americans that has steadily risen in recent years, nor to Martyrs' general hostility to pluralism. My point is that continued rhetorical cage matches about why religion is so dangerous or is so endangered have proven ineffective at dealing with precisely these realities.

Outside of bland invocations of "religious freedom," Americans spend little or no time interrogating the conceptual particulars that enshrine this freedom: self-limitation, a "proper" sphere, shared rights and immunities. What is more, these particulars are not nearly satisfying enough for the maximal expression of Life as Action Movie, which seeks victory rather than conciliation. For both reasons, then, Americans unconsciously invest faith in law as absolute in its protection of their particular selves, a faith that does not acknowledge the obvious ambivalences this chapter has traced. This inflexibility, then, demands the Embattled's reliance on a "real" religion that will defang opponents while also absolving them from acknowledging that politics and law require the acceptance of different (and even divergent) worldviews as an unremarkable, even desirable product of democracy. All too many Americans have adopted the easier, and more exciting, attitude that law is for them alone, and that other citizens are devils illegitimately claiming liberties to which they are not entitled.

The right to the free exercise of religion (tangled and muddled as it is) exists on a continuum with others, like freedom of speech, or the right to equal personhood. To presume that it does not, or that it is politically prior in some sense, leads us to precisely these kinds of choke points in public life; we shrilly proclaim that our misfortune is worse than yours, and tolerance of one's religious others is read as compliance with a system rigged against you. When the Embattled feel offended, their privilege gone wobbly, they protest that simply to *have* the feeling is a sign of the violation of the Constitution, a whiplash away from the mainline of American history. Simple exposure to the notion that one's ideas about religion, even one's very ways of being in the world, are not universally acclaimed is taken as an offense. And yet Embattled Americans require the tension they seek to escape: the friction of difference provides vitality, yet it is backed up by the unconscious association between voluntarism and negative liberty with the complete absence of coercion.[69]

Currently, nearly an entire political party has coalesced around the claims central to Martyrs' understanding of law. The question of law and religion, or religious law, reached an apotheosis in the era of Trump. From a uniquely lawless administration, under scrutiny but calamitously effective in judicial stonewalling and in navigating an impeachment "trial" without witnesses or evidence, there issued a large number of policies affecting religion's legal status. It is common to encounter the notion that the Trump presidency was a divine opportunity because, for all his crudeness and calamity, he rewarded evangelical supporters with Justices Amy Coney Barrett, Neil Gorsuch, and Brett Kavanaugh.

So what do Americans expect from the law? Religion and the emotions it provokes—among champions and despisers—have not helped interrogate Americans' desire to use law as a shield against mutual responsibility or self-restraint based on shared norms and procedures. The Embattleds' complaints about law's effects on religion collapse law's content into an emotional experience that can be performed in public life. And because of the Whirl's capacities for customizable truth, law's independence and stability are everything for everyone.

Left unchanged by spasms of outrage are a corporate power and elite hegemony that law protects, grounded in the illusion that law is independent of other dimensions of the political. Via transference, law becomes the hero and the villain in the Action Movie that Americans simply watch. Discontented citizens express their alienation from law's power by protesting that it protects undeserving others: homosexuals, Muslims, self-righteous evangelicals, or smug liberal secularists. By making law at once the object of hope and of scorn, mirroring American attitudes about religion, Americans effectively accept the unspoken limits on their own political capacities.

How do we get outside this condition? The solution will not come through bland reassertions of liberal tolerance. As Wendy Brown has demonstrated, while tolerance "took shape as an instrument of civic peace and an alternative to the violent exclusion or silencing of religious dissidents," its role in contemporary liberal polities is largely to enshrine a settled politics of caution that effectively organizes "good" citizenship.[70] On the face of it, the centrality of Embattlement to American politics would seem to belie this claim. And yet, as I have argued throughout this book, Embattlement quite simply *is* the politics of convention, the default mode, the performance that prevents us from thinking seriously about what being political actually requires. Because to claim one is Embattled is to claim that fairness has been violated, that the system is worthless, and that what is needed is not a reassessment of civic responsibility but a knockout victory.

The problems of law and Embattlement cannot be solved without the frank acknowledgment that law only works if in concert with civic education, local activism, and a redoubled commitment to fostering a genuinely democratic culture. What this means is not a consistently, inflexibly leftist orientation to law, nor anything as simple-minded and unachievable as a "secular public sphere." Rather, law (and those who seek things from it) must understand that it is accountable not to program, ideology, or religion in isolation but to fostering the conditions for democratic practice itself. And this practice in turn requires better citizenship.

It is past time to think about what broader sets of values and practices are associated with constitutional norms. The Constitution does not afford special protections to citizens on the basis of race, gender, sexuality, or class, protections that might complicate those afforded to religion qua religion. Yet it clearly stipulates a range of protections and rights to citizens qua citizens. This has been obscured by thinking about religion only via the most extreme hypotheticals—Stalinist prohibitions or theocracy—or by invoking commitments not to allow religions to do things that are already manifestly illegal, like torturing homosexuals or beating Muslims. Neither of these gets us to the kind of reconceptualization we need if we are to reduce Embattlement's hold on us.

The point is to remake democratic culture from the ground up. For without this, other forms of legislation—to oppose discrimination or to ensure equal pay, for example—will remain out of reach. The vengeful, zero-sum approach to public life that has triumphed in Embattled America will not shift until law as winning gives way to a conception of law as a *context*, a framework in which mutual obligations are recognized and acknowledged, until Americans accept that democracy fails when citizens feel entitled to use law to Embattle someone else.

Clarifications of the scope of law should be linked to elucidation of the implicit responsibilities of citizens in each sphere of social life. Whether in the realm of commerce, education, or political service, law has—treating religion as isolated from other sets of political obligations—too often treated religion as exempt from public, civic responsibilities. I do not mean to paint exemptions with a broad brush, as the legitimacy of, for example, conscientious objection to military service is clear. In Embattled America, however, no heterosexual is being compelled to marry a gay person, no Christian is ordered to bow toward Mecca, no atheist is forced to attend Jesus Camp. No commandment or injunction is being annulled by laws that allow others to live differently from you.

Law is an index of the buy-in to the social contract that citizens share. Recognition of this mutuality, and the implied mutual accountability that ensues from this conception of citizenship, is obscured by Embattled religion. While it might be tempting to see such flare-ups, along with the political favoritism that now mars the judiciary more than ever, as signs of the end, those with any remaining hope for American democracy might reframe them as a challenge to reckon with our own expectations and responsibilities.

One component of such progress would be a new commitment to rational public discourse, of the sort described by John Rawls and by Jürgen Habermas as fully transparent and self-reflective. Certainly this might make legal conflagrations like anti-sharia proposals less frequent.[71] Yet the desire for free-standing norms of rationality begs the question we hope such norms will answer. Without large-scale commitments to renewed civic education and to creating open, permanent outlets for deliberation, simply pointing to the need for such discourse has the feel of "thoughts and prayers." Rational discourse can be inflexible, after all, in its demand that different groups of citizens "translate" their convictions into mutually recognizable terms. It is also true that some of the finest transformations in American public life have come through movements animated by robust religious convictions. Perhaps the problems of law, then, can be addressed by locating linkages and congruences between different conceptions of citizenship, history, free speech, and free exercise. This is a notion with some appeal, and intentionally echoes Rawls's well-known arguments for what he called overlapping consensus. But it runs up against the sheer resistance of Embattled Americans to admit even the possibility of conciliation as a political desire: in Martyrs' zeal for court-stacking, gerrymandering, and Religious Liberty Task Forces, and the parallel complaints from Whistleblowers that public life would hum like a V-8 if we could just purge it of religion they distrust.

Law's purpose is not to bar religious conservatives from public life. This was never at stake. Rather, assessments of law—and our responsibilities in its orbit—should focus on law's capacity to ensure that public life remains a place of contestation, where citizens are not guaranteed any insulation from competing viewpoints, not just the irreligious but the differently religious. Law's purpose is not simply to block outlandish efforts like anti-sharia legislation but to contrast fantasy and fear with education: judicial reasoning, opinions, briefs, and the like might enhance law's legitimacy by acknowledging and strengthening links to the spaces of interactivity and different models for realizing democratic norms that thrive within the United States. If local and national democracy are to flourish, there must be space for multiple conceptions of law, places where arguments are assessed not on the basis of their religiosity as such but on the basis of their resonance with a broader set of democratic convictions.

What is really at stake then, instead of "religious liberty" narrowly conceived or the terrors of religion narrowly conceived, is something like law as the grounding of mutual civic respect. Given the depredations of the judiciary and of political religion, it may seem somewhat naive to invoke such categories here. But politics is also the work of the imagination, and one method of achieving what seems impossible is to reject the stale reminder that politics is the art of the possible in favor of politics *as if*. It is for citizens and jurists alike to perform not just a religious self-inventory but a democratic one in determining where and how the rule of law is enacted around religions.

No deliberation about the scope of law—its burden, its exemptions, its compelling interests—can be detached from concerns about the legitimacy of citizens who are the targets of religious speech or antireligious speech, and, importantly, about the legitimacy and stability of institutions. Religion is perhaps too many things: a protected class, a category that secures legitimacy, and the force behind law in all its punitive power. In the Whirl's emotional vortex, the most alarmist claims with the deepest histories and most grievous injuries are those that circulate the most: everyone is a Bonhoeffer witnessing bravely against tyranny; each citizen is a Martin Luther King Jr. breaking an unjust law.

But despite the Embattleds' dreams of perfect freedom, which depend on their cinematic imagination of persecution, law must have the power to constrain in order to secure its own legitimacy as well as the conditions for democratic life. And though this very power, so central to law, fuels disgruntlement, this is in part because we fail to see law as contrapuntal rather than singular and static. Embattlement depends on the idea that "law" and "religion" are perfectly monolithic in protecting or vexing us. But if we shift our understanding of law to one that is more dialogic and interactive—with our conceptions making sense only in relation to others, in a mutually constituting rhythm that relates to civic education and public accountability—law's purposes might be broadened, contributing to the revitalization of public life.

Self-styled victims, in short, cannot use law to become killers. It is obvious that the volatility of religion and law exists partly because of a failure to go for nuance and flexibility, backed by self-limiting citizenship. Outside the difficulty of defining religion or its public demarcation, the law is precisely what it says it is not: a medium of sustained political contestation. And in this, law picks up Embattled America's larger confusions about legitimate political action, public discourse, and rights. Law cannot easily deflect questions about its own political management of religious life, evident in its assumptions about the inner life of citizens, the designated spheres of religious participation, and the effects of juridical power. If we are committed to remaking the law a vehicle of justice, rather than a mirror that we pretend is innocent of our construction, let it embrace its own political qualities, its pedagogical force and its ability do what conscience alone will not: protect the fundamental dignity of human persons. When loss of privilege is construed as an attack, and when fair rules for all are felt as hostile, it is we, and not the law, who need adjustment.

# 9

# Locked and Loaded

## On Birth, Death, Guns, and Citizenship

> Our worst misfortunes never happen, and most miseries lie in anticipation.
> —Honoré de Balzac

> [That was] how the Old Man's mind worked. Whatever he believed, he believed. It didn't matter to him whether it was really true or not. He just changed the truth until it fit him. He was a real white man.
> —James McBride, *The Good Lord Bird*

In the years following September 11, 2001, we became used to existing in an intense atmosphere of edgy, technologically imbued urgency, the continual anxiety that bad things are imminent precisely where they seem not to be actually happening. And yet, to many millions of Americans, November 2016 seemed not just politically but ontologically unexpected: it felt as if the weightlessness of the Whirl had just been sucked away—even though everything about the moment had been enabled by its weird epistemologies—and a great burden had brought everything heavily back to earth, wrecked and stunned. For there, in the White House, sat Donald J. Trump, the businessman and reality show huckster who had championed the "birther" movement, with President Barack H. Obama, the first African American president, whose legitimacy and authority and character had been questioned from the moment his national ambitions were announced. Whether or not one considered the social and historical import of this symbolically charged meeting, it certainly felt like some kind of emphatic punctuation, after eight years of intense conversation about and denial of ongoing racism in the United States.

*Embattled America*. Jason C. Bivins, Oxford University Press. © Oxford University Press 2022.
DOI: 10.1093/oso/9780197623503.003.0009

Obama's presidency was unique, not just because of his racial identity but also because of the excess of imagery and interpretation produced around it. One saw this in the endless Photoshopping that transformed Obama's face, most frequently applied to Shepard Fairey's iconic "Hope" campaign poster from 2008. Obama became Heath Ledger in *The Dark Knight*, or Adolf Hitler, or the Grim Reaper, among others from the bestiary of his critics' imagination. Now the words for which he was once celebrated were lampooned ("Nope"), or his name transformed to become Nobama or Obummer. Of course, the true face of this anxiety was everywhere, in those unashamed and unsettling statements on bathroom walls, on signs, and elsewhere in the world of texts, tweets, and emails.

With each mind-bending, Brueghelesque day of the Trump presidency, which in its final year was marked by openly racist tweets and speeches during a movement for racial justice, it grew clearer that Obama captured the enduring Embattlements of America and the peculiar intensities of the twenty-first-century freakout: Obama was not simply nonwhite; he was president when the most glaring failures of America™ became impossible to ignore: the paper-thin economy, the scorched social safety net, the blaring narcissism, and the white supremacy, among the more obvious examples. Obama was also the subject of Embattled America's peculiar, inflammatory investments in religion. Aside from the baseless allegations of "birthers," who insisted along with Trump that Obama was born outside of the United States and was thus illegitimately occupying the Oval Office, Obama was said to be a Muslim, a secular humanist, and the wrong kind of Christian simultaneously. He was thus judged, in multiple ways, to be beyond the pale of American political legitimacy.

In this chapter I discuss how Obama Embattlement's focus on Kenyan Muslim socialism obscured necessary conversations about citizenry, birthright, and belonging in a democracy. Obama the fearsome unicorn provoked the most widespread and hyperbolic complaint of all the Martyrs' foci. He was hanged in effigy, pictured in innumerable crosshairs, Jim Crow mocked, and more. And then the guns came, affixed like beepers to the khakis of suburban dads or displayed in all their hugeness at rallies on Martin Luther King Jr.'s birthday. Guns were also pointed and fired at African Americans with disturbing regularity. So there is no reckoning with the fearful apocalypticism of 2020 and 2021 without reckoning with white America's obsession with guns. To assess religion in Obama Embattlement requires addressing the power of death and sovereignty.

## Race and War

Imaginations of the horrific have regularly accompanied (and defined) American politics, as has ubiquitous racism, but something about Obama unleashed the mentality of war. In "Thoughts for the Times on War and Death," Sigmund Freud anticipated something of the militarized uncertainty of our decentered, reeling moment: "Swept as we are into the vortex of this war-time, our information one-sided . . . we are incapable of apprehending the significance of thronging impressions, and we know not what value to attach to the judgments we form."[1] Freud intuited that the warlike response to experiences of informational disorientation was produced by a crisis for "the great ruling powers among the white nations."[2] The great fiction of the modern state, Freud observed, was its ability to break older assumptions "that 'foreigner' and 'enemy' . . . [were] regarded as synonymous."[3] Yet while modern states and cities boasted of their cosmopolitanism, in practice they were uneasy with a multiplicity of information and people. The cosmopolis became the breeding ground for suspicions that something "unhindered and unsuspected" moved among us.[4]

In a world that is unsettlingly protean, war assures people in the face of their own insignificance, and the horror this brings about; likewise, the very proximity to otherness produces a revulsion that demands flushing out the interloper. While democracy is described as a system that nourishes "difference"—the census, polling, the accumulation of likes online and in the cloud—America is ever reminded of how difficult it is for millions of its citizens to live comfortably amid such difference. The experience of alienation thus ascribes itself to the existence of a war for the soul of a nation, and the experience also justifies participation in such a struggle.

Given that related dramas and fantasies of persecution multiplied so visibly during Obama's eight years in office, it is instructive to reflect on the topics such fantasies avoid. There is great resistance among many white Americans to acknowledging the constitutive nature of white supremacy: how it lives in patterns of consumption; how seldom white Americans recognize the oppressions nonwhite Americans suffer; how clearly white privilege benefits from the labor of others. Silence about these things does the work of whiteness; the fantasy of Embattlement is a ritual of denial.

The furor surrounding Obama, and the religio-racial panic about his birthright, was therefore never a conversation about the rights owed to human beings. It was a powerful reminder of the salience of race in every period of American history, and the way religions have authorized racial representations and the cultural power of white supremacy.[5] This furor expressed a denial that racism continues to be an issue in the United States, a denial that has, at every stage of post–Civil War history, enabled the continued disempowerment of nonwhite citizenship.

This point needs little rehearsing at present, when the Republican Party has openly, and with little penalty, engaged in race-motivated voter suppression: closing polling places in African American communities, suspending Sunday voting, "accidentally" sending voters to the wrong polling place, rejecting tens of thousands of new voter registrations (that just so happen to be majority nonwhite), gutting portions of the 1965 Voting Rights Act, and demanding street addresses for voter registration from Native Americans on reservations (where 40 percent of the population do not have street addresses), and the hundreds of hastily written laws sent to state legislatures after the 2020 election, to name just some of a plethora of examples.[6] These instances are part of a long political history aimed at the disenfranchisement of African Americans. For centuries, public life and law have been organized explicitly around opposition to (and panic about) free bodies of color organizing themselves.

As Ibram X. Kendi notes, in the early 1700s "every Virginia county had a militia of landless Whites 'ready in case of any sudden eruption of Indians or insurrection of Negroes.'"[7] Since that time, Americans have expressed their racial anxieties at least partly through debates about citizenship, or who belongs to America. Formal understandings of American citizenship were framed racially from the outset. At the Constitutional Convention of 1787, the "three fifths compromise" held that, when determining congressional representation, electors, and taxation, slaves would be counted as only 60 percent of their personhood. The 1790 United States Naturalization Law held that citizenship was available "only to 'free white persons' of 'good moral character.'"[8]

The logic and the execution of the 1850 Fugitive Slave Law gave license to an infinite prosecutorial suspicion, justifying the capture of any African American even suspected of being in public illicitly, that is, not possessed of authentic freedom or personhood. Then and now, citizenship meant whiteness and maleness, with all other persons considered guilty until proven innocent. Passed in the wake of formal freedoms conferred on African American males after the Civil War, the Black Codes and Jim Crow expanded impediments to nonwhite participation in public life. And in addition to racist initiatives at the local level, the federal court authorized law and policy that limited nonwhite popular power. As Carol Anderson shows, 1874's *Minor v. Happersett* decided that "the Constitution of the United States does not confer the right of suffrage upon anyone"; the right to vote "was not coexistent with citizenship."[9] Legally and philosophically this (along with women's inability to vote) was clearly inconsistent with liberalism's assumption that atomistic personhood (endowed with rights) is the foundation of all such constitutional order, yet such legal sophistry is common in the history of American struggles for equality. In the Civil Rights Cases of 1883, the Supreme Court cynically employed the Fourteenth Amendment itself—with its promises of due process and equal treatment under the law—to rule that "the 1875 Force Act that banned discrimination in public accommodations was also unconstitutional," asserting that any form of discrimination not specifically enacted by law fell outside the amendment's scope.[10]

Such efforts did not end with the nineteenth century. In a cultural context populated by groups ranging from the Ku Klux Klan to the White Citizens' Council of the 1950s, bent on harassing and intimidating nonwhite citizens, legal decisions like the above muddied the distinction between de facto and de jure white supremacy. Conservatives of all stripes, and many tepid white liberals, resisted the civil rights movement. Since then, it has become common for conservatives to cherry-pick Martin Luther King Jr's remarks about color-blindness and the content of our character, and suggest that, after passage of the Civil Rights Act, we no longer need to talk about race. Indeed, to "play the race card" is taken by conservatives as an expression *of* racism. Even as Republican Party leadership has (sometimes) shifted how it talks about race, its policies have consistently undermined the liberties of people of color. All of this was explicit and obvious, unless to those who had a vested interest in pretending it was not true. As New Right architect Paul Weyrich put it bluntly in 1980, "I don't want everybody to vote."[11] Post-Reagan Democrats, seeking to prove they could be "tougher" than the Republicans, sponsored omnibus crime bills, denounced welfare queens, and invoked fear of black "superpredators." Obama did not come out of nowhere, then. The history leading up to his election was replete with African Americans who succeeded despite the systematic attempts of white Americans to make their failure inevitable and then to blame it on the "natural" attributes of race.

So when Obama capitalized on the frisson of excitement accompanying his 2004 Democratic National Convention speech and emerged as the Democratic nominee for the presidency in 2008, the Whirl roared into overdrive. There was talk about race, to be sure, much of it starry-eyed. "Finally!" people exhaled, America can atone for its original sin. Perhaps now that this milestone had been achieved, many mused, America can become postracial. But Obama was immediately transformed into a subject of disappointment: he was not left enough, not black enough, not white enough, not "normal" enough. Obama wore a tan suit. The republic was doomed.

While America™ aggressively marketed the idea of consensus, of the at-last achievement of *e pluribus unum*, the electorate sank once more into the satisfactions of rage-tweeting and conspiracy theory. The sense of stunned unreality that accompanied Obama's political ascent led to the manufacture of realities preposterous and evidence-free enough to fit the mood. And Obama stood for it all. The first black POTUS was also the first true meme POTUS. He was Photoshopped with bling and gold teeth, or with bin Laden's beard. The racial imagery was shocking in its bluntness. One 2008 image featured a portrait of "Ten Dollars Obama Bucks."[12] It featured the Obama's face pasted onto a crudely drawn donkey. And scattered around the faux currency (clearly designed, with its legend "United States Food Stamps," to tap into long-standing gripes about "big government handouts" or "free stuff") were watermelon, a bucket of Kentucky Fried Chicken, a rack of ribs, and the Kool-Aid logo.[13] At the 2012 North Carolina State Fair, an Obama effigy was hung from a noose. The 2012 campaign season also saw anti-Obama bumper stickers with the phrase "Don't Re-Nig in 2012."[14]

The 2012 "documentary" *2016: Obama's America* predicted that an Obama reelection would cause "the death and dismemberment of the United States of America."[15] The film is rooted in the observations of neoconservative pundit Dinesh D'Souza, according to whom "Obama espouses an anticolonialist worldview that imperils America."[16] The film derides Obama's achievements as being "largely because of his skin color," intimating that he was an affirmative action president. Such an interloper, viewers were warned, would be joined by "his fellow activists and his professors" in transforming America "into a socialist state . . . and permitting a 'United States of Islam' to . . . squelch Israel."[17]

Could a mundane, pro-corporate centrist like Obama actually inspire such a dystopian scenario? These apocalyptic musings should not be read as merely anxious, for we cannot ignore how integral visions of fantastical violence and morbidity are to an American public culture that increasingly embraces them as a surrogate for politics. They are rotting inversions of the smiling optimism we present to the world. Obama imagery traded in the category of foreignness, built on the assumption that "real" Americans must also have "real" religion.

## Proof and Consequences

In June 2008, in response to the claims of the "birthers," the Obama campaign publicized the candidate's certification of live birth issued in Hawaii. To the confusion of many, there immediately arose a small but persistent opposition claiming that this document was a forgery.[18] This anxious faction was fearful that an actual "foreigner" had somehow made an end run around electoral procedure and was on the cusp of presidential power.

From conservative Orange County, California, emerged an improbable figurehead: Orly Taitz, dentist and Israeli émigré, with frosted hair and a meme-rich name ("O rly?"). Taitz, who had earned an online law degree, alleged that Obama was concealing his past in ways she recognized from Moldova, the former Soviet republic where she was born.[19] Taitz was irate that the "mainstream media" was not doing more to expose the truth. She went public and gained attention by speaking ominously about an "all-civilian army," about "footage of children dressed in uniforms, saluting Obama and doing drills."[20] This imagery evoked old, conspiracy-soaked fears about foreign armies or government thugs robbing Americans of their civil liberties. To Taitz, Americans had been suckered by multicultural optimism into courting disaster.

Beginning in early 2009, Taitz claimed repeatedly that Obama "didn't meet the constitutional requirements to be president."[21] She was soon buoyed by support from Wiley Drake, an influential radio host and pastor who had become infamous for praying for Obama's death. Taitz appeared on Drake's show, where the two pledged to expose Obama's secret. Birthers soon appeared everywhere. Rush Limbaugh said that Obama "has yet to prove that he's a citizen."[22] Nine congressional representatives proposed redundant legislation "that would require prospective presidents to affirm their U.S. citizenship."[23] CNN's Lou Dobbs publicly aired his sympathy for birthers.[24] Liz Cheney explained to Larry King that "people are uncomfortable with a president who is reluctant to defend the nation overseas."[25]

Callers to radio shows, editorials, internet comments, the fully overwhelming density of the Whirl gave substance to these accusations. Obama had spoken openly about change, looked like change, advocated policies understood as change. From these vaporous concerns about national sovereignty and tradition emerged an identity that resonated with Martyrs. Birthers proudly embraced this identity as a "badge of honor, as if they were a persecuted minority."[26] With each refuted conspiracy theory, with each detail of the birth certificate explained, the Action Movie somehow grew convinced that the plot had more layers to expose.

If nothing else, it was exciting to living with an "imposter" in the White House. If Obama was not foreign by birth, perhaps he was concealing his true identity as a secret Muslim. Birthers had always contended that part of the president's very foreignness was his suspected "allegiance" to Islam, and throughout Obama's first term the Whirl produced a tide of Islamophobic discourse. Critics noted that Obama's grandfather, Hussein Onyango, and his Indonesian stepfather, Lolo Soetero, were both Muslim. How could exposure to such a baneful religion be resisted? What is more, Obama was "instructed in Islam at a school in Jakarta" and "many of his college friends were Muslim."[27] Critics noted even more urgently that Obama was "listed as a Muslim on school documents."[28] Was this yet more "evidence" of Martyrs' deepest fears? Who cared that none of this mattered in terms of democracy or the Constitution? Who cared that these claims were also refuted?[29] Feelings this powerful could not be erased by facts.

Islam was a contagion, rendering POTUS Muslim by contact or osmosis; Islam was a "cult," with the irresistible power of a false religion; or it was a transparent fraud. Just behind Obama's sham Christianity was a foreign faith, which, if exposed, would reveal the socialist behind the neoliberal policy nerd, the bomb-throwing radical behind the meek community organizer's facade, or the affirmative action baby who could not get into all those Ivy League schools on his own.[30] These fears, expressed in the language of law and policy, ignored the rich opportunity to consider what one was actually entitled to as a citizen, as one's birthright. Instead Obama was at the center of panic over "Dark Conspiracies and ... Threats to the Republic, of a bastard prince born in Kenya and of soldiers fighting halfway around the world, of forged documents and an endangered flag."[31] As early as the 2008 campaign, an ominous email was circulated (allegedly originating with Christian missionaries in Kenya) that "repeated the secret Muslim claim and said the would-be forty-fourth president was bent on starting a race war."[32]

Words like "madrassa" and "Jihad" and "Koran" did the thinking for Americans already anxious about declining Protestantism and whiteness. In the University of Central Florida's basketball arena, thousands gathered to perform a kind of presidential exorcism, to "cast out . . . the evil spirits they believe inhabit the United States—the socialists, the Marxists, the totalitarian wannabes and their imposter-in-chief, Barack Hussein Obama."[33] Imposter or no, it was through Obama that an identity was conjured into being, one fearful of its own dissolution in the growing tide of unfamiliar Americans. As one birther put it succinctly: "There's more of them."[34] Another said of Obama's "minions" that "they represent the welfare America, the handout America—what do they call it, the nanny state, [where] everybody is taken care of."[35] The Obama voter was some grim amalgam of a Malbec-sipping elitist, a "welfare queen" (Gingrich called Obama the "food stamp president"), and part of a radical political faction that would "change everything."[36] Think about it, one suspicious mind urged: "All the people that they turned everybody against us . . . was all the people that Obama was associated with, and it doesn't take a rocket scientist to put two and two together. He is not American."[37] And they knew it because of Islam.

Obama himself shrugged off the outrage of Glenn Beck, Sean Hannity, Bill O'Reilly, and the rest: "Those folks were exercising their rights under our Constitution exactly as they should."[38] He did note, however, that "there is . . . a network of misinformation, that in a new media era can get churned out there constantly."[39] In his more candid moments, Obama went further: "I can't spend all my time with my birth certificate plastered on my forehead. . . . The facts are the facts."[40] But in his insistence on this point—as with his insistence on his country of birth, on his support for the so-called Park 51 Mosque, and other issues—the POTUS was also doing what precisely what so enraged his critics, which in their own minds was all that mattered.

Throughout 2009 these critics weaponized their speech. South Carolinian Republican representative Joe Wilson interrupted Obama's congressional address with a peremptory "You lie!" When Obama criticized police for arresting black academic Henry Louis Gates on his own doorstep, "A third of whites said the remark made them feel less favorably toward the president, and nearly two-thirds claimed that Obama had 'acted stupidly' by commenting."[41] Elected officials from Missouri and California described Obama as a "monkey" and a "chimp."[42] In addition to multiple state-sponsored "birther bills," GOP-controlled state legislatures nationwide began passing legislation to make voting more difficult that targeted black voters with, in the reckoning of the federal court that struck down such a North Carolina law in 2016, "almost surgical precision."[43]

These were the conditions that produced Trump, the chief birther who became the first president after the first black president. Trump, in the dead-on assessment of Ta-Nehisi Coates, "understood... the great power in not being a nigger."⁴⁴ Throughout the intervening years, the majority of Republicans continued to doubt Obama's Americanness. And as protesters filled the streets after the lonely, gray Trump inaugural, Bill O'Reilly warned that the Left was trying to destroy white America: "It's not a traditional America."⁴⁵ Perhaps in some way he was correct.

## Armed and/as Patriotic

As the birther movement grew, what increasingly stitched together these concerns about birthrights and freedoms, about wrong religions and citizenship, was guns. On the heels of Kenyan birth and Islam by osmosis came the ominous allegation that Obama's thugs would come for the right to bear arms that was an American's by birthright. This would, in Martyrs' imagining, prevent good citizens from armed and righteous revolt once the real attacks on Christianity began. Dobbs mused that the Federal Emergency Management Agency had been instructed by White House "Maoists" to build detainee camps, to be converted—after their use in legitimate emergency situations—into quarantines for noncompliant citizens.⁴⁶ (Dobbs was unmoved by the brutal activities of ICE at the border during the Trump presidency, when such camps were regular scenes of inhumane treatment of migrants.) As they had in the 1990s, self-styled citizen "militias" began to organize, ready to defend what they felt was at risk. Backed by the publicity and self-aggrandizement of social media, these groups flamboyantly, cinematically announced their resistance to things that would never happen.

Armed, white citizens appearing in public was nothing new in the Obama years. There were numerous appearances of sidearm-packing citizens at Obama's 2010 town hall meetings. The links between the normalization of such appearances and the increase of white Christian terrorism during the Trump era have been well documented.⁴⁷ The same Martyrs who protested Obama's presidency predictably disavow this connection. Yet throughout Obama's time in office, they gave voice to all manner of alarmist speech, urging self-defense in the face of imminent genocidal extinction.⁴⁸ One social media maven, "Liberty Belle," warned people that the Obama administration's stimulus package was the beginning of America's ruin, while another wrote that "the American Taxpayers Are the Jews for Obama's Ovens."⁴⁹

What is happening when citizens compare their tax rates with genocide, in protest against a thing that hasn't happened? The emotional enthusiasm of public gun displays was felt and understood to prove the veracity of patently absurd claims; one cannot "prove" that an emotion is baseless. One can only deny the facts associated with these emotions, which themselves are inevitably construed as offense, or discrimination. The ritualized defenses of gun laws, which assert that citizens' rights are above legal constraint, not only represent Americans' ambiguous relationship with authority and power (feel free to tread on the other guy, just don't tread on me); they underscore white anxiety about time and identity. Charges of "generational theft" pepper these rituals and their fantastical allegations, which paved the way for proliferating claims about white genocide. Obama was the law that must be resisted in the name of #freedom. The law, specifically as personified by those associated with law enforcement, was also that which might contain America's Obamafication.

The spectacle of armed "patriots" at the local Starbucks was common in the Obama years, a pre-echo of armed QAnon supporters marching to "Liberate Michigan" during the Covid-19 pandemic or storming the Capitol to overturn a lawful election. It was as if gun owners were daring non-gun owners to say anything, to question the wisdom (as opposed to the legality) of these actions. Critics would not hear that Obama was the most gun-friendly president in decades.⁵⁰ Instead, gun merchant Brian Kitts said of the president, "At the very core, he's un-American. The rest of the world sees him as weak and that's going to bite us in the ass."⁵¹ Ex-marine Russ Murphy, member of the Delaware 9-12 Patriots and the Constitution Party, barked indignantly that "as Christians we absolutely will no longer tolerate attacks or attempts to disparage us."⁵² The deprivileging of Christianity in public life was inseparable from anxiety about self-defense and American tradition itself.

But would an Antichrist seem so safely wonky as Obama? Would his very Dad-ness cover for global violence or theocidal intent? One patriot wondered, "What am I afraid of? I don't know—but I feel far more comfortable knowing that I have my nine-millimeter in my car."⁵³ Birther mainstay Joe Gayan regularly predicted that if Obama could not seize patriots' guns, he would "tax the bejeezus out of bullets instead."⁵⁴ Indeed, so thoroughly did birthers conflate identity, religion, and guns that Alabama's My Holy Smoke provided a cremation service which stuffed the ashes of the deceased into bullets. One could even kill after death, surely the deepest expression of Second Amendment panic among Obama's detractors.[55]

Birtherism grew on gun ranges. When Gayan first heard Phil Berg's radio interview about the president's supposed Kenyan birth, "Right away I just thought it was true."[56] Gayan ripped the interview to CD-Rs and sold them three dollars each at gun ranges. It also thrived on YouTube, which in these years grew crowded with the faces of hollering critics, with upside-down flags in the background, in dimly lit rooms, as if the solitary freedom fighter must be ever vigilant against those who would deny him his broadband connection. Their dark, factless imaginings convinced them to engage in paramilitary-style training.

One of the earliest groups organized to protect whiteness from Obama was the Oath Keepers, made up of (mostly former) soldiers and police officers who pledged—among other things—not to "put Americans in concentration camps."[57] The Oath Keepers formed as a kind of law enforcement organization outside the law, "claiming their allegiance was to the U.S. Constitution and not the president."[58] They have become quite well-known in recent years, for supporting ICE agents on the southern border, "defending" attendees of Trump rallies, and their organizational efforts in the January 2021 insurrection. Cofounded by Stewart Rhodes (a former army paratrooper who helped run Ron Paul's 2008 presidential campaign) and Celia Hyde, they regularly staged pre-enactments of the invasions they believe will eventually lead to the internment of Christian patriots. This is theater that parallels David Barton's history (moving in the opposite direction) even as it shares with the rise of weekend warrior games a broad reenactment of Vietnam-era trauma.[59] The Ohio Valley Freedom Fighters "organized 'open carry' church services and held paramilitary training exercises in the woods."[60] New Mexico's Second Amendment Task Force assembled simply "to wave their handguns and semi-automatics . . . at passing cars in a show of force" against what was said to be the Obama's plot to confiscate guns nationally.[61] In rural Montana at a Celebrating Conservatism rally presenters urged local politicians "to create mandatory militia service in the county and prevent forced inoculations as well as any attempts at enforcement of federal gun laws."[62] The strains of 2020–2021 resounded in advance.

Unlike routine American grumbling about the intrusiveness of the state, Twitter-era militias tap into a deep sense of bristling against coercion, filtered through the grandiose self-importance of social media profiles. The Three Percenters, for example, take their name from the common (albeit discredited) assertion that during the American Revolution "only 3% of the colonists were actively fighting."[63] We few, we brave citizens, this moniker suggests, resist Obama's assault on good citizenship and good religion. Such perceptions resonate with the apocalyptic sensibility that has regularly urged that, at the first sign of governmental persecution, the devout must make themselves ready for holy struggle. Always self-fulfilling, these pronouncements of righteous otherness do not exactly make every Oath Keeper a David Koresh or a Jim Jones, nor do Oath Keepers protest the "tyranny" of seatbelts; but when Rhodes and others continually warn that the state is eager for a terrorist attack or some similar excuse to impose martial law and seize guns, it is as if it has already happened, a suspected truth now being revealed because the depths of our feelings cannot mean anything else.[64]

Aside from Obama's racial otherness, critics insisted that in 2008 he had tipped his hand with his remark about Americans who cling to their guns and religion. Denounced as caricature and as evidence of Obama's Ivy League snobbishness, there is no denying that the nexus of guns and religion was in fact central to the identities of these militia groups. The Southern Poverty Law Center reported that in 2009 alone, far-right paramilitary groups grew by 244 percent.[65] And despite the alarm that has accompanied the rise in violent rhetoric and high-powered weaponry in public life, which has continued to rise since the group's founding, participants responded that "there's no law against declaring what you won't do."[66] This was an odd acknowledgment of the unreality of their outrage; while they incessantly declared that they would not knuckle under to government oppression if it actually arose, every scenario was deferred into a heroic future.

As if to bring this future into being, Oath Keepers spoke enthusiastically about "resistance and guerilla war."[67] Though Rhodes suspected such Action Movie fantasy might repel active-duty military supporters, the excitement of resisting things that hadn't happened proved contagious. In the group's first year of existence, Oath Keepers' Facebook wall was covered with headlines like "Obama Signs Martial Law Order." In response, Whistleblowers like Chris Matthews tweaked Rhodes, asking, "When you put your head on the pillow at night, are you afraid that at some point in your lifetime, the black helicopters from the UN will arrive in the United States and deny American sovereignty?" Rhodes responded, "It's possible . . . look at Germany, an advanced civilization, they fell into a despotism in a dictatorship, a murderous dictatorship in the span of ten years after an economic collapse. It could happen here. Think it can't happen here? Ask the Japanese-Americans whether it can happen here."[68] In this tangle of claims—where sympathy for the historical wrongs of a different racial other is invoked to support dystopian imaginations of a racially other president—Rhodes imagined Obama's neoliberal America as a barely disguised Weimar Republic, whereas he openly supported the transparently authoritarian Trump and helped plan the January 2021 insurrection. Once more Embattled Americans tap into the craving for historical significance, to be part of an epic narrative whose very urgency and intensity contrast with an otherwise unremarkable moment.

Of all the impulses in Embattled America, birtherism and Obama frenzy were the most explicitly violent. In its varied iterations we find clear forecasts of 2016's electoral earthquake and the ratcheting up of political violence that exploded in January 2021. Birthers' violent fantasies made telling references to slavery in their fantasies of weaponized resistance to the foreign mob, the latter so central to the Trump era's xenophobia. Candidates for office picked up the refrains echoing throughout this book. Their nearly apocalyptic scenarios drew their righteousness from a backward glance at a sanctified past, that fiction just waiting for Trump to convert it into a campaign.

Birther websites by the dozen began to sell prepper guides like *Understanding and Surviving Martial Law: How to Survive and Even Prosper during the Coming Police State*.[69] The title is telling, as if even in the apocalyptic police state there is some kind of twelve-step plan for business success and personal transformation. And yet it is impossible to interpret this phenomenon outside that other ritual violence that repeated itself in the Obama and Trump eras: the dead black bodies in streets or in police custody—the bodies of George Floyd, Breonna Taylor, Trayvon Martin, Michael Brown, Tamir Rice, Sandra Bland, Rekia Boyd, Eric Garner, Philando Castile, Freddie Gray, Charleena Lyles, and so, so many more—these bodies apparently less troubling to some white Americans than the massed bodies who filled the streets in protest against the killings, the terror they inspire in white people apparently more important than the terror of African Americans living in the reality that exists for privileged white gun owners merely as fantasy. Something more is happening when typical conservative nostalgia and laments about government bigness are expressed in the idea that "the system" is going to enslave white people.

History itself became a kind of gated community. The entire political sphere was transformed into Florida's "Stand Your Ground" law. With Obama, Embattled America converted conspiracy and political panic into expressions of identity: it was no longer just the corruption of institutions or offices that was driving birthers crazy; it was the inner experience of legitimacy or authenticity felt to be slipping away. When Martyrs began to sense they might not be able to have it all, visions of oppression become a way of surviving the experience of not mattering more than everyone else.

The story of Obama Embattlement shows us why gun sales and stocks spiked after the 2008 and 2012 elections.[70] The outward fear about being denied guns concealed the deeper fear that the black POTUS was coming for your privilege. These armed, white citizens felt themselves to be the *real* majority who had been made minor by illegitimates and thugs. The National Rifle Association's executive director, Wayne LaPierre, warned that "Obama wants to put every private, personal firearms transaction right under the thumb of the federal government . . . [so he can] either tax 'em or take 'em."[71]

Nothing had been done to threaten gun owners. Nothing had actually happened other than the shootings themselves. And it was still a half-decade before actual Nazis marched in Charlottesville during Trump's first year in office, and even further from the white riot of January 2021, its visual landscape overrun with far-right racist signage, tattoos, insignia, and slogans.[72] It seems that it was the order and tranquility themselves that were so unsettling to Obama's critics, who seemed unable to accept that he was anything other than the fearful black man of their collective imagination. Bellicose rocker Ted Nugent feared the Europeanization of America, complete with madrassas and higher taxes. In the mind of the libertarian rocker, the new tax rate that never came to pass entailed one dire result above all: "Bands will be dying left and right . . . everything America has been built on will be destroyed."[73] Obama was even going to kill rock and roll.

Nugent had sworn, during the 2012 campaign, "If Barack Obama becomes the president in November again, I will either be dead or in jail by this time next year."[74] While the Obama administration was "wiping its ass with the Constitution, you're living under a rock some place."[75] Man up, America! Nugent urged listeners to join the Action Movie: "We need to ride into that battlefield and chop their heads off in November."[76] It is hard not to hear in these fevered sentiments the pre-echo of the war rhetoric of the Trump era. Consider a 2013 survey by Fairleigh-Dickinson University's Public Mind Poll, assessing support for tighter gun control legislation in the wake of the Sandy Hook Elementary School shootings in which twenty small children and six adults perished. Forty-four percent of self-identified Republicans did not just oppose such legislation; they agreed with the statement that "an armed revolution in order to protect liberties might be necessary in the next few years."[77] A Virginia Republican openly called for such revolution. Many others predicted a new civil war, a prediction that became even more regular during the Trump era, most obviously manifested in the violence of the MAGA insurrection.[78]

Martyrs kept insisting that Obama was concealing the anti-Christian aggression of his "true agenda," which would lead the United States to the brink of "socialism or something much worse," likely the End of Days.[79] Robert Ringer, Ayn Rand devotee and self-help advocate, warned that Obama sought to confer "instant citizenship [on] all Third World immigrants."[80] This was the anxiety—a fresh start, a new birth, a universalization of Obama's citizenship ruse—that begat Trump. Ringer also predicted that Obama would jail his critics, the "real" citizens, suspend habeas corpus (the world cum Guantánamo), and "end fossil fuel production," and thus presumably the American way of life.[81] World Net Daily's webmaster Joseph Farah warned that "if he is re-elected, it's gonna be war. We will be hunted down like dogs."[82] Farah alleged further that the government was using drones to spy on him for simply issuing such warnings. This is the Action Movie: Embattled Americans insist, despite the outward appearance of Farah's comfortable life as a mostly insignificant middle-class white male in northern Virginia, that they are important enough to be spied on or hunted down like dogs.

On the eve of the 2012 election Paul Ryan warned of the "dangerous path" Obama would tread if reelected: "It's a path that grows government, restricts freedom and liberty, and compromises those values, those Judeo-Christian, Western civilization values that made us such a great and exceptional nation in the first place."[83] Religion was both danger (Obama's foreign hostility) and endangered. Critics ranging from Franklin Graham to Rick Santorum to Trump declared themselves aghast that, in supporting disaffected non-Christian populations in various places around the world, Obama was implicitly thumbing his nose at Christians murdered in the Middle East and China. Obama's emphasis on expanding voting rights and celebrating diversity were likened by Georgia state representative Bobby Franklin to "Soviet style central planning."[84] It all amounted to "secular oppression of Christians" such that one day simply to confess that Jesus is one's savior would be denounced as "hate speech."[85]

Never was the experience of white masculinity so publicly insistent on its own victimization, when the mere existence of other humans who would not be silent about their own histories, experiences, and actual oppression was understood to be an attack. Indeed, reacting to Black Lives Matter marches in response to the extrajudicial execution of George Floyd in May 2020, activists like Charlie Kirk and Trump himself repeatedly intoned that a Biden victory would mean the end of the suburbs and churches. Obama thus flipped a powerful switch in Martyrs' collective unconscious. He was the embodiment of every conservative Other distilled since the 1960s: the black male sexual predator and the un-American superprofessor; the champion of bloated bureaucracy, the purloiner of tax dollars, the foreign agent. In the inverted mirror of the Embattled psyche, Obama's very mundaneness could not have been real. He must, therefore, have been a dictator, overlord, or tyrant. That was the only way that the Martyrs' lust for living in times of great historical importance could be authenticated. Stopping him was an exercise of #freedom.

Whistleblowers dove in eagerly to address the issue of "real" religion and bogus conservatism. They gleefully castigated Martyrs' ignorance: how do they not know, for example, that there was an earlier birther controversy focused on Chester Arthur's alleged Canadian birth?[86] How can they be taken seriously when even "the top crazy of the Republican Conservative nutty right-wing movement," Glenn Beck, thinks birthers are nuts?[87] Apostate conservative Francis Schaeffer lamented the role of "Trump-like crass carnival barker opportunism" in conservative Christian critics of Obama.[88] Fevered at their keyboards, Whistleblowers ginned up epithet after acidic epithet for the Martyrs: "that rabid crop of self-appointed patriots," or "incurable wackjobs."[89] Birthers were infantilized but also likened to witch-hunters wielding the internet instead of the *Malleus Maleficarum*.[90] Obama saved global capitalism, so who were the yahoos in "this KKK Redux ... sans sheets and sans brains in [their] ridiculous Pagan rural obsessionism"? America was getting more woke, thinking green jobs and new apps, and yet "Whackadoodles Wearing Tinfoil Caps" tweeted conspiracies "from the caves of ignorance and hatred."[91]

America was beta-testing the epistemology of the Trump era. This was the way of being in the world that Embattlement required: Americans simply had to take the overwhelming volume of data and interpretations and make it fit their unperturbable Self. The seductions of Embattlement were the most durable way to carve out a space in the din of public life. This was the grim holding pattern Americans had settled into during Obama's second term. Would there emerge some way out of this condition in 2016?

## Locked and Loaded

Things become clear in retrospect. The AR-15 was less regulated than the uterus, but Americans claimed that their freedoms were about to be violently wrested from them. This is, of course, not the only time that political realignment has made gun rights central. After the tumultuous 1960s, Charlton Heston landed a starring role in a near-future America where white people, their cities ruined, were held captive and weaponless by apes. The 1994 Republican House victories came in part because the NRA spent considerable money and energy mobilizing rural conservatives. Grassroots Christian groups in the 1990s worked steadily to weaken gun laws, framing this as an expansion of freedom.[92]

Now, when such arguments intersect with fever-dreams about outlawed Christianity and the disappearance of whiteness, there are more ominous implications. This is also the moment of Sandy Hook and Orlando, of Las Vegas and Parkland, of El Paso and the Capitol, the moment when wedding vows are exchanged with AR-15s strapped to the beloveds' backs.[93] The moment where defiant Trump supporters, those who thrill in the vitality of his scorn for convention, are more likely to be gun owners than not.[94] Because Trump is the fighter-in-chief, the protagonist in a collective Action Movie which, upon Obama's election, shifted from a prominent position in the Coming Attractions to IMAX 3-D. Exploding into fearful life, Obama was the dark inversion of *The Secret*: he was all the ominous portents of the abundantly precarious universe brought to life.

Multiple states introduced legislation to ban gun control.[95] And all the while, militias and hate groups kept growing in number and influence.[96] As America's birther-in-chief, Trump's zeal to undo everything Obama had accomplished led to even greater weakening of gun regulation.[97] To watch all this happening, the boiling white rage targeting masks and other safety measures during a global pandemic, is to suspect that the Nietzschean maxim about victims becoming killers is America's unofficial national slogan. The absolute ontological fear of demographic change—of having whiteness sacrificed to the false god of multiculturalism and political correctness—worms its way through a segment of the electorate that wants to turn the tables before it's too late. In return, scornful Whistleblowers denounce them as rubes and con artists.

Even in the wake of the Capitol siege, those seeking to understand how America got to this point continue to focus overmuch on whether non-Trump voters should feel more empathy for Trump voters. Twitter rages on. There is anxiety that talking "too much" about "identity politics" is what led to Trump's election. How dare leftists make Trump voters feel bad enough about themselves to vote for Trump? Please overlook billboards that say "Make America White Again."[98] Please disregard the voluminous literature connecting white intolerance of difference with support for authoritarianism.[99] Feel free to turn a blind eye to the National Academy of Science's or professional psychologists' findings, on the basis of extensive peer-reviewed research, that anxiety about status and racial animosity figured much more largely in support for Trump than did economic anxiety.[100] Obama's change had scared people so much that even the word "hope" became frightening, so out of touch with "traditional American values" was he. Trump vowed to keep America distinct from all those "shithole countries" where black people lived, where AIDS was rampant, where MS-13 gangs plotted to rape white girls in the northern Virginia suburbs, and whatever other dark fantasy festered in the white imagination.

In the smoldering wake of the Trump administration, the national conversation has shown signs of opening up to larger considerations of belonging, entitlement, and, indeed, birthright. This has taken place in response to the humanitarian crisis at the United States' southern border, in response to the Trump administration's repeated efforts to impose a ban on immigration from majority Muslim countries (and to curtail many forms of legal immigration), and as a result of Covid-19, which has revealed the manifold brokenness of American politics with renewed clarity. And yet, think of the opportunity to focus more robustly on the implications of America's conferral of birthright citizenship, still a rarity in much of the world. Despite the Trump administration's flirtation with curtailing it, an impulse as heart-stopping as it was predictable, something about this rarity remains powerful even in a moment of fragility.[101] It is on some level at the center of all the aspirational stories America tells about itself. It propels liberation movements, and it anchors Americans to a common legal and political reality. Or at least it can, when conceptualized and realized properly.

After the Thirteenth Amendment's abolition of slavery, the Fourteenth Amendment stated, in its first section, "All persons born or naturalized in the United States, and subject to the jurisdiction thereof, are citizens of the United States and of the state wherein they reside." Birthright citizenship was upheld against several legal challenges in the late nineteenth century, usually drawing on English common law combined with the principle of *jus soli*, which holds that "citizenship of a person is determined by the place where a person was born."[102] According to Title 8 of the US Code, section 1401, *jus soli* citizenship shall be granted to "a person born in the U.S., and subject to its jurisdiction," among a range of other possibilities that includes children of "unknown parentage found in the United States while under the age of five."[103]

There has been much uncertainty about the merits of such entitlements. Democrats in Congress, such as Nevada's Harry Reid, have flirted with curtailing immigration, but it has been Republicans who have pushed reconsideration of the birthright citizenship. In 2013, Louisiana senator David Vitter and Iowa's representative Steve King (who has openly affiliated with white supremacist organizations) introduced into Congress legislation that would abolish birthright citizenship. South Carolina's mercurial senator Lindsey Graham said that he would support a constitutional amendment to achieve this end.[104] Graham had also complained about immigrants who "drop and leave" their babies to become bogus Americans, and about immigrants who benefit unworthily from birthing "anchor babies" on US soil.[105]

These debates about birthright and citizenship flow back at least to the 1830s–1840s, when immigration to the United Stats grew rapidly. Since then, the papists, the "Yellow Peril," the Jewish international conspiracy, and the undeserving freed slaves overrunning America's cities, all have been the target of popular mob violence and barbed words (like Josiah Strong's *Our Country*). Most significant here, though, is how the long-developing idea of Trump's wall—the material fantasy of the birther mindset—has its roots in the Second Klan, which emerged in the early twentieth century as a phenomenon that spread outside the South. Though Congress had passed anti-Klan laws in the 1870s, the Klan of the 1920s boasted four million members and considered their ideas to be mainstream American. And as Kelly J. Baker shows, they actually understood their actions as modeled after Jesus's life and ministry.[106]

This Klan marched on Washington. They rioted at Notre Dame. They developed their own literature, clothing, institutions, and more. And in D. W. Griffith's film *Birth of a Nation*, the Klan was depicted as the true exemplar of a fighting Christ, a white Jesus who would rescue America from racial degradation.[107] In the film this was illustrated by white actors in blackface pretending to rape white women. This was representational violence authorizing the real violence taking place in the world around it. Less seldom remarked in Klan histories are Georgia governor Clifford Walker's 1924 remarks at the Second Imperial Klonvocation. There, Walker acknowledged that northern European immigration would be acceptable if immigrants committed to becoming "one hundred percent Americans."[108] Against "those Southern Europeans" who never "spoke the language of a democracy," Walker "would build a wall of steel, a wall as high as Heaven."[109]

The Klan reared up again after the 1954 Supreme Court decision in *Brown v. Board of Education* lit a match beneath the cauldron of racial anxiety. No one reading this needs reminding that the Klan has survived into our day. Most famously, Louisiana's David Duke has used conventional politic channels to advocate for the Klan's defense of white American Protestantism. In the 1970s, Duke promised that the Klan would restore America's glory days. He wanted to roll back illegal immigration, and for a time worked to organize a Klan border watch on the Mexican line.[110]

In short, what is old is new in America; it just gets louder and more violent. Our politics is the result of decades of haranguing about "tradition" and "the American dream" rather than what citizenship and the good society substantively require. It is the result of thinking that the politics of economic materialism can or should be meaningfully distinguished from identity politics. It is the result of decades of hucksters and antidemocrats convincing large swaths of the American people that if someone else is allowed to count as part of the "we" in "we the people," our own status will immediately be threatened. And, it must be admitted, the academy plays a role in this, having become so nervous about the genuinely social critical role scholars should play. Thus we are left with a cultural shutdown, and a good portion of the electorate who worried about Trump that "he's not hurting the people he needs to be hurting."[111]

If these Embattlements signal anything, it is the radical instability of the category of "the people" in American life. Despite the inevitability of demographic change, and the obviousness of white backlash to it, Americans are still not doing enough to focus on the actual democracy that is their birthright. Though still invested in the idea of *e pluribus unum*, Americans seem more motivated by the inverse, the idea that they and they alone are the righteous, true Americans. What is at stake is one group's particular freedom—of guns, of shopping, of religion, of maskless faces, and elections where they always win—rather than a shared, general freedom that must accommodate and make concessions and actually impose demands and self-limitation on all citizens. The guns that Americans brandished in the Obama-to-Trump era were meant to protect this fantasy from being intruded on by the actual existence of unruly American manyness.

Americans too often accept that religion is either dangerously volatile or wholly exempt from criticism. The sense of creeping minoritarianism quickly propels Martyrs not just to act like an entitled majority, but to overreach with both rhetorical and real violence. In the years when America's chief birther replaced America's first black POTUS, we learned that some white Americans have a limitless ability to see themselves as the real victims, because Obama made them feel so uncomfortable at having to think about race at all. You could almost hear the thinking: what more do they want? Can the naive hope for an attitudinal shift possibly be enough when the Affordable Care Act was described as an act of "reparations" or when Iowa's Steve King wondered what was wrong with talking about white supremacy?[112]

So if Embattled Americans wage war for the sovereignty of selves untroubled by others, in this chapter we see what is basically a war for the sovereignty of whiteness. Aside from rhetoric and imagery, this took the form of a spike in cross burnings, church burnings, and membership in racist groups.[113] And it was somehow made the fault of the very people who wanted to discuss the dangers of white supremacy. Race was belittled as a card game, and cited as a material antagonism. It was everything and also dismissed as beside the point, just like Obama.[114]

The many citizens who identify structural and institutional racism as precisely the object of such necessary reassessment are correct, but their voices have been shouted down by choruses bemoaning "white genocide" or hostility to American greatness, and thus also by the Whistleblowing, however well intentioned, that takes this particular bait. The immovable certainty of these positions seems to stand absolutely in the way of reassessing citizenship and belonging. And so Embattlement's repertoire of melancholies and angers maintains the very conditions that give them life: a fog of numbed consumption, a shrinking social safety net, a blaring culture that tells us we must live up to an America defined by overcompensating swagger.

The feeling of being overwhelmed, of being unable to escape this America, is also the feeling of proximity to all the other bodies trapped with anxious citizens, who will claw over them to make it, to fight their way to the end of the dystopian movie and then take a selfie next to a statue of Gerald Ford. This is what replaces politics when the state and the law wither from neglect or succumb to outright attack.[115] So people are left to double down on extremism and its costar, the glittering possibility of America™—becoming a star on Instagram or a reality show—both concealing the terror at the heart of America's history. There is the fear of "undeserving" people participating in public life. There is the fear of scarcity and the collapse of the cloud. There is the ontological terror of limits and mortality. And there is, at every moment of American history, a horror-show imagination that produces visions of a fiery end, and displaces charity and goodwill. What should we make of the fact that Americans are largely reconciled to a state that possesses the power to kill in multiple ways but not to that state's power to confer entitlements in the name of birthright?

When Embattlement becomes the marker of citizenship, birthright is converted into the idiom of survival. I am here making observations about a broadly shared condition. Let me be clear, though: I agree that birthers are paranoid, racist, guilty of distorting truth, and uncomfortable with religious pluralism. My argument is not some species of false equivalency or some suggestion that we need to group-hug until we feel the deep economic anxiety of birthers. My point is rather that it is both simplistic and ineffective to presume that either this, or the lambasting of conservative Christianity, is a sufficient response to the conditions that created birtherism. To sling mud back at the slingers, to retweet, endlessly fact-checking and counterlinking, does not persuade anyone; it merely replicates the political condition we lament and avoids our civic and ethical obligations to create a culture less likely to descend into such paranoia and madness.

At least in the short term, the legacy of Obama is inseparable from the burden of weaponized nonfacts and of actual weapons, both dependent on the unhinged imagination in which too many citizens find comfort. For in Trump's America, solid facts—the lifeless bodies of schoolchildren or unarmed citizens, the realities of institutional racism, the norms and laws hourly flouted—have been commuted into things that can be ignored, as if their hold on us were mere fantasy. In turn, the fantasy of revenge against all those "other" Americans who chide right-wingers for their intolerance morphs into the "again" that is central to the MAGA phenomenon, which is a yearning for the erasure of black bodies, women's bodies, Muslim bodies, or the dead who bear the marks of our complicity.

We cannot think this era without thinking of the status of nonwhite bodies, too many black bodies assembled to ignore any longer, because too many black bodies had been filmed being felled by too many guns. And we cannot think those bodies without the fact of guns stockpiled by white people. White "patriots" claimed that they were breaking no laws, but were in fact keeping the streets safer. Confronted with the seeming unreality of their fever visions of UN troops helicoptering into their homes at night, or of "political correctness" finally outlawing Christianity, Oath Keepers and their sympathizers stubbornly insisted that just because it hasn't happened doesn't mean it won't. Who could possibly profess shock, then, at the massive increase in American hate groups since 2016, or at the rise in public violence like the Capitol siege, after years of open carry racism, of hoarding bullets before Obama can tax them, of attempts to intimidate crowds at Black Lives Matter marches, or of a president ordering unidentified troops into American cities to rough up protesters? The links between Oath Keepers, racial violence, and Christian nationalism were on full display in the brutal seventy-seven days following the November 2020 election. Rhodes pleaded with Trump to invoke the Insurrection Act to "stop the steal," and vowed to "resist" Biden's "illegitimate" presidency. Perhaps most telling of the Martyr mindset run rampant was its confirmation that white entitlement and armed lawlessness were part of Action Movie vigilantism.[116] Throughout 2020 and into 2021, Trump's armed, ostensibly Christian supporters pronounced their refusal to "let liberal cities dictate the terms for the rest of the country," or to give in to a "narrow majority trampling on our rights." As fearsome as it all sounded, one militia leader conceded that because of the attention the rallies and protests attracted, "I'm not going to lie to you, man. I feel like a movie star."[117]

In the face of this mad imagination's triumph, which even enabled Trump to wonder whether Oakland, California-born Kamala Harris was a US citizen, the only durable future is one that reckons honestly with our past, which is our historical birthright. But what needs to be acknowledged is that while Trump is truly exceptional in his disregard for laws, norms, and institutions, the fearful times we live in did not drop out of the sky; Trump just turned up the volume on what has been cultivated for at least a half-century: a steady, shrill white noise that drowns out other voices in America. It is much easier to double down on the idea of Embattlement than to admit that Americans still need to rethink certain fundamental realities: like who "the people" are.[118]

While white racists, defined through imaginings of their own heroic resistance, implicitly acknowledge the erosion of their historic privilege, now there are also skyrocketing numbers of African American gun owners and gun clubs.[119] For all that Richard Spencer or Stephen Miller might wish otherwise, for all the fearsomeness of alt-righters in the streets, for all the pieties about "our way of life" and the whiteness of its religion, ours is a time of things refusing to conceal themselves, to be swept under nostalgia's rug. It is still possible that Americans might make it through this bleak time with an increased readiness to listen and practice a different politics, rather than indulge in carnival and braggadocio and self-serving fantasies of white Embattlement. But if privileged Americans keep drowning out the voices of those who actually, materially suffer, new noise will get louder too.

In the end, what we learn from Obama Embattlement is that Americans are both too certain about what true religion and true freedom are, and insufficiently comfortable with uncertainty. If the Long Con of anti-politics doesn't get reversed, and if we cannot rekindle a spirit of civic investment for a post-Trump era (in order to address the authoritarian energies that are growing so openly), then Americans will remain trapped in the holding pattern of Embattlement. The problem isn't that talking meaningfully about race distracts us from class (as if there is no black or Latinx working class). Rather, treating conversations about birthright as only xenophobic in their implication robs us of an opportunity to reassess just what American citizens are entitled to in this time of shrinking resources.

We need to change the subject. Obviously anyone who voted for Trump, despite the vigor with which they deny the implications, was at the very least comfortable voting for someone who supported white supremacy in word and deed. But instead of focusing on declining whiteness as if that were the only thing, let us actually think about what Americans are owed as a matter of citizenship and membership in the human family. We need to reclaim and reframe the notion of entitlement, and once again think aspirationally about building the good society. This is a richer, more collective vector of dreaming than the toxic stew I have been describing. If the expectation of substantive, material progress is one component of an American's birthright, how might we achieve it?

# 10
# How to Be an American

## An Address to Citizens

> Jollity and gloom were contending for an empire.
> —Nathaniel Hawthorne

America is free and everywhere in chains. We are chained to our very American dreams. The dream of progress. The dream of making it. Dreams whose unreality has increasingly allowed strange impulses to move to the center of our America. The mad-eyed, demon-haunted, doom-saying violence that's been there all along has wended its way into every crack in every foundation. We fight. We prep. We tweet. We march. And little changes except the density, velocity, and storm of our self-imagining, ever hotter and fiercer.

It seems like it will never end. Not the country. That might end sometime, and, indeed, imaginings of that possibility have proven an attractive medium through which Americans conceive of their importance. But what seems so endless is America's ability to overwhelm itself, to drown in the sheer too-muchness of inherited stories, which move with flickering speed and weigh down simultaneously, all of it making for an immensity that cannot power down or be unseen. And because it seems so impossible to change the structure and the context of our politics, many Americans have turned to outrage.

But don't forget to smile, everyone; you're Americans and you are on camera. You live in a country that can barely begin a sporting season without a Blue Angels flyover. A country with a surfeit of porn and gambling, and a moralism to match. A country that is a burden, a brand, a myth, and a weapon. These last years have prompted me to wonder if it—and we—can be anything else. If there is a path ahead, it starts with a question: how did we learn to be an America like this? A boilerplate response might be simply that we have failed to renew our commitment to the languages (if not the practices) of pluralism and tolerance. After all, the invocation of such civic pieties has proved a sturdily reliable way of assuring ever-anxious Americans that new groups of people are not to be feared. The political arrangements and norms that have historically framed the commitment to pluralism have been piecemeal and regularly contested. But behind America's public self-regard is a nearly unwavering assumption that religious liberty is at the core of a durable American identity.

We tell ourselves that religion is a constitutionally privileged index of identity, whose importance is manifested in public ritual and private conviction, and whose protected status is visible in the long history of denominational creativity that has marked American history since its beginnings. We are told to appreciate a uniquely accommodationist "American way of life" that allows maximal personal (though possibly not communal) freedom, and welcomes under its capacious canopy any tradition that can abide by the rule of law and a code of public conduct rooted in what is avowed to be mutual respect. In other words, what it means to be an American is, fundamentally, to accept a series of stories, all of which, we are told, dovetail with an inevitable pluralist epic. But what we actually hear and experience of religion are its outrages: fervid anxieties among different groups of citizens, each of them trumpeting their defense of an "authentic" or "real" American religion against the depredations or oppressions of their fellow citizens, who have it in for the good guys.

I have written this book not to assail the wrong religion of the Martyrs or the inadequate religion of the Whistleblowers, but because I regard the entire conversation about Embattlement as a distraction that has undermined what politics requires in this moment of democracy's crisis. We have mistaken echoes for authenticity. We have misconstrued the meaning of political representation. We have confused cosplay with civic activism. We have made a caricature of history's complex textures. We have used the law to shield ourselves from the responsibilities of citizenship. And we have allowed the categories of entitlement and birthright to be perverted in the service of conspiracy theory. No citizen is off the hook for what has happened.

What we learn from the preceding episodes of Embattlement is that what we call "politics" in America is often simply the name we give to the intoxicating atmosphere of our own unshakable feeling. America today is filled with privileged people documenting their anger, the point-and-click jeremiads replicating endlessly to create the swirling atmosphere that is the new normal, with religion both vehicle and substance of an endless furor. How does any of this help us get through this dangerous moment in American democracy, which is the product of a half-century of Embattlement's ascendancy?

We need a wholesale reconceptualization of American democracy, but our largest and most volatile habits of talking about religion are getting in the way. Religions are not inherently antagonistic to social order, though many assume that religious liberty allows them to prioritize particular religious ends instead of shared public ones. Religions are also not inherently benevolent regarding pluralism, with discrimination or violence mere exceptions. What is most notable in Embattled America, though, is how religion has come to weaken consensus around shared conceptions of law, political order, and citizenship. Coupled with acute anxiety about the future, fragility has become the baseline experiences of our America. These are products of the Long Con.

## Failure and the Long Con

One reason our politics has failed is because of the way rights-talk and demands for recognition are wielded by Embattled Americans. Behind claims that one is persecuted, or is the object of bigotry, is the idea that politics must be grounded in respect. This, we assume unconsciously, is how pluralism and tolerance work. But our political unconscious assumes that our rights exist not only as abstract capacities, but as bulwarks against the inevitable conflict between citizens with competing claims on public life. When conflict overwhelms the system, as it has in Embattled America, we learn that it is difficult to achieve abstract freedom when citizens refuse to reconcile themselves with institutions, principles, and languages that require trade-offs and compromises. The Trump insurrection was, thus, somehow unsurprising.

The feeling that we are part of an Embattled Majority consoles us with the sense that we are all stars in our own Action Movie, that our ordinariness is mere prelude to some glorious overcoming, that the din of the polis might evolve into our very own theme music. This was a feeling Americans leaned into after the 1960s, hoping it would sustain us in a time of shrinking public resources and uncertain futures. Now, after decades of attacks on politics and government, too many Americans have been convinced that indignation itself is enough for an identity and that public life is about prevailing in blood sport.

Psychologically this works to justify systemic disparities in power: we want to make it out of the struggle rather than change the conditions producing it.[1] Since we've already decided that a meaningful life is an Action Movie, simply to assert that a villain opposes us means we're on the right path. This is only possible in an America whose politics have been severed from arguments and evidence in favor of claims that are justified by the intensity of their convictions. Spectacle, especially involving "wrong religion" or a "war" on faith, injects the mundane with a bit of elan and the enthusiasms of historical significance at just those points where we suspect how trivial we are.

But Embattlement is also the product of actual horrors lived by other human beings whose labor creates the comforts the Embattled deny they possess. For it is not the poor in their millions who are performing their aggrievement in this way, nor the victims of the police state. As long as American politics is trapped in the spin cycle of Embattlement claims, not only do we deflect our attention from the failures of our political system; in so doing we also turn away from the real pain of others, committing suicide because there are no jobs, or working in dehumanizing conditions to make shoes in Sri Lanka, or simply struggling for recognition in a country whose narratives do not match the reality.

With this in mind, and in order to frame my proposals for reform, let me return to some of the historical developments that have shaped Embattled America. As historian Scott Sandage notes, economic precarity and unequal access to public institutions are fundamental to American self-imaginings, from Henry Ward Beecher and Henry Hill to the Gilded Age.[2] As they did for these historical figures, contemporary premonitions of a dire future lead to the conviction that only personal overcoming will save us. This preserves the habit of thinking of one another as competitors rather than allies in remaking the political. Embattlement is thus unthinkable without the unconscious assumption that we are all winners, stars in the most triumphal Action Movie. In this, Embattlement doesn't just pick up on the anxiousness at the heart of the system; it sustains a presumption about persons and institutions that requires this anxiousness: Embattlement reveals our collective investment in the idea that democracy's problems can be addressed through the right kind of emotional experience.

It is important to understand that this is a condition of remainders: this is what is left of politics after decades of coordinated assault on popular power and egalitarianism. For all the racism that was coded into New Deal programs, one could reasonably celebrate the New Deal's nationalization of social welfare that, by means of a robust and growing state, ensured the distribution of social liberties.³ The mid-twentieth-century critique of statism was not merely an expression of concern about communism, as conservatives often held; it was also a clear effort to contest the expansion of liberties under the New Deal as an intrusion on the actual guarantor of social freedom, which neoconservative thinkers like Friedrich Hayek, Ludwig von Mises, and Leo Strauss located in the market. Their descendant Milton Friedman defined the terms of this freedom as wealth generation for investors, market deregulation, and trickle-down effects that would help all boats rise on a phantom tide that citizens are still waiting for.

Think tanks and law schools and politicians without number assured us that this dream was the perfect realization of the America™ that the Framers intended. The very idea that the market might be limited in the name of social goods was a plot to rob someone of their opportunity for an Awesome Journey. The triumph of this vision is seen in the therapeutic neoliberalism that feels your pain, sending you thoughts and prayers, having already resigned itself to the negation of government's moral responsibility for citizens. So the rage of Embattled America is a sublimated acknowledgment of our decline, our optimism inverted. To be all in on this lonely future requires a magnification of other explanatory forces, like Embattled Religion.

Religion thus becomes central to the triumph of a neoliberal order defined by the removal of barriers to trade.⁴ The Long Con is the product of corporate (usually conservative) elites protecting their interests by convincing Americans that politics and policy do not matter. This order defines itself in possessive individualism (occasionally grafted onto communitarian rhetoric). Privatization is now taken for granted as the sine qua non of social relations. This receives its most obvious expression in antigovernment platforms seeking to trade off the social safety net for tax cuts; it is also a key register of the emotional politics circulating in America. Structurally, as David Harvey notes, neoliberalism's priorities breed the "anarchy of the market" and "unbridled individualism" that make things "increasingly ungovernable."⁵ This notion of the private is what hardwires us to engage fellow citizens with suspicion, primed to accuse them of crashing our boundaries through offense and affront. The avatar of this condition is not so much the self-governing citizen as the troll who jams up your Twitter feed.

Neoliberalism is not only the institutional face of the Long Con's antipolitics, but also the atmosphere preventing us from seeing what is behind Embattlement. In a time of weakening commitment to democracy around the globe, the combination of alienation, irrationality, and declining confidence in future prosperity have pressed many citizens to seek power at the expense of others.[6] It is easy to see how this orientation to social life, which resonates deeply with the all-American social atomism of "Don't Tread on Me," becomes mistaken for political and religious freedom. For Whistleblowers, religion is an impediment to social freedom while for Martyrs it has been circumscribed by unfairly erected barriers. In neither case do the Embattled locate a language that helps us think beyond this shrunken political horizon, and in continuing to obsess over religious acrimony we allow ourselves to be managed in the way neoliberalism requires.

So turn that frown upside down, America. We now share space in a giant self-help lesson masquerading as a culture. The imperative to be efficient, to be positive, to happily find a seat on the wreck: the impossibility and unreality of it all is felt in the outrage that wells up when America doesn't resemble the smile we are told to wear.[7] We know that the boundless possibility of the American dreamscape does not exist. We pursue self-creation at the expense of the commons, and blame those who question our own dreams. In this way we produce a politics of ephemera, precisely because politics itself is so ephemeral now: an emotional medium rather than an arena of achievable change.

It is no surprise, then, that America's madhouse decades have incubated such profound corruption and attacks on the legitimacy of our institutions. Indeed, Watergate, the Iran-Contra scandal, the attacks on civil liberties following September 11, 2001, the protection of corporate "free speech" by *Citizens United*, the militarization of public space, and the ongoing assault on voting rights have all helped weaken Americans' confidence in politics. If we do not understand the appeal of passion, conviction, and ferocity in the face of all this, we will not be able to unseat the dark romanticism at Embattlement's heart. As Trump himself put it at a March 28, 2019, rally in Grand Rapids, Michigan, "We want us and that's what we got."[8]

But this is not the only way to be an American. If we accept that we're not special by virtue of our Embattlement, we might be forced to think freshly about who we are in relation to each other and what we might accomplish together in an entirely different kind of movie. We need to imagine that the political community to which we all actually belong is also a moral community, wherein the suffering of our fellow citizens must trouble us to action. With Trump and his scorched-earth petulance, we have all been forced to live squarely inside the narrative of Embattlement: a white male conservative victimhood that wants revenge. We must now decide with whom we stand. None of us has the luxury any longer of imagining we have no complicity in where we are. If we are to remake American democracy, we must kill the narrative of Embattlement rather than each other.[9]

It is past time. Are you not also sick of being presented with an America chiefly recognizable for its flag-wrapped brokenness? The scale of our problems has left people of goodwill clueless as to how to begin making a difference, or even to have their voices heard. Too many voices have told us that differences of opinion are differences of ontology, and that we don't need to think about them so much as stamp them out. This is politics as a first-person shooter game. Embattlement invokes the moral authority to silence other perspectives without being held accountable to the idea of independent moral authority as such.[10] Which means that Embattlement is, finally, a sign that anti-politics has won.

I have written this book with the hope of signaling that this victory is not permanent. It is in this spirit that I turn, in the pages remaining, to the very democratic culture and processes that Embattlement evades. My thoughts are framed by the insistence that religious rights do not exempt citizens from criticism when their vision of political life is insufficiently egalitarian, appropriately calibrated to democratic culture, and accountable to the rule of law. For what is politically and civically serious about America's political religions is ill served by the politics of Embattlement too frequently associated *with* these religions. To say that it is serious means that it can be criticized, not on the basis of theological conviction or any hazy sincerity but as a mode of political speech that is subject to the standards and expectations of political speech and practice common to all who enter public life. The challenges of our situation require that we admit some claims simply do not pass as legitimate in public life. A requirement to participate in a diversity workshop is not Stalinism. Medicaid is not comparable to slavery. Talking about racism is not a form of racism. The principles we claim to share, in other words, also come with implied practices of reasonability that ought to weaken splenetic claims like these. If such claims are found unconvincing on their face, those making them cannot reasonably protest that religion has been prevented from being heard.

The challenges American democracy faces can be met by both the religious and the nonreligious in the name of good policy and sound principle. Instead of construing politics as an arena of conquest, doubt and fragility can be converted into opportunities to collaborate rather than states to be avoided. After all, it is the absolute certitude of the Embattled that scorns information or dialogue in favor of dunking over fellow citizens. Embattled America imagines that individual rights—bearing arms or the free exercise of religion, for example—exist in isolation from others. This is no more convincing than the idea that we exist in isolation from other people. We are actively harming ourselves by claiming that we are harmed by the viewpoints, even the mere existence of, our fellow humans. As George Orwell wrote in 1946, "If thought corrupts language, language can also corrupt thought."[11] Let us think and speak differently so as to imagine different social outcomes.

If we are to address the conditions of Embattlement, something like a complete institutional overhaul is necessary. If democracy is to thrive, it is necessary to get dark money out of politics, overturn *Citizens United*, establish institutions connecting citizens and the political class, and begin the generational marathon of re-envisioning education and citizenship. For now, there are some things we can do in the name of persuading ourselves and our fellow citizens to abandon the comforts of hermetically sealed identity in favor of democratic openness, with all its uncertainty. Political principles must be rearticulated so as to make clearer their grounding in human, not only political, rights. For without such clarity, it is too easily for powerful voices to justify their discrimination against the marginalized in the name of exercising an abstract, isolated political right.

In earlier chapters I have partly spelled out my vision for reforming democracy by attending to the fault lines in categories like representation or authenticity. Below I flesh out further the features of a reimagined American politics, not to deny the humanity or the citizenship of Embattled Americans but to starve their discourse of oxygen. To change the condition that angers them in order to focus on broader maladies is not to give up, but to propose a different way of doing citizenship. Instead of gnashing our teeth about whether religions will form the basis of public identities (they will and they won't, as ever) or whether religious language and display will be a part of the political (they will and they won't, as ever), the best way we can defuel the politics of Embattled religion is to treat religion seriously by not treating it specially.

## Check Yourself

I propose four interlocking areas where we can reasonably shore up our relationship to democracy. This is the logical next step after this book's argument that in focusing on religion's inflammatory and/or sacrosanct status in public life we misdiagnose America's ills. There are good religious reasons for supporting this observation. There are also abundant roles for religious actors and communities in any functioning democracy. The key, however, is to reestablish the priority of democracy itself. Doing so will also reframe how Americans think about, and what we expect from, public religions.

In what follows, you might disagree with the way I frame my proposals, their content, or even the specifics of my recommendations. The scale of the problems revealed by Embattlement, however, positively demands us to think concretely about reforming democracy, and resist the impulse to produce yet another lament for America's unstable pluralism; to focus generically on pluralism or constitutionalism keeps things high above the gritty terrain of real political work.

As a practical, and not just a scholarly matter, I think that citizens who—like me—feel overwhelmed by and disconnected from the gargantuan mess of American politics must begin with a focus on ourselves. There are abundant resources for thinking about conceptual and personal self-inventory in American history, traditions ready-to-hand but in many ways forgotten. These are not the tools of self-help, prayer, or mindfulness meditation, though I derogate none of these. I think, rather, of the expressive, critical tradition connecting figures as diverse as W. E. B. Du Bois, Ralph Waldo Emerson, Reinhold Niebuhr, and John Rawls. What connects these figures is neither idiom, subject matter, nor method, but an insistence that criticism in the name of social justice be tethered to individuals' ability to see beyond self-interest. Americans do not necessarily need to read these authors' books (although it would help) nor become public intellectuals themselves, of course. But the necessary procedural and institutional reforms facing Americans cannot be accomplished without individuals overhauling their sense of their own citizenship and their orientation to others.

I have made it clear that I think the vast majority of the policy positions advocated by Martyrs are insufficiently inclusive to work in a democracy. The work ahead of us, though, will not be accomplished by scolding evangelicals when they fail to support LGBTQ Americans, nor by mocking Wallbuilders for some of their more outlandish redescriptions of history. I am also not proposing another condescending, and ultimately trivial, call for "civility" in the face of "tribalism." Rather, the work of reconceptualizing American democracy begins with the willingness to practice self-limitation when faced with the temptations of maximizing our own interests. No stable public life can exist without individuals feeling they will benefit to at least some degree; this is basic psychology. But these benefits cannot be realized through the practices and concepts of possessive individualism, especially those that turn on ontological claims that are restrictive.

In order to end the harm to other persons that is the actual, material product of particular worldviews, it is strategically and morally superior to engage those who disagree with us not as candidates for the Darwin award or as ineligible for the same rights we claim for ourselves, but only as fellow citizens in the public arena. American attitudes about free speech are muddled at best; and at worst, a tendency to tolerate viewpoints in the abstract has given comfort to antidemocratic tendencies now on obvious display. Citizens must develop the habit of questioning the integrity of their political convictions relative to standards of human rights and democratic norms. Any hope for a reasonable democratic future depends on this. There are compelling ethical and civic reasons to ask, even if we are neither Whistleblower nor Martyr, whether we have contributed to an America where Embattlement thrives. Have we indulged in the kinds of caricature and stereotyping that sustain it? Are we consuming inflammatory Whistleblowing media or spooning up Martyr indignation?

Habits of thought that perpetuate dualisms or reject the common bonds of citizenship will never be able to overcome the distance between good policy and bad. These habits are also too lazy to recognize nuance. What is more, they effectively give up on our fellow citizens, absolving us of the need to change anything about ourselves and also of the difficult work of persuasion. Shifting to suasion and reasonability is no easy task, and certainly nothing that can be accomplished by lone individuals. Suspicions about truthfulness did not begin with Twitter, and they will not be diminished easily. But if we still lack confidence in reason's ability to disclose a mutual standpoint more convincing than everyone's customizable "truth," it may be more fruitful to think about institutionalizing practices and techniques whereby different citizens can come together in good-faith efforts to enact provisional forms of reason and consensus.

Such efforts don't require a conception of truth and reason as independent of time and history. Reason doesn't require such critical distance and monastic reflection; it can be achieved through public agency and deliberation. The sovereignty of conscience and opinion in a talking democracy has always depended on some sort of consensus regarding the real. Because the Whirl has fragmented and undermined such consensus, there has been a loss of confidence in collaboration. This is partly what accounts for Americans' highly divergent uses of the languages of liberal constitutionalism. While we want to confine the worldviews of others to the private sphere, we demand full public expression of our own. Even such obviously selective use of foundational liberal notions as the autonomy of spheres keeps alive the idea that "religion" is a thing independent of other rights, identities, or social responsibilities, and thus endlessly able to assuage or to vex our feelings. This condition also preserves the false assumption that politics must not ask much of us, lest it undermine the self's triumph, to which we feel entitled, whose narrative destiny is America's, written as possibility into each heart's democratic vistas, which are now built from the Whirl's accretions of information.

Without concerted efforts to change, citizens will be left with a default social position of, at best, mere "tolerance," which political theorist Wendy Brown sharply describes as "a breeding ground for . . . resentments."[12] The spectacles of Embattled Religion are moments where revulsions and resentments are transferred both consciously and unconsciously onto those whom we are told to tolerate. In allowing for these habits of thought, religion has become a ubiquitous subject of outrage at the expense of politics itself, which we overlook in our anger at our others. With self-interrogation we might learn to discipline ourselves to regard our own identities, our very selves, as nonstatic and nonessential. We are open and porous, from the molecular level to the social. Failure to acknowledge this is one reason for our furious anxiety to maintain our own boundaries.

This perspective harmonizes with multiple religious norms and with most readings of universal human rights.[13] Seeing rights as interdependent, rather than exclusive (for that, at least, is how many citizens have construed their rights unconsciously) yields a far more generous social ethic. I don't think American citizens should abandon the idea that they belong to a liberal constitutional polity; but the attitude that negative liberty means immunity from the views, experiences, and practices of other citizens is unsustainable.

Any reasonable citizen's scrutiny of their own commitments to democratic norms and practices should result in the conviction that we must prioritize the demands of injury grounded in material harm over the attitudinal discomfort of the privileged. Our self-interrogation ought to yield a sense of selfhood and citizenship that does not construe democracy's failures as primarily failures of respect and intolerance, as if these did not require action or institutionalization. Framing religion as deserving of protections—without attention to competing considerations—not only preserves such insulated attitudinal politics, but does so by harmonizing with the notion that if "tolerance" exists and "intolerance" does not, we needn't be troubled overmuch by things like "equality" and "justice."

The idea that the problems of American injustice are interiorized, as if housing discrimination or glass ceilings don't exist because no one really *feels* like a bigot, is part of the same strategy as avoiding self-limitation or self-sacrifice. Embattled Religion is the mirror of the ambition to achieve personal glory, making it all the way to a gated community heaven with Google Fiber; but this ambition ensures our failure, because it does not question the conformity necessary for making it on the system's terms. Embattlement is thus complicit in the actual injustice that is everywhere in America.

I am well aware that democratic structural change will not occur just because un-Embattled citizens commit to reflection and reassessment. Such altered thinking is, however, a meaningful part of a broader remaking of American democracy. It requires of us one additional responsibility: we must be willing not only to examine ourselves but to educate ourselves about our fellow citizens and about America itself. For the norms of American democracy depend not only on freedom from harm but on realizing the fundamental dignity and respect owed to others. If, for example, a Whistleblower believes that a Martyr is supporting the wrong kind of educational policy, nothing is achieved by mocking fundamentalism or assuming that Martyrs are ignorant yokels. Treat political speech as political speech, which is subject to the norms attending thereto. At the same time, do not assume that Martyrs' narrow definition of religion is all there is. Citizens should investigate multiple viewpoints, must take care with their presuppositions and distinctions, must avoid exaggeration and overgeneralization, and must above all avoid the pitfalls of media feedback loops that confirm rather than challenge.

None of this happens magically, nor is it guaranteed to make Embattlement less attractive. But it does suggest just how much work there is to do, including a generations-long effort to produce different kinds of citizens through different modes of civic education. A world without ambiguity is a comfortable one. But it is also a fantasy. There is some good in being able to imagine ourselves inhabiting something other than permanent certainty at the expense of others, of situating ourselves in a space where we cannot resolve things with any finality and cannot win politics. The chief implication of this perspective is that it leaves us with obligations to solidarity and human rights. These can be realized, initially, in our communities.

## Communities of Difference

If responsible self-interrogation presumes a kind of civic education, common investment in institutions and habits, and dialogic ground rules that are currently absent in American politics, where does all of this get housed? Clearly the triumph of Embattlement reveals the impoverishment of American conceptions of community. I raise this point not because I find value in old-school communitarian nostalgia. Nor do I pretend to have any rigorous policy ideas about how to reverse the generational inattention to systematically disenfranchised communities of color in America, although this is clearly essential.

Instead, I would want Americans to focus on the interrelationship of legislation, institutional reform, and grassroots citizenship, as a way of making the appeal of democratic civil society stronger than the appeal of righteous Embattlement. The broad questions that should shape our communities are related to justice and equality. There is no a priori consensus on just what justice and equality actually mean, of course. But community should be grounded in the conviction that protesting that one's culture is Embattled—by the very existence of Muslims, or by the acknowledgment of trans rights, for example—can never justify constraining the opportunities and fair treatment of other citizens who simply live differently.

It is also in community that citizens can help promote the sort of civic education mentioned above. While we clearly are in need (nationally) of richer and more effective public education, civic groups like Black Lives Matter and Indivisible provide a model for organizing and educating in the name of more inclusive publics. Communities should look to partnerships with local school boards and universities to create civic forums for conversation around religion and the public good. Public space is available, even if public monies increasingly aren't. But community is an effective space for harnessing the energies of social media for something like the educational equivalent of a flash mob or a pop-up restaurant, spontaneous, temporary publics of the sort that have been occurring elsewhere in American life. There is no guarantee, of course, that a convergence of actual American humans will be free from the outlandish ideas one encounters in the kingdom of the Embattled: the vitriol, stereotype, and scorn that have become the norm. But it is in face-to-face encounter that we can enact the basic civic skills of intersubjectivity that I continue to believe can undermine the lure of Embattlement.

If one key dimension of the problems of democracy is scale, shifting emphasis to the local can conduct energy into public life while also overcoming the distance between citizens, even if slowly and imperfectly. One of the many obstacles impeding participation is the sheer lack of confidence that our public life can effectively safeguard values like solidarity and respect. It is in revived communities that citizens can deliberate freely and openly about the substance of these values, and how to transform institutional life in ways that better reflect them collectively. School boards and city councils and neighborhood alliances matter; through them groups of citizens can contest injustice and can shift the emphasis of public discourse through redescription. Redescription is also a practice, something that can happen through the force of bodies in streets; it creates rupture and renewed opportunity for clarity about the ground rules for public language and action, what common investment in institutions requires, and what habits civic education should inculcate.

Of course people disagree about what meaningful debate is, and about how shared rationality and respect are defined. But the point is to try, in however piecemeal a fashion, to move to a space where *that* is the conversation we are having: trying to figure out what rational debate requires rather than who gets to win the game of Embattlement. This requires work on multiple scales, from neighborhood to state to nation, in thinking about how best to normalize and institutionalize such conversations. The fact is that citizens already do this kind of thing, but they are disconnected in ways that favor the powerful forces who for decades have poisoned the political well. More spontaneous civic initiatives, brave enough to reach across communities and invite the other into your midst, might go a very long way in beginning these necessary conversations. This in turn might establish bonds of solidarity and identity between citizens. The Whirl has in many ways contributed to feelings of isolation among citizens, but it might also be a vehicle for change; the amplification of different messages could play a substantive role in persuading publics of the legitimacy of policies geared toward justice and fairness. If we are to reduce distortions in truth and power, then some sort of common world must be posited. The great political struggle going forward will likely not be between conventional ideologies but between disinformation and shared knowledge. With this in mind, the work of community is ever more crucial, as it is here that citizens might reflect on what it means to occupy space and institutions with other people, and how this relationship might be leveraged against authoritarianism.[14]

Communities can also help clarify distinctions between real and imagined persecution. For, let us be clear: feeling uneasy around those who are different is in no way morally or materially equivalent to being isolated from public life, scorned or harassed, or even legally barred for one's religious identification (or any other feature of one's identity, for that matter); if one's religious identification is rooted in opposition to another social group, the rule of law exists to curtail the harmful speech and action that such perspectives too often produce. The work of dialogue can militate against conceptual discrimination, while the law works elsewhere. We have implied duties to others when we enter the spheres of public life, whether education, the state house, or the market. Let us honor them.

Religious communities themselves will be vital in this work of overcoming Embattlement. This turns on the willingness of citizens and the coreligious to engage in introspection about the necessary trade-offs and accommodations required of membership in any society, especially one that claims to value equality of opportunity and religious liberty. Religious traditions are complex historically, textually, and sociologically, it goes without saying. But since the most powerful justifications for political life often come from sacred texts and authorities within religious communities, religious citizens might more responsibly investigate those aspects of tradition that respond to the challenges of contemporary American life, rather than privileging those that militate against it. What I mean here is not that communitarian groups must be forcibly integrated into public institutions but that traditions consider investigating more reflectively those aspects of their genealogies—individuals, scriptures, social experiments—that exemplify inclusivity, generosity toward the other or the neighbor (the violation of which was the chief sin of Sodom, after all), and points of convergence among different civic and religious orientations.

There are many civic groups already engaged in this work. It is vital for communities to find resources—not just financial but social—to promote them, amplifying their voices so as to contrast with the Embattled. I do not naively believe that every hypothetical conversation between a narrow-minded theophobe and a conservative evangelical around, say, fair immigration policies will proceed amicably. But avoiding these conversations leaves things mired in current conditions. So challenge the Whistleblower to accept the vitality of religious groups that promote the ethic of Jesus embracing the migrant and the outcast. Challenge the Martyr to accept that criticizing the Trump administration's antidemocratic policies did not amount to an attack on Christianity. Religion either does or does not advance policies that are prodemocratic and egalitarian; it cannot supersede them. To say this is simply to acknowledge that if religions participate in public life, they will necessarily be evaluated according to broadly shared standards of speech and suasion that may ultimately find them wanting. If religious communities think they can successfully argue against equal treatment for homosexuals on nonreligious grounds, they may try; I have confidence they will fail.

In our communities, we citizens can work together to explain and demonstrate that proximity and sharing do not amount to threat. We can hopefully build and sustain the kinds of institutions that make joint projects and shared social goods more appealing than triumphalism. These efforts will not always work. They will not reach everyone. But it is vital that Americans strive in these directions so that the imagery of Embattlement weakens.

Whistleblowers must abandon their hesitancy around the religious. While many rightly criticized the George W. Bush administration's endeavors to award faith-based initiatives funding (largely on the grounds that these tended to favor one set of Christians, and often did not promote widely shared interests), there is a role for local and state agencies cooperating with religious communities, and for encouraging interreligious and religious/nonreligious solidarity. What is more, it is not only the state that should recognize good civic initiatives that happen to come from religious communities (provided, importantly, that no social rights are infringed on in these efforts); religious communities serious about participation in public life must also reconcile with statism. Too often, conservative antistatism has drowned out other religious voices. These other voices must be vocal in their support for the shared norms of law, human solidarity, and social justice.

The outcomes of civic debate will never look exactly like any of our communities alone, nor should they. Communities must honestly accept that this does not make them Embattled. If communities can recognize some fair portion of themselves in particular norms and policies, that must be enough. Religious and nonreligious communities should be invested not in one-upping each other in the machismo of suffering but in promoting the idea that it is social justice that provides the surest foundation for a thriving democracy (and which also realizes diverse religious ends).

More democracy, in other words, is the answer to the problems of democracy. We are quite simply wasting our time in talking about Embattled Religion. When "trolling the libs" has become the substance of a major political party, it is irresponsible to take the bait. As I write this in the early months of the Biden presidency, it should be noted that the return of establishment politics in no way obscures how very much work is left to be done. I have no confidence that QAnon and Oath Keepers possess an appropriate degree of shame such that merely exposing them will turn the tide of this toxic conversation, nor do I expect much from the vast majority of the Republican Party bent on exploiting these energies. Thus, precisely because that is not enough, other citizens must redirect focus to the long project of institutional and cultural change on behalf of democracy itself.

Our efforts should be invested in creating a flexible, open-ended politics of radical democracy—one that ensures fairness, and demands mutual responsibility and accountability from citizens and elected officials alike—that addresses the issues Embattlement only conceals. Citizens and communities have a moral and civic responsibility to accept one of the fundamental truths of democracy: that our self-interest can only ever partly be realized in a form of governance designed for the dispersal rather than the concentration of power, and that is designed to be ongoing and revisable, not static. The trick is not to rid ourselves of difference, as the Embattled might have it, but to live peacefully and creatively with it.

## "Real" America?

One of the most powerful components of the Long Con is the disconnectedness from politics that is the baseline experience of most Americans. In a country of this scale and complexity, with its myriad and overlaid discrepancies of power, not to mention its truly archaic political architecture, it is awfully hard to feel that one matters. The electoral college, court-packing, corporate lobbying as protected free speech, and nakedly partisan gerrymandering all contribute to the sense that our efforts and the intensity of our convictions cannot match the half-century success of conservatives in gaming the system, which continues with brazen assaults on voting rights. While leftists continue to have the same old conversations about whether identity politics and materialist policies can coexist, the Right has been successfully changing the rules to benefit themselves. Nonetheless, mobilization at the first two levels could in time produce the numbers necessary to de-rig institutions and policies nationally. This is far more urgent a focus than arguing with Martyrs about the latest red herring. So if we want to shore up the conditions enabling authentic representative democracy, we have to attend to the gaps in law and social justice extant at the national level, too.

Nationally, America would benefit from the same kind of values-assessment that I proposed for individual citizens. The rise of the new authoritarianism is one clear sign that democratic values are wobbly on our planet.[15] Trump's presidency was built on a national identity that is transparently hostile to a wide range of political, religious, and sexual orientations. It would be false to call such an identity ahistorical, because American history quite simply is the history of white supremacy, patriarchy, and political repression (though other tendencies, happily, have also existed). So how can we get past this?

As with the self-inventory of religious traditions and local communities, America at the broadest level of imagination and history has multiple options to choose from for its self-image. There is the rabid racism connecting Andrew Jackson to the alt-right. There is America the war machine, which has only seldom not been involved in a serious military venture. There is America the greedy, home of the multinational corporation and the tycoon. These Americas converge in principle and purpose. But there is another America. It is not simply an America of the Left, but rather an America of expansive inclusivity, transformative art, shared purpose, and the continual ambition to live up to ideals to which we often give lip service but imperfectly institutionalize.

Embattlement thrives in part because of the power of Martyrs and Whistleblowers to generalize about each other, and to assume that there is something called a "real America" that looks just like them. Bellicosity and exclusivism provide comforts for citizens who are so thoroughly frozen out of the process. Yet it is precisely when we turn on each other, reducing the stakes of national life to oppositional imagery, that we are so easily manipulable. After all, it is likely that Embattlement would not have grown so powerful without the fraying of the social safety net, the rise of corporatism in public life (and not just electoral politics), social media, and deeply rooted alienation. Reclaiming citizen power depends on escaping these conditions. This requires understanding that the powerful benefit from them.

This will not happen simply because we wish it. Too often, Americans' self-understandings consist only of language and symbolism promoting how glorious America is. Leaving aside how that rhetoric plays internationally, and what it has given comfort to, America is defined by a national self-image that sanctifies the market, demonizes statism, and promotes showy patriotism above authentic collective community. It is, in many ways, a colossal burden being an American. We are taught in so many ways that patriotism requires ignorance, and to ask tough questions, to stare down honestly the awful bloody past, or to point out structural inequality, is somehow to be undermining America.

Yet the kind of principled critique that is thus discouraged reflects precisely that abstract commitment to national self-improvement which many Americans learned in civics class. It is a collective commitment to the fullest realization of the norms and aspirations we claim to cherish.[16] Law and policy are absolutely vital, ranging from enhanced voting rights to the realization of full human rights in our society, attending especially to the "least of these," ranging from people of color to immigrants to trans Americans, from the marginalized to America's many forgotten communities. Only when us and them are no longer divided by the zip codes' school budgets, by access to basic social goods, by obviously discrepant life opportunities, and by inclusion in the political process can we speak meaningfully of equal opportunity and the pursuit of happiness. Being told to lift yourself up by your bootstraps is cruel advice if the rest of you is pinned down.

The state's material provisions play an additional role. It is my conviction that raising the social floor much higher and distributing basic social goods (among which I include fair housing, robust healthcare, family leave, equal opportunity for work, and free public education through university) more broadly will play an important role in settling some of the anxiety that neoliberalism arouses in citizens. While such robust distribution will not of itself make it more difficult for Americans to profess their Embattlement (the white privilege characterizing both Martyrs and Whistleblowers has not given them pause), changing the structure and the tone of the culture will help winnow energy from these discourses over time. In this, it will be crucial to combat disinformation on the national level, beginning with congressional hearings, stricter social media policy, and establishing a federal agency to function as the Fairness Doctrine once did.

Law and policy are not free, of course. If we are to get past this toxic condition of Embattlement and reach a place where America can actually start to do democracy properly, many trillions of dollars will be necessary. The money is there; we have simply been taught to accept that it can rightly go to tax breaks for the rich and to the war machine rather than to the poor and the outcast. Indeed, the triumph of the market has led to such a thoroughly possessive approach to public life and resources that it is all but impossible to think these structural alternatives. It is common to observe, with Michael Sandel, that citizenship itself has been framed in the idiom of consumer choice.[17] It is even more obvious that many investments in the public good are still demonized as socialism. Against this, good citizenship and good government require a careful, ongoing balance between public goods that are primary, a shared culture of democratic conviction to back them up, and hopefully the opportunity for personal satisfaction that exists because of these conditions. As it is, our politics is not giving Americans a chance to be better citizens, interested in solving problems rather than competing with each other.

This substantive shift in public priorities and social goods is necessary because "free" markets and the charity of individuals have manifestly failed to achieve social justice, or even basic decency across the board. A fair and just America would be more preoccupied with the problems of the least advantaged than with fantasies of Embattled religion. It is a great and obvious failure that the Long Con continues to work through our arguments about religion, indeed possibly because of them. The fraying of the social safety net has been permitted because of conservatism's relentless insistence that big government is the devil, which itself has impeded attention to climate change and justice, among other trenchant issues.

Too often American politics has turned on platitudes and generalizations like those that pit big government against "constitutionalism," the bland emptiness of which can be yoked into the service of just about any ideological conviction. These are enough for the vast majority of citizens, many of whom are overworked, uninterested, and often understandably disappointed at the narrow political options presented to them. A fair and just America might try to restore the confidence of such citizens not with a newer, better set of platitudes but through efforts to strengthen the bonds between communities, schools, NGOs, and federal agencies more adaptive and responsive to the needs of citizens on the ground. In this, public religions either will or will not make arguments and propose policies that are recognizable to citizens that don't share their convictions. In national life as in communities, if they cannot do this their arguments and proposals will fail, not because they are explicitly religious but because they are unconvincing.

These observations come from my conviction that the foundational purpose of governments is to protect its citizens in the nonmilitaristic sense: to make sure that the conditions of social life are not tilted in the direction of the powerful; to ensure that basic rights and liberties are not just given lip service but are fleshed out in franchise, access to political representatives, and in fair treatment under a robust rule of law, and to guarantee a sense of safety that is achieved through socioeconomic justice and inclusivity.

The state's value, aside from law and policy as protecting the conditions for social life, can be expressed in championing a particular *kind* of social life. Both Martyrs and Whistleblowers have reduced public life, in different ways, to an arena of threat. They reproduce the logic of the security state and of the terrorism index in their paranoiac scan for malefactors in their midst. Neither spends sufficient time or energy on changing the broader conditions in which Embattlement emerges as an easy path to social capital. In this, each has an insufficiently democratic vision of the relation between religion and public life. Religious communities should be encouraged to participate in politics, but not with the sense that "religion" is a distinct thing that either survives unperturbed in the political sphere or is wholly frozen out of it. Religions should aim to connect creatively to political institutions in the hope that they might persuade or influence them, not that these institutions might unilaterally reflect their priorities. Our national institutions must be shaped in accordance with the political rights conferred upon democratic citizens as well as robustly defended human rights, not the narrower set of rights and immunities the Embattled have consistently sought.

## Fear of a Just Planet

Lastly, it is worth reminding ourselves of the interdependence that is now increasingly characteristic of humans and our societies. The scale of Embattlement, of course, reaches beyond America into a most surprising world. Instead of the anticipated spread of egalitarianism across our planet, it is authoritarianism that is having a renaissance, in Hungary's Viktor Orbán, Brazil's Jair Bolsanaro, Rodrigo Duterte in the Philippines, and the growth of reactionary nationalism in Britain, Germany, and elsewhere. Instead of floating cars and global prosperity, there is manifold bigotry; there is still war, endlessly reinventing itself and sucking up tax dollars; the lie of trickle-down economics is retold in the service of an ever-narrower percentage of the megarich; and the seas and skies and earth are imperiled. Religion is on all sides of all these problems, but in America it is the Embattled who continue to drive the conversation.

What it means to be an American must involve reconsidering our relationship with the rest of the planet, and aligning these relations through revivified international institutions that safeguard justice, fairness, climate, and, above all, human rights. Whether we Americans like it or not, our response to democracy's crisis will be go a long way in shaping how other nations respond. That is still the measure of our global influence. As it stands now, we look back on a Trump administration that related to the rest of the planet as a Martyr does to America: anything that does not enable freedom as complete noncoercion and guaranteed victory—whether this is fossil fuels regulation, international efforts to secure gay rights, or even conventional diplomacy—is framed as an assault on America itself.

Instead of this way of being in the world, scoping our problems at least partly through the lens of international human rights and the rule of law reminds us of two things. There are many populations and cultures around the planet that face actual persecution by state power and/or nonstate actors. These people are often acknowledged by American administrations and by the State Department, and even by many religious organizations that devote considerable resources to protecting minority populations elsewhere. Americans must, however, resist the temptation to respond as Martyrs have done to religious persecution abroad: to cite this as "evidence" somehow that their own Embattlement must be real. Not only is that kind of instrumentalization unethical on its face, it fundamentally mistakes the political and economic contextual differences between a first-world nation with freedom of religion (including the realities of being offended and of disagreement) and a nation without the guardrails of a democracy, the same guardrails that in America have proven less sturdy than we thought.

The second reminder from international law has to do with its legacy for how humans envision each other, and the lessons this has for democracies today. Aside from the bedrock assumption that human beings are defined by the possession of rights and dignities that cannot be abridged in the name of economic gain or political power or religion, the flourishing of human rights discourse over the last century issues a powerful reminder to citizens of democracies that we are responsible for the maintenance of a public life where the good order depends on our responsibility to protect our least fortunate members.

In America, this is a necessary lesson because so much of the discord pitting citizens against each other is of clear benefit to corporate power, rather than to those who are actually dispossessed. I have very little sympathy with the "economic anxiety" of a white male from Bucks County, Pennsylvania, or

Raleigh, North Carolina, when the wealth gap suffered by African Americans, or the gig economy that weighs down the aspirations of younger citizens, or the crippling costs of social services that are taken for granted in other democracies do not foreground assumptions about economic life. What we learn from these considerations in international perspective is that—following the 1948 Universal Declaration of Human Rights and the 1975 Helsinki Accords—we must insist that economic survival is a basic human right, without which citizens cannot realize their other rights and capacities. The fundamental disparities of wealth so blatantly on display in the Land of Corporate Free Speech, and the precarity of the future, stand against these rights in a starkly clear fashion. Faced with the impossibility of making it, we are taught to turn on each other, at the local, national, and global levels alike.

It has been difficult to name the problems behind the problem since Embattled Americans seek liberal political protections for their particular identities (often obscuring their naked self-interest with the liberal language of equality, fairness, and rights) while at the same time resisting being subject to the authority of these same political norms and practices. Without transparent norms and procedures, open access to institutions, and the guarantees of robust social goods, American humans turn to a kind of moral perfectionism that excludes others and exempts the self from critique. This leaves all politics as a game of domination.

Instead of thinking about religious and nonreligious communities as inevitable antagonists in politics, we would do better to think carefully about how to identify their convergences around issues of peace, prosperity, and justice, to think concretely about how to produce a society that asks different questions than Embattled America does. Democracy is not about the validation of particular identities; it is, rather, a framework for procedure and deliberation, grounded in a rule of law that protects all citizens equally, and backed up by robust social goods that address discontent, alienation, and marginalization. None of this is a road map to the peaceable kingdom. Democracy isn't about that, either. It is a way of restoring commitment to the work of dignity, equality, and progress for all.

## Organizing the Din

I spend a lot of time being angry at how things have gone in America. I cannot believe that America is still miles away from decency and fairness.

The America that could have been burns ever in my mind. Still, the measure of my ferocity is the measure of my bruised hope for the future. And that is why I have written this concluding chapter as I have. I believe in the power of human cooperation more than the institutions or the traditions deposited to American humans at birth. Beyond the practical questions of resources and power and implementation, conversation and collaboration yield results, often surprising ones. Look at the joyful defiance of Americans resisting the madness in recent years, resistance I have been proud to join. Look at the new, young faces involved in politics: their energy not just a good in its own right but a sign of possibility that effort and conviction can work. Look at the art that American humans make, glorious and rambunctious and not a thing separate from politics but a vein that feeds it.

Writing about Embattled Majorities has surprised me, too. I have found myself learning to balance outrage and exhaustion with joy as a subversive response. I know not everyone has the luxury of feeling this, which itself is part of the larger condition in my sights. I know, too, that the pleasures of Embattlement reveal a hunger for meaning waiting for a different outlet. And by joy I mean not vapid glee but a critical, engaged, aesthetically focused response to the immediacies of existence, including to the real suffering of others, which appears to us as joy's absence and demands of us a compassion that comes from the same emotional wellspring, which refuses ironic distance and despair alike. When I took time off from this project to write a book about jazz, some of my readers and colleagues wondered why I was apparently sidestepping politics. I explained to them that I wasn't; I was simply balancing my reckoning with American culture, focusing on the sensibilities without which I could not focus my rage at my country's failure to be what it should be.

The ascendance of the Embattled can only happen when we are resigned to an America where all decent social programs will be defunded, leaving us with the insistence that charity, rather than the state, is responsible for our well-being. Embattled religion is the vanguard of this sensibility, which opens further room for antidemocratic tendencies: the abjuration of the slow, halting processes by which common life proceeds and is sustained. As political theorist Wendy Brown writes, this is moralism rather than morality; and "It does not want to talk or argue but rather seeks to abort conversation with its prohibitions and reproaches."[18]

My proposals are pitched antithetically to such a sensibility. They are intentionally pitched idealistically, as extensions of my understanding of politics as the *principled conciliation of reasonable differences with regard to matters of public life*. When I proposed this formulation in the introduction, I noted there that every single word of it is contestable. But is not now precisely when we should be insisting on the reintroduction of such notions into our shared life? I see the fourfold proposals above, building on my reassessment of norms in earlier chapters, as vehicles through which we might reinvest in the idea that we can meaningfully distinguish reasonable from unreasonable conciliation, principled from unprincipled differences, arguments and policies rooted in common life from those that seek to impose the particular on the general. Being overwhelmed by the seeming impossibility of such notions is part of being disempowered; Embattlement has done the service of a corporatist politics that prevents imagination outside of itself, palliating citizens with fantasies of glory rather than plans for reform.

We could, in short, reframe the condition of Embattlement as an opportunity. In order to do the things I have proposed, we need to flex our heads and see things differently.[19] We live among all these limits and blockages, and no metaphoric shift alone will save us. But a shift might prepare us for the work. Because authentic democracy quite simply *is* a condition of limits and instability, which Claude Lefort crisply describes as a "form of society in which [people] consent to live under the stress of uncertainty."[20] If Americans can recognize this, we might be able to enter into a state where mutual engagement and responsiveness can be channeled into our politics. After all, if nothing is stable, if terms are malleable (though material conditions less so), this at least ought to resonate with democratic incrementalism. And if we cannot each write the Great American Novel about our glorious selves, perhaps we could think differently about creativity and improvise together in our common lives. Democracy tests and pushes and revises and never permanently arrives. The frustrations and the slowness and the lack of clarity that ensue can breed the disappointments of the Embattled, who respond with the fervor of Life as Action Movie. But citizens who wish to be taken as politically serious must not gripe that they are frozen out of public life if they will not also accept its responsibilities and burdens. If the Embattled are not willing to measure their performance of the suffering citizen against the full range of material deprivations and historical disenfranchisements of Americans who have marched and fought and died for their basic rights, then their claims should frankly be ignored.

The idea that some Americans and some religions are exempt from all these considerations is a fundamentally undemocratic one. The idea that stand-alone rights and entitlements allow us to slip loose of our obligations to other people is cynical and evasive. As Ian Shapiro writes, democracy rejects this viewpoint by "tak[ing] seriously the political implications of nothing in life being unconditional."[21] In other words, to assert that all traditions, norms, and institutions are provisional makes it much harder to self-aggrandize, or to go for broke in politics. The overcompensating attempt to own America that we see among the Embattled is antidemocratic in its refusal to acknowledge its own moral and political limits.

The Embattled have constructed a religion that is either impervious to critique or unfit for public life, neither of which squares with what democracy requires. What is more, since each of them posits that religion is beyond the reach of democratic reason, each is complicit in our fractious politics by fundamentally disrespecting religions. There are so many other ways of being religious in America, past and present, that both Martyrs and Whistleblowers actively crowd out. If religion is worthy of political respect, it must be allowed to fail on the terms of the political. Or to succeed.

If we can reclaim a sense of democracy as high-stakes but noncinematic, we might be able to see the benefits of reinvesting meaning in common purpose.[22] This in turn depends on our willingness to be self-limiting, commit to the long haul of reform, and get into the streets again and again. It is unproductive to seek to expose the religion of the Embattled Majority as fraudulent, lest we risk energizing the narrative. It is simply a thing that cannot address the seriousness of rethinking representation, public life, and those categories that ought to have political priority in rehabilitating American democracy. For this religion is actually a refusal to allow other speech, other thinking: it insists on its own priority, sucking up all the oxygen for itself.

Citizens who are serious about their religious convictions are not exempted from their fundamental obligation, as citizens of a democracy, to respect the dignity of persons. This entails not only rational debate and self-determination, but yields what ought to be a self-limiting politics. Indeed, there are abundant ways in which religions might enthusiastically endorse changing the subject as well, whether from a Niebuhrian tradition of accepting limits or socially engaged Buddhism's application of selflessness to a politics of human solidarity. Religions that ease human suffering, petition the state for moral change, or focus on healing and inclusiveness have always been valuable contributors to the expansion of equality in this country. My point is that religions that overreach, dominate, or demonize—of the sort that have flooded American politics for decades—must be contested in the name of the political and of human rights, not because they are religious.

Some readers may accuse me of privileging some religions over others. I would remind them that I have not described this book as something other than what it is: an act of social criticism, which is openly partial in its politics and its recommendations for public life. The pursuit of what is theoretically au courant, or conforms to dusty methodological aversions, in particular corners of academia can still, in the memorable words of Richard J. Bernstein, give comfort to thugs.[23] I see no reason to think that non-Embattled conservatives could not agree wholeheartedly that we need to get to a place where we rethink the political fundaments in which all Americans have a stake, and which are so obviously in need of rehabilitation.

If a just society needs to establish limits, we might profit in these efforts by reminding ourselves that, in the words of John Rawls, "while an intolerant sect does not itself have title to complain of intolerance, its freedom should be restricted only when the tolerant sincerely and with reason believe that their own security and that of the institutions of liberty are in danger."[24] To be blunt, not all forms of knowledge and not all public claims possess equal value. The work before us as democratic citizens depends on recognizing that an "argument" is more than a series of disconnected rantings and assertions guaranteed a hearing simply because they are vigorously presented. As Karl Popper wrote many decades ago, the mindless commitment to treating viewpoints as equal in kind could lead—as it has in America—to the unchecked seizure of social power by the intolerant.[25] It has also left us with an emotional politics less concerned with the substantiation of claims than with producing atmospheres of appeal.

To be clear, then: not winning all the time is *not* a form oppression. If your ideas make for bad politics, this is not cause for armed revolt. The rage that is everywhere in America, the same rage that would have been there even if Trump had lost in 2016 (and conceded it), is unproductive. But can we think about rage serving a purpose, not a crowdsourced fantasy that leads to an insurrection but as a vehicle for creative direction and purpose in the political sphere? Think about the possibility of tapping into this energy, using it to rearrange our categories and institutions as we would a musical composition. After all, in both performance and debate, there ought to be an implied, shared conviction that different parties are mutually interested in creating something meaningful. And if that is the case, one must limit one's own impulse to play continually, to play over others, or be endlessly self-indulgent.

The shared work of creation might, indeed, require you to simply be silent and listen. This holds true for democracy in real time, where there is not always a composer or conductor to guide us.

If we're going to find new ways to be American, we need to embrace an entirely different sensibility. We might think not about stopping the Whirl but about how to organize its roaring din in the service of a different history, different publics, different institutions, and thus a different future. Dissonance and difference are not threats to be avoided. Imagine a politics where we don't impose a false consonance or resolution on matters relating to the common good but instead think about even far-flung ideas as notes in a chord whose ultimate shape and resonance might surprise us. Let us learn to describe ourselves differently: as citizens first, built to learn and listen, attuned to the generative and constructive.

Embattlement has undermined the possibility of creative revision that is at the heart of America at its best: its exploratory thought, its creative communities, its soaring art, its willingness at times to take to the streets for justice. Are we content to let America be the kind of place populated by the kind of people who can be Embattled *so hard*? Or can we feed a different narrative, where we inhibit authoritarian and isolationist tendencies by exploring our similarities through what Romand Coles calls agonistic respect?[26] Assuming the worst of each other is an evasion of our responsibility *to* each other.

If you could see America from above, through contrails and clouds, what might you learn about its future? In the streets of America, white power signs flash. Women gather in *Handmaid's Tale* red. Americans march in all their motley glory, faces masked and fists up, chanting down white supremacy. And still another black man is killed. And Martyrs mob the Capitol, their hearts filled with entitled rage. So many Americans stare at each other and see only dying suns in the eyes staring back at them. A planet spins in space. We all race toward death. And we resign ourselves to the idea that none of it can ever possibly change. That is wrong. But to get there, we must learn to live with each other differently, and make from these strange fires something new.

# Notes

## Chapter 1

1. Randall Balmer and Jeffrey Sharlet—whose works are diametrically opposed in many different ways—have each limned the institutional or movement contours of this sense of embattlement. See Balmer, *Thy Kingdom Come: How the Religious Right Distorts Faith and Threatens America* (New York: Basic Books, 2006) and Sharlet, *The Family: The Secret Fundamentalism at the Heart of American Power* (New York: Harper Perennial, 2009). Elizabeth Castelli has sharply located some of the discursive features of this notion in her important article "Persecution Complexes: Identity Politics and the 'War on Christians,'" *differences* 18(3) (2007), pp. 152–180. Historian Grace Elizabeth Hale's *A Nation of Outsiders: How the White Middle Class Fell in Love with Rebellion in Postwar America* (New York: Oxford University Press, 2014) contains a provocative chapter on the 1970s conservative Christian appropriation of erstwhile leftist outsider tropes.
2. See Ronald Brownstein, "This Group of Voters Could Swing the 2020 Election," *CNN* (November 5, 2019): https://www.cnn.com/2019/11/05/politics/white-non-college-evangelicals-election-2020/index.html.
3. Elana Schor, "Rev. Graham's Tour Evokes Evangelical Support for Trump," *Associated Press* (October 7, 2019): https://apnews.com/5cfef4941efd4d23b06f7b4db8ca546a?utm_campaign=SocialFlow&utm_medium=AP&utm_source=Twitter.
4. Freedom from Religion Foundation, "Pence Distorted 'Christian Persecution' Tale, FFRF Contends," *FFRF* (August 30, 2019): https://www.cnn.com/2019/08/30/politics/mike-pence-bible-veterans-affairs-fact-check/index.html .
5. See Ralph Reed, *For God and Country: The Christian Case for Trump* (Washington, DC: Regnery Publishing, 2020).
6. Paul Bedard, "Liberty University Opens Falkirk Center to Fight Attacks on Jesus, Constitution," *Washington Examiner* (November 30, 2019): https://www.washingtonexaminer.com/washington-secrets/liberty-university-opens-falkirk-center-to-fight-attacks-on-jesus-constitution.
7. https://www.reuters.com/article/us-twitter-trump/twitter-removes-image-tweet-by-trump-over-nyt-copyright-complaint-idUSKBN243062. See also Rich Lowry, "The Victim President," *Politico* (December 18, 2019): https://www.politico.com/news/magazine/2019/12/18/trump-impeachment-victim-087534.
8. There is abundant literature exploring the relationship between technology and public life. Sources I have found especially illuminating are Jodi Dean, *Blog Theory: Feedback and Capture in the Circuits of Drive* (New York: Polity Books, 2010); Harold A. Innis, *Empire and Communications* (Lanham, MD: Rowman & Littlefield, 1994); Friedrich Kittler, *Gramophone, Film, Typewriter* (Stanford, CA: Stanford University

Press, 1999); John Durham Peters, *Speaking into the Air: A History of the Idea of Communication* (Chicago: University of Chicago Press, 2001); and Fred Turner, *The Democratic Surround: Multimedia and American Liberalism from World War II to the Psychedelic Sixties* (Chicago: University of Chicago Press, 2013).

9. See Elisabeth Robin Anker, *Orgies of Feeling: Melodrama and the Politics of Freedom* (Durham, NC: Duke University Press, 2014) and Brenton J. Malin, *Feeling Mediated: A History of Media Technology and Emotion in America* (New York: New York University Press, 2014).

10. See Nicholas Carr, *The Shallows: What the Internet Is Doing to Our Brains* (New York: Norton, 2011).

11. Sources like these, as well as the aforementioned Jacoby text, often fall well short of the standards scholars might hold for public discourse. This is, in a certain sense, the point of their citation here and throughout. More obviously, texts like these are far more influential in shaping American public discourse than most scholarship. See Chris Hedges, *American Fascists: The Christian Right and the War on America* (New York: Free Press, 2007) and Christopher Hitchens, *God Is Not Great: How Religion Poisons Everything* (New York: Twelve Publishing, 2007).

12. See John Fea, *Was America Founded a Christian Nation? A Historical Introduction*, rev. ed. (Louisville, KY: Westminster John Knox Press, 2016) and Robert Kagan, *Dangerous Nation: America's Foreign Policy from Its Earliest Days to the Dawn of the Twentieth Century* (New York: Vintage Books, 2006).

13. For two sides of these histories, see Chris Beneke, *Beyond Tolerance: The Religious Origins of American Pluralism* (New York: Oxford University Press, 2009) and David Harrington Watt, *Antifundamentalism in Modern America* (Ithaca, NY: Cornell University Press, 2017).

14. The subject continues to fuel a cottage industry, much of it invested in primary source assessment. Many texts are valuable in terms of furnishing detail but do not interrogate the larger conceptual and practical discrepancies between the revolutionary era and the political present that seems to propel these historical investigations like clockwork. See David L. Holmes, *The Faiths of the Founding Fathers* (New York: Oxford University Press, 2006) and Frank Lambert, *The Founding Fathers and the Place of Religion in America* (Princeton, NJ: Princeton University Press, 2003).

15. For suggestive analyses of changes among white evangelicals, see Robert P. Jones, *The End of White Christian America* (New York: Simon & Schuster, 2017) and Justin Farrell, "The Young and the Restless? The Liberalization of Young Evangelicals," *Journal for the Scientific Study of Religion* 50(3) (September 2011), pp. 517–532.

16. The classic text is James Davison Hunter's *Culture Wars: The Struggle to Define America* (New York: Basic Books, 1992). More recent entries in this literary lineage include James E. Campbell, *Polarized: Making Sense of a Divided America* (Princeton, NJ: Princeton University Press, 2016) and Andrew Hartman, *A War for the Soul of America: A History of the Culture Wars* (Chicago: University of Chicago Press, 2016).

17. See Sean Wilentz, *The Politicians and the Egalitarians: The Hidden History of American Politics* (New York: Norton, 2017) and Sheldon Wolin, *Democracy Incorporated: Managed Democracy and the Specter of Inverted Totalitarianism* (Princeton, NJ: Princeton University Press, 2017).
18. See Edward J. Balleisen, *Fraud: An American History from Barnum to Madoff* (Princeton, NJ: Princeton University Press, 2017).
19. See Gilles Chatelet, *To Live and Think Like Pigs: The Incitement of Envy and Boredom in Market Democracies* (Cambridge, MA: Urbanomic/Sequence Press, 2018).
20. See Winnifred Fallers Sullivan, *The Impossibility of Religious Freedom* (Princeton, NJ: Princeton University Press, 2005) and Tisa Wenger, *Religious Freedom: The Contested History of a Religious Ideal* (Chapel Hill: University of North Carolina Press, 2017).
21. David L. Bigler and Will Bagley, *The Mormon Rebellion: America's First Civil War, 1857–1858* (Norman: University of Oklahoma Press, 2011); Anson Shupe, "The North American Anticult Movement," pp. 117–142 in James R. Lewis and Inga B. Toellefson, eds., *The Oxford Handbook of New Religious Movements*, vol. 2 (New York: Oxford University Press, 2016); George E. Tinker, *Missionary Conquest: The Gospel and Native American Genocide* (Minneapolis: Augsburg Fortress Press, 1993); Eric Williams, *Capitalism and Slavery* (Chapel Hill: University of North Carolina Press, 1994).
22. This actually happened in Raleigh, North Carolina, in 2020.
23. See Teresa M. Bejan, *Mere Civility: Disagreement and the Limits of Toleration* (Cambridge, MA: Harvard University Press, 2017). A crankier look at related issues is found in Alan Wolfe, *The Politics of Petulance: America in an Age of Immaturity* (Chicago: University of Chicago Press, 2018).
24. My thinking here is inspired by Wendy Brown's *Regulating Aversion: Toleration in the Age of Identity and Empire* (Princeton, NJ: Princeton University Press, 2006).
25. See Bonnie Honig, *Democracy and the Foreigner* (Princeton, NJ: Princeton University Press, 2003). For a practical assessment of these ideas in American history, see Sylvester Johnson's magisterial *African-American Religions, 1500–2000: Colonialism, Democracy, and Freedom* (Cambridge: Cambridge University Press, 2015).
26. Immanuel Kant's *Perpetual Peace* is the most obvious touchstone. See Kant, *Perpetual Peace and Other Essays* (Indianapolis, IN: Hackett Classics, 1983).
27. See Edmund Burke, *Reflections on the Revolution in France* (Indianapolis, IN: Hackett Classics, 1987) and Sigmund Freud, *Civilization and Its Discontents* (New York: Norton, 2010).
28. G.W. F. Hegel, *Phenomenology of Spirit* (New York: Oxford University Press, 1977).
29. See Todd Gitlin, *The Twilight of Common Dreams: Why America Is Wracked by Culture Wars* (New York: Henry Holt, 1996) and Mark Lilla, *The Once and Future Liberal: After Identity Politics* (New York: Harper Books, 2017). See also Jeffrey C. Isaac's devastating takedown of Lilla in "Does Liberalism Still Have a Future?," *Los Angeles Review of Books* (November 22, 2017): https://lareviewofbooks.org/article/does-liberalism-still-have-a-future/#.

30. Didier Fassin and Richard Rechtman, *The Empire of Trauma: An Inquiry into the Condition of Victimhood* (Princeton, NJ: Princeton University Press, 2009), p. 5.
31. Ibid., p. 7.
32. Ibid., pp. 78–79.
33. The basic Nietzschean insight derives from the concept of ressentiment in *On the Genealogy of Morals* (New York: Oxford University Press, 2009). The specific terminology of victims and killers comes from Mahmood Mamdani's extraordinary *When Victims Become Killers: Colonialism, Nativism, and the Genocide in Rwanda* (Princeton, NJ: Princeton University Press, 2002).
34. Catherine Bell, *Ritual: Perspectives and Dimensions* (New York: Oxford University Press, 2009), p. 208. Italics mine.
35. See Jean-Yves Camus and Nicolas Lebourg, *Far-Right Politics in Europe* (Cambridge, MA: Belknap Press, 2017) and Steven Levitsky and Daniel Ziblatt, *How Democracies Die* (New York: Broadway Books, 2019).
36. See John Corrigan and Lynn Neal, eds., *Religious Intolerance in America: A Documentary History* (Chapel Hill: University of North Carolina Press, 2010), Peter Gottschalk, *American Heretics: Catholics, Jews, Muslims, and the History of American Intolerance* (New York: St. Martin's Press, 2013), and Richard Moon, *Putting Faith in Hate: When Religion Is the Source or Target of Hate Speech* (Cambridge: Cambridge University Press, 2018).
37. See Jeffrey Stout, *Blessed Are the Organized: Grassroots Democracy in America* (Princeton, NJ: Princeton University Press, 2009). Stout's volume builds on the long-standing work of Harry Boyte and other theorists of new social movements in the 1980s–1990s.
38. See Jason C. Bivins, *Religion of Fear: The Politics of Horror in Conservative Evangelicalism* (New York: Oxford University Press, 2008); and Kevin Mattson, *Rebels All! A Short History of the Conservative Mind in Postwar America* (New Brunswick, NJ: Rutgers University Press, 2008).
39. See Sean Wilentz, *The Age of Reagan: A History, 1974–2008* (New York: Harper Perennial, 2009).
40. See, for example, John Fea, *Believe Me: The Evangelical Road to Donald Trump* (Grand Rapids, MI: Eerdmans Publishing, 2018) and Michael Gerson, "The Last Temptation," *The Atlantic* (April 2018): https://www.theatlantic.com/magazine/archive/2018/04/the-last-temptation/554066/.
41. George Orwell, "Politics and the English Language," p. 139 in Sonia Orwell and Ian Angos, eds., *The Collected Essays, Journalism and Letters of George Orwell*, vol. 4 (New York: Harcourt, Brace, Jovanovich, 1968).
42. Ibid.
43. See Arlie Russell Hochschild, *Strangers in Their Own Land: Anger and Mourning on the American Right* (New York: New Press, 2016) and J. D. Vance, *Hillbilly Elegy: A Memoir of a Family and Culture in Crisis* (New York: Harper Books, 2018). For a wholly convincing alternate perspective, see Ashley Jardina, *White Identity Politics* (Cambridge: Cambridge University Press, 2019).
44. See Christian Smith, *American Evangelicalism: Embattled and Thriving* (Chicago: University of Chicago Press, 1998).

## Chapter 2

1. Lucy Pasha-Robinson, "White Evangelical Christians Believe They Are More Discriminated Against Than Muslims, US Poll Finds," *The Independent* (March 21, 2017). See also Perry Chiaramonte, "Christians the Most Persecuted Group in World for Second Year: Study," *Fox News* (January 6, 2017): http://www.foxnews.com/world/2017/01/06/christians-most-persecuted-group-in-world-for-second-year-study.html and Taylor Link, "White Evangelicals Say Christians Face More Persecution Than Muslims: Poll," *Salon* (March 10, 2017): http://www.salon.com/2017/03/10/white-evangelicals-say-christians-face-more-persecution-than-muslims-poll/.
2. Zach Ford, "One of the GOP's 'Young Guns' Wishes We Still Had Sodomy Laws," *ThinkProgress* (August 10, 2018): https://thinkprogress.org/north-carolina-candidate-congress-criminalize-homosexuality-05e8b5914d7b/.
3. Kyle Feldscher, "Steve King Says He Relates to What Christ 'Went Through for Us' after Controversies," *CNN* (April 24, 2019): https://www.cnn.com/2019/04/24/politics/steve-king-jesus-christ/index.html.
4. Peter Beinart, "Breaking Faith," p. 17 in *The Atlantic* (April 2017).
5. See Nelson Blackstock, *COINTELPRO: The FBI's Secret War on Political Freedom* (New York: Pathfinder Press, 1988); John P. Bowes, *Land Too Good for Indians: Northern Indian Removal* (Norman: University of Oklahoma Press, 2017); Maura Jane Farrelly, *Anti-Catholicism in America, 1620–1860* (Cambridge: Cambridge University Press, 2017); Christopher Finan, *From the Palmer Raids to the Patriot Act: A History of the Fight for Free Speech in America* (Boston: Beacon Press, 2008); Terri Diane Halperin, *The Alien and Sedition Acts of 1798: Testing the Constitution* (Baltimore: Johns Hopkins University Press, 2016); Sylvester A. Johnson and Steven Weitzman, eds., *The FBI and Religion: Faith and National Security before and after 9/11* (Berkeley: University of California Press, 2017); Richard Reeves, *Infamy: The Shocking Story of the Japanese American Internment in World War II* (New York: Picador Books, 2016); and James A. Warren, *God, War, and Providence: The Epic Struggle of Roger Williams and the Narraganset Indians against the Puritans of New England* (New York: Scribner's Books, 2018).
6. See David E. Rosenbaum, "THE NATION: Buchanan and the Convention; Now, This is the Message from Our Tormentor," *New York Times* (March 17, 1996): https://www.nytimes.com/1996/03/17/weekinreview/the-nation-buchanan-and-the-convention-now-this-message-from-our-tormentor.html; and James Davison Hunter, *Culture Wars: The Struggle to Define America* (New York: Basic Books, 1992).
7. The literature here is particularly rich, though usually ensconced in larger histories of early Christianity. For an excellent comprehensive study, see William W. H. C. Frend, *Martyrdom and Persecution in the Early Church: A Study of Conflict from the Maccabees to Donatus* (Eugene, OR: Wipf and Stock, 2014). An engaging anthology of comparative perspectives is Margo Kitts, ed., *Martyrdom, Self-Sacrifice, and Self-Immolation: Religious Perspectives on Suicide* (New York: Oxford University Press, 2018). See also Candida Moss, *The Myth of Persecution: How Early Christians Invented a Story of Martyrdom* (New York: Harper One, 2013).

8. Mircea Eliade, *A History of Religious Ideas*, vol. 1: *From the Stone Age to the Eleusinian Mysteries* (Chicago: University of Chicago Press, 1978), p. 358.
9. See Alan Noble, "The Evangelical Persecution Complex," *The Atlantic* (August 14, 2014): https://www.theatlantic.com/national/archive/2014/08/the-evangelical-persecution-complex/375506/.
10. John Locke, *Second Treatise of Government* (Indianapolis, IN: Hackett Classics, 1980), p. 29.
11. Adrian Chastain Weimer, *Martyrs' Mirror: Persecution and Holiness in Early New England* (New York: Oxford University Press, 2014).
12. Peter Gottschalk, *American Heretics: Catholics, Jews, Muslims, and the History of Religious Intolerance* (New York: Palgrave MacMillan, 2013), p. 21.
13. Quoted in Sean Wilentz, *The Rise of American Democracy: Jefferson to Lincoln* (New York: Norton, 2005), p. 32.
14. See Amanda Porterfield, *Conceived in Doubt: Religion and Politics in the New American Nation* (Chicago: University of Chicago Press, 2012).
15. For insight into this range of debates, see Woody Holton, *Unruly Americans and the Origins of the Constitution* (New York: Hill & Wang, 2008); and Gordon S. Wood's classic *The Radicalism of the American Revolution* (New York: Vintage Books, 2011).
16. Nathan O. Hatch, *The Democratization of American Christianity* (New Haven, CT: Yale University Press, 1989), p. 25.
17. R. Laurence Moore, *Selling God: American Religion in the Marketplace of Culture* (New York: Oxford University Press, 1994), p. 128.
18. See Gottschalk, *American Heretics*; and John Corrigan and Lynn S. Neal, eds., *Religious Intolerance in America: A Documentary History* (Chapel Hill: University of North Carolina Press, 2010).
19. Michael Kazin, *American Dreamers: How the Left Changed a Nation* (New York: Vintage Books, 2011), p. 26.
20. See Michael Lienesch, *Redeeming America: Power, Piety, and Politics in the New Christian Right* (Chapel Hill: University of North Carolina Press, 1993).
21. See Alan Brinkley, *Voices of Protest: Huey Long, Father Coughlin, and the Great Depression* (New York: Vintage Books, 1983).
22. Kevin M. Schultz, *Tri-Faith America: How Catholics and Jews Held Postwar America to Its Protestant Promise* (New York: Oxford University Press, 2011), p. 10.
23. Quoted in ibid., p. 95.
24. See Jason C. Bivins, *The Fracture of Good Order: Christian Antiliberalism and the Challenge to American Politics* (Chapel Hill: University of North Carolina Press, 2003).
25. See D. J. Molloy, *The World of the John Birch Society: Conspiracy, Conservatism, and the Cold War* (Nashville, TN: Vanderbilt University Press, 2014).
26. Sasha Issenberg, "Barnstorming America," p. 47 in *Smithsonian Magazine* (September 2018).
27. Ibid., p. 46.
28. Ibid., p. 36.
29. Ibid., p. 50.

30. Robert Alan Goldberg, *Enemies Within: The Culture of Conspiracy in Modern America* (New Haven, CT: Yale University Press, 2001), p. 23. See also Andrew Burt, *American Hysteria: The Untold Story of Mass Political Extremism in the United States* (Lanham, MD: Lyons Press, 2015).
31. See Kevin Mattson, *Rebels All! A Short History of the Conservative Mind in Postwar America* (New Brunswick, NJ: Rutgers University Press, 2008). See also Corey Robin, *The Reactionary Mind: Conservatism from Edmund Burke to Donald Trump*, 2nd ed. (New York: Oxford University Press, 2017).
32. Cited in Mark Lilla, *The Shipwrecked Mind: On Political Reaction* (New York: New York Review of Books, 2016), p. xiii.
33. See J. William Middendorf II, *A Glorious Disaster: Barry Goldwater's Presidential Campaign and the Origins of the Conservative Movement* (New York: Basic Books, 2006).
34. Mattson, *Rebels All!*, pp. 92–93.
35. See Matthew D. Lassiter, *The Silent Majority: Suburban Politics in the Sunbelt South* (Princeton, NJ: Princeton University Press, 2007).
36. Rick Perlstein, "Exclusive: Lee Atwater's Infamous 1981 Interview on the Southern Strategy," *The Nation* (November 13, 2012): https://www.thenation.com/article/exclusive-lee-atwaters-infamous-1981-interview-southern-strategy/.
37. Sam Tanenhaus, "The Architect of the Radical Right," p. 41 in *The Atlantic* (July–August 2017). See Warren Nutter, *Political Economy and Freedom: A Collection of Essays* (Carmel, IN: Liberty Fund Books, 1983). On the conservative Christian response to desegregation, see Randall Balmer, *Thy Kingdom Come: How the Religious Right Distorts the Faith and Threatens America* (New York: Basic Books, 2006). On Christian school systems and curricula, see Bivins, *Fracture of Good Order*.
38. See Steven M. Teles, *The Rise of the Conservative Legal Movement: The Battle for Control of the Law* (Princeton, NJ: Princeton University Press, 2010); and Luke O'Brien, "The Making of an American Nazi," *The Atlantic* (December 2017), pp. 54–67. On Martyrs and the law generally; see also Daniel Bennett, *Defending Faith: The Politics of the Christian Conservative Legal Movement* (Lawrence: University of Kansas Press, 2017); and Andrew R. Lewis, *The Rights Turn in Conservative Christian Politics: How Abortion Transformed the Culture Wars* (Cambridge: Cambridge University Press, 2018).
39. O'Brien, "American Nazi," p. 64.
40. Lewis Franklin Powell Jr., "Attack of American Free Enterprise System" at https://www.thirteen.org/wnet/supremecourt/personality/sources_document13.html. For discussion and analysis of the memo, see Earl Wysong, Robert Perucci, and David Wright, *The New Class Society: Goodbye American Dream?* (Lanham, MD: Rowman and Littlefield, 2008).
41. Philip Jenkins, *Decade of Nightmares: The End of the Sixties and the Making of the Eighties* (New York: Oxford University Press, 2006), p. 78.
42. See Lisa McGirr, *Suburban Warriors: The Origins of the New American Right*, updated ed. (Princeton, NJ: Princeton University Press, 2015).

43. Rick Perlstein, *The Invisible Bridge: The Fall of Nixon and the Rise of Reagan* (New York: Simon & Schuster, 2014), p. 89.
44. Sean Wilentz, *The Age of Reagan: A History, 1974–2008* (New York: Harper Perennial, 2008), p. 43.
45. Rick Perlstein, *Nixonland: The Rise of a President and the Fracturing of America* (New York: Simon & Schuster, 2008), p. 265.
46. Ibid., p. 743.
47. Balmer, *Thy Kingdom Come*, p. 5.
48. Randall Balmer, "The Real Origins of the Religious Right," *Politico* (May 27, 2014): https://www.politico.com/magazine/story/2014/05/religious-right-real-origins-107133/.
49. Grace Elizabeth Hale, *A Nation of Outsiders: How the White Middle Class Fell in Love with Rebellion in Postwar America* (New York: Oxford University Press, 2011), p. 168.
50. See Jefferson Cowie, *Stayin' Alive: The 1970s and the Last Days of the Working Class* (New York: New Press, 2012).
51. Daniel T. Rodgers, *Age of Fracture* (Cambridge, MA: Harvard University Press, 2011), p. 76.
52. Ibid., p. 30.
53. Rick Perlstein, *Reaganland: America's Right Turn, 1976–1980* (New York: Simon & Schuster, 2020), p. 627.
54. Ulf Hannerz, "The World in Creolisation," p. 551 in *Africa* 57:4 (1987), pp. 546–559.
55. Mattson, *Rebels All!*, p. 82.
56. Michael Rogin, *Ronald Reagan, the Movie and Other Episodes in Political Demonology* (Berkeley: University of California Press, 1987), p. xiii.
57. David Greenberg, "Dog Whistling Dixie," *Slate* (November 20, 2007): https://slate.com/news-and-politics/2007/11/what-reagan-meant-by-states-rights.html.
58. See Dan T. Carter, *From George Wallace to Newt Gingrich: Race in the Conservative Counterrevolution, 1963–1994* (Baton Rouge: Louisiana State University Press, 1996).
59. McKay Coppins, "Newt Gingrich Says You're Welcome," p. 54 in *The Atlantic* (November 2018), pp. 50–60.
60. Ibid., p. 54.
61. Quoted in George Packer, *The Unwinding: An Inner History of the New America* (New York: Farrar, Straus and Giroux, 2013), p. 22.
62. Lienesch, *Redeeming America*, p. 169.
63. Ibid., pp. 37, 170.
64. See Dan Cassino, *Fox News and American Politics: How One Channel Shapes American Politics and Society* (New York: Routledge Press, 2016).
65. Emily Shugerman, "Who Was Roger Ailes and Why Was He So Controversial: Five Things You Need to Know," *The Independent* (May 18, 2017): https://www.independent.co.uk/news/world/americas/roger-ailes-who-was-he-fox-news-murdoch-trump-founder-life-career-what-you-need-to-know-a7743281.html.
66. Ibid.
67. See Julian Borger, "US Inquiry into Claims Black Voters Were Stripped of Rights," *The Guardian* (December 4, 2000): https://www.theguardian.com/world/2000/dec/04/

uselections2000.usa1. See also the executive summary from the US Commission on Civil Rights: https://www.usccr.gov/pubs/vote2000/report/exesum.htm.
68. The brashest example of this is Christian Reconstruction, which holds that all public institutions should be aligned with strict understandings of Christian morality. See Michael McVicar, *Christian Reconstruction: R.J. Rushdoony and American Religious Conservatism* (Chapel Hill: University of North Carolina Press, 2015).
69. Todd Starnes, "Roger Ailes Is Our Gun-Toting, Bible-Clinging Culture War General," *Fox News* (July 14, 2016): https://www.foxnews.com/opinion/starnes-roger-ailes-is-our-gun-toting-bible-clinging-culture-war-general.
70. See Amy DeRogatis, *Saving Sex: Sexuality and Salvation in American Evangelicalism* (New York: Oxford University Press, 2014).
71. Bob Moser, "The Crusaders," *Rolling Stone* (April 8, 2005).
72. Balmer, *Thy Kingdom Come*.
73. Richard Dawkins, Daniel Dennett, Sam Harris, and Christopher Hitchens's orgy of self-importance, *The Four Horsemen: The Discussion That Sparked an Atheist Revolution* (New York: Bantam Books, 2019); Andrew Seidel's *The Founding Myth: Why Christian Nationalism Is Un-American* (New York: Sterling Publishing, 2019); and Jay Wexler's *Our Non-Christian Nation: How Atheists, Satanists, Pagans, and Others Are Demanding Their Rightful Place in Public Life* (Stanford, CA: Redwood Press, 2019).
74. Christian Smith, *Christian America? What Evangelicals Really Want* (Berkeley: University of California Press, 2000), p. 4.
75. Robert Putnam and David E. Campbell, *American Grace: How Religion Divides and Unites Us* (New York: Simon & Schuster, 2012); and Alan Wolfe, *One Nation, after All: What Middle-Class Americans Really Think about God, Country, Family, Racism, Welfare, Immigration, Homosexuality, Work, the Right, the Left, and Each Other* (New York: Viking Books, 1998).
76. Nina Mandell, "Pat Robertson Slams 'Saturday Night Live' over Jesus-Tim Tebow Skit for 'Anti-Christian Bigotry,'" *New York Daily News* (December 20, 2011): https://www.nydailynews.com/entertainment/tv-movies/pat-robertson-slams-saturday-night-live-jesus-tim-tebow-skit-article-1.994366.
77. See Philip Bump, "There's a Virus in Trumpland," *Washington Post* (August 3, 2018): https://www.washingtonpost.com/news/politics/wp/2018/08/03/theres-a-virus-in-trumpland/; Jack Hitt, "Lunar-tics," *New York Times Magazine* (February 9, 2003):https://www.nytimes.com/2003/02/09/magazine/lunar-tics.html; and Isaac Stanley-Becker, "'We Are Q': A Deranged Conspiracy Cult Leaps from the Internet to the Crowd at Trump's 'MAGA' Tour," *Washington Post* (August 1, 2018): https://www.washingtonpost.com/news/morning-mix/wp/2018/08/01/we-are-q-a-deranged-conspiracy-cult-leaps-from-the-internet-to-the-crowd-at-trumps-maga-tour/.
78. Miranda Blue, "Franklin Graham: 'Only One Election Left' to Save America from Godless Secularists," *Right Wing Watch* (February 12, 2016): http://www.rightwingwatch.org/content/franklin-graham-only-one-election-left-save-america-godless-secularists.

79. Elizabeth Stoker Bruenig, "The Right's Ayn Rand Hypocrisy: Why Their 'Religious' Posture Is a Total Sham," *Salon* (February 28, 2014): http://www.salon.com/2014/02/28/the_rights_ayn_rand_hypocrisy_why_their_religious_posture_is_a_total_sham/.
80. Sarah Posner, "The Movie the Faithful Want You to See," *Politico* (March 9, 2014): https://www.politico.com/magazine/story/2014/03/persecution-cpac-movie-the-faithful-want-you-to-see-104471.
81. See Paul Lyons, *New Left, New Right, and the Legacy of the Sixties* (Philadelphia: Temple University Press, 1996), p. 68.
82. See Charles M. Blow, "White Male Victimization Anxiety," *New York Times* (October 10, 2018): https://www.nytimes.com/2018/10/10/opinion/trump-white-male-victimization.html; and Tim Marcin, "Trump Voters Say Men Face More Discrimination Than Women, African-Americans or LGBT People, Poll Says," *Newsweek* (October 17, 2018): https://www.newsweek.com/men-face-more-discrimination-women-african-americans-lgbt-trump-voters-poll-1175395?utm_source=Twitter&utm_medium=Social&utm_campaign=NewsweekTwitter.
83. Davis Richardson, "Lindsey Graham Wants You to Know He's a 'Single White Man' Who Doesn't Forget," *The Observer* (September 28, 2018): https://observer.com/2018/09/lindsey-graham-the-single-white-male-will-not-shut-up/.
84. Stephen J. Ducat, *The Wimp Factor: Gender Gaps, Holy Wars, & the Politics of Anxious Masculinity* (Boston: Beacon Press, 2004), p. 62.
85. For two exceptional readings of masculinity and American Christianity, see Seth Dowland, *Family Values and the Rise of the Christian Right* (Philadelphia: University of Pennsylvania Press, 2015); and Jessica Johnson, *Biblical Porn: Affect, Labor, and Pastor Mark Driscoll's Evangelical Empire* (Durham, NC: Duke University Press, 2018). See also Michael Kimmel, *Angry White Men: American Masculinity at the End of an Era* (New York: Bold Type Books, 2017).
86. See Richard Slotkin, *Gunfighter Nation: The Myth of the Frontier in Twentieth-Century America* (Norman: University of Oklahoma Press, 1998).
87. James William Gibson, *Warrior Dreams: Violence and Manhood in Post-Vietnam America* (New York: Hill and Wang, 1994), p. 12.
88. See Ducat, *Wimp Factor*; and also Michael Kimmel, *Guyland: The Perilous World Where Boys Become Men* (New York: HarperCollins, 2008).
89. The benchmark study in American masculinity is Susan Jeffords's *The Remasculinization of America: Gender and the Vietnam War* (Bloomington: Indiana University Press, 1989). See also Stewart M. Hoover and Curtis D. Coats, *Does God Make the Man? Media, Religion, and the Crisis of Masculinity* (New York: New York University Press, 2015).
90. See Lizabeth Cohen, *A Consumers' Republic: The Politics of Mass Consumption in Postwar America* (New York: Vintage Books, 2003). See also Daniel Marcus, *Happy Days and Wonder Years: The Fifties and the Sixties in Contemporary Cultural Politics* (New Brunswick, NJ: Rutgers University Press, 2004).
91. There is a rich literature on religious outsiderdom. R. Laurence Moore's *Religious Outsiders and the Making of Americans* (New York: Oxford University Press, 1986)

is an overview of pluralism and accommodation, couched in a modest complication of standard, post-Baird narratives that flow from the unchanging source that is Puritanism. Moore shows that "outsider" groups embody "mainstream" traits and that this is wholly American. Hale's *s*casts the broadest of nets, drawing together Norman Mailer, hippies, the Christian Right, and the Black Panthers, all of whom "provided an imaginary resolution for an intractable mid-century cultural and political conflict, the contradiction between the desire for self-determination and autonomy and the desire for a grounded, morally and emotionally meaningful life" (3).

92. The scholar of religion Elizabeth Castelli gets closest to the mark in her focus on identity and authenticity in the "self-referential and self-generating logic" of organizations like Battle Cry, Liberty Sunday, and the JCCCR. Elizabeth A. Castelli, "Persecution Complexes: Identity Politics and the 'War on Christians,'" *differences* 18:5 (2007), pp. 152–180.

93. Anne Rothe, *Popular Trauma Culture: Selling the Pain of Others in the Mass Media* (New Brunswick, NJ: Rutgers University Press, 2011), p. 165. See also Alyson M. Cole, *The Cult of True Victimhood: From the War on Welfare to the War on Terror* (Stanford, CA: Stanford University Press, 2007).

# Chapter 3

1. Marc Fisher, John Woodrow Cox, and Peter Hermann, "Pizzagate: From Rumor, to Hashtag, to Gunfire in D.C.," *Washington Post* (December 6, 2016): https://www.washingtonpost.com/local/pizzagate-from-rumor-to-hashtag-to-gunfire-in-dc/2016/12/06/4c7def50-bbd4-11e6-94ac-3d324840106c_story.html?noredirect=on&utm_term=.8c26583d8316.
2. See David Christian, *Maps of Time: An Introduction to Big History* (Berkeley: University of California Press, 2011). See also Feras A. Batarseh, "Thoughts on the Future of Human Knowledge and Machine Intelligence," *LSE Business Review* (September 20, 2017): https://blogs.lse.ac.uk/businessreview/2017/09/20/thoughts-on-the-future-of-human-knowledge-and-machine-intelligence/.
3. Quoted in James Parker, "Why We Still Miss Jon Stewart," p. 36 in *The Atlantic* (March 2016), pp. 34–36.
4. See Theodor Adorno, *The Culture Industry: Selected Essays on Mass Culture* (New York: Routledge, 2001).
5. See Marshall McLuhan, *Understanding Media: The Extensions of Man* (Cambridge, MA: MIT Press, 1994).
6. Neil Postman, *Amusing Ourselves to Death: Public Discourse in the Age of Show Business* (New York: Penguin, 1985), p. 6.
7. Cardi B, "Best Life," *Invasion of Privacy* (Atlantic Records, 2018).
8. Manuel De Landa, *A Thousand Years of Nonlinear History* (New York: Zone Books, 1997), p. 16.

9. See David Harvey, *A Brief History of Neoliberalism* (New York: Oxford University Press, 2007); Daniel T. Rodgers, *The Age of Fracture* (Cambridge, MA: Belknap Press, 2012); and Robert O. Self, *All in the Family: The Realignment of American Politics since the 1960s* (New York: Hill & Wang, 2013). A superb reading of the varied configurations of religion in these developments is Kathryn Lofton, *Consuming Religion* (Chicago: University of Chicago Press, 2017).
10. See Katie Hafner and Matthew Lyon, *Where Wizards Stay Up Late: The Origins of the Internet* (New York: Simon & Schuster, 1998). See also http://www.nethistory.info/index.html.
11. This is a reference to Francis Fukuyama's famed confidence that, with the fall of the Iron Curtain, the great ideological struggle of Western history had been fully resolved. See Fukuyama, *The End of History and the Last Man*, reissue ed. (New York: Free Press, 2006).
12. Kurt Andersen, "How America Lost Its Mind," p. 86 in *The Atlantic* (September 2017), pp. 76–91.
13. Cass R. Sunstein, *Republic.com 2.0* (Princeton, NJ: Princeton University Press, 2007), p. xi.
14. See Richard Dawkins, *The Selfish Gene*, 2nd ed. (New York: Oxford University Press, 1989).
15. See Emerson T. Brooking and P. W. Singer, "War Goes Viral: How Social Media Is Being Weaponized," *The Atlantic* (November 2016), pp. 70–83.
16. See Sarah Ahmed, *The Cultural Politics of Emotion*, 2nd ed. (New York: Routledge, 2014).
17. Emerson, "Society and Solitude." Accessed at https://archive.org/details/in.ernet.dli.2015.43434/page/n15.
18. C. Wright Mills, *The Power Elite*, new ed. (New York: Oxford University Press, 2000).
19. See, for example, Todd P. Newman, Erik C. Nisbet, and Matthew C. Nisbet, "Climate Change, Cultural Cognition, and Media Effects: Worldviews Drive News Selectivity, Biased Processing, and Polarized Attitudes," *Public Understanding of Science* 27:8 (November 2018), pp. 985–1002.
20. Thomas Mulholland, "Cortical Activation during Steady and Changing Visual Stimulation," *Electroencephalography and Clinical Neurophysiology* 17:4 (November 1964), pp. 371–375.
21. Nathaniel Hawthorne, *Tales and Sketches* (New York: Library of America, 1996), p. 480.
22. Teresa Brennan, *The Transmission of Affect* (Ithaca, NY: Cornell University Press, 2004), p. 12.
23. James Gleick, *The Information: A History, a Theory, a Flood* (New York: Vintage Books, 2011), p. 403. The term actant is from Bruno Latour, *Reassembling the Social: An Introduction to Actor-Network-Theory* (New York: Oxford University Press, 2007). See also Gary S. Cross and Robert N. Proctor, *Packaged Pleasures: How Technology and Marketing Revolutionized Desire* (Chicago: University of Chicago Press, 2014); Adam Gazzaley and Larry D. Rosen, *The Distracted Mind: Ancient Brains in a High-Tech World* (Cambridge, MA: MIT Press, 2017); Michael Harris, *The End of Absence: Reclaiming What We've Lost in a World of Constant Connection*

(New York: Current Books, 2014), Caroline A. Jones, David Mather, and Rebecca Uchill, eds., *Experience: Culture, Cognition, and Common Sense* (Cambridge, MA: MIT Press, 2016); and Judy Wajcman, *Pressed for Time: The Acceleration of Life in Digital Capitalism* (Chicago: University of Chicago Press, 2014).

24. Quoted in David Shenk, *Data Smog: Surviving the Information Glut* (New York: HarperCollins, 1997),</IBT> p. 24.

25. Ibid., p. 38.

26. Michael Shermer, *The Believing Brain: From Ghosts and Gods to Politics and Conspiracies—How We Construct Beliefs and Reinforce Them as Truths* (New York: Henry Holt, 2011), p. 209.

27. See Jodi Dean, *Blog Theory: Feedback and Capture in the Circuits of Drive* (Malden, MA: Polity Press, 2010). My thinking about the Swirl and mediation more generally has been influenced significantly not only by Dean but by the Lacanian theorists who shape her thinking. The Lacanian emphasis on the drive entails a symbolic reading of the compensatory lack that fundamentally rewrites individual and social identity after the retreat of the symbolic Big Other which once grounded the Real. Clearly this thinking is of a time, when Lyotard and other social theorists explored what they asserted was a time of retreating metanarratives. Yet as a way of reconceptualizing the bizarre turns of post–Cold War American politics, it is hard to deny that this theory has a certain explanatory merit to it.

28. Paul Kedrosky, "The Large Information Collider, BDTs, and Gravity Holidays on Tuesdays," p. 47 in John Brockman, ed., *Is the Internet Changing the Way You Think? The Net's Impact on Our Minds and Future* (San Francisco: Harper Perennial, 2010).

29. Anyone seeking further insight into the reach of these powers is advised to consult Shoshana Zuboff's *The Age of Surveillance Capitalism: The Fight for a Human Future at the New Frontier of Power* (New York: Hachette Book Group, 2019).

30. I wrote this section long before Covid-19. It has been deeply surreal to revisit it.

31. The above account indebted to Nicholas H. Acheson, *Fundamentals of Molecular Virology*, 2nd ed. (Hoboken, NJ: Wiley Books, 2011).

32. See Arjun Appadurai, *Modernity at Large: Cultural Dimensions of Globalization* (Minneapolis: University of Minnesota Press, 1996); and Ulf Hannerz, *Transnational Connections: Culture, People, Places* (New York: Routledge, 1996). See also Stewart M. Hoover and Lynn Schofield Clark, eds., *Practicing Religion in the Age of Media: Explorations in Media, Religion, and Culture* (New York: Columbia University Press, 2002).

33. Hawthorne, "Alice Doane's Appeal," p. 206 in Nathaniel Hawthorne, *Tales and Sketches* (New York: Library of America, 1996)</IBT>.

34. "Passages from a Relinquished Work," p. 176 in ibid.

# Chapter 4

1. See Nathan Schneider, *Thank You, Anarchy: Notes from the Occupy Apocalypse* (Berkeley: University of California Press, 2013). Older theorists of crowds

and mass movements remain illustrative. See Elias Canetti, *Crowds and Power* (New York: Farrar, Straus and Giroux, 1984); Eric Hoffer, *The True Believer: Thoughts on the Nature of Mass Movements* (New York: Harper Perennial, 2010); Gustave LeBon, *The Crowd: A Study of the Popular Mind*, reprint ed. (Mineola, NY: Dover Books, 2002); and José Ortega y Gasset, *The Revolt of the Masses* (New York: Norton Books, 1994).

2. See Lincoln A. Mullen's fascinating *The Chance of Salvation: A History of Conversion in America* (Cambridge, MA: Harvard University Press, 2017).
3. Useful surveys of the philosophical development of these understandings can be found in James Miller, *Examined Lives: From Socrates to Nietzsche* (New York: Picador Books, 2012); Doug Rossinow, *Visions of Progress: The Left-Liberal Tradition in America* (Philadelphia: University of Pennsylvania Press, 2009); and Charles Taylor, *Sources of the Self: The Making of Modern Identity* (Cambridge, MA: Harvard University Press, 1992).
4. Michael Warner, Jonathan VanAntwerpen, and Craig Calhoun, "Editor's Introduction," pp. 7, 10, in Warner, VanAntwerpen, and Calhoun, eds., *Varieties of Secularism in a Secular Age* (Cambridge, MA: Harvard University Press, 2010).
5. Ibid., p. 10.
6. Cited in Amanda Anderson, *The Way We Argue Now: A Study in the Cultures of Theory* (Princeton, NJ: Princeton University Press, 2006), p. 163.
7. This account indebted also to Alan Ryan, *On Politics: A History of Political Thought: From Herodotus to the Present* (New York: Liveright Publishing, 2012).
8. Anderson, *Way We Argue Now*, p. 163.
9. These formulations also depend on particular juridical formulations of religion in the United States, particularly the use of "sincerity" as a standard for distinguishing between religion and nonreligion, with sincerity understood as nonfraudulent, and in this authentic.
10. Charles Taylor, "Western Secularity," p. 35 in Craig Calhoun, Mark Juergensmeyer, and Jonathan Van Antwerpen, eds., *Rethinking Secularism* (New York: Oxford University Press, 2011).
11. Ibid., p. 37.
12. Ibid., p. 39.
13. Will Bunch, *The Backlash: Right-Wing Radicals, High-Def Hucksters, and Paranoid Politics in the Age of Obama* (New York: Harper Books, 2010), p. 257.
14. Todd S. Purdum, "Beck and the Beast," *Vanity Fair* (May 2012): https://archive.vanityfair.com/article/2012/5/beck-and-the-beast.
15. Alexander Zaitchik, "Glenn Beck Rises Again," *Salon* (September 23, 2009): https://www.salon.com/2009/09/23/glenn_beck_three/.
16. Ibid.
17. Keach Hagey, "Glenn Beck Signs Off from Fox," *Politico* (June 30, 2011): www.politico.com/news/stories/0611/58175.html.
18. Dana Milbank, *Tears of a Clown: Glenn Beck and the Tea Bagging of America* (New York: Doubleday, 2010), p. 24.

19. See Matthew L. Harris, ed., *Thunder from the Right: Ezra Taft Benson in Mormonism and Politics* (Urbana: University of Illinois Press, 2019).
20. Quoted in Steve Rabey, "Exploring Glenn Beck's Beliefs," *Get Religion* (October 8, 2009): http://www.getreligion.org/2009/10/exploring-glenn-beck%E2%80%99s-beliefs/.
21. Skousen published dozens of books expounding on such themes. Though he is widely influential on a certain strain of millennial thought that Beck shares, he is considered outside the mainline of LDS politics. This is reflected in the fact that he is referenced merely twice in Randall Balmer and Jana Riess, eds., *Mormonism and American Politics* (New York: Columbia University Press, 2015).
22. Kathy Riordan, "Understanding Glenn Beck," *Salon* (August 27, 2010). Archived at http://slinkingtowardretirement.com/?p=28101.
23. www.the912project.com.
24. Ibid.
25. Ibid.
26. See Glenn Beck, *Glenn Beck's Common Sense: A Case against an Out-Of-Control Government, Inspired by Thomas Paine* (New York: Threshold Editions, 2009).
27. Radio interview transcribed at http://www.glennbeck.com/content/articles/article/196/10221/.
28. Matthew Continetti, "The Two Faces of the Tea Party," *Weekly Standard* 15:39 (June 28, 2010). Archived at https://www.washingtonexaminer.com/weekly-standard/the-two-faces-of-the-tea-party.
29. See Paul E. Gottfried, *Leo Strauss and the Conservative Movement in America*, reprint ed. (Cambridge: Cambridge University Press, 2013).
30. Mark Leibovich, "Being Glenn Beck," *New York Times Magazine* (September 29, 2010): https://www.nytimes.com/2010/10/03/magazine/03beck-t.html.
31. David Bauder, "Fox's Glenn Beck: President Obama Is a Racist," *Associated Press* (July 28, 2009): https://www.delcotimes.com/news/fox-s-glenn-beck-president-obama-is-a-racist/article_320fb049-347e-5d84-9d9d-5d960f365170.html.
32. Brian Montopoli, "ACORN Sting Lands Housing Group in Conservative Crosshairs," *CBS News* (September 16, 2009): http://www.cbsnews.com/8301-503544_162-5315657-503544.html.
33. See Andrew Newman, "Advice to Fake Pimp Was No Crime, Prosecutor Says," *New York Times* (March 1, 2010): https://www.nytimes.com/2010/03/02/nyregion/02acorn.html; and Chris Rovar, "Damaging Brooklyn ACORN Sting Video Ruled 'Heavily Edited,' No Charges to Be Filed," *New York Magazine* (March 2, 2010): https://nymag.com/intelligencer/2010/03/damaging_brooklyn_acorn_sting.html.
34. Tobin Grant, "Glenn Beck: 'Leave Your Church,'" *Christianity Today* (March 12, 2010): http://www.christianitytoday.com/ct/2010/marchweb-only/20-51.0.html.
35. Radio interview transcribed at http://www.glennbeck.com/content/articles/article/198/42573/.
36. Ibid.
37. Ibid.
38. Ibid.

39. Ibid.
40. Quoted in "Common Good Death Camps" (no author), *The Revealer* (May 29, 2010): https://therevealer.org/common-good-death-camps/.
41. Ibid.
42. Nate Anderson, "Glenn Beck Loses Domain Dispute, Still Ends Up with Domain," *Ars Technica* (November 9, 2009): https://arstechnica.com/tech-policy/2009/11/glenn-beck-loses-domain-dispute-still-ends-up-with-domain/.
43. Nina Mandell, "Glenn Beck Apologizes for Comparing Reform Judaism to Radical Islam," *New York Daily News* (February 24, 2011): https://www.nydailynews.com/news/national/glenn-beck-apologizes-comparing-reform-judaism-radical-islam-bad-analogy-article-1.134374.
44. Ibid.
45. See Andrew M. Shocket, *Fighting over the Founders: How We Remember the American Revolution* (New York: New York University Press, 2015).
46. Jason Easley, "Glenn Beck the Mormon Blames Progressives for Perverting Religion," *Politics USA* (April 30, 2010): http://www.politicususa.com/en/beck-progressives-religion.
47. Ibid.
48. Ibid.
49. Glenn Beck, "We Are All Catholics Now," *Washington Post* (February 19, 2012): http://www.washingtonpost.com/blogs/guest-voices/post/why-we-are-all-catholics-now/2012/02/19/gIQAZFYVOR_blog.html.
50. Ibid.
51. On these religious sources, see Ann Braude, *Radical Spirits: Spiritualism and Women's Rights in Nineteenth-Century America*, 2nd ed. (Bloomington: Indiana University Press, 2001); Stephen J. Stein, *The Shaker Experience in America: A History of the United Society of Believers* (New Haven, CT: Yale University Press, 1994); and Hugh B. Urban, *New Age, Neopagan, and New Religious Movements: Alternative Spirituality in Contemporary America* (Berkeley: University of California Press, 2015).
52. On the riotous, unstable features of this era so often thought to be singular in its democratic enthusiasms, see Thaddeus Russell's marvelous *A Renegade History of the United States* (New York: Free Press, 2010).
53. See text at http://www.simonandschuster.com/books/The-Original-Argument/Glenn-Beck/9781451650617.
54. See Jon Elster, ed., *Tocqueville: The Ancien Régime and the French Revolution* (Cambridge: Cambridge University Press, 2012).
55. Michael Sean Winters, "Glenn Beck's Rally and the Banality of Goodness," *National Catholic Reporter* (August 28, 2010): https://www.ncronline.org/blogs/distinctly-catholic/glenn-becks-rally-banality-goodness.
56. Cathy Lynn Grossman, "Glenn Beck: Politicians Should Give Voice to God's Will," *USA Today* (August 28, 2010): http://content.usatoday.com/communities/Religion/post/2010/08/glenn-beck-god-obama-mormon/1.

57. Elizabeth Tenety, "Beck Sets Religious Tone for Restoring Honor Rally," *Washington Post* (August 28, 2010). Archived at https://www.democraticunderground.com/discuss/duboard.php?az=view_all&address=389x9031372.
58. Quoted in Miller, *Examined Lives*, p. 293.
59. Bunch, *The Backlash*, p. 327. Italics mine.
60. Kate Zernike, Carl Hulse, and Brian Knowlton, "At Lincoln Memorial, a Call for Religious Rebirth," *New York Times* (August 29, 2010): https://www.nytimes.com/2010/08/29/us/politics/29beck.html.
61. Ibid. See Juan M. Floyd-Thomas and Anthony Pinn, eds., *Religion in the Age of Obama* (London: Bloomsbury Academic, 2018).
62. Julie Ingersoll, "Glenn Beck Has a Plan," *Religion Dispatches* (August 10, 2010): http://www.religiondispatches.org/dispatches/julieingersoll/3115/glenn_beck_has_a_plan.
63. Zernike, Hulse, and Knowlton, "At Lincoln Memorial."
64. Key to the advancement of these notions has been the work of African American conservatives like Thomas Sowell and Shelby Steele.
65. Zernike, Hulse, and Knowlton, "At Lincoln Memorial."
66. Sam Dillon, "Wisdom of Leaders and Guidance for Graduates," *New York Times* (June 20, 2010): https://www.nytimes.com/2010/06/21/education/21commence-web.html.
67. David Von Drehle, "Mad Man: Is Glenn Beck Bad for America," *Time* (September 17, 2009): http://content.time.com/time/subscriber/article/0,33009,1924495,00.html. Beck is reported to prefer the term "doom room."
68. Sam Stein, "Sen. Graham Calls Beck 'a Cynic' and Birthers 'Crazy,'" *Huffington Post* (December 1, 2009): https://www.huffpost.com/entry/sen-graham-calls-beck-a-c_n_306434.
69. Laura Miller, "The Paranoid Style of American Punditry," *Salon* (September 15, 2010): https://www.salon.com/2010/09/15/hofstadter/.
70. See Brad Knickerbocker, "Glenn Beck Goes Home to Face—What Else?—Controversy," *Christian Science Monitor* (September 26, 2009): https://www.csmonitor.com/USA/Politics/2009/0926/glenn-beck-goes-home-to-face-what-else-controversy; *The Daily Show*, Comedy Central (November 5, 2009 and March 18, 2010); *The Colbert Report*, Comedy Central (March 4, 2009); Chris Good, "South Park Does Glenn Beck," *The Atlantic* (November 12, 2009): https://www.theatlantic.com/politics/archive/2009/11/south-park-does-glenn-beck/30090/; Bill Maher, "Bill Maher Talks Glenn Beck's 'Diabetic Mall-Walkers,' Summer of Racism," *Huffington Post* (September 14, 2010): http://www.huffingtonpost.com/2010/09/14/bill_maher_glenn_beck_n_716897.html?view=print.
71. James Martin, "Glenn Beck to Jesus: Drop Dead," *Huffington Post* (May 8, 2010): http://www.huffingtonpost.com/rev-james-martin-sj/glenn-beck-to-catholics-l_b_490669.html. For historical backdrop, see Jay P. Dolan, *The American Catholic Experience: A History from Colonial Times to the Present* (New York: Doubleday, 1985).
72. Joe Carter, "Glenn Beck Thinks Catholics Should 'Leave Their Church,'" *First Things* (March 8, 2010): http://www.firstthings.com/blogs/firstthoughts/2010/03/08/glenn-beck-thinks-catholics-should-leave-their-church/.

73. Laurie Goodstein, "Outraged by Glenn Beck's Salvo, Christians Fire Back," *New York Times* (March 12, 2010): https://www.nytimes.com/2010/03/12/us/12justice.html?searchResultPosition=9.
74. Reverend Robert Thompson, "Jesus Is Glenn Beck's Worst Nightmare," *Chicago Tribune* (March 16, 2010): http://newsblogs.chicagotribune.com/religion_theseeker/2010/03/rev-robert-thompson-jesus-is-glenn-becks-worst-nightmare-.html.
75. Paul Harvey, "American Idiot and Glenn Beck," *US Religion* (March 29, 2009): http://usreligion.blogspot.com/2009/03/american-idiot-and-glen-beck.html.
76. Sarah Posner, "Glenn Beck's Social Justice Heresies," *Religion Dispatches* (July 19, 2010):http://www.religiondispatches.org/archive/politics/2988/glenn_beck%E2%80%99s_%E2%80%98social_justice%E2%80%99_heresies.
77. Joanna Brooks, "Who Says the Tea Party Isn't a Religious Movement?," *Religion Dispatches* (June 3, 2010): http://www.religiondispatches.org/dispatches/joannabrooks/2736/who_says_the_tea_party_isn%E2%80%99t_a_religious_movement%2C_part_ii.
78. Kathryn Joyce, "Can Mormon Glenn Beck Unite the Christian Right?," *Religion Dispatches* (September 21, 2010): http://www.religiondispatches.org/archive/politics/3334/can_mormon_glenn_beck_unite_the_christian_right.
79. Michelle Boorstein, "Glenn Beck May Be Unlikely Leader for Conservative Christians," *Washington Post* (August 31, 2010). Archived at https://madison.com/ct/news/glenn-beck-may-be-unlikely-leader-for-conservative-christians/article_cca2c0d4-b514-11df-9e71-001cc4c002e0.html.
80. Becky Garrison, "What Beck's Marching For: Making Social Justice Unjust," *The Revealer* (August 28, 2010): http://therevealer.org/archives/4771.
81. Annette Powers, "Reform Movement Denounces Glenn Beck's Attack on Religious Values," *Progressive Jewish Voice* (February 23, 2011): http://blog.pjvoice.com/diary/316/reform-movement-denounces-glenn-becks-attack-on-religious-values.
82. Gloria Goodale, "Glenn Beck Sticks Liberation Theology Label on Obama's Christianity," *Christian Science Monitor* (August 25, 2010): https://www.csmonitor.com/USA/Politics/The-Vote/2010/0825/Glenn-Beck-sticks-liberation-theology-label-on-Obama-s-Christianity.
83. Stevens-Arroyo, "Is Glenn Beck Preaching Mormon 'Restoration' Theology?," *Washington Post* (August 31, 2010).
84. Andrew Murphy, "Beck Plays Prophet—Politics Pervade": https://blog.oup.com/2010/09/beck-plays-prophet/.
85. Moore, "God, the Gospel, and Glenn Beck": www.russellmoore.com/2010/08/29/god-the-gospel-and-glenn-beck/.
86. Ibid.
87. Ibid.
88. Milbank, *Tears of a Clown*, p. 87.
89. The term "fort-da" is, as many readers will know, from Sigmund Freud's work. It refers to a kind of perceptual reversal that children learn to enact against their parents. Freud interpreted the interplay between these colloquial terms for "gone" and "there" to the child's ability to transform situations of negativity or constraint into one's of joy and possibility. See Freud, *Beyond the Pleasure Principle* (New York: Norton Books, 1990).

90. Dan Gilgoff, "Glenn Beck: Hurricane Irene Is a Blessing," *CNN* (August 27, 2011): http://religion.blogs.cnn.com/2011/08/27/glenn-beck-hurricane-irene-is-a-blessing/.
91. Elizabeth Tenety, "Mormon Glenn Beck: Hurricane Irene and East Coast Earthquake a 'Blessing' from God," *Washington Post* (August 26, 2011). Quoted at https://thinkprogress.org/bachmann-hurricane-was-a-message-from-god-to-washington-about-spending-updated-fb997f46a606/.
92. Shalom Goldman, "The Auspicious Timing of Glenn Beck's Zeal for Zion," *Religion Dispatches* (July 19, 2011): http://www.religiondispatches.org/archive/politics/4860/the_auspicious_timing_of_glenn_beck%E2%80%99s_zeal_for_zion_/.
93. Bunch, *The Backlash*, p. 333.
94. Ibid., p. 255.
95. Ibid., pp. 334–335.
96. Bob Cesca, "Welcome to Glenn Beck's Grifter Theme Park," *Huffington Post* (August 1, 2014): http://www.huffingtonpost.com/bob-cesca/welcome-to-glenn-becks-gr_b_2497307.html.
97. See Bradley Burston, "Not Jewish Enough for Glenn Beck," *Haaretz* (August 19, 2011): https://www.haaretz.com/1.5049163.
98. Quoted in ibid.
99. Joshua Holland, "Glenn Beck's Absurd Jerusalem Rally: Why Religious Conservatives Are Obsessed with Israel," *Alternet* (May 18, 2011). Archived at https://www.greanvillepost.com/2011/05/25/glenn-becks-absurd-jerusalem-rally-why-religious-conservatives-are-obsessed-with-israel/.
100. See Yaakov Ariel, *Evangelizing the Chosen People: Missions to the Jews in America, 1880–2000* (Chapel Hill: University of North Carolina Press, 2000); and Gershom Gorenberg, *The End of Days: Fundamentalism and the Struggle for the Temple Mount* (New York: Oxford University Press, 2002).
101. Karl Vick, "Among His Believers: With Glenn Beck's Posse in Jerusalem," *Time Magazine* (August 25, 2011): http://content.time.com/time/world/article/0,8599,2090466,00.html.
102. Ibid.
103. Ibid.
104. Lisa Schencker, "Politics, Religion Draw Utahans to Glenn Beck's Holy Land Events," *Salt Lake Tribune* (August 12, 2011): https://archive.sltrib.com/article.php?id=52355250&itype=CMSID.
105. See James Downie, "The Decline of Glenn Beck," *New Republic* (March 3, 2011): https://newrepublic.com/article/84662/the-decline-glenn-beck; Mark Engler, "Boycott Power and the Fall of Glenn Beck," *Dissent* (June 29, 2011): https://www.dissentmagazine.org/blog/boycott-power-and-the-fall-of-glenn-beck; and Hendrik Hertzberg, "Beck's Last Tapes," *New Yorker* (April 6, 2011): https://www.newyorker.com/news/hendrik-hertzberg/becks-last-tapes.
106. James Parker, "Glenn Beck in Exile," *The Atlantic* (June 2012), pp. 40–41.
107. All examples and quotations from ibid., p. 40.

108. Erik Hedegaard, "Glenn Beck's Regrets," p. 46 in *Rolling Stone* (November 3, 2016), pp. 44–47, 56–57. See also Peter Beinart, "Glenn Beck's Regrets," *The Atlantic* (January–February 2017), pp. 16–19.
109. This inheritance of modernist conceptions of authenticity as truthful and self-authoring generally does not yield an implied ethic for Embattled Americans. See Charles Taylor, *The Ethics of Authenticity*, reprint ed. (Cambridge, MA: Harvard University Press, 2018). On legitimacy, the conversation usually turns on notions of law and the right to govern. See Arthur Isak Applbaum, *Legitimacy: The Right to Rule in a Wanton World* (Cambridge, MA: Harvard University Press, 2019).
110. Ibid., p. 56.
111. Ibid., p. 57.
112. Matt Sheedy, "Trump and the Tyranny of Authenticity": http://bulletin.equinoxpub.com/2016/11/trump-and-the-tyranny-of-authenticity/.
113. Leslie Savan, "The Beck Identity, Supremacy, and Ultimatum," *The Nation* (June 28, 2011): http://www.thenation.com/blog/161691/beck-identity-supremacy-and-ultimatum.
114. Kyle Mantyla, "Glenn Beck's Latest Conspiracy Theory: Women's March Was George Soros, Radical Islam 'Astroturf,'" *Salon* (January 24, 2017): http://www.salon.com/2017/01/24/glenn-becks-latest-conspiracy-theory-womens-march-was-george-soros-radical-islam-astroturf_partner/.
115. Danny Gallagher, "Glenn Beck Might Be Losing More Than His Media Empire after Tense CNN Interview," *Dallas Observer* (July 11, 2018): https://www.dallasobserver.com/news/glenn-beck-his-media-company-tanking-becomes-a-trump-fan-10845643.
116. Ed Mazza, "'I'd Rather Die': Glenn Beck Urges Older Americans to Work Despite Coronavirus," *Huffington Post* (March 24, 2020):https://www.huffpost.com/entry/glenn-beck-coronavirus_n_5e7ab2d6c5b620022ab30851.
117. Glenn Beck Radio (August 25, 2020): https://www.glennbeck.com/radio/glenn-reacts-to-rnc-night-1-i-havent-felt-that-way-at-a-convention-since-ronald-reagan.
118. Aila Sisco, "Glenn Beck Suggests It's Americans 'Duty to Overthrow' Government If Election Is 'Stolen' by Dems," *Newsweek* (November 4, 2020): https://www.newsweek.com/glenn-beck-suggests-its-americans-duty-overthrow-government-if-election-stolen-dems-1544994. Lee Moran, "Glenn Beck Slammed for Comparing Trump Social Media Ban to Holocaust," *Huffington Post* (January 13, 2021): https://www.huffpost.com/entry/glenn-beck-tucker-carlson-fox-news-big-tech_n_5ffeb5e9c5b691806c4dbb57.
119. Milbank, *Tears of a Clown*, pp. 1–2.
120. Ian Schwartz, "Glenn Beck Chalkboard Lesson: Chicago Marxists Are Pulling the Strings on the Attack on Our Border," *Real Clear Politics* (April 11, 2019): https://www.realclearpolitics.com/video/2019/04/11/glenn_beck_chalkboard_lesson_chicago_marxists_are_pulling_the_strings_on_the_attack_on_our_border.html.
121. Milbank, *Tears of a Clown*, p. 83.
122. Ibid.

123. Nietzsche, *Human, All Too Human: A Book for Free Spirits* (Cambridge: Cambridge University Press, 1996), p. 78.
124. My account here is indebted to Taylor, *Sources of the Self*.
125. See Walter Benn Michaels, *The Problem with Diversity: How We Learned to Love Identity and Ignore Inequality* (New York: Metropolitan Books, 2006).
126. Lauren Berlant, *The Female Complaint: The Unfinished Business of Sentimentality in American Culture* (Durham, NC: Duke University Press, 2008), p. 35.
127. See Martin Heidegger, *The Question Concerning Technology and Other Essays* (New York: Harper Perennial, 2013).
128. My thanks to Ann Burlein for this insight into Bataille. See Georges Bataille, *On Nietzsche* (Saint Paul, MN: Paragon House Publishers, 1988).
129. Ian Shapiro, *Political Criticism* (Berkeley: University of California Press, 1992), p. 270.
130. Melissa A. Orlie, *Living Ethically, Acting Politically* (Ithaca, NY: Cornell University Press, 1997), p. 2.
131. See Václav Havel, *Living in Truth: 22 Essays Published on the Occasion of the Award of the Erasmus Prize to Vaclav Havel*, 2nd ed. (London: Faber & Faber, 1990).
132. Shapiro, *Political Criticism*, p. 271.
133. Aristotle, *The Nicomachean Ethics* (New York: Oxford University Press 2009).

# Chapter 5

1. Herman Melville, *Billy Budd & Other Stories* (New York: Penguin Books, 1986), p. 61.
2. Jean Bethke Elshtain, *Real Politics: At the Center of Everyday Life* (Baltimore: Johns Hopkins University Press, 1997), p. 77.
3. See Jason C. Bivins, *Religion of Fear: The Politics of Horror in Conservative Evangelicalism* (New York: Oxford University Press, 2008).
4. Manya Bracher, "How Religion Guides Palin," *Chicago Tribune* (September 6, 2008). For a solid scholarly assessment, see Linda Beail and Rhonda Kinney Longworth, *Framing Sarah Palin: Pit Bulls, Puritans, and Politics* (New York: Routledge Books, 2012).
5. Brachear, "How Religion Guides Palin."
6. Kirk Johnson and Kim Severson, "In Palin's Life and Politics, Goal to Follow God's Will," *New York Times* (September 6, 2008): https://www.nytimes.com/2008/09/06/us/politics/06church.html?searchResultPosition=2.
7. Ibid.
8. See Kate Bowler, *Blessed: A History of the American Prosperity Gospel* (New York: Oxford University Press, 2013).
9. Stephen Braun, "Palin Canny on Religion and Politics," *Los Angeles Times* (September 28, 2008): https://www.latimes.com/archives/la-xpm-2008-sep-28-na-palinreligion28-story.html.

10. Ibid.
11. http://www.ontheissues.org/sarah_palin.htm.
12. Ibid.; and Sarah Palin, *America by Heart: Reflections on Family, Faith, and Flag* (New York: HarperCollins, 2010), pp. 103–104.
13. Ibid., p. 153.
14. While Jodi Dean does not theorize precisely these connections, her work has been influential on my thinking in this area. See Dean, *Democracy and Other Neoliberal Fantasies: Communicative Capitalism and Left Politics* (Durham, NC: Duke University Press, 2009).
15. Palin, *America by Heart*, pp. 76–77.
16. http://www.ontheissues.org/2010_Tea.htm.
17. Palin, *America by Heart*, pp. 87–88.
18. http://www.ontheissues.org/Archive/New_Energy_Budget_+_Economy.htm.
19. Ibid.
20. https://eagleforum.org/political/candidate-questionnaire.html.
21. Palin, *America by Heart*, pp. 130–31.
22. Ibid., pp. 111–112.
23. Ibid., pp. 165–166.
24. Ibid., pp. xii–xiii.
25. Ibid., p. 37.
26. http://www.ontheissues.org/2006_AK_Governor.htm.
27. Palin, *America by Heart*, pp. 228–229.
28. Ibid., p. 12.
29. Ibid., p. 215.
30. Ibid.
31. http://www.ontheissues.org/2008_AK_Governor.htm.
32. Ed Pilkington, "This Person Loves Jesus," *The Guardian* (September 6, 2008): http://www.guardian.co.uk/world/2008/sep/06/uselections2008.sarahpalin.
33. Adam Rose, "Sarah Palin Supports Dr. Laura via Twitter: 'Don't Retreat . . . Reload!,'" *Huffington Post* (August 18, 2010): http://www.huffingtonpost.com/2010/08/18/sarah-palin-supports-dr-laura_n_687148.html. All punctuation from the original tweets.
34. Amy Sullivan, "Does Palin Have a Pentecostal Problem?," *Time Magazine* (October 9, 2008): http://content.time.com/time/politics/article/0,8599,1848420,00.html.
35. Welton Gaddy, "The Car Wreck That Is Sarah Palin and the National Day of Prayer," *Religion Dispatches* (April 22, 2010): http://www.religiondispatches.org/archive/politics/2499/the_car_wreck_that_is_sarah_palin_and_the_national_day_of_prayer.
36. Braun, "Palin Canny."
37. Jeffrey Weiss, "Religion and Sarah Palin—Her History," *Dallas Morning News* (September 28, 2008): https://www.dallasnews.com/news/faith/2008/08/29/religion-and-sarah-palin-her-history/.
38. Ibid.
39. Ibid.

40. Mary E. Hunt, "Sarah Palin and the Clarence Thomas Factor," *Religion Dispatches* (June 11, 2009): http://www.religiondispatches.org/archive/politics/480/sarah_palin_and_the_clarence_thomas_factor.
41. Randall Balmer, "Sarah Palin and the Politics of Victimization," *Religion Dispatches* (January 3, 2011): http://www.religiondispatches.org/books/politics/3972/sarah_palin_and_the_politics_of_victimization.
42. Ibid.
43. Kathleen Kennedy Townsend, "Sarah Palin Is Wrong about JFK, Religion and Politics," *Washington Post* (December 7, 2010): https://live.washingtonpost.com/outlook-kathleen-kennedy-townsend.html.
44. Bruce Wilson, "A Buzzflash Interview," *Buzzflash* (September 22, 2008): http://legacy.buzzflash.com/commentary/sarah-palins-extremist-religious-beliefs-the-republic-is-at-risk.
45. Ibid.
46. Ibid.
47. On the social and political significance of Third Wave spiritual warfare, see Sean McCloud, *American Possessions: Fighting Demons in the Contemporary United States* (New York: Oxford University Press, 2015).
48. "Sarah Palin: Dominionist Stalking Horse" (no author), *The Daily Kos* (August 29, 2008): http://www.dailykos.com/story/2008/08/29/579213/-Sarah-Palin:-Dominionist-Stalking-Horse.
49. Ibid.
50. Andy Birkey, "Religious Right Watch: Sarah Palin at a Glance," *Twin Cities Daily Planet* (September 10, 2008): https://www.tcdailyplanet.net/religious-right-watch-sarah-palin-glance/.
51. Bruce Wilson, "Palin's Prayer Leader Hinted Terrorist Attack Could Make Sarah President," *Talk to Action* (November 16, 2009): http://www.talk2action.org/story/2009/11/16/172837/58.
52. Bruce Wilson, "Katherine Harris, Sarah Palin Linked to Same Prayer Warfare Network," *Talk to Action* (November 2, 2008): http://www.talk2action.org/story/2008/11/2/115526/519; and Wilson, "Palin Movement Urges 'Godly' to 'Plunder' Wealth of 'Godless,'" *Talk to Action* (November 1, 2008): http://www.talk2action.org/story/2008/11/1/14522/8804/.
53. Bruce Wilson, "Palin Linked to Second Witch Hunter," *Talk to Action* (October 24, 2008): http://www.talk2action.org/story/2008/10/24/125017/31.
54. P. J. Gladnick, "WaPo Religion Blogger Attacks Sarah Palin's Religion," *Newsbusters* (September 11, 2008): http://www.newsbusters.org/blogs/p-j-gladnick/2008/09/11/wapo-religion-blogger-attacks-sarah-palins-religion.
55. Anthea Butler, "Whom Will She Wreck? The Real Sarah Palin Question," *Religion Dispatches* (September 6, 2011): http://www.religiondispatches.org/archive/politics/5061/whom_will_she_wreck%3A_the_real_sarah_palin_question/.
56. Two excellent scholarly sources on the cultural construction of the generic category "religion" are Daniel Dubuisson, *The Western Construction of Religion: Myths, Knowledge, and Identity* (Baltimore: Johns Hopkins University Press, 2007); and

Tomoko Masuzawa, *The Invention of World Religions: Or, How European Universalism Was Preserved in the Language of Pluralism* (Chicago: University of Chicago Press, 2006).

57. Carol Jensen, "Sarah Palin's Religious Beliefs Too Extreme for America," *ExChristian* (September 28, 2008): http://news.exchristian.net/2008/09/sarah-palins-religious-beliefs-too.html.
58. Ibid.
59. Bonnie Erbe, "Sarah Palin's Lies about Obamacare Are Based on Religion," *U.S. News & World Report* (August 11, 2008): http://www.usnews.com/opinion/blogs/erbe/2009/08/11/sarah-palins-lies-about-obamacare-are-based-on-religion.
60. Mary Fairchild, "Sarah Palin's Faith," *Learn Religions* (March 6, 2017): https://www.learnreligions.com/sarah-palins-faith-701386.
61. Balmer, "Sarah Palin."
62. Sarah Posner, "The Perry v. Bachmann Primary at Liberty University," *Religion Dispatches* (July 11, 2011): http://www.religiondispatches.org/dispatches/sarahposner/4841/the_perry_v._bachmann_primary_at_liberty_unversity/.
63. Bob Moser, "God Help Us," *American Prospect* (December 2011): https://prospect.org/labor/god-help-us/.
64. Philip Rucker, "Perry Casts Himself as Spiritual, Says His Life is Shaped by Faith," *Washington Post* (September 14, 2011): http://www.washingtonpost.com/politics/perry-casts-himself-as-anti-intellectual-says-his-life-shaped-by-faith/2011/09/14/gIQAUNgASK_story.html.
65. Ibid.
66. Dana Milbank, "Rick Perry Is No Libertarian," *Washington Post* (August 30, 2011):http://www.washingtonpost.com/opinions/rick-perry-is-no-libertarian/2011/08/30/gIQA6IsbqJ_story.html.
67. Ibid.
68. Moser, "God Help Us."
69. Ibid.
70. Ibid.
71. Ibid.
72. Ibid.
73. Ibid.
74. Scott Keyes, "Top 10 Things Rick Perry Doesn't Want You to Know about Him," *ThinkProgress* (June 10, 2011): http://thinkprogress.org/politics/2011/06/10/241830/top-10-thing-texas-gov-rick-perry/.
75. Ibid.
76. Moser, "God Help Us."
77. Grace Wyler, "Rick Perry Defends Threatening Ben Bernanke," *Business Insider* (August 16, 2011): https://www.businessinsider.com/rick-perry-defends-bernanke-threats-says-hes-just-venting-frustration-2011-8.
78. Moser, "God Help Us."
79. Mark Halperin and John Heilemann, *Double Down: Game Change 2012* (New York: Penguin Press, 2013), p. 172.

80. Sarah Posner, "Blankets, Booties, and Jesus: Spiritual War on the Uterus in Rick Perry's Texas," *Religion Dispatches* (March 19, 2012): http://www.religiondispatches.org/archive/politics/5372/blankets%2C_booties%2C_and_jesus%3A_spiritual_war_on_the_uterus_in_rick_perry%E2%80%99s_texas/.
81. Forrest Wilder, "Rick Perry's Army of God: Is Rick Perry God's Man for President?," *Texas Observer* (August 3, 2011): http://www.texasobserver.org/cover-story/rick-perrys-army-of-god.
82. Maggie Haberman, "Perry Back to 'Ponzi Scheme,' 'Monstrous Lie' on Social Security," *Politico* (August 28, 2011): https://www.politico.com/story/2011/08/perry-back-to-ponzi-scheme-monstrous-lie-on-social-security-062201.
83. "Rick Perry's Religious Revival Sparks a Holy War," *National Public Radio* (August 5, 2011): http://www.npr.org/templates/transcript/transcript.php?storyId=138995325.
84. Abby Ohlheiser, "Perry's Cross-Section of the Body of Christ," *The Revealer* (August 18, 2011): https://therevealer.org/perrys-cross-section-of-the-body-of-christ/.
85. Ibid.
86. Maggie Haberman, "The GOP Debate: 8 Takeaways," *Politico* (September 8, 2011): https://www.politico.com/story/2011/09/the-gop-debate-8-takeaways-062963.
87. David Nakamura, "White House to Rick Perry: We Won't Respond to 'Struggling . . . Campaigns,'" *Washington Post* (December 9, 2011): http://www.washingtonpost.com/blogs/44/post/white-house-to-rick-perry-we-wont-respond-to-struggling--campaigns/2011/12/09/gIQATQvfiO_blog.html.
88. "Rick Perry's Religious Revival."
89. Manny Fernandez and Erik Eckholm, "Texas Governor Draws Criticism on Prayer Event," *New York Times* (June 12, 2011): https://www.nytimes.com/2011/06/12/us/politics/12prayer.html.
90. Manny Fernandez, "Governor Leads Prayer Rally for 'Nation in Crisis,'" *New York Times* (August 7, 2011): http://www.nytimes.com/2011/08/07/us/politics/07prayer.html?_r=1&hp.
91. Halperin and Heilemann, *Double Down*, p. 176.
92. Jason Cohen, "When the Governor Talks to God," *Texas Monthly* (January 21, 2013): https://www.texasmonthly.com/articles/when-the-governor-talks-to-god/.
93. Wilder, "Rick Perry's Army of God."
94. Richard Dawkins, "Attention Gov. Perry: Evolution Is a Fact," *The Oregonian* (August 7, 2011): https://www.oregonlive.com/opinion/2011/08/attention_gov_perry_evolution.html.
95. Bill Keller, "Asking Candidates Tougher Questions about Faith," *New York Times Magazine* (August 28, 2011): http://www.nytimes.com/2011/08/28/magazine/asking-candidates-tougher-questions-about-faith.html?_r=1.
96. Michael Medved, "*New York Times* Editor Bill Keller's Religious Test for Presidential Candidates," *Daily Beast* (August 30, 2011): http://www.thedailybeast.com/articles/2011/08/30/new-york-times-editor-bill-keller-s-religious-test-for-presidential-candidates.html.

97. Steve Kornacki, "Rick Perry's Descent into Birtherism," *Salon* (October 24, 2011): http://www.salon.com/2011/10/24/now_rick_perry_is_flirting_with_birtherism/.
98. Sarah Posner, "Rick Perry and the New Apostolic Reformation," *Religion Dispatches* (July 19, 2011): http://www.religiondispatches.org/dispatches/sarahposner/4874/rick_perry_and_the_new_apostolic_reformation/.
99. For a crisp distillation of the "economic anxiety" argument, see Daniel Kreiss, Joshua O. Barker, and Shannon Zenner, "Trump Gave Them Hope: Studying the Strangers in Their Own Land," *Political Communication* 34:3 (2017), pp. 470–478.
100. For a series of insights into Trump's relationship with evangelicalism, see *Religion and American Culture* 27:1 (Winter 2017).
101. On these grim economic realities, see Drew Desilver, "For Most U.S. Workers, Real Wages Have Barely Budged for Decades," *Fact Tank* (August 7, 2018): https://www.pewresearch.org/fact-tank/2018/08/07/for-most-us-workers-real-wages-have-barely-budged-for-decades/.
102. See Sahil Chinoy, "What Happened to America's Political Center of Gravity?," *New York Times* (June 26, 2019): https://www.nytimes.com/interactive/2019/06/26/opinion/sunday/republican-platform-far-right.html.
103. Habermas's classic historical portrait is found in Jürgen Habermas, *The Structural Transformation of the Public Sphere: An Inquiry into a Category of Bourgeois Society* (Cambridge, MA: MIT Press, 1991).
104. On the complicated history of majoritarianism and its associated fears, see Tamás Nyirkos, *The Tyranny of the Majority: History, Concepts, Challenges* (New York: Routledge, 2018).
105. For a recent theoretical intervention into these debates, see Chantal Mouffe, *The Democratic Paradox* (New York: Verso Books, 2009).
106. See Sean Wilentz, *The Rise of American Democracy: Jefferson to Lincoln* (New York: Norton, 2005).
107. The standard resource for this line of thinking is Robert Dahl's *Polyarchy: Participation and Opposition* (New Haven, CT: Yale University Press, 1972).
108. See Francis Fukuyama, *The End of History and the Last Man*, reissue ed. (New York: Free Press, 2006).
109. Stuti Mishra, "Sarah Palin Hits Campaign Trail in Georgia, Denying Trump Lost alongside Q-Anon-Supporting Republican," *The Independent* (December 15, 2020): https://www.independent.co.uk/news/world/americas/us-election-2020/sarah-palin-trump-qanon-georgia-election-b1774085.html.
110. A vivid critical assessment of rational choice theory is Donald P. Green and Ian Shapiro, *Pathologies of Rational Choice Theory: A Critique of Applications in Political Science* (New Haven, CT: Yale University Press, 1994).
111. Amy Brittain and David Willman, "'A Place to Fund Hope': How Proud Boys and Other Fringe Groups Found Refuge on a Christian Fundraising Website," *Washington Post* (January 18, 2021): https://www.washingtonpost.com/investigations/a-place-to-fund-hope-how-proud-boys-and-other-fringe-groups-found-ref

uge-on-a-christian-fundraising-website/2021/01/18/14a536ee-574b-11eb-a08b-f1381ef3d207_story.html.
112. I refer here to the *Citizens United* case: https://www.oyez.org/cases/2008/08-205. For insight into the difficulties of campaign finance reform, consider the stalled efforts of bills like: https://www.congress.gov/bill/116th-congress/house-bill/1.
113. Hannah Arendt, *On Revolution* (New York: Penguin Classics, 2006), p. 237.
114. Ibid.
115. Ibid., pp. 237–238.
116. Ibid., p. 239.
117. John Dewey, *The Public and Its Problems* (Athens: Ohio University Press, 1994), p. 184.
118. Ibid., p. 82.
119. Walter Lippmann, *Public Opinion* (New York: Harcourt, Brace and Company, 1922).
120. Jonathan Rauch, "What's Ailing American Politics?," p. 58 in *The Atlantic* (July–August 2016).
121. Geoffrey Kabaservice documents this sentiment in "The Great Performance of Our Failing President," *New York Times* (June 9, 2017): https://www.nytimes.com/2017/06/09/opinion/great-performance-of-donald-trump-our-failing-president.html.
122. James Madison, "Federalist #10": https://www.congress.gov/resources/display/content/The+Federalist+Papers#TheFederalistPapers-10.
123. Lawrence Lessig, *They Don't Represent Us: Reclaiming Our Democracy* (New York: Dey Street Books, 2019), pp. 174–191.

# Chapter 6

1. Thaddeus Russell, *A Renegade History of the United States* (New York: Free Press, 2010).
2. John Fea, *Was America Founded as a Christian Nation? A Historical Introduction* (Louisville, KY: Westminster John Knox Press, 2011), p. 102.
3. See Steven Perlberg, "Rick Santelli Started the Tea Party with a Rant Exactly 5 Years Ago Today—Here's How He Feels Now," *Business Insider* (February 19, 2014): https://www.businessinsider.com/rick-santelli-tea-party-rant-2014-2.
4. See Catherine McNicol Stock, *Rural Radicals: Righteous Rage in the American Grain*, new ed. (Ithaca, NY: Cornell University Press, 2017).
5. A representative montage can be seen here: http://www.youtube.com/watch?v=S38VioxnBaI&feature=player_embedded.
6. See, for example: Devin Fergus, *Land of the Fee: Hidden Costs and the Decline of the American Middle Class* (New York: Oxford University Press, 2018); Jacob S. Hacker, *The Great Risk Shift: The New Economic Insecurity and the Decline of the American Dream*, 2nd ed. (New York: Oxford University Press, 2019); and Dale L. Johnson, *Social Inequality, Economic Decline, and Plutocracy: An American Crisis* (New York: Palgrave Macmillan, 2017).

7. See Theda Skocpol and Vanessa Williamson, *The Tea Party and the Remaking of American Conservatism* (New York: Oxford University Press, 2012). See also Ruth Braunstein, *Prophets and Patriots: Faith in Democracy across the Political Divide* (Berkeley: University of California Press, 2017); and Christopher S. Parker and Matt A. Barreto, *Change They Can't Believe In: The Tea Party and Reactionary Politics in America* (Princeton, NJ: Princeton University Press, 2014).
8. See Michael Brendan Dougherty, "Tea Party Crashers," *American Conservative* (April 2010), pp. 6–9. Also Mary Katharine Ham, "Grand Old Tea Party: The Insurgents Meet the Insiders," *Weekly Standard* (March 1, 2010): https://www.washingtonexaminer.com/weekly-standard/grand-old-tea-party.
9. "Who Is the Tea Party? There's No Short Answer," *National Public Radio* (September 15, 2010): http://www.npr.org/templates/story/story.php?storyId=129874282. See also Amy Gardner, "Gauging the Scope of the Tea Party Movement in America," *Washington Post* (October 23, 2010): https://www.washingtonpost.com/wp-dyn/content/article/2010/10/23/AR2010102304000.html; and Kate Zernike and Megan Thee-Brenan, "Poll Finds Tea Party Backers Wealthier and More Educated," *New York Times* (April 15, 2010): http://www.nytimes.com/2010/04/15/us/politics/15poll.html.
10. See Charles S. Bullock, "The 2010 Elections," p. 4 in Charles S. Bullock III, ed., *Key States, High Stakes: Sarah Palin, the Tea Party, and the 2010 Elections* (Lanham, MD: Rowman and Littlefield, 2012). See also Geoffrey Kabaservice, *Rule and Ruin: The Downfall of Moderation and the Destruction of the Republican Party, from Eisenhower to the Tea Party* (New York: Oxford University Press, 2012).
11. "Who Is the Tea Party?"
12. See Matthew Continetti, "The Two Faces of the Tea Party: Rick Santelli, Glenn Beck, and the Future of the Populist Insurgency," *Weekly Standard* 15:39 (June 28, 2010): https://www.washingtonexaminer.com/weekly-standard/the-two-faces-of-the-tea-party; and Paul Gottfried, "Not One, but Three Tea Parties," *American Conservative* (October 29, 2010): https://www.theamericanconservative.com/not-one-but-three-tea-parties/.
13. This rhetoric is ubiquitous in TP literature. See John O'Hara, *A New American Tea Party: The Counterrevolution against Bailouts, Handouts, Reckless Spending, and More Taxes* (Hoboken, NJ: John Wiley & Sons, 2010).
14. Skocpol and Williamson, *Tea Party*, p. 39.
15. All quotations from Matt Welch, "What the Left Can Learn from the Tea Party," *Reason* 43:5 (October 2011): https://reason.com/2011/09/06/what-the-left-can-learn-from-t/.
16. Katrina Trinko, "NPR Exec: Tea Partiers Are 'White, Middle-America, Gun-Toting Racists,'" *National Review* (March 8, 2011): https://www.nationalreview.com/corner/npr-exec-tea-partiers-are-white-middle-america-gun-toting-racists-katrina-trinko/.
17. Mike Mullen, "Bachmann Warns Obama to Fear the Tea Party, Who Are Not All Toothless Hillbillies," *City Pages* (July 6, 2011): http://www.citypages.com/news/bachmann-warns-obama-to-fear-the-tea-party-who-are-not-all-toothless-hillbillies-6548764.

18. Scott Wong, "Matthews: Tea Party Miners Would Have Killed Each Other," *Politico* (October 14, 2010): https://www.politico.com/story/2010/10/matthews-tea-party-miners-would-have-killed-each-other-043592.
19. Mark Lloyd, "Why the Left Will Never Understand the Tea Party," *Tea Party Review* 1:1 (March 2011), p. 7.
20. Justin Elliott, "Michigan Dems Charged in Fake Tea Party Scheme," *Salon* (March 17, 2011): https://www.salon.com/2011/03/17/dems_tea_party_charges/.
21. Tom Tillison, "Taking a Close Look at the Tea Party," *Red State* (February 14, 2011): https://www.redstate.com/diary/tomtflorida/2011/02/14/taking-a-close-look-at-the-tea-party/.
22. Lauren Ritchie, "Tea Party Should Look Closely—at Itself," *Orlando Sentinel* (February 13, 2011), cited in ibid.
23. Hussein Rashid, "Tea Party Organizes Islamophobic Hate Rally," *Religion Dispatches* (March 3, 2011): http://www.religiondispatches.org/dispatches/husseinrashid/4333/tea_party_organizes_islamophobic_hate_rally.
24. William Hogeland, "Real Americans," *Boston Review* (September–October 2010): http://bostonreview.net/hogeland-real-americans.
25. Frank Rich, "The Rage Is Not about Health Care," *New York Times* (March 27, 2010): https://www.nytimes.com/2010/03/28/opinion/28rich.html.
26. "Who Is the Tea Party?"
27. "New McCarthy Era?," *The Revealer* (June 25, 2010): http://therevealer.org/archives/4326.
28. Mark Lilla, "The Tea Party Jacobins," *New York Review of Books* (May 27, 2010): https://www.nybooks.com/articles/2010/05/27/tea-party-jacobins/.
29. Chris Mooney, "The Reality Gap," p. 19 in *American Prospect* (July–August 2011), pp. 18–25.
30. Amitai Etzioni, "The Tea Party Is Half Right," p. 197 in *Society* 48:3 (2011), pp. 197–202.
31. Kate Zernike, *Boiling Mad: Inside Tea Party America* (New York: Times Books, 2010).
32. Jill LePore, *The Whites of Their Eyes: The Tea Party's Revolution and the Battle over American History* (Princeton, NJ: Princeton University Press, 2010), p. 13.
33. Thomas Kidd, "The Tea Party, Fundamentalism, and the Founding," *Patheos* (December 1, 2010): http://www.patheos.com/Resources/Additional-Resources/Tea-Party-Fundamentalism-and-the-Founding.html.
34. See Tracy Fessenden, *Culture and Redemption: Religion, the Secular, and American Literature* (Princeton, NJ: Princeton University Press, 2006); Kathryn Lofton, *Oprah: The Gospel of an Icon* (Berkeley: University of California Press, 2011); and John Modern, *Secularism in Antebellum America* (Chicago: University of Chicago Press, 2011).
35. All quotations from Stephen Eichler, "Invisible Tea Party Heroes," *Canada Free Press* (February 3, 2011): http://canadafreepress.com/index.php/article/32902. For those keeping score, "vile disembowelment" is also the name of an obscure death metal band, as well as an attack skill performed by Harvesters in the game *Dragon Age*.

36. Paul A. Rahe, "How to Think about the Tea Party," *Commentary* 131:2 (February 2011), pp. 13–18.
37. See Andrew M. Shocket, *Fighting over the Founders: How We Remember the American Revolution* (New York: New York University Press, 2015).
38. Andrew Romano, "America's Holy Writ: Tea Party Evangelists Claim the Constitution as Their Sacred Text. Why That's Wrong," *Newsweek* (October 17, 2010).
39. "The New Republic: Paladino and the Politics of Anger," *National Public Radio* (October 14, 2010): https://www.npr.org/templates/story/story.php?storyId=130559117.
40. David Weigel, "The Dark Horse," *Slate* (January 8, 2011): www.slate.com/id/2281516/pagenum/all/#p2.
41. Sarah Posner, "Conservative Activist Says Tea Party Movement Needs 'Reverence to God,'" *Religion Dispatches* (February 19, 2010): http://www.religiondispatches.org/dispatches/sarahposner/2287/conservative_activist_says_tea_party_movement_needs_%E2%80%9Creverence_to_god%E2%80%9D.
42. Julie Ingersoll, "Candidate Sharron Angle Accuses Opponent of Idolatry," *Religion Dispatches* (August 5, 2010): http://www.religiondispatches.org/dispatches/julieingersoll/3098/candidate_sharron_angle_accuses_opponent_of_idolatry.
43. Sarah Posner, "Tea Party Leader Hates United Methodist Church," *Real Clear Religion* (December 20, 2010): http://www.tngovwatch.org/2010/12/my-dream-no-more-methodist-church.
44. Jeff Sharlet, "Is the Tea Party Becoming a Religious Movement?" *CNN* (October 27, 2010): http://www.cnn.com/2010/OPINION/10/27/sharlet.tea.party.evangelical/.
45. Lepore, *Whites of Their Eyes*, pp. 5, 112.
46. Sarah Posner, "Children of God," *American Prospect* (February 19, 2010): http://prospect.org/article/children-god-0.
47. Frederick Clarkson, "The Eliminationists: How Hate Talk Radicalized the American Right," *Religion Dispatches* (October 20, 2009): http://www.religiondispatches.org/archive/politics/1893/the_eliminationists%3A_how_hate_talk_radicalized_the_american_right.
48. Skocpol and Williamson, *Tea Party*, pp. 32–33.
49. Sarah Posner, "Tea Partiers and Religious Right Court at Values Voter Summit," *Religion Dispatches* (September 24, 2009): http://www.religiondispatches.org/archive/politics/1857/tea_partiers_and_religious_right_court_at_values_voter_summit.
50. Julie Ingersoll and Sarah Posner, "Gun Ownership: 'An Obligation to God,'" *Religion Dispatches* (July 13, 2010): http://www.religiondispatches.org/archive/politics/2910/gun_ownership%3A_%E2%80%98an_obligation_to_god%E2%80%99.
51. Jamelle Bouie, "The Tea Party Is Still Basically the Religious Right," *American Prospect* (February 24, 2011): https://prospect.org/article/tea-party-still-basically-religious-right/.
52. David E. Campbell and Robert D. Putnam, "Crashing the Tea Party," *New York Times* (August 17, 2011): http://www.nytimes.com/2011/08/17/opinion/crashing-the-tea-party.html?_r=3.

53. Louis A. Ruprecht, "It's Not a Tea Party, Silly, It's a Rebellion," *Religion Dispatches* (June 1, 2010): http://www.religiondispatches.org/archive/politics/2652/it%E2%80%99s_not_a_tea_party%2C_silly%2C_it%E2%80%99s_a_rebellion.
54. Michael Gerson, "An Unholy War on the Tea Party," *Washington Post* (August 22, 2011): https://www.washingtonpost.com/opinions/a-holy-war-on-the-tea-party/2011/08/22/gIQAYRcOXJ_story.html?wprss=rss_opinions.
55. Julie Ingersoll, "Tea Partiers Say Slavery Not Race-Related," *Religion Dispatches* (July 15, 2010): http://www.religiondispatches.org/archive/politics/2832/tea_partiers_say_slavery_not_race-related.
56. Sarah Posner, "Religious Right Very Much Alive in Tomorrow's Elections," *Religion Dispatches* (November 3, 2009): http://www.religiondispatches.org/dispatches/sarahposner/1970/religious_right_very_much_alive_in_tomorrow%E2%80%99s_elections.
57. Jacob Weisberg, "The Tea Party and the Tucson Tragedy," *Slate* (January 10, 2011): https://slate.com/news-and-politics/2011/01/jared-loughner-gabrielle-giffords-and-the-tea-party.html.
58. See James William Gibson, *Warrior Dreams: Violence and Manhood in Post-Vietnam America* (New York: Hill & Wang, 1994); Tony Horwitz, *Confederates in the Attic: Dispatches from the Unfinished Civil War* (New York: Vintage Books, 1999); and Susan Jeffords, *The Remasculinization of America: Gender and the Vietnam War* (Bloomington: Indiana University Press, 1989).
59. Curtis D. Coats and Stewart M. Hoover, "Broadswords and Face Paint: Why *Braveheart* Still Matters," p. 415 in Bruce David Forbes and Jeffrey H. Mahan, eds., *Religion and Popular Culture in America*, 3rd ed. (Berkeley: University of California Press, 2017).
60. Ibid., p. 413.
61. It is worth noting that only in a revision of this manuscript, in the summer of 2020, did it strike me as necessary to include the qualifier "likely" in this sentence.
62. See Alexis de Tocqueville, *Democracy in America and Two Essays on America* (New York: Penguin Classics, 2003).
63. John Jay, Alexander Hamilton, and James Madison, *The Federalist Papers* (Mineola, NY: Dover Books, 2014), p. 37.
64. One of the most consistently thoughtful theorists of such work is Harry C. Boyte. See, among his recent works, *Awakening Democracy through Public Work: Pedagogies of Empowerment* (Nashville, TN: Vanderbilt University Press, 2018). For a different range of theoretical resources, grounded in his notion of publics as a mode of paying attention, see Michael Warner, *Publics and Counterpublics* (New York: Zone Books, 2005).
65. See, for example, Nadia Marzouki, Duncan McDonnell, and Olivier Roy, eds., *Saving the People: How Populists Hijack Religion* (New York: Oxford University Press, 2016); and Jan-Werner Mueller, *What Is Populism?* (Philadelphia: University of Pennsylvania Press, 2016).
66. Anthea Butler, "Weak Uni-Tea," *Religion Dispatches* (August 3, 2010): http://www.religiondispatches.org/dispatches/antheabutler/3084/weak_uni-tea_.

67. Clarence Walker, " 'We're Losing Our Country': Barack Obama, Race & the Tea Party," p. 126 in *Daedalus* (Winter 2011), pp. 125–130.
68. Shannon Travis, "NCAA Passes Resolution Blasting Tea Party 'Racism,'" *CNN* (July 16, 2010): http://www.cnn.com/2010/POLITICS/07/14/naacp.tea.party/index.html.
69. On the performative in populism, see Benjamin Arditi, "The People as Representation and Event," pp. 91–112 in Carlos de la Torre, ed., *The Promise and Perils of Populism: Global Perspectives* (Lexington: University of Kentucky Press, 2015); and Benjamin Moffitt, *The Global Rise of Populism: Performance, Political Style, and Representation* (Stanford, CA: Stanford University Press, 2016).
70. Moffitt, *Global Rise of Populism*, p. xi.
71. Richard Rorty, *Philosophy as Cultural Politics: Philosophical Papers* (Cambridge: Cambridge University Press, 2007), p. 58.
72. John Lukacs, *Democracy and Populism: Fear and Hatred* (New Haven, CT: Yale University Press, 2005), p. 177. Theorists of crowds—from Alexander Hamilton to José Ortega y Gasset to Michel Foucault—have sought to assess the regulation of collective purpose amidst these transitions. See Elias Canetti, *Crowds and Power* (New York: Farrar, Straus and Giroux, 1984) and José Ortega y Gasset, *The Revolt of the Masses* (New York: Norton Books, 1994). Foucault in particular, in his 1976 lectures at the Collège de France, introduced ideas of biopower as a way of theorizing the dispersed populations and industrialization characteristic of mass democracy. With biopolitics, Foucault says, we move beyond the disciplinary apparatus and even the surveilling apparatus of the early modern into a period where power moves through not just new bodies but new mechanisms: "forecasts, statistical estimates, and overall measures. And their purpose is not to modify any given phenomenon as such, or to modify a given individual insofar as he is an individual, but, essentially, to intervene at the level at which these general phenomena are determined." Foucault, *"Society Must Be Defended": Lectures at the Collège de France, 1975–1976* (New York: Picador Books, 2003), p. 246.
73. Lauren Berlant, "Cruel Optimism," p. 93 in Melissa Gregg and Gregory J. Seigworth, eds., *The Affect Theory Reader* (Durham, NC: Duke University Press, 2010). For suggestive links to technology, see Manuel Castells, *Networks of Outrage and Hope: Social Movements in the Internet Age* (Cambridge: Polity Press, 2015).
74. On this notion of felt experiences prior to their actual occurrence, see my *Religion of Fear: The Politics of Horror in Conservative Evangelicalism* (New York: Oxford University Press, 2008); Brian Massumi's *Parables for the Virtual: Movement, Affect, Sensation* (Durham, NC: Duke University Press, 2002); and Meaghan Morris's *Too Soon Too Late: History in Popular Culture* (Bloomington: Indiana University Press, 1998).
75. In *Democracy Incorporated: Managed Democracy and the Specter of Inverted Totalitarianism* (Princeton, NJ: Princeton University Press, 2008), Sheldon Wolin called these "demotic moments."
76. Keith Mines, quoted in Robin Wright, "Is America Headed for a New Kind of Civil War?," *New Yorker* (August 14, 2017): https://www.newyorker.com/news/news-desk/is-america-headed-for-a-new-kind-of-civil-war.

77. Graeme Wood, "His Kampf," p. 50 in *The Atlantic* (June 2017), pp. 40–52.
78. William Galston, "Steve Bannon and the 'Global Tea Party,'" *Wall Street Journal* (February 28, 2017): https://www.wsj.com/articles/steve-bannon-and-the-global-tea-party-1488327459.
79. Wood, "His Kampf," p. 49.
80. See Grace Elizabeth Hale, *A Nation of Outsiders: How the White Middle Class Fell in Love with Rebellion in Postwar America* (New York: Oxford University Press, 2014); and Kevin Mattson, *Rebels All! A Short History of the Conservative Mind in Postwar America* (New Brunswick, NJ: Rutgers University Press, 2008).
81. See Hannah Arendt, "A Special Supplement: Reflections on Violence," *New York Review of Books* (February 27, 1969).
82. Wood, "His Kampf," p. 49.
83. Melissa A. Orlie, *Living Ethically, Acting Politically* (Ithaca, NY: Cornell University Press, 1997), p. 19.

# Chapter 7

1. Mikal Gilmore, "Bob Dylan Unleashed," *Rolling Stone* (September 27, 2012): https://www.rollingstone.com/music/music-news/bob-dylan-unleashed-189723/.
2. Walter Benjamin, *Illuminations: Essays and Reflections* (New York: Schocken Books, 2007), p. 225.
3. See Randall Balmer, *Thy Kingdom Come: How the Religious Right Distorts Faith and Threatens America* (New York: Basic Books, 2007). On the establishment of Christian schools and homeschooling, see my *The Fracture of Good Order: Christian Antiliberalism and the Challenge to American Politics* (Chapel Hill: University of North Carolina Press, 2003).
4. See www.education.com/schoolfinder/us/texas/aledo/aledo-christian-school/ and www.aledocc.org/hillhistory.pdf.
5. See Nate Blakeslee, "King of the Christocrats," *Texas Monthly* (September 2006): https://www.texasmonthly.com/articles/king-of-the-christocrats/; Rob Boston, "Sects, Lies and Videotape," *Church & State* 46:4 (April 1993), pp. 8–12; and Eric Eckholm, "Using History to Mold Ideas on the Right," *New York Times* (May 4, 2011): https://www.globalpolicy.org/nations-a-states/general-analysis-on-states-and-their-future/50177-using-history-to-mold-ideas-on-the-right.html.
6. John Fea, *Was America Founded as a Christian Nation? A Historical Introduction*, rev. ed. (Louisville, KY: Westminster John Knox, 2016), p. 58.
7. See Randall J. Stephens and Karl W. Giberson, *The Anointed: Evangelical Truth in a Secular Age* (Cambridge, MA: Belknap Press of Harvard University Press, 2011).
8. Ibid., p. 76.
9. Rick Perlstein, *Reaganland: America's Right Turn, 1976–1980* (New York: Simon & Schuster, 2020), p. 24.

10. Cynthia Miller-Idriss, *Hate in the Homeland: The New Global Far Right* (Princeton, NJ: Princeton University Press, 2020), pp. 124–125.
11. Stephens and Giberson, *The Annointed*, p. 73.
12. David Barton, "The Separation of Church and State," *Wallbuilders* (January 2001): http://www.wallbuilders.com/libissuesarticles.asp?id=123.
13. https://www.logos.com/product/17337/wallbuilders-american-foundations-digital-library.
14. Ibid.
15. See "History of the Republican Party of Texas": https://www.collincountygop.org/collin-county-republican-resources/history-republican-party-texas/.
16. Ibid.
17. David Barton, "God: Missing in Action in American History," *Wallbuilders* (June 2005): https://wallbuilders.com/god-missing-action-american-history/.
18. David Barton, "Evolution and the Law: 'A Death Struggle between Two Civilizations,'" *Wallbuilders* (Spring 2002): https://wallbuilders.com/spring-2002/.
19. David Barton, "Political Parties and Morality," *Wallbuilders* (December 21, 1998): http://www.wallbuilders.com/LIBissuesArticles.asp?id=109.
20. Ibid.
21. Quotations from promotional literature for Barton's ten-disc DVD set: http://www.christiancinema.com/catalog/product_info.php?products_id=2792.
22. http://www.youtube.com/watch?v=fGvTdN5ko10. Transcription by the author supplies all quotations in this paragraph.
23. Texas Freedom Network, "Barton on the Issues": https://tfn.org/david-barton-watch/barton-on-the-issues/.
24. Connor Perrett, "Trump Threatens to Investigate and Pull Federal Funding from Schools That Teach NYT's 1619 Project on the Consequences of Slavery," *Business Insider* (September 6, 2020): https://www.businessinsider.com/trump-pull-funding-california-schools-1619-project-2020-9.
25. All quotations from Barton's books in this and subsequent paragraphs from https://shop.wallbuilders.com/books.
26. "It's Time to Hold Federal Judges Accountable," *Phyllis Schlafly Report*, Eagle Forum (March 1997): https://eagleforum.org/psr/1997/mar97/psrmar97.html.
27. Right Wing Watch Staff, "David Barton: Propaganda Masquerading as History," *Right Wing Watch* (September 2006): http://www.pfaw.org/media-center/publications/david-barton-propaganda-masquerading-history.
28. Ibid.
29. See Stephens and Giberson, *The Annointed*, pp. 9, 26.
30. By 2010, "555 school districts in 38 states used their materials" and "over 360,000 students had taken their courses." Ibid., p. 88.
31. Kayla Webley, "Perusing the Glenn Beck University Curriculum Guide," *Time* (July 7, 2010): https://newsfeed.time.com/2010/07/07/glenn-beck-university/.
32. Ibid.
33. Ibid.

34. Julie Ingersoll, "Tea Party Bullies on Homosexuality: 'No Punishment Too Severe,'" *Religion Dispatches* (October 8, 2010): https://religiondispatches.org/tea-party-bullies-on-homosexuality-no-punishment-too-severe/.
35. See Rob Boston, "Dissecting the Religious Right's Favorite Bible Curriculum," *The Humanist* (November 1, 2007): https://www.thefreelibrary.com/Dissecting+the+religious+right%27s+favorite+Bible+Curriculum.-a0170729742; and Arlen Specter, "Defending the Wall: Maintaining Church/State Separation in America," *Harvard Journal of Law & Public Policy* 18:2 (Spring 1995), pp. 575–590.
36. Eckholm, "Using History"; and Jennifer Schuessler, "And the Worst Book of History Is . . . ," *New York Times* (July 16, 2012): https://artsbeat.blogs.nytimes.com/2012/07/16/and-the-worst-book-of-history-is/.
37. Siddhartha Mahanta, "GOP's Favorite Fake Historian Spins *The New York Times*," *Mother Jones* (May 2011): https://www.motherjones.com/politics/2011/05/david-barton-new-york-times-huckabee/.
38. Peter Montgomery, "Glenn Beck's Salvation Army," *Religion Dispatches* (September 9, 2010): http://www.religiondispatches.org/archive/atheologies/3266/glenn_beck%E2%80%99s_salvation_army.
39. See ibid.
40. Julie Ingersoll, "Beck's "Dream"—Our Nightmare," *Religion Dispatches* (August 25, 2010): http://www.religiondispatches.org/archive/politics/3199/beck%E2%80%99s_%E2%80%9Cdream%E2%80%9D%E2%80%94our_nightmare.
41. Bob Moser, "The Crusaders: Christian Evangelicals Are Plotting to Remake America in Their Own Image," *Rolling Stone* (April 7, 2005): https://newslog.cyberjournal.org/bob-moser-the-dominionists-far-right-threat-to-u-s/.
42. Ibid.
43. Martin Marty, "David Barton's Christian America," *Christian Post* (May 10, 2011): https://divinity.uchicago.edu/sightings/articles/david-bartons-christian-america-martin-e-marty.
44. See Frederick Clarkson, "Top Christian Nationalist on Hot Seat," *Daily Kos* (April 11, 2005): https://m.dailykos.com/stories/2005/4/11/105896/-.
45. Ibid.
46. Deborah Caldwell, "David Barton & the 'Myth' of Church-State Separation," *Beliefnet* (October 2004): http://www.beliefnet.com/News/Politics/2004/10/David-Barton-The-Myth-Of-Church-State-Separation.aspx.
47. Chris Rodda, "David Barton Keeps Up His Lies at Glenn Beck Event," *Huffington Post* (June 1, 2010): http://www.huffingtonpost.com/chris-rodda/david-barton-glenn-beck_b_521485.html.
48. Julie Ingersoll, "Beck's Historian Bringing Seminar to Congressional Tea Partiers," *Religion Dispatches* (February 2, 2011): http://www.religiondispatches.org/dispatches/julieingersoll/4165/beck%E2%80%99s_historian_bringing_seminar_to_congressional_tea_partiers_.
49. For a useful perspective on such civic engagement, see Jon A. Shields, *The Democratic Virtues of the Christian Right* (Princeton, NJ: Princeton University Press, 2009).

50. Mariah Blake, "Revisionaries: How a Group of Texas Conservatives Are Rewriting Your Kids' Textbooks," *Washington Monthly* (January 1, 2010): https://washingtonmonthly.com/2010/01/01/revisionaries/.
51. Ibid.
52. Ibid.
53. Ibid.
54. Ross Ramsey, "Green Days," *Texas Weekly* (July 20, 2009): https://texasweekly.texastribune.org/texas-weekly/vol-26/no-28/green-days/.
55. Ibid.
56. Ibid.
57. Ibid.
58. See Antony Alumkal, *Paranoid Science: The Christian Right's War on Reality* (New York: New York University Press, 2017); Michael Lienesch, *In the Beginning: Fundamentalism, the Scopes Trial, and the Making of the Antievolution Movement* (Chapel Hill: University of North Carolina Press, 2007); Ronald L. Numbers, *The Creationists: From Scientific Creationism to Intelligent Design*, expanded ed. (Cambridge, MA: Harvard University Press, 2006); and Robert T. Pennock, ed., *Intelligent Design Creationism and Its Critics: Philosophical, Theological, and Scientific Perspectives* (Cambridge, MA: MIT Press, 2001).
59. Lauri Lebo, "Texas Textbook Massacre," *Religion Dispatches* (May 12, 2010): https://religiondispatches.org/texas-textbook-massacre/.
60. John G. West, "Intelligent Design and Creationism Just Aren't the Same," *Discovery Institute* (December 1, 2002): https://www.discovery.org/a/1329/.
61. Justin Elliott, "What a Long, Strange Trip It's Been: TX Textbooks Rules Set for Final Vote," *Talking Points Memo* (May 19, 2010): http://tpmmuckraker.talkingpointsmemo.com/2010/05/texas_textbooks_what_a_long_strange_trip.php. See also Jeff Sharlet, "Through a Glass Darkly: How the Christian Right Is Reimagining U.S. History," *Harper's* (December 2006): http://harpers.org/archive/2006/12/through-a-glass-darkly/.
62. Elliott, "Long, Strange Trip."
63. Justin Elliott, "Conservative Bloc Prevails in Latest TX Textbooks Standards Vote," *Talking Points Memo* (March 12, 2010): http://tpmmuckraker.talkingpointsmemo.com/2010/03/conservative_bloc_dominates_latest_texas_textbooks.php?ref=mp.
64. Right Wing Watch Staff, "Texas Textbooks: What Happened, What It Means, and What We Can Do about It," *Right Wing Watch* (June 2010): http://www.pfaw.org/rww-in-focus/texas-textbooks-what-happened-what-it-means-and-what-we-can-do-about-it.
65. Ibid.
66. Ibid.
67. Amanda Paulson, "Texas Textbook War: 'Slavery' or 'Atlantic Triangular Trade'?," *Christian Science Monitor* (May 19, 2010): https://www.csmonitor.com/USA/Education/2010/0519/Texas-textbook-war-Slavery-or-Atlantic-triangular-trade.
68. Ibid.

69. Ellen Bresler Rockmore, "How Texas Teaches History," *New York Times* (October 21, 2015): https://www.nytimes.com/2015/10/22/opinion/how-texas-teaches-history.html.
70. Ibid.
71. Lebo, "Texas Textbook Massacre."
72. Ibid.
73. Ibid.
74. Justin Elliott, "TX Textbooks Proposal: Students Must Discuss Gutting Social Security, Explain How U.N. Undermines U.S.," *Talking Points Memo* (May 17, 2010): http://tpmmuckraker.talkingpointsmemo.com/2010/05/tx_textbooks_proposal_students_must_discuss_guttin.php.
75. http://video.pbs.org/video/1481758920/.
76. Ibid.
77. *Nightline* (March 11, 2010): http://abcnews.go.com/Nightline/video/texas-textbook-controversy-10080731. Author transcription.
78. Ibid.
79. Ibid.
80. http://www.youtube.com/watch?v=ZUVrT_My_ro. Author transcription. All quotations in this and the following paragraph are from this source.
81. Blake, "Revisionaries."
82. Right Wing Watch Staff, "Texas Textbooks."
83. Ibid.
84. Ibid.
85. Ibid.
86. Elliott, "Long, Strange Trip."
87. Ibid.
88. Michael Birnbaum, "Historians Speak Out against Proposed Texas Textbook Changes," *Washington Post* (March 18, 2010): http://journalofeducationalcontroversy.blogspot.com/2010/03/historians-speak-out-against-proposed.html.
89. Sam Tanenhaus, "In Texas Curriculum Fight, Identity Politics Leans Right," *New York Times* (March 21, 2010): https://www.nytimes.com/2010/03/21/weekinreview/21tanenhaus.html.
90. American Historical Association, "Advocacy in Action: AHA Sends Letter to the Texas Board of Education Regarding Proposed Mexican American Studies Textbook," *AHA Today* (September 28, 2016): https://www.historians.org/publications-and-directories/perspectives-on-history/september-2016/advocacy-in-action-aha-sends-letter-to-the-texas-board-of-education-regarding-proposed-mexican-american-studies-textbook.
91. David Cannadine, "History with Rose-Tinted Hindsight," *BBC News Magazine* (June 25, 2010): http://news.bbc.co.uk/2/hi/uk_news/magazine/8762969.stm.
92. Quoted in Tanenhaus, "Texas Curriculum Fight."
93. Birnbaum, "Historians Speak Out."
94. T. J. Holmes, "Texas Textbook Fallout," *CNN Newsroom* (May 22, 2010): http://newsroom.blogs.cnn.com/2010/05/22/textbook-fallout/.

95. See John Bodnar, *Remaking America: Public Memory, Commemoration, and Patriotism in the Twentieth Century* (Princeton, NJ: Princeton University Press, 1993), which contains two excellent background chapters on early American public memory.
96. Quoted in Anne Norton, *Republic of Signs: Liberal Theory and American Popular Culture* (Chicago: University of Chicago Press, 1993), p. 13.
97. Ibid., p. 14.
98. Charles Taylor, *Modern Social Imaginaries* (Durham, NC: Duke University Press, 2004), p. 167.
99. Friedrich Nietzsche, *Beyond Good and Evil* (New York: Cosimo Classics, 2006), p. 62. Italics mine.
100. Thanks to Mike Michalson for pointing out this distinction.
101. See Chris Mooney, "The Reality Gap," *American Prospect* (July–August 2011), pp. 18–25. Stephens and Giberson in *The Annointed* focus on the cultures of evangelical expertise.
102. Mooney, "The Reality Gap," p. 21.
103. Anthony Giddens, *The Consequences of Modernity* (Cambridge: Polity Press, 1990).
104. See Katherine Stewart, "Betsy DeVos and God's Plan for Schools," *New York Times* (December 13, 2016): http://www.nytimes.com/2016/12/13/opinion/betsy-devos-and-gods-plan-for-schools.html; and Stewart, "A Christian Nationalist Blitz," *New York Times* (May 26, 2018): https://www.nytimes.com/2018/05/26/opinion/project-blitz-christian-nationalists.html?action=click&pgtype=Homepage&clickSource=story-heading&module=opinion-c-col-top-region&region=opinion-c-col-top-region&WT.nav=opinion-c-col-top-region. On the 1619 Project, see https://wallbuilderslive.com/the-1619-project-ken-blackwell/.
105. Vincent P. Pecora, *Secularization and Cultural Criticism: Religion, Nation, & Modernity* (Chicago: University of Chicago Press, 2006), pp. 77–78.
106. Quoted in George Lipsitz, *Time Passages: Collective Memory and American Popular Culture* (Minneapolis: University of Minnesota Press, 1990), p. 29.
107. Quoted in Jean Bethke Elshtain, *Democracy on Trial* (New York: Basic Books, 1995), p. 36.
108. Nikhil Pal Singh, *Race and America's Long War* (Berkeley: University of California Press, 2017), p. x. Martyrs' preference for this "propaganda of history" continues. See Dana Goldstein, "Two States, Eight Textbooks, Two American Stories," *New York Times* (January 12, 2020): https://www.nytimes.com/interactive/2020/01/12/us/texas-vs-california-history-textbooks.html?smid=nytcore-ios-share.

# Chapter 8

1. On the older historical wellsprings of this diversity, see David Hall, *Worlds of Wonder, Days of Judgment: Popular Religious Belief in Early New England* (New York: Knopf, 1989).

2. See, among many others, Talal Asad, *Formations of the Secular: Christianity, Islam, Modernity* (Stanford, CA: Stanford University Press, 2003); Janet Jakobsen and Ann Pellegrini, eds., *Secularisms* (Durham, NC: Duke University Press, 2008); Saba Mahmood, *Religious Difference in a Secular Age: A Minority Report* (Princeton, NJ: Princeton University Press, 2015); and John Modern, *Secularism in Antebellum America* (Chicago: University of Chicago Press, 2011).
3. Winnifred Fallers Sullivan, *The Impossibility of Religious Freedom* (Princeton, NJ: Princeton University Press, 2005).
4. Two very different overviews of and engagements with this condensed legal history are Joshua Dubler and Isaac Weiner, eds., *Religion, Law, USA* (New York: New York University Press, 2019); and Mark Douglas McGarvie, *Law and Religion in American History: Public Values and Private Conscience* (Cambridge: Cambridge University Press, 2016).
5. https://www.oyez.org/cases/1970/89.
6. See Catharine Cookson, *Regulating Religion: The Courts and the Free Exercise Clause* (New York: Oxford University Press, 2001).
7. https://www.congress.gov/bill/103rd-congress/house-bill/1308.
8. See Elizabeth Castelli, "Persecution Complexes: Identity Politics and the 'War on Christians,'" *differences* 18:3 (2007), pp. 152–180.
9. http://www.advocatesinternational.org/; http://www.clsnet.org/; and http://aclj.org/.
10. http://www.aclj.org.
11. See Christine Leigh Heyrman, *American Apostles: When Evangelicals Entered the World of Islam* (New York: Hill and Wang, 2015); Thomas Kidd, *American Christians and Islam: Evangelical Culture and Muslims from the Colonial Period to the Age of Terrorism* (Princeton, NJ: Princeton University Press, 2013); and Timothy Marr, *The Cultural Roots of American Islamicism* (Cambridge: Cambridge University Press, 2006).
12. See, for example, Khaled A. Beydoun, *American Islamophobia: Understanding the Roots and Rise of Fear* (Berkeley: University of California Press, 2018); Peter Gottschalk, *Islamophobia and Anti-Muslim Sentiment: Picturing the Enemy*, 2nd ed. (Lanham, MD: Rowman & Littlefield, 2018); and Erik Love, *Islamophobia and Racism in America* (New York: New York University Press, 2017). For an important rejoinder, see Nadia Marzouki, *Islam: An American Religion* (New York: Columbia University Press, 2017).
13. See Megan P. Goodwin, *Abusing Religion: Literary Persecution, Sex Scandals, and American Minority Religions* (New Brunswick, NJ: Rutgers University Press, 2020).
14. The entire bill is available at http://www.capitol.tn.gov/Bills/107/Bill/SB1028.pdf.
15. Ibid., p. 1.
16. Ibid., p. 2.
17. Ibid., p. 3.
18. Ibid., p. 4.
19. https://action.politicalmedia.com/ctas/stop-sharia-in-america-tell-leaders-to-reintroduce-hr-973/comments/page/543.

20. "Wyoming Legislation Targets Islamic, International Law," *Casper Star-Tribune* (January 20, 2011): https://billingsgazette.com/news/state-and-regional/wyoming/wyoming-legislation-targets-islamic-international-law/article_abc1a5ff-96dc-5b2e-ab34-f46d4b68f0ec.html.
21. I am grateful to Finbarr Curtis for this observation about two senses of honor and violence.
22. See, for example: Hussein Rashid, "Texas Man Indicted for Mosque Bomb Threat," *Religion Dispatches* (June 23, 2012): http://www.religiondispatches.org/dispatches/husseinrashid/6112/texas_man_indicted_for_mosque_bomb_threat/.
23. Muslim Diaspora Initiative, "Anti-Muslim Activities in the United States: Violence, Threats, and Discrimination at the Local Level," *New America*: https://www.newamerica.org/in-depth/anti-muslim-activity/. There has been an equally significant spike in anti-Semitism.
24. My account here relies heavily on Wajahat Ali, Eli Clifton, Matthew Duss, Scott Keyes, and Faiz Shakir, "Fear Inc.: The Roots of the Islamophobia Network in the U.S.," *Center for American Progress* (August 2011): https://cdn.americanprogress.org/wp-content/uploads/issues/2011/08/pdf/islamophobia.pdf.
25. Ibid., p. 27.
26. Ibid., p. 35.
27. Ibid., p. 41.
28. Ibid., p. 43.
29. Ibid.
30. Ibid., p. 49.
31. Ibid., p. 33.
32. Ibid., p. 41.
33. Andrea Elliott, "The Man behind the Anti-shariah Movement," *New York Times* (July 31, 2011): http://www.nytimes.com/2011/07/31/us/31shariah.html?_r=1&hp.
34. Ibid.
35. Ibid.
36. See Matthew Schmitz, "Anti-sharia Laws Are Magic," *National Review* (June 18, 2012): http://www.nationalreview.com/corner/303135/anti-sharia-laws-are-magic-matthew-schmitz.
37. Ali et al., "Fear Inc.," p. 5.
38. See "CPAC: Former CIA Director Tells of Sharia Threat," *Judicial Watch* (February 12, 2011): https://www.judicialwatch.org/blog/2011/02/cpac-former-cia-director-tells-of-sharia-threat/.
39. Brian Tashman, "Anti-Muslim Extremist James Lafferty Angry He Was Quoted Verbatim," *Right Wing Watch* (February 15, 2012): https://www.rightwingwatch.org/post/cpac-anti-muslim-activist-james-lafferty-says-hes-proud-of-attacks-against-mosques/.
40. Ali et al., "Fear Inc.," p. 66.
41. Tanya Somanader, "Tennessee Bill Dubs Sharia Law 'Treasonous,' Would Punish Muslims with 15 Years in Jail," *Think Progress* (February 23, 2011): http://thinkprogress.org/politics/2011/02/23/145849/tennessee-bill-dubs-sharia-law-treason

ous-would-punish-muslims-with-15-years-in-jail/. See also Bridge Initiative Team, "Factsheet: Brigitte Gabriel," *Bridge Initiative* (December 4, 2018): https://bridge.georgetown.edu/research/factsheet-brigitte-gabriel-2/.
42. Ali et al., "Fear Inc.," p. 67.
43. Scott Shane, "In Shariah, Gingrich Sees a Mortal Threat to U.S.," *New York Times* (December 22, 2011): http://www.nytimes.com/2011/12/22/us/politics/in-shariah-gingrich-sees-mortal-threat-to-us.html?hp.
44. Ali et al., "Fear Inc.," p. 99.
45. Ibid.
46. Right Wing Watch Staff, "The Right Wing Playbook on Anti-Muslim Extremism," *Right Wing Watch* (July 2011): http://www.pfaw.org/rww-in-focus/the-right-wing-playbook-anti-muslim-extremism.
47. Ibid.
48. For historical context on these barbaric remarks, see Kunal M. Parker, *Making Foreigners: Immigration and Citizenship Law in America, 1600–2000* (Cambridge: Cambridge University Press, 2015).
49. Ed Mazza, "Laura Ingraham Targets Even Legal Immigrants in Off-the-Rails Rant," *Huffington Post* (August 9, 2018): https://www.huffingtonpost.com/entry/laura-ingraham-immigration-rant_us_5b6bbfd7e4b0bdd0620646fa.
50. Christian Mathias, "A Fascist Trump Rally in Greenville," *Huffington Post* (July 18, 2019): https://www.huffpost.com/entry/fascist-trump-rally-greenville-ilhan-omar-send-her-back_n_5d30529fe4b0419fd328b270.
51. ADL Staff, "Disinformation: Claims about Black Lives Matter and Antifa Collaborating with Muslim Groups to Impose Sharia Law" (June 2020): https://www.adl.org/disinformation-claims-about-black-lives-matter-and-antifa-collaborating-with-muslim-groups-to.
52. Jonathan S. Tobin, "Backlash against Muslims? Then Why Are Their Numbers Growing?," *Commentary* (May 3, 2012): http://www.commentarymagazine.com/2012/05/03/backlash-against-muslims-then-why-are-numbers-growing/.
53. Conor Friedersdorf, "Was There Really a Post-9/11 Backlash against Muslims?," *The Atlantic* (May 4, 2012): http://www.theatlantic.com/politics/archive/2012/05/was-there-really-a-post-9-11-backlash-against-muslims/256725/.
54. Jack Jenkins, "Sorry, Newt Gingrich: That's Not How Shariah Works," *Think Progress* (July 15, 2016): https://thinkprogress.org/sorry-newt-gingrich-thats-not-how-shariah-works-88b23d0cf353/. See also Omid Safi, "What Islam Says and Doesn't Say about Democracy," *New York Times* (October 4, 2012): https://www.nytimes.com/roomfordebate/2012/10/04/is-islam-an-obstacle-to-democracy/what-islam-says-and-doesnt-say-about-democracy.
55. "What Is Shariah?," *Defending Religious Freedom*: http://www.defendingreligiousfreedom.com/faqst/.
56. Ibid.
57. "Anti-sharia Law Unconstitutional and 'Stupid' Says Court," *Dirty South News* (January 10, 2012): http://dirtysouthnews.com/2012/01/10/oklahoma-anti-sharia-law-unconstitutional-and-stupid-says-court/.

58. Ibid.
59. Ibid.
60. Melissa Jeltsen, "Tennessee Jumps on the Anti-sharia Bandwagon," *Talking Points Memo* (February 24, 2011): http://tpmmuckraker.talkingpointsmemo.com/2011/02/tennessee_state_sen_joins_effort_to_criminalize_sh.php.
61. See, for example, Tim Murphy, "Meet the White Supremacist Leading the GOP's Anti-shariah Crusade," *Mother Jones* (March 1, 2011): https://www.motherjones.com/politics/2011/03/david-yerushalmi-sharia-ban-tennessee/.
62. Americans United, "Hypocrisy Alert: Ex-Christian Coalition Staffer Now Opposes Religious Control of Courts—at Least for Muslims," *Wall of Separation* (August 1, 2011): http://au.org/blogs/wall-of-separation/hypocrisy-alert-ex-christian-coalition-staffer-now-opposes-religious.
63. This refers not to John Walker Lindh but to books like Daily Kos founder Markos Moulitsas, *American Taliban: How War, Sex, Sin, and Power Bind Jihadists and the Radical Right* (Sausalito, CA: Polipoint Press, 2010).
64. See Kirstie M. McClure, "Difference, Diversity, and the Limits of Toleration," *Political Theory* 18:3 (August 1990), pp. 361–391.
65. Rafia Zakaria, "The Sharia Charade," *Dissent* (September 1, 2011): https://www.dissentmagazine.org/online_articles/the-sharia-charade.
66. Ibid.
67. Winnifred Fallers Sullivan, "Religion Naturalized: The New Establishment," p. 84 in Courtney Bender and Pamela E. Klassen, eds., *After Pluralism: Reimagining Religious Engagement* (New York: Columbia University Press, 2010). In legal studies, see Caroline Corbin, "Secularism and U.S. Jurisprudence," pp. 467–481 in Phil Zuckerman and John R. Shook, eds., *The Oxford Handbook of Secularism* (New York: Oxford University Press, 2017); Paul W. Kahn, "The Jurisprudence of Religion in a Secular Age: From Ornamentalism to *Hobby Lobby*," *Law & Ethics of Human Rights* 10:1 (May 2016), pp. 1–30; Christine L. Niles, "Epistemological Nonsense—the Secular/Religious Distinction," *Notre Dame Journal of Law, Ethics & Public Policy* 17:2 (2012), pp. 561–592; and Laura Underkuffler-Freund, "The Separation of the Religious and the Secular: A Foundational Challenge to First Amendment Theory," *William and Mary Law Review* 36:3 (March 1995), pp. 837–988.
68. Sullivan, "Religion Naturalized," p. 95.
69. On this point, see Talal Asad, "Thinking about Religion, Belief, and Politics," pp. 36–57 in Robert A. Orsi, ed., *The Cambridge Companion to Religious Studies* (Cambridge: Cambridge University Press, 2012). Excellent resources for thinking broadly and comparatively about these issues are Benjamin L. Berger, *Law's Religion: Religious Difference and the Claims of Constitutionalism* (Toronto: University of Toronto Press, 2015); Elizabeth Shakman Hurd, *Beyond Religious Freedom: The New Global Politics of Religion* (New York: Oxford University Press, 2015); Peter Irons, *God on Trial: Dispatches from America's Religious Battlefields* (New York: Viking Books, 2007); Matthew Scherer, *Beyond Church and State: Democracy, Secularism, and Conversion* (Cambridge: Cambridge University Press, 2015); Winnifred Fallers Sullivan, Elizabeth Shakman Hurd, Saba Mahmood, and Peter G. Danchin, eds.,

*Politics of Religious Freedom* (Chicago: University of Chicago Press, 2015); and Nelson Tebbe, *Religious Freedom in an Egalitarian Age* (Cambridge, MA: Harvard University Press, 2017).

70. Wendy Brown, *Regulating Aversion: Tolerance in the Age of Identity and Empire* (Princeton, NJ: Princeton University Press, 2006), p. 5.
71. In some sense, this has been the project of all of Habermas's writing since the 1960s. I would single out as particularly instructive his *Between Facts and Norms: Contributions to a Discourse Theory of Law and Democracy* (Cambridge, MA: MIT Press, 1996). Rawls's "overlapping consensus" is most usefully described in *Political Liberalism*, expanded ed. (New York: Columbia University Press, 2005).

## Chapter 9

1. Sigmund Freud, *On Creativity and the Unconscious* (New York: Harper Perennial Modern Thought, 2009), p. 206.
2. Ibid., p. 207.
3. Ibid., p. 208.
4. Ibid.
5. See Sylvester Johnson, *African-American Religions, 1500–2000: Colonialism, Democracy, and Freedom* (Cambridge: Cambridge University Press, 2015).
6. See Carol Anderson, *One Person, No Vote: How Voter Suppression Is Destroying Our Democracy* (New York: Bloomsbury Press, 2018); Keith J. Bentele and Erin E. O'Brien, "Jim Crow 2.0? Why States Consider and Adopt Restrictive Voter Access Policies," *Perspectives on Politics* 11:4 (December 2013), pp. 1088–1116; and Zoltan Hajnal, Nazita Lajevardi, and Lindsay Nielson, "Voter Identification Laws and the Suppression of Minority Votes," *Journal of Politics* 79:2 (April 2017), pp. 363–379.
7. Ibram X. Kendi, *Stamped from the Beginning: The Definitive History of Racist Ideas in America* (New York: Nation Books, 2016), p. 54.
8. Matthew W. Hughey and Gregory S. Parks, *The Wrongs of the Right: Language, Race, and the Republican Party in the Age of Obama* (New York: NYU Press, 2014), p. 39.
9. Carol Anderson, *White Rage: The Unspoken Truth of Our Racial Divide* (New York: Bloomsbury Press, 2016), p. 33.
10. Ibid., p. 34.
11. Hughey and Parks, *Wrongs of the Right*, p. 41.
12. Amanda Terkel, "Racist GOP Mailing Depicts Obama Surrounded by KFC, Watermelon, and Food Stamps," *Think Progress* (October 16, 2008): https://thinkprogress.org/racist-gop-mailing-depicts-obama-surrounded-by-kfc-watermelon-and-food-stamps-bc992e34c693/.
13. Image reproduced in Jamelle Bouie, "The Rising Tide of Anti-black Racism," *American Prospect* (February 7, 2013): http://prospect.org/article/rising-tide-anti-black-racism.

14. Daily Kos Staff, "Our Post-racial America," *Daily Kos* (March 15, 2012): http://www.dailykos.com/story/2012/03/15/1074757/-Our-post-racial-America.
15. Dan Zak, "Documentary Film '2016: Obama's America' Takes Michael Moore-esque Approach," *Washington Post* (August 27, 2012): https://www.washingtonpost.com/lifestyle/style/documentary-film-2016-obamas-america-takes-michael-moore-esque-approach/2012/08/27/3ecb5198-f07e-11e1-adc6-87dfa8eff430_story.html.
16. Ibid.
17. Ibid.
18. See Matthew W. Hughey, "Show Me Your Papers! Obama's Birth and the Whiteness of Belonging," *Qualitative Sociology* 35 (June 2012), pp. 163–181.
19. Kyle Mantyla, "The Birth of the Birthers," *Right Wing Watch* (June 19, 2009): http://www.rightwingwatch.org/content/birth-birthers.
20. Ibid.
21. All quotations from ibid.
22. Chelsea Schilling, "Limbaugh: 'Obama Has Yet to Prove He's a Citizen,'" *World Net Daily* (July 20, 2009): http://www.wnd.com/2009/07/104595/.
23. Ibid.
24. Ibid.
25. Joan Walsh, "Liz Cheney Defends the Birthers," *Salon* (July 23, 2009): https://www.salon.com/2009/07/23/liz_cheney_and_birthers/.
26. Marc Ambinder, "Should the GOP Take the Birther Threat Seriously? Rush Does . . . ," *The Atlantic* (July 21, 2009): https://www.theatlantic.com/politics/archive/2009/07/should-the-gop-take-the-birther-threat-seriously-rush-does/21787/.
27. Ibid.
28. Ibid.
29. Ibid. Obama's father was an atheist; the President never met his Muslim grandfather; Obama's Kenyan relatives were deeply influenced by evangelicalism; and Indonesian school documents always listed students "in the religion of their fathers."
30. Ibid.
31. Will Bunch, *The Backlash: Right-Wing Radicals, High-Def Hucksters, and Paranoid Politics in the Age of Obama* (New York: HarperCollins, 2010), p. 1.
32. Ibid., p. 15.
33. Ibid., p. xi.
34. Ibid., p. 32.
35. Ibid., p. 33.
36. Ibid., p. 34.
37. Ibid.
38. Glynnis MacNicol, "Obama on Glenn Beck Rally: Folks Exercising Their Rights Exactly as They Should," *Mediaite* (August 30, 2010): https://www.mediaite.com/online/obama-on-glenn-becks-rally-folks-exercising-their-rights-exactly-as-they-should/.
39. Glenn Thrush, "Obama Blasts Lies, Disinformation," *Politico* (August 29, 2010): https://www.politico.com/story/2010/08/obama-blasts-lies-disinformation-041575.

40. Ibid.
41. Ta-Nehisi Coates, "My President Was Black," p. 63 in *The Atlantic* (January–February 2017), pp. 46–66.
42. Ibid., p. 63.
43. Washington Post Editorial Board, "An Assault on Minority Voting Continues in North Carolina," *Washington Post* (August 12, 2018): https://www.washingtonpost.com/opinions/an-assault-on-minority-voting-continues-in-north-carolina/2018/08/12/b60ea52c-9a8f-11e8-8d5e-c6c594024954_story.html?utm_term=.4af0dc49792a.
44. Ta-Nehisi Coates, "The First White President," p. 87 in *The Atlantic* (October 2017), pp. 74–87.
45. Margaret Hartman, "Bill O'Reilly Laments Left's Desire to Take Power from 'White Establishment,'" *New York Magazine* (December 21, 2016): https://nymag.com/intelligencer/2016/12/oreilly-white-establishment.html.
46. Bunch, *The Backlash*, p. 14.
47. See Kathleen Belew's extraordinary *Bring the War Home: The White Power Movement and Paramilitary America* (Cambridge, MA: Harvard University Press, 2018). See also Trevor Aaronson, "Homegrown Material Support: The Domestic Terrorism Law the Justice Department Forgot," *The Intercept* (March 23, 2019): https://theintercept.com/2019/03/23/domestic-terrorism-material-support-law/; Weiyi Cai and Simone Landon, "Attacks by White Supremacists Are Growing. So Are Their Connections," *New York Times* (April 3, 2019): https://www.nytimes.com/interactive/2019/04/03/world/white-extremist-terrorism-christchurch.html; Mark Hamm and Ramon Spajj, "Lone Wolf Terrorism in America: Using Knowledge of Radicalization Pathways to Forge Prevention Strategies," *National Institute of Justice Publications* (February 2015): https://www.ncjrs.gov/pdffiles1/nij/grants/248691.pdf; Rachel Pain, "Everyday Terrorism: Connecting Domestic Violence and Global Terrorism," *Progress in Human Geography* 38:4 (August 2014), pp. 531–550; Matt Stieb, "Report: Domestic Terrorism Is Still a Greater Threat Than Islamic Extremism," *NY Magazine* (March 10, 2019): https://nymag.com/intelligencer/2019/03/domestic-terror-still-greater-threat-than-islamic-extremism.html; and Kevin Sullivan, "Primed to Fight the Government," *Washington Post* (May 21, 2016): http://www.washingtonpost.com/sf/national/2016/05/21/armed-with-guns-and-constitutions-the-patriot-movement-sees-america-under-threat/. For an important religious history that helps unpack this zeal for weapons, see Patrick Blanchfield, "God and Guns, Part One," *The Revealer* (September 25, 2015): https://wp.nyu.edu/therevealer/2015/09/25/god-and-guns/.
48. Far-right panic about "white genocide" is not new. See Barbara Perry, "'White Genocide': White Supremacists and the Politics of Reproduction," pp. 75–96 in Abby L. Ferber, ed., *Home-Grown Hate: Gender and Organized Racism* (New York: Routledge, 2004).
49. Bunch, *The Backlash*, pp. 37, 39.
50. The Hill, "Obama, Congress Have Been Gun Friendly," *Real Clear Politics* (August 27, 2010): https://www.realclearpolitics.com/2010/08/27/obama_congress_have_been_gun_friendly_240507.html.

51. Bunch, *The Backlash*, p. 88.
52. Ibid., p. 53.
53. Ibid., p. 95.
54. Ibid., p. 96.
55. http://www.myholysmoke.com/.
56. Bunch, *The Backlash*, p. 103.
57. Ibid., pp. 4–5.
58. Ibid., p. 40. The Oath Keepers had been energized by Trump's border rhetoric beginning in the 2016 presidential campaign. See Shane Bauer, "Undercover with a Border Militia," *Mother Jones* (November–December 2016): https://www.motherjones.com/politics/2016/10/undercover-border-militia-immigration-bauer/. See also Pete Kotz, "Armed Conspiracy Group Will Defend Republicans at Minneapolis Trump Rally," *Minneapolis City Pages* (October 9, 2019): http://www.citypages.com/news/armed-conspiracy-group-will-defend-republicans-at-minneapolis-trump-rally/562562061.
59. See Belew, *Bring the War Home*; and James William Gibson, *Warrior Dreams: Violence and Manhood in Post-Vietnam America* (New York: Hill and Wang, 1994).
60. Bunch, *The Backlash*, p. 40.
61. Ibid., p. 35.
62. Ibid., p. 36.
63. https://www.thethreepercenters.org/about-us.
64. See Anti-Defamation League, "The Oath Keepers: Anti-government Extremists Recruiting Military and Police," *Anti-Defamation League* (2015): https://www.adl.org/sites/default/files/documents/assets/pdf/combating-hate/The-Oath-Keepers-ADL-Report.pdf.
65. Southern Poverty Law Center, "Oath Keepers," *SPLC*: https://www.splcenter.org/fighting-hate/extremist-files/group/oath-keepers.
66. Bunch, *The Backlash*, p. 121.
67. On the appeal of such rhetoric to men experiencing a collective crisis in their masculine self-image, see Michael Kimmel, *Angry White Men: American Masculinity at the End of an Era*, 2nd ed. (New York: Bold Type Books, 2017).
68. Ibid., p. 127.
69. https://www.martiallawsurvival.com/.
70. German Lopez, "Study: President Obama's Election Scared Americans into Buying More Guns," *Vox* (January 21, 2016): https://www.vox.com/2016/1/21/10801664/obama-gun-sales.
71. Ed Pilkington, "NRA's LaPierre Accuses Obama of Trying to Steal Gun Owners' Weapons," *The Guardian* (January 23, 2013): https://www.theguardian.com/world/2013/jan/23/nra-wayne-lapierre-obama-stealing-weapons.
72. Washington Post Staff, "Identifying Far-Right Symbols That Appeared at the U.S. Capitol Riot," *Washington Post* (January 15, 2021): https://www.washingtonpost.com/nation/interactive/2021/far-right-symbols-capitol-riot/.
73. Mary Oulette, "Megadeth Frontman Dave Mustaine Chalks Up Obama Re-election Comments as 'Stage Fodder,'" *Metalscene* (November 17, 2012): http://metalsc

enenews.com/megadeth-frontman-dave-mustaine-chalks-up-obama-re-election-comments-as-stage-fodder/.
74. CNN Political Unit, "Nugent Threatens Death If Obama Wins in November," *CNN* (April 17, 2012): http://politicalticker.blogs.cnn.com/2012/04/17/nugent-threatens-death-if-obama-wins-in-november/comment-page-37/.
75. Ibid.
76. Ibid.
77. Dan Cassino, "Beliefs about Sandy Hook Cover-Up, Coming Revolution Underlie Divide on Gun Control," *Public Mind Poll* (May 1, 2013): http://publicmind.fdu.edu/2013/guncontrol/final.pdf.
78. On the Virginia GOP, see "Is This True? Virginia Republicans Call for Armed Revolution If Obama Wins in November," *Daily Kos* (August 20, 2012): http://www.dailykos.com/story/2012/08/20/1122295/-Is-this-true-Virginia-Republicans-Call-for-Armed-Revolution-if-Obama-Wins-in-November. On imagery in response to gun control legislation, see Matt Gertz, "Drudge Links Potential Obama Executive Order on Guns to Hitler, Stalin," *Media Matters* (January 1, 2013): http://mediamatters.org/blog/2013/01/09/drudge-links-potential-obama-executive-order-on/192118.
79. Booth Gunter, "Six Most Paranoid Fears for Obama's Second Term," *Salon* (November 4, 2012): https://www.salon.com/2012/11/04/six_most_paranoid_fears_for_obamas_second_term/.
80. Robert Ringer, "Is an Obama Dictatorship in the Air?," *World Net Daily* (April 11, 2012): http://www.wnd.com/2012/04/is-an-obama-dictatorship-in-the-air/.
81. Ibid.
82. Leah Nelson, "Farah: If Obama Re-elected 'We Will Be Hunted Down Like Dogs,'" *Southern Poverty Law Center Hatewatch* (July 9, 2012): http://www.splcenter.org/blog/2012/07/09/farah-if-obama-re-elected-we-will-be-hunted-down-like-dogs/.
83. Amy Davidson Sorkin, "Paul Ryan's Judeo-Christian Values," *New Yorker* (November 5, 2012): https://www.newyorker.com/news/amy-davidson/paul-ryans-judeo-christian-values.
84. Robert Parham, "Fringe Christian Politicians Feed 'Birther' Movement," *Ethics Daily* (February 21, 2011): http://www.ethicsdaily.com/fringe-christian-politicians-feed-birther-movement-cms-17484.
85. Frank Schaeffer, "Understanding the 'Reason' Why Fundamentalists Must Exclude Gays (and Other 'Sinners')," *Huffington Post* (May 25, 2011): https://www.huffpost.com/entry/understanding-the-reason_b_628079.
86. John Curran, "Early 'Birthers' Targeted Chester Arthur," *Los Angeles Times* (August 23, 2009): https://www.latimes.com/archives/la-xpm-2009-aug-23-adna-chester23-story.html.
87. Ezra Grant, "Glenn Beck Attacks Donald Trump and the Birther Movement," *EZKool* (April 26, 2011): http://ezkool.com/2011/04/glenn-beck-attacks-donald-trump-and-the-birther-movement/.

88. Francis Schaeffer, "Franklin Graham Is Big Time Religion's 'Donald Trump,'" *Huffington Post* (April 28, 2011): https://www.huffpost.com/entry/franklin-graham-is-big-ti_b_854758.
89. Liliana Segura, "Racism Is the Prime Cause for the Debunked Obama Birth Certificate Conspiracy Theory," *Alternet* (July 28, 2009): https://www.alternet.org/2009/07/racism_is_the_prime_cause_for_debunked_obama_birth_certificate_conspiracy_theory/.
90. Tina Dupuy, "The Birther Movement: Beyond Unreasonable Doubt," *Huffington Post* (August 31, 2009): http://www.huffingtonpost.com/tina-dupuy/the-birther-movement-beyo_b_248786.html.
91. Walter Brasch, "The Audacity of Hate: Birthers, Deathers, Deniers, and Barack Obama," *Public Record* (May 20, 2011): http://pubrecord.org/commentary/9398/audacity-hate-birthers-deathers/.
92. E. J. Dionne, "The Beginning of the End of the Gun Lobby's Power," *Salt Lake Tribune* (December 17, 2018): https://www.sltrib.com/opinion/commentary/2018/12/17/ej-dionne-beginning-end/.
93. Eduardo Munoz, "Couples Lug AR-15 Assault Rifles to Pennsylvania Church Blessing," *Reuters* (February 28, 2018): https://www.reuters.com/article/us-usa-guns-church/couples-lug-ar-15-assault-rifles-to-pennsylvania-church-blessing-idUSKCN1GC2V3?feedType=RSS&feedName=domesticNews&utm_medium=Social&utm_source=Twitter.
94. Dionne, "Beginning of the End."
95. David Daley, "Creationism, Ayn Rand, and Gun Control: Actual Laws Proposed This Month," *Salon* (February 24, 2013): http://www.salon.com/2013/02/24/creationism_ayn_rand_and_gun_control_six_terrible_state_laws_proposed_this_month/.
96. Statistics are tracked at https://www.splcenter.org/issues/hate-and-extremism.
97. Z. Byron Wolf, "Trump's One Piece of Gun-Related Legislation Undid Restrictions Aimed at Mental Illness," *CNN* (February 15, 2018): https://www.cnn.com/2018/02/15/politics/trump-gun-legislation-mental-health/index.html.
98. Lindsey Bever, "'Make America White Again': A Politician's Billboard Ignites Uproar," *Washington Post* (June 23, 2016): https://www.washingtonpost.com/news/the-fix/wp/2016/06/23/make-america-white-again-a-politicians-billboard-ignites-uproar/?hpid=hp_no-name_hp-in-the-news%3Apage%2Fin-the-news.
99. Noah Berlatsky, "The Trump Effect: New Study Connects White American Intolerance and Support for Authoritarianism," *NBC News* (May 27, 2018): https://www.nbcnews.com/think/opinion/trump-effect-new-study-connects-white-american-intolerance-support-authoritarianism-ncna877886.
100. See Daniel Sullivan, "Psychology Explains How Trump Won by Making White Men Feel Like Victims," *Quartz* (November 11, 2016): http://qz.com/834713/us-election-psychology-explains-how-donald-trump-won-by-making-white-men-feel-like-victims/. See also Diana C. Mutz, "Status Threat, Not Economic Hardship Explains the 2016 Presidential Vote," *Proceedings of the National Academy of Sciences of the*

*United States of America* (April 18, 2018): http://www.pnas.org/content/early/2018/04/18/1718155115.
101. See Joon K. Kim, Ernesto Sagás, and Karina Cespedes, "Genderacing Immigrant Subjects: 'Anchor Babies' and the Politics of Birthright Citizenship," *Social Identities: Journal for the Study of Race, Nation and Culture* 24:3 (2018), pp. 312–326.
102. https://definitions.uslegal.com/j/jus-soli/.
103. https://www.law.cornell.edu/uscode/text/8/1401.
104. The Times Editorial Board, "The 'Birthright Citizenship' Debate," *Los Angeles Times* (October 26, 2014): https://www.latimes.com/nation/la-ed-birthright-citizenship-20141026-story.html.
105. Andy Barr, "Graham Eyes 'Birthright Citizenship,'" *Politico* (July 29, 2010): https://www.politico.com/story/2010/07/graham-eyes-birthright-citizenship-040395.
106. Kelly J. Baker, *Gospel According to the Klan: The KKK's Appeal to Protestant America, 1915–1930* (Lawrence: University of Kansas Press, 2011).
107. See Michael Rogin's *Ronald Reagan, the Movie and Other Episodes in Political Demonology* (Berkeley: University of California Press, 1988).
108. "Full Text of 'Proceedings of the Second Imperial Klonvocation of the Knights of the Ku Klux Klan, held in Kansas City, MO in September 1924,'" *Internet Archive*: https://archive.org/stream/ProceddingsOfTheSecondImperialKlonvocation/Klon_djvu.txt.
109. Ibid.
110. "Ku Klux Klan Plans Border Patrol to Help Fight Illegal Alien Problem," *New York Times* (October 18, 1977): https://www.nytimes.com/1977/10/18/archives/ku-klux-klan-plans-border-patrol-to-help-fight-illegal-alien.html.
111. Zack Beauchamp, "'He's Not Hurting the People He Needs to Be': A Trump Voter Says the Quiet Part Out Loud," *Vox* (January 8, 2019): https://www.vox.com/policy-and-politics/2019/1/8/18173678/trump-shutdown-voter-florida.
112. See Peter Gottschalk, *American Heretics: Catholics, Jews, Muslims, and the History of Religious Intolerance* (New York: Palgrave Macmillan, 2013).
113. Randall Kennedy, *The Persistence of the Color Line: Racial Politics and the Obama Presidency* (New York: Vintage Books, 2011), p. 65. See also David R. Roediger, *How Race Survived U.S. History: From Settlement and Slavery to the Obama Phenomenon* (New York: Verso Books, 2008).
114. See Edward J. Blum and Paul Harvey, *The Color of Christ: The Son of God and the Saga of Race in America* (Chapel Hill: University of North Carolina Press, 2012).
115. See Rosi Braidotti, "The Politics of 'Life Itself' and New Ways of Dying," pp. 201–218 in Diana Coole and Samantha Frost, eds., *New Materialisms: Ontology, Agency, and Politics* (Durham, NC: Duke University Press, 2010).
116. See Stewart Rhodes, "Open Letter to President Trump" (December 2020): https://oathkeepers.org/2020/12/open-letter-to-president-trump-you-must-use-insurrection-act-to-stop-the-steal-and-defeat-the-coup/. See also Griffin Connolly and Richard Hall, "America's Largest Militia Says It Will Refuse to Recognise Biden as President," *The Independent* (November 15, 2020): https://www.independent.co.uk/

news/world/americas/us-election-2020/oath-keepers-militia-donald-trump-joe-biden-2020-election-b1723323.html.

117. Mike Giglio, "'Civil War is Here, Right Now': The President's Supporters on the Militant Right Are Bracing for Conflict," pp. 70–71 in *The Atlantic* (November 2020), pp. 62–73.

118. On these matters, consider Arjun Appadurai, *Fear of Small Numbers: An Essay on the Geography of Anger* (Durham, NC: Duke University Press, 2006). See also Erika Lee, *America for Americans: A History of Xenophobia in the United States* (New York: Basic Books, 2019); and Elaine Tyler May, *Fortress America: How We Embraced Fear and Abandoned Democracy* (New York: Basic Books, 2017).

119. Brakkton Booker, "With a Growing Membership since Trump, Black Gun Group Considers Getting Political," *National Public Radio* (July 10, 2019): https://www.npr.org/2019/07/10/738493491.

# Chapter 10

1. See Jojanneke Van der Toorn et al., "A Sense of Powerlessness Fosters System Justification," *Political Psychology* (February 2015).
2. Scott Sandage, *Born Losers: A History of Failure in America* (Cambridge, MA: Harvard University Press, 2005). See also Jackson Lears, *Rebirth of a Nation: The Making of Modern America, 1877–1920* (New York: HarperCollins, 2009).
3. See Richard Rothstein, *The Color of Law: A Forgotten History of How Our Government Segregated America* (New York: Liveright Publishing, 2017); and Eric Schickler, *Racial Realignment: The Transformation of American Liberalism, 1932–1965* (Princeton, NJ: Princeton University Press, 2016).
4. See David Harvey, *A Brief History of Neoliberalism* (New York: Oxford University Press, 2005). On the impact for democracies, see Wendy Brown, *Undoing the Demos: Neoliberalism's Stealth Revolution* (New York: Zone Books, 2015).
5. Harvey, *Brief History of Liberalism*, p. 82.
6. See Larry Bartels, *Unequal Democracy: The Political Economy of the New Gilded Age* (Princeton, NJ: Princeton University Press, 2010); Jason Brennan, *Against Democracy* (Princeton, NJ: Princeton University Press, 2017); Freedom House, "Democracy in Retreat": https://freedomhouse.org/report/freedom-world/freedom-world-2019/democracy-in-retreat; and Frida Ghitis, "Why 2019 Was a Turning Point in the Global Battle for Democracy," *Washington Post* (December 27, 2019): https://www.washingtonpost.com/opinions/2019/12/27/why-was-turning-point-global-battle-democracy/.
7. See Barbara Ehrenreich, *Bright-Sided: How the Relentless Promotion of Positive Thinking Has Undermined America* (New York: Metropolitan Books, 2009).
8. Mark Landler and Katie Rogers, "Trump Tells Grand Rapids Rally: 'The Russian Hoax Is Finally Dead," *New York Times* (March 28, 2019): https://www.nytimes.com/2019/03/28/us/politics/trump-rally-grand-rapids.html.

9. James Edgar Poague Bell has convinced me of the need to kill narratives. I thank him for the gift of his insight.
10. See Timothy Hinton, "'Sentiments of the Understanding, Perceptions of the Heart'—Constitutional Sentimentalism and the Authority of Morals," unpublished paper, courtesy of the author.
11. George Orwell, "Politics and the English Language," p. 167 in *A Collection of Essays* (New York: Harvest/HBJ, 1946).
12. Wendy Brown, *Regulating Aversion: Tolerance in the Age of Identity and Empire* (Princeton, NJ: Princeton University Press, 2006), p. 29.
13. See Samuel Moyn, *Never Enough: Human Rights in an Unequal World* (Cambridge, MA: Belknap Press of Harvard University Press, 2018).
14. See Bernard Debarbieux, "Hannah Arendt's Spatial Thinking: An Introduction," *Territory, Politics, Governance* 5:4 (2017), pp. 351–367.
15. See James Aho, *Far-Right Fantasy: A Sociology of American Religion and Politics* (New York: Routledge, 2015); Wendy Brown, *In the Ruins of Neoliberalism: The Rise of Antidemocratic Politics in the West* (New York: Columbia University Press, 2019); Jean-Yves Camus and Nicolas Lebourg, *Far-Right Politics in Europe* (Cambridge, MA: Harvard University Press, 2017); Nancy Fraser, *The Old Is Dying and the New Cannot Be Born: From Progressive Neoliberalism to Trump and Beyond* (New York: Verso Books, 2019); William A. Galston, *Anti-pluralism: The Populist Threat to Liberal Democracy* (New Haven, CT: Yale University Press, 2020); George Hawley, *Making Sense of the Alt-Right* (New York: Columbia University Press, 2017); Bonnie Honig, *Public Things: Democracy in Disrepair* (New York: Fordham University Press, 2017); Steven Levitsky and Daniel Ziblatt, *How Democracies Die* (New York: Crown Books, 2018); and Angela Nagle, *Kill All Normies: Online Culture Wars from 4Chan and Tumblr to Trump and the Alt-Right* (London: Zero Books, 2017).
16. See Michael Walzer, *Interpretation and Social Criticism* (Cambridge, MA: Harvard University Press, 1987).
17. See Michael Sandel, *What Money Can't Buy: The Moral Limits of Markets* (New York: Farrar, Straus and Giroux, 2013).
18. Wendy Brown, *Politics Out of History* (Princeton, NJ: Princeton University Press, 2001), pp. 37–38.
19. The phrase "flex your head" derives from an important compilation released by Dischord Records in 1982. The vibrant harDCore scene Dischord represented was a crucial part of the musical milieu of my adolescence, instrumental in the social and political outlooks of many listeners from that time.
20. Quoted in Daniel Bensaid, "Permanent Scandal," p. 32 in Giorgio Agamben et al., *Democracy in What State?* (New York: Columbia University Press, 2011).
21. Ian Shapiro, *Political Criticism* (Berkeley: University of California Press, 1992), p. 279.
22. My thinking about the terrors and possibilities of ordinariness have been shaped by Thomas L. Dumm's *A Politics of the Ordinary* (New York: New York University Press, 1999). See also John Corrigan, *Emptiness: Feeling Christian in America* (Chicago: University of Chicago Press, 2015).

23. See Richard J. Bernstein, "One Step Forward, Two Steps Backward: Rorty on Liberal Democracy and Philosophy," *Political Theory* 15:4 (1987), pp. 538–563.
24. John Rawls, *A Theory of Justice* (Cambridge, MA: Harvard University Press, 1971), p. 220.
25. See Karl Popper, *The Open Society and Its Enemies*, vol. 1: *The Spell of Plato* (Princeton, NJ: Princeton University Press, 2013).
26. See Romand Coles, *Beyond Gated Politics: Reflections for the Possibility of Democracy*, 2nd ed. (Minneapolis: University of Minnesota Press, 2005); James Miller, *Can Democracy Work? A Short History of a Radical Idea, from Ancient Athens to Our World* (New York: Farrar, Straus and Giroux, 2018); Ian Shapiro, *Politics against Domination* (Cambridge, MA: Belknap Press of Harvard University Press, 2018) and *The Real World of Democratic Theory* (Princeton, NJ: Princeton University Press, 2010); and Karen Stenner, *The Authoritarian Dynamic* (Cambridge: Cambridge University Press, 2005). For a rich meditation on related possibilities, see Luke Bretherton, *Resurrecting Democracy: Faith, Citizenship, and the Politics of Common Life* (Cambridge: Cambridge University Press, 2014).

# Bibliography

Aaronson, Trevor. "Homegrown Material Support: The Domestic Terrorism Law the Justice Department Forgot." *The Intercept* (March 23, 2019): https://theintercept.com/2019/03/23/domestic-terrorism-material-support-law/.

Acheson, Nicholas H. *Fundamentals of Molecular Virology*, 2nd ed. (Hoboken, NJ: Wiley Books, 2011).

ADL Staff. "Disinformation: Claims about Black Lives Matter and Antifa Collaborating with Muslim Groups to Impose Sharia Law" (June 2020): https://www.adl.org/disinformation-claims-about-black-lives-matter-and-antifa-collaborating-with-muslim-groups-to.

Adorno, Theodor. *The Culture Industry: Selected Essays on Mass Culture* (New York: Routledge, 2001).

Ahmed, Sara. *The Cultural Politics of Emotion*, 2nd ed. (New York: Routledge, 2014).

Aho, James. *Far-Right Fantasy: A Sociology of American Religion and Politics* (New York: Routledge, 2015).

Ali, Wajahat, Eli Clifton, Matthew Duss, Scott Keyes, and Faiz Shakir. "Fear Inc.: The Roots of the Islamophobia Network in the U.S." *Center for American Progress* (August 2011): https://cdn.americanprogress.org/wp-content/uploads/issues/2011/08/pdf/islamophobia.pdf.

Alumkal, Antony. *Paranoid Science: The Christian Right's War on Reality* (New York: New York University Press, 2017).

Ambinder, Marc. "Should the GOP Take the Birther Threat Seriously? Rush Does . . . ." *The Atlantic* (July 21, 2009): https://www.theatlantic.com/politics/archive/2009/07/should-the-gop-take-the-birther-threat-seriously-rush-does/21787/.

American Historical Association. "Advocacy in Action: AHA Sends Letter to the Texas Board of Education Regarding Proposed Mexican American Studies Textbook." *AHA Today* (September 28, 2016): https://www.historians.org/publications-and-directories/perspectives-on-history/september-2016/advocacy-in-action-aha-sends-letter-to-the-texas-board-of-education-regarding-proposed-mexican-american-studies-textbook.

Americans United. "Hypocrisy Alert: Ex-Christian Coalition Staffer Now Opposes Religious Control of Courts—at Least for Muslims." *Wall of Separation* (August 1, 2011): http://au.org/blogs/wall-of-separation/hypocrisy-alert-ex-christian-coalition-staffer-now-opposes-religious.

Andersen, Kurt. "How America Lost Its Mind." *The Atlantic* (September 2017), pp. 76–91.

Anderson, Amanda. *The Way We Argue Now: A Study in the Cultures of Theory* (Princeton, NJ: Princeton University Press, 2006).

Anderson, Carol. *One Person, No Vote: How Voter Suppression Is Destroying Our Democracy* (New York: Bloomsbury Press, 2018).

Anderson, Carol. *White Rage: The Unspoken Truth of Our Racial Divide* (New York: Bloomsbury Press, 2016).

Anderson, Nate. "Glenn Beck Loses Domain Dispute, Still Ends Up with Domain." *Ars Technica* (November 9, 2009): https://arstechnica.com/tech-policy/2009/11/glenn-beck-loses-domain-dispute-still-ends-up-with-domain/.

Anker, Elisabeth Robin. *Orgies of Feeling: Melodrama and the Politics of Freedom* (Durham, NC: Duke University Press, 2014).

Anti-Defamation League. "The Oath Keepers: Anti-government Extremists Recruiting Military and Police." *Anti-Defamation League* (2015): https://www.adl.org/sites/defa ult/files/documents/assets/pdf/combating-hate/The-Oath-Keepers-ADL-Report.pdf.

"Anti-sharia Law Unconstitutional and 'Stupid' Says Court." *Dirty South News* (January 10, 2012): http://dirtysouthnews.com/2012/01/10/oklahoma-anti-sharia-law-uncon stitutional-and-stupid-says-court/.

Appadurai, Arjun. *Fear of Small Numbers: An Essay on the Geography of Anger* (Durham, NC: Duke University Press, 2006).

Appadurai, Arjun. *Modernity at Large: Cultural Dimensions of Globalization* (Minneapolis: University of Minnesota Press, 1996).

Applbaum, Arthur Isak. *Legitimacy: The Right to Rule in a Wanton World* (Cambridge, MA: Harvard University Press, 2019).

Arditi, Benjamin. "The People as Re-presentation and Event." In Carlos de la Torre, ed., *The Promise and Perils of Populism: Global Perspectives* (Lexington: University of Kentucky Press, 2015), pp. 91–112.

Arendt, Hannah. *On Revolution* (New York: Penguin Classics, 2006).

Arendt, Hannah. "A Special Supplement: Reflections on Violence." *New York Review of Books* (February 27, 1969).

Ariel, Yaakov. *Evangelizing the Chosen People: Missions to the Jews in America, 1880–2000* (Chapel Hill: University of North Carolina Press, 2000).

Aristotle. *The Nicomachean Ethics* (New York: Oxford University Press 2009).

Asad, Talal. *Formations of the Secular: Christianity, Islam, Modernity* (Stanford, CA: Stanford University Press, 2003).

Asad, Talal. "Thinking about Religion, Belief, and Politics." In Robert A. Orsi, ed., *The Cambridge Companion to Religious Studies* (Cambridge: Cambridge University Press, 2012), pp. 36–57.

Baker, Kelly J. *Gospel According to the Klan: The KKK's Appeal to Protestant America, 1915–1930* (Lawrence: University of Kansas Press, 2011).

Balleisen, Edward J. *Fraud: An American History from Barnum to Madoff* (Princeton, NJ: Princeton University Press, 2017).

Balmer, Randall. "The Real Origins of the Religious Right." *Politico* (May 27, 2014): https://www.politico.com/magazine/story/2014/05/religious-right-real-origins-107133_Pa ge3.html.

Balmer, Randall. "Sarah Palin and the Politics of Victimization." *Religion Dispatches* (January 3, 2011): http://www.religiondispatches.org/books/politics/3972/sarah_ palin_and_the_politics_of_victimization.

Balmer, Randall. *Thy Kingdom Come: How the Religious Right Distorts Faith and Threatens America* (New York: Basic Books, 2006).

Balmer, Randall and Jana Riess, eds. *Mormonism and American Politics* (New York: Columbia University Press, 2015).

Barr, Andy. "Graham Eyes 'Birthright Citizenship.'" *Politico* (July 29, 2010): https://www. politico.com/story/2010/07/graham-eyes-birthright-citizenship-040395.

Bartels, Larry. *Unequal Democracy: The Political Economy of the New Gilded Age* (Princeton, NJ: Princeton University Press, 2010).
Barton, David. "Evolution and the Law: A Death Struggle between Two Civilizations." *Wallbuilders* (Spring 2002): https://wallbuilders.com/spring-2002/.
Barton, David. "God: Missing in Action in American History." *Wallbuilders* (June 2005): https://wallbuilders.com/god-missing-action-american-history/.
Barton, David. "Political Parties and Morality." *Wallbuilders* (December 21, 1998): http://www.wallbuilders.com/LIBissuesArticles.asp?id=109.
Barton, David. "The Separation of Church and State." *Wallbuilders* (January 2001). http://www.wallbuilders.com/libissuesarticles.asp?id=123.
Bataille, Georges. *On Nietzsche* (Saint Paul, MN: Paragon House Publishers, 1988).
Batarseh, Feras A. "Thoughts on the Future of Human Knowledge and Machine Intelligence." *LSE Business Review* (September 20, 2017): https://blogs.lse.ac.uk/businessreview/2017/09/20/thoughts-on-the-future-of-human-knowledge-and-machine-intelligence/.
Bauder, David. "Fox's Glenn Beck: President Obama Is a Racist." *Associated Press* (July 28, 2009): https://www.delcotimes.com/news/fox-s-glenn-beck-president-obama-is-a-racist/article_320fb049-347e-5d84-9d9d-5d960f365170.html.
Bauer, Shane. "Undercover with a Border Militia." *Mother Jones* (November/December 2016): https://www.motherjones.com/politics/2016/10/undercover-border-militia-immigration-bauer/.
Beauchamp, Zack. "'He's Not Hurting the People He Needs to Be': A Trump Voter Says the Quiet Part Out Loud." *Vox* (January 8, 2019): https://www.vox.com/policy-and-politics/2019/1/8/18173678/trump-shutdown-voter-florida.
Beail, Linda and Rhonda Kinney Longworth. *Framing Sarah Palin: Pit Bulls, Puritans, and Politics* (New York: Routledge, 2012).
Beck, Glenn. *Glenn Beck Radio* (August 25, 2020): https://www.glennbeck.com/radio/glenn-reacts-to-rnc-night-1-i-havent-felt-that-way-at-a-convention-since-ronald-reagan.
Beck, Glenn. *Glenn Beck's Common Sense: A Case against an Out-of-Control Government, Inspired by Thomas Paine* (New York: Threshold Editions, 2009).
Beck, Glenn. "We Are All Catholics Now." *Washington Post* (February 19, 2012): http://www.washingtonpost.com/blogs/guest-voices/post/why-we-are-all-catholics-now/2012/02/19/gIQAZFYVOR_blog.html.
Bedard, Paul. "Liberty University Opens Falkirk Center to Fight Attacks on Jesus, Constitution." *Washington Examiner* (November 30, 2019).
Beinart, Peter. "Breaking Faith." *The Atlantic* (April 2017), pp. 15–17.
Beinart, Peter. "Glenn Beck's Regrets." *The Atlantic* (January–February 2017), pp. 16–19.
Bejan, Teresa M. *Mere Civility: Disagreement and the Limits of Toleration* (Cambridge, MA: Harvard University Press, 2017).
Belew, Kathleen. *Bring the War Home: The White Power Movement and Paramilitary America* (Cambridge, MA: Harvard University Press, 2018).
Bell, Catherine. *Ritual: Perspectives and Dimensions* (New York: Oxford University Press, 2009).
Beneke, Chris. *Beyond Tolerance: The Religious Origins of American Pluralism* (New York: Oxford University Press, 2009).
Benjamin, Walter. *Illuminations: Essays and Reflections* (New York: Schocken Books, 2007).

Bennett, Daniel. *Defending Faith: The Politics of the Christian Conservative Legal Movement* (Lawrence: University of Kansas Press, 2017).

Bensaid, Daniel. "Permanent Scandal." In Giorgio Agamben et al., *Democracy in What State?* (New York: Columbia University Press, 2011), pp. 16–43.

Bentele, Keith J. and Erin E. O'Brien. "Jim Crow 2.0? Why States Consider and Adopt Restrictive Voter Access Policies." *Perspectives on Politics* 11:4 (December 2013), pp. 1088–1116.

Berger, Benjamin L. *Law's Religion: Religious Difference and the Claims of Constitutionalism* (Toronto: University of Toronto Press, 2015).

Berlant, Lauren. "Cruel Optimism." In Melissa Gregg and Gregory J. Seigworth, eds., *The Affect Theory Reader* (Durham, NC: Duke University Press, 2010), pp. 93–117.

Berlant, Lauren. *The Female Complaint: The Unfinished Business of Sentimentality in American Culture* (Durham, NC: Duke University Press, 2008).

Berlatsky, Noah. "The Trump Effect: New Study Connects White American Intolerance and Support for Authoritarianism." *NBC News* (May 27, 2018): https://www.nbcnews.com/think/opinion/trump-effect-new-study-connects-white-american-intolerance-support-authoritarianism-ncna877886.

Bernstein, Richard. "One Step Forward, Two Steps Backward: Rorty on Liberal Democracy and Philosophy." *Political Theory* 15:4 (1987), pp. 538–563.

Bever, Lindsey. "'Make America White Again': A Politician's Billboard Ignites Uproar." *Washington Post* (June 23, 2016): https://www.washingtonpost.com/news/the-fix/wp/2016/06/23/make-america-white-again-a-politicians-billboard-ignites-uproar/?hpid=hp_no-name_hp-in-the-news%3Apage%2Fin-the-news.

Beydoun, Khaled A. *American Islamophobia: Understanding the Roots and Rise of Fear* (Berkeley: University of California Press, 2018).

Bigler, David L. and Will Bagley. *The Mormon Rebellion: America's First Civil War, 1857–1858* (Norman: University of Oklahoma Press, 2011).

Birkey, Andy. "Religious Right Watch: Sarah Palin at a Glance." *Twin Cities Daily Planet* (September 10, 2008): https://www.tcdailyplanet.net/religious-right-watch-sarah-palin-glance/.

Birnbaum, Michael. "Historians Speak Out against Proposed Texas Textbook Changes." *Washington Post* (March 18, 2010): http://journalofeducationalcontroversy.blogspot.com/2010/03/historians-speak-out-against-proposed.html.

Bivins, Jason C. *The Fracture of Good Order: Christian Antiliberalism and the Challenge to American Politics* (Chapel Hill: University of North Carolina Press, 2003).

Bivins, Jason C. "How Christian Media Is Shaping American Politics." https://theconversation.com/how-christian-media-is-shaping-american-politics-95910.

Bivins, Jason C. *Religion of Fear: The Politics of Horror in Conservative Evangelicalism* (New York: Oxford University Press, 2008).

Blackstock, Nelson. *COINTELPRO: The FBI's Secret War on Political Freedom* (New York: Pathfinder Press, 1988).

Blake, Mariah. "Revisionaries: How a Group of Texas Conservatives Are Rewriting Your Kids' Textbooks." *Washington Monthly* (January 1, 2010): https://washingtonmonthly.com/2010/01/01/revisionaries/.

Blakeslee, Nate. "King of the Christocrats." *Texas Monthly* (September 2006): https://www.texasmonthly.com/articles/king-of-the-christocrats/.

Blanchfield, Patrick. "God and Guns, Part One." *The Revealer* (September 25, 2015): https://wp.nyu.edu/therevealer/2015/09/25/god-and-guns/.

Blow, Charles M. "White Male Victimization Anxiety." *New York Times* (October 10, 2018): https://www.nytimes.com/2018/10/10/opinion/trump-white-male-victimization.html.
Blue, Miranda. "Franklin Graham: 'Only One Election Left' to Save America from Godless Secularists." *Right Wing Watch* (February 12, 2016): http://www.rightwingwatch.org/content/franklin-graham-only-one-election-left-save-america-godless-secularists.
Blum, Edward J. and Paul Harvey. *The Color of Christ: The Son of God and the Saga of Race in America* (Chapel Hill: University of North Carolina Press, 2012).
Bodnar, John. *Remaking America: Public Memory, Commemoration, and Patriotism in the Twentieth Century* (Princeton, NJ: Princeton University Press, 1993).
Booker, Brakkton. "With a Growing Membership Since Trump, Black Gun Group Considers Getting Political." *National Public Radio* (July 10, 2019): https://www.npr.org/2019/07/10/738493491/with-a-growing-membership-since-trump-black-gun-group-considers-getting-political.
Boorstein, Michelle. "Glenn Beck May Be Unlikely Leader for Conservative Christians." *Washington Post* (August 31, 2010). Archived at https://madison.com/ct/news/glenn-beck-may-be-unlikely-leader-for-conservative-christians/article_cca2c0d4-b514-11df-9e71-001cc4c002e0.html.
Borger, Julian. "US Inquiry into Claims Black Voters Were Stripped of Rights." *The Guardian* (December 4, 2000): https://www.theguardian.com/world/2000/dec/04/uselections2000.usa1.
Boston, Rob. "Dissecting the Religious Right's Favorite Bible Curriculum." *The Humanist* (November 1, 2007): https://www.thefreelibrary.com/Dissecting+the+religious+right%27s+favorite+Bible+Curriculum.-a0170729742.
Boston, Rob. "Sects, Lies and Videotape." *Church & State* 46:4 (April 1993), pp. 8–12.
Bouie, Jamelle. "The Rising Tide of Anti-black Racism." *American Prospect* (February 7, 2013): http://prospect.org/article/rising-tide-anti-black-racism.
Bouie, Jamelle. "The Tea Party Is Still Basically the Religious Right." *American Prospect* (February 24, 2011): https://prospect.org/article/tea-party-still-basically-religious-right.
Bowes, John P. *Land Too Good for Indians: Northern Indian Removal* (Norman: University of Oklahoma Press, 2017).
Bowler, Kate. *Blessed: A History of the American Prosperity Gospel* (New York: Oxford University Press, 2013).
Boyte, Harry C. *Awakening Democracy through Public Work: Pedagogies of Empowerment* (Nashville, TN: Vanderbilt University Press, 2018).
Bracher, Manya. "How Religion Guides Palin." *Chicago Tribune* (September 6, 2008).
Braidotti, Rosi. "The Politics of 'Life Itself' and New Ways of Dying." In Diana Coole and Samantha Frost, eds., *New Materialisms: Ontology, Agency, and Politics* (Durham, NC: Duke University Press, 2010), pp. 201–218.
Brasch, Walter. "The Audacity of Hate: Birthers, Deathers, Deniers, and Barack Obama." *Public Record* (May 20, 2011): http://pubrecord.org/commentary/9398/audacity-hate-birthers-deathers/.
Braude, Ann. *Radical Spirits: Spiritualism and Women's Rights in Nineteenth-Century America*, 2nd ed. (Bloomington: Indiana University Press, 2001).
Braun, Stephen. "Palin Canny on Religion and Politics." *Los Angeles Times* (September 28, 2008): https://www.latimes.com/archives/la-xpm-2008-sep-28-na-palinreligion28-story.html.

Braunstein, Ruth. *Prophets and Patriots: Faith in Democracy across the Political Divide* (Berkeley: University of California Press, 2017).
Brennan, Jason. *Against Democracy* (Princeton, NJ: Princeton University Press, 2017).
Brennan, Teresa. *The Transmission of Affect* (Ithaca, NY: Cornell University Press, 2004).
Bretherton, Luke. *Resurrecting Democracy: Faith, Citizenship, and the Politics of Common Life* (Cambridge: Cambridge University Press, 2014).
Bridge Initiative Team. "Factsheet: Brigitte Gabriel." *Bridge Initiative* (December 4, 2018): https://bridge.georgetown.edu/research/factsheet-brigitte-gabriel-2/.
Brinkley, Alan. *Voices of Protest: Huey Long, Father Coughlin, and the Great Depression* (New York: Vintage Books, 1983).
Brittain, Amy and David Willman. "'A Place to Fund Hope': How Proud Boys and Other Fringe Groups Found Refuge on a Christian Fundraising Website." *Washington Post* (January 18, 2021): https://www.washingtonpost.com/investigations/a-place-to-fund-hope-how-proud-boys-and-other-fringe-groups-found-refuge-on-a-christian-fundraising-website/2021/01/18/14a536ee-574b-11eb-a08b-f1381ef3d207_story.html.
Brooking, Emerson T. and P. W. Singer. "War Goes Viral: How Social Media Is Being Weaponized." *The Atlantic* (November 2016), pp. 70–83.
Brooks, Joanna. "Who Says the Tea Party Isn't a Religious Movement?" *Religion Dispatches* (June 3, 2010): http://www.religiondispatches.org/dispatches/joannabrooks/2736/who_says_the_tea_party_isn%E2%80%99t_a_religious_movement%2C_part_ii.
Brown, Wendy. *In the Ruins of Neoliberalism: The Rise of Antidemocratic Politics in the West* (New York: Columbia University Press, 2019).
Brown, Wendy. *Politics Out of History* (Princeton, NJ: Princeton University Press, 2001).
Brown, Wendy. *Regulating Aversion: Tolerance in the Age of Identity and Empire* (Princeton, NJ: Princeton University Press, 2006).
Brown, Wendy. *Undoing the Demos: Neoliberalism's Stealth Revolution* (New York: Zone Books, 2015).
Brownstein, Ronald. "This Group of Voters Could Swing the 2020 Election." *CNN* (November 5, 2019): https://www.cnn.com/2019/11/05/politics/white-non-college-evangelicals-election-2020/index.html.
Bruenig, Elizabeth Stoker. "The Right's Ayn Rand Hypocrisy: Why Their 'Religious' Posture Is a Total Sham." *Salon* (February 28, 2014): http://www.salon.com/2014/02/28/the_rights_ayn_rand_hypocrisy_why_their_religious_posture_is_a_total_sham/.
Bullock, Charles S. "The 2010 Elections." In Charles S. Bullock III, ed., *Key States, High Stakes: Sarah Palin, the Tea Party, and the 2010 Elections* (Lanham, MD: Rowman and Littlefield, 2012), pp. 1–9.
Bump, Philip. "There's a Virus in Trumpland." *Washington Post* (August 3, 2018): https://www.washingtonpost.com/news/politics/wp/2018/08/03/theres-a-virus-in-trumpland/.
Bunch, Will. *The Backlash: Right-Wing Radicals, High-Def Hucksters, and Paranoid Politics in the Age of Obama* (New York: Harper Books, 2010).
Burke, Edmund. *Reflections on the Revolution in France* (Indianapolis, IN: Hackett Classics, 1987).
Burston, Bradley. "Not Jewish Enough for Glenn Beck." *Haaretz* (August 19, 2011): https://www.haaretz.com/1.5049163.
Burt, Andrew. *American Hysteria: The Untold Story of Mass Political Extremism in the United States* (Lanham, MD: Lyons Press, 2015).

Butler, Anthea. "Weak Uni-Tea." *Religion Dispatches* (August 3, 2010): http://www.religiondispatches.org/dispatches/antheabutler/3084/weak_uni-tea_.

Butler, Anthea. "Whom Will She Wreck? The Real Sarah Palin Question." *Religion Dispatches* (September 6, 2011): http://www.religiondispatches.org/archive/politics/5061/whom_will_she_wreck%3A_the_real_sarah_palin_question/.

Cai, Weiyi and Simone Landon. "Attacks by White Supremacists Are Growing. So Are Their Connections." *New York Times* (April 3, 2019): https://www.nytimes.com/interactive/2019/04/03/world/white-extremist-terrorism-christchurch.html.

Caldwell, Deborah. "David Barton & the 'Myth' of Church-State Separation." *Beliefnet* (October 2004): http://www.beliefnet.com/News/Politics/2004/10/David-Barton-The-Myth-Of-Church-State-Separation.aspx.

Campbell, David E. and Robert D. Putnam. "Crashing the Tea Party." *New York Times* (August 17, 2011): http://www.nytimes.com/2011/08/17/opinion/crashing-the-tea-party.html?_r=3.

Campbell, James E. *Polarized: Making Sense of a Divided America* (Princeton, NJ: Princeton University Press, 2016).

Camus, Jean-Yves and Nicolas Lebourg. *Far-Right Politics in Europe* (Cambridge, MA: Harvard University Press, 2017).

Canetti, Elias. *Crowds and Power* (New York: Farrar, Straus and Giroux, 1984).

Cannadine, David. "History with Rose-Tinted Hindsight." *BBC News Magazine* (June 25, 2010): http://news.bbc.co.uk/2/hi/uk_news/magazine/8762969.stm.

Carr, Nicholas. *The Shallows: What the Internet Is Doing to Our Brains* (New York: Norton, 2011).

Carter, Dan T. *From George Wallace to Newt Gingrich: Race in the Conservative Counterrevolution, 1963–1994* (Baton Rouge, LA: Louisiana State University Press, 1996).

Carter, Joe. "Glenn Beck Thinks Catholics Should 'Leave Their Church.'" *First Things* (March 8, 2010): http://www.firstthings.com/blogs/firstthoughts/2010/03/08/glenn-beck-thinks-catholics-should-leave-their-church/.

Cassino, Dan. *Fox News and American Politics: How One Channel Shapes American Politics and Society* (New York: Routledge, 2016).

Cassino, Dan. "Beliefs about Sandy Hook Cover-Up, Coming Revolution Underlie Divide on Gun Control." *Public Mind Poll* (May 1, 2013): http://publicmind.fdu.edu/2013/guncontrol/final.pdf.

Castelli, Elizabeth. "Persecution Complexes: Identity Politics and the 'War on Christians.'" *differences* 18:3 (2007), pp. 152–180.

Castells, Manuel. *Networks of Outrage and Hope: Social Movements in the Internet Age* (Cambridge: Polity Press, 2015).

Cesca, Bob. "Welcome to Glenn Beck's Grifter Theme Park." *Huffington Post* (August 1, 2014): http://www.huffingtonpost.com/bob-cesca/welcome-to-glenn-becks-gr_b_2497307.html.

Chatelet, Gilles. *To Live and Think Like Pigs: The Incitement of Envy and Boredom in Market Democracies* (Cambridge, MA: Urbanomic/Sequence Press, 2018).

Chiaramonte, Perry. "Christians the Most Persecuted Group in World for Second Year: Study." *Fox News* (January 6, 2017): http://www.foxnews.com/world/2017/01/06/christians-most-persecuted-group-in-world-for-second-year-study.html.

Chinoy, Sahil. "What Happened to America's Political Center of Gravity?" *New York Times* (June 26, 2019): https://www.nytimes.com/interactive/2019/06/26/opinion/Sunday/republican-platform-far-right.html.

Christian, David. *Maps of Time: An Introduction to Big History* (Berkeley: University of California Press, 2011).

Clarkson, Frederick. "The Eliminationists: How Hate Talk Radicalized the American Right." *Religion Dispatches* (October 20, 2009): http://www.religiondispatches.org/archive/politics/1893/the_eliminationists%3A_how_hate_talk_radicalized_the_american_right.

Clarkson, Frederick. "Top Christian Nationalist on Hot Seat." *Daily Kos* (April 11, 2005): https://m.dailykos.com/stories/2005/4/11/105896/-.

CNN Political Unit. "Nugent Threatens Death If Obama Wins in November." *CNN* (April 17, 2012): http://politicalticker.blogs.cnn.com/2012/04/17/nugent-threatens-death-if-obama-wins-in-november/comment-page-37/.

Coats, Curtis D. and Stewart M. Hoover. "Broadswords and Face Paint: Why *Braveheart* Still Matters." In Bruce David Forbes and Jeffrey H. Mahan, eds., *Religion and Popular Culture in America*, 3rd ed. (Berkeley: University of California Press, 2017), pp. 413–430.

Coates, Ta-Nehisi. "The First White President." *The Atlantic* (October 2017), pp. 74–87.

Coates, Ta-Nehisi. "My President Was Black." *The Atlantic* (January/February 2017), pp. 46–66.

Cohen, Jason. "When the Governor Talks to God." *Texas Monthly* (January 21, 2013): https://www.texasmonthly.com/articles/when-the-governor-talks-to-god/.

Cohen, Lizabeth. *A Consumers' Republic: The Politics of Mass Consumption in Postwar America* (New York: Vintage Books, 2003).

Cole, Alyson M. *The Cult of True Victimhood: From the War on Welfare to the War on Terror* (Stanford, CA: Stanford University Press, 2007).

Coles, Romand. *Beyond Gated Politics: Reflections for the Possibility of Democracy*, 2nd ed. (Minneapolis: University of Minnesota Press, 2005).

"Common Good Death Camps." *The Revealer* (May 29, 2010): https://therevealer.org/common-good-death-camps/.

Connolly, Griffin and Richard Hall. "America's Largest Militia Says It Will Refuse to Recognise Biden as President." *The Independent* (November 15, 2020): https://www.independent.co.uk/news/world/americas/us-election-2020/oath-keepers-militia-donald-trump-joe-biden-2020-election-b1723323.html.

Continetti, Matthew. "The Two Faces of the Tea Party." *Weekly Standard* (June 28, 2010). Archived at https://www.washingtonexaminer.com/weekly-standard/the-two-faces-of-the-tea-party.

Cookson, Catharine. *Regulating Religion: The Courts and the Free Exercise Clause* (New York: Oxford University Press, 2001).

Coppins, McKay. "Newt Gingrich Says You're Welcome." *The Atlantic* (November 2018), pp. 50–60.

Corbin, Caroline. "Secularism and U.S. Jurisprudence." In Phil Zuckerman and John R. Shook, eds., *The Oxford Handbook of Secularism* (New York: Oxford University Press, 2017), pp. 467–481.

Corrigan, John. *Emptiness: Feeling Christian in America* (Chicago: University of Chicago Press, 2015).

Corrigan, John and Lynn Neal, eds. *Religious Intolerance in America: A Documentary History* (Chapel Hill: University of North Carolina Press, 2010).
Cowie, Jefferson. *Stayin' Alive: The 1970s and the Last Days of the Working Class* (New York: New Press, 2012).
"CPAC: Former CIA Director Tells of Sharia Threat." *Judicial Watch* (February 12, 2011): https://www.judicialwatch.org/blog/2011/02/cpac-former-cia-director-tells-of-sharia-threat/.
Cross, Gary S. and Robert N. Proctor. *Packaged Pleasures: How Technology and Marketing Revolutionized Desire* (Chicago: University of Chicago Press, 2014).
Curran, John. "Early 'Birthers' Targeted Chester Arthur." *Los Angeles Times* (August 23, 2009): https://www.latimes.com/archives/la-xpm-2009-aug-23-adna-chester23-story.html.
Dahl, Robert. *Polyarchy: Participation and Opposition* (New Haven, CT: Yale University Press, 1972).
Daily Kos Staff. "Our Post-racial America." *Daily Kos* (March 15, 2012): http://www.dailykos.com/story/2012/03/15/1074757/-Our-post-racial-America.
Daley, David. "Creationism, Ayn Rand, and Gun Control: Actual Laws Proposed This Month." *Salon* (February 24, 2013): http://www.salon.com/2013/02/24/creationism_ayn_rand_and_gun_control_six_terrible_state_laws_proposed_this_month/.
Dawkins, Richard. "Attention Gov. Perry: Evolution Is a Fact." *The Oregonian* (August 7, 2011): https://www.oregonlive.com/opinion/2011/08/attention_gov_perry_evolution.html.
Dawkins, Richard. *The Selfish Gene*, 2nd ed. (New York: Oxford University Press, 1989).
Dawkins, Richard, Daniel Dennett, Sam Harris, and Christopher Hitchens. *The Four Horsemen: The Discussion That Sparked an Atheist Revolution* (New York: Bantam Books, 2019).
Dean, Jodi. *Blog Theory: Feedback and Capture in the Circuits of Drive* (New York: Polity Books, 2010).
Dean, Jodi. *Democracy and Other Neoliberal Fantasies: Communicative Capitalism and Left Politics* (Durham, NC: Duke University Press, 2009).
Debarbieux, Bernard. "Hannah Arendt's Spatial Thinking: An Introduction." *Territory, Politics, Governance* 5:4 (2017), pp. 351–367.
De Landa, Manuel. *A Thousand Years of Nonlinear History* (New York: Zone Books, 1997).
de Tocqueville, Alexis. *Democracy in America and Two Essays on America* (New York: Penguin Classics, 2003).
DeRogatis, Amy. *Saving Sex: Sexuality and Salvation in American Evangelicalism* (New York: Oxford University Press, 2014).
Desilver, Drew. "For Most U.S. Workers, Real Wages Have Barely Budged for Decades." *Fact Tank* (August 7, 2018): https://www.pewresearch.org/fact-tank/2018/08/07/for-most-us-workers-real-wages-have-barely-budged-for-decades/.
Dewey, John. *The Public and Its Problems* (Athens: Ohio University Press, 1994).
Diiulio, John J., Jr. "Getting Faith-Based Programs Right." *Public Interest* 155 (Spring 2004), pp. 75–88.
Dillon, Sam. "Wisdom of Leaders and Guidance for Graduates." *New York Times* (June 20, 2010): https://www.nytimes.com/2010/06/21/education/21commence-web.html.
Dionne, E. J. "The Beginning of the End of the Gun Lobby's Power." *Salt Lake Tribune* (December 17, 2018): https://www.sltrib.com/opinion/commentary/2018/12/17/ej-dionne-beginning-end/.

Dolan, Jay P. *The American Catholic Experience: A History from Colonial Times to the Present* (New York: Doubleday, 1985).

Dougherty, Michael Brendan. "Tea Party Crashers." *American Conservative* (April 2010), pp. 6–9.

Dowland, Seth. *Family Values and the Rise of the Christian Right* (Philadelphia: University of Pennsylvania Press, 2015).

Downie, James. "The Decline of Glenn Beck." *New Republic* (March 3, 2011): https://newrepublic.com/article/84662/the-decline-glenn-beck.

Dubler, Joshua and Isaac Weiner, eds. *Religion, Law, USA* (New York: New York University Press, 2019).

Dubuisson, Daniel. *The Western Construction of Religion: Myths, Knowledge, and Identity* (Baltimore: Johns Hopkins University Press, 2007).

Ducat, Stephen J. *The Wimp Factor: Gender Gaps, Holy Wars, & the Politics of Anxious Masculinity* (Boston: Beacon Press, 2004).

Dumm, Thomas L. *A Politics of the Ordinary* (New York: New York University Press, 1999).

Dupuy, Tina. "The Birther Movement: Beyond Unreasonable Doubt." *Huffington Post* (August 31, 2009): http://www.huffingtonpost.com/tina-dupuy/the-birther-movement-beyo_b_248786.html.

Easley, Jason. "Glenn Beck the Mormon Blames Progressives for Perverting Religion." *Politics USA* (April 30, 2010): http://www.politicususa.com/en/beck-progressives-religion.

Eckholm, Eric. "Using History to Mold Ideas on the Right." *New York Times* (May 4, 2011): https://www.globalpolicy.org/nations-a-states/general-analysis-on-states-and-their-future/50177-using-history-to-mold-ideas-on-the-right.html.

Ehrenreich, Barbara. *Bright-Sided: How the Relentless Promotion of Positive Thinking Has Undermined America* (New York: Metropolitan Books, 2009).

Eichler, Stephen. "Invisible Tea Party Heroes." *Canada Free Press* (February 3, 2011): http://canadafreepress.com/index.php/article/32902.

Eliade, Mircea. *A History of Religious Ideas*, vol. 1: *From the Stone Age to the Eleusinian Mysteries* (Chicago: University of Chicago Press, 1978).

Elliott, Andrea. "The Man behind the Anti-shariah Movement." *New York Times* (July 31, 2011): http://www.nytimes.com/2011/07/31/us/31shariah.html?_r=1&hp.

Elliott, Justin. "Conservative Bloc Prevails in Latest TX Textbooks Standards Vote." *Talking Points Memo* (March 12, 2010): http://tpmmuckraker.talkingpointsmemo.com/2010/03/conservative_bloc_dominates_latest_texas_textbooks.php?ref=mp.

Elliott, Justin. "Michigan Dems Charged in Fake Tea Party Scheme." *Salon* (March 17, 2011): https://www.salon.com/2011/03/17/dems_tea_party_charges/.

Elliott, Justin. "TX Textbooks Proposal: Students Must Discuss Gutting Social Security, Explain How U.N. Undermines U.S." *Talking Points Memo* (May 17, 2010): http://tpmmuckraker.talkingpointsmemo.com/2010/05/tx_textbooks_proposal_students_must_discuss_guttin.php.

Elliott, Justin. "What a Long, Strange Trip It's Been: TX Textbooks Rules Set for Final Vote." *Talking Points Memo* (May 19, 2010): http://tpmmuckraker.talkingpointsmemo.com/2010/05/texas_textbooks_what_a_long_strange_trip.php.

Elshtain, Jean Bethke. *Democracy on Trial* (New York: Basic Books, 1995).

Elshtain, Jean Bethke. *Real Politics: At the Center of Everyday Life* (Baltimore: Johns Hopkins University Press, 1997).

Elster, Jon, ed. *Tocqueville: The Ancien Régime and the French Revolution* (Cambridge: Cambridge University Press, 2012).

Emerson, Ralph Waldo. "Society and Solitude." Accessed at https://archive.org/details/in.ernet.dli.2015.43434/page/n15.

Engler, Mark. "Boycott Power and the Fall of Glenn Beck." *Dissent* (June 29, 2011): https://www.dissentmagazine.org/blog/boycott-power-and-the-fall-of-glenn-beck.

Erbe, Bonnie. "Sarah Palin's Lies about Obamacare Are Based on Religion." *U.S. News & World Report* (August 11, 2008): http://www.usnews.com/opinion/blogs/erbe/2009/08/11/sarah-palins-lies-about-obamacare-are-based-on-religion.

Etzioni, Amitai. "The Tea Party Is Half Right." *Society* 48:3 (2011), pp. 197–202.

Fairchild, Mary. "Sarah Palin's Faith." *Learn Religions* (March 6, 2017): https://www.learnreligions.com/sarah-palins-faith-701386.

Farrell, Justin. "The Young and the Restless? The Liberalization of Young Evangelicals." *Journal for the Scientific Study of Religion* 50:3 (September 2011), pp. 517–532.

Farrelly, Maura Jane. *Anti-Catholicism in America, 1620–1860* (Cambridge: Cambridge University Press, 2017).

Fassin, Didier and Richard Rechtman. *The Empire of Trauma: An Inquiry into the Condition of Victimhood* (Princeton, NJ: Princeton University Press, 2009).

Fea, John. *Believe Me: The Evangelical Road to Donald Trump* (Grand Rapids, MI: Eerdmans, 2018).

Fea, John. *Was America Founded a Christian Nation? A Historical Introduction*, rev. ed. (Louisville, KY: Westminster John Knox Press, 2016).

Feldscher, Kyle. "Steve King Says He Relates to What Christ 'Went through for Us' after Controversies." *CNN* (April 24, 2019): https://www.cnn.com/2019/04/24/politics/steve-king-jesus-christ/index.html.

Fergus, Devin. *Land of the Fee: Hidden Costs and the Decline of the American Middle Class* (New York: Oxford University Press, 2018).

Fernandez, Manny. "Governor Leads Prayer Rally for 'Nation in Crisis.'" *New York Times* (August 7, 2011): http://www.nytimes.com/2011/08/07/us/politics/07prayer.html?_r=1&hp.

Fernandez, Manny and Erik Eckholm. "Texas Governor Draws Criticism on Prayer Event." *New York Times* (June 12, 2011): https://www.nytimes.com/2011/06/12/us/politics/12prayer.html.

Fessenden, Tracy. *Culture and Redemption: Religion, the Secular, and American Literature* (Princeton, NJ: Princeton University Press, 2006).

Finan, Christopher. *From the Palmer Raids to the Patriot Act: A History of the Fight for Free Speech in America* (Boston: Beacon Press, 2008).

Fisher, Marc, John Woodrow Cox, and Peter Hermann. "Pizzagate: From Rumor, to Hashtag, to Gunfire in D.C." *Washington Post* (December 6, 2016).

Floyd-Thomas, Juan M. and Anthony Pinn, eds. *Religion in the Age of Obama* (London: Bloomsbury Academic, 2018).

Ford, Zach. "One of the GOP's 'Young Guns' Wishes We Still Had Sodomy Laws." *ThinkProgress* (August 10, 2018): https://thinkprogress.org/north-carolina-candidate-congress-criminalize-homosexuality-05e8b5914d7b/.

Foucault, Michel. *"Society Must Be Defended": Lectures at the Collège de France, 1975–1976* (New York: Picador Books, 2003).

Fraser, Nancy. *The Old Is Dying and the New Cannot Be Born: From Progressive Neoliberalism to Trump and Beyond* (New York: Verso Books, 2019).

Freedom from Religion Foundation. "Pence Distorted 'Christian Persecution' Tale, FFRF Contends." *FFRF* (August 30, 2019): https://ffrf.org/news/news-releases/item/35502-pence-distorted-christian-persecution-tale-ffrf-contends.

Freedom House. "Democracy in Retreat." https://freedomhouse.org/report/freedom-world/freedom-world-2019/democracy-in-retreat.

Frend, William W. H. C. *Martyrdom and Persecution in the Early Church: A Study of Conflict from the Maccabees to Donatus* (Eugene, OR: Wipf and Stock, 2014).

Freud, Sigmund. *Beyond the Pleasure Principle* (New York: Norton, 1990).

Freud, Sigmund. *Civilization and Its Discontents* (New York: Norton, 2010).

Freud, Sigmund. *On Creativity and the Unconscious* (New York: Harper Perennial Modern Thought, 2009).

Friedersdorf, Conor. "Was There Really a Post-9/11 Backlash against Muslims?" *The Atlantic* (May 4, 2012): http://www.theatlantic.com/politics/archive/2012/05/was-there-really-a-post-9-11-backlash-against-muslims/256725/.

Fukuyama, Francis. *The End of History and the Last Man*, reissue ed. (New York: Free Press, 2006).

Gaddy, Welton. "The Car Wreck That Is Sarah Palin and the National Day of Prayer." *Religion Dispatches* (April 22, 2010): http://www.religiondispatches.org/archive/politics/2499/the_car_wreck_that_is_sarah_palin_and_the_national_day_of_prayer.

Gallagher, Danny. "Glenn Beck Might Be Losing More Than His Media Empire after Tense CNN Interview." *Dallas Observer* (July 11, 2018): https://www.dallasobserver.com/news/glenn-beck-his-media-company-tanking-becomes-a-trump-fan-10845643.

Galston, William. *Anti-pluralism: The Populist Threat to Liberal Democracy* (New Haven, CT: Yale University Press, 2020).

Galston, William. "Steve Bannon and the 'Global Tea Party.'" *Wall Street Journal* (February 28, 2017): https://www.wsj.com/articles/steve-bannon-and-the-global-tea-party-1488327459.

Gardner, Amy. "Gauging the Scope of the Tea Party Movement in America." *Washington Post* (October 23, 2010): https://www.washingtonpost.com/wp-dyn/content/article/2010/10/23/AR2010102304000.html.

Garrison, Becky. "What Beck's Marching For: Making Social Justice Unjust." *The Revealer* (August 28, 2010): http://therevealer.org/archives/4771.

Gazzaley, Adam and Larry D. Rosen. *The Distracted Mind: Ancient Brains in a High-Tech World* (Cambridge, MA: MIT Press, 2017).

Gerson, Michael. "The Last Temptation." *The Atlantic* (April 2018): https://www.theatlantic.com/magazine/archive/2018/04/the-last-temptation/554066/.

Gerson, Michael. "An Unholy War on the Tea Party." *Washington Post* (August 22, 2011): https://www.washingtonpost.com/opinions/a-holy-war-on-the-tea-party/2011/08/22/gIQAYRcOXJ_story.html?wprss=rss_opinions.

Gertz, Matt. "Drudge Links Potential Obama Executive Order on Guns to Hitler, Stalin." *Media Matters* (January 1, 2013): http://mediamatters.org/blog/2013/01/09/drudge-links-potential-obama-executive-order-on/192118.

Ghitis, Frida. "Why 2019 Was a Turning Point in the Global Battle for Democracy." *Washington Post* (December 27, 2019).

Gibson, James William. *Warrior Dreams: Violence and Manhood in Post-Vietnam America* (New York: Hill and Wang, 1994).

Giddens, Anthony. *The Consequences of Modernity* (Cambridge: Polity Press, 1990).

Giglio, Mike. "'Civil War Is Here, Right Now': The President's Supporters on the Militant Right Are Bracing for Conflict." *The Atlantic* (November 2020), pp. 62–73.

Gilgoff, Dan. "Glenn Beck: Hurricane Irene Is a Blessing." *CNN* (August 27, 2011): http://religion.blogs.cnn.com/2011/08/27/glenn-beck-hurricane-irene-is-a-blessing/.

Gilmore, Mikal. "Bob Dylan Unleashed." *Rolling Stone* (September 27, 2012): https://www.rollingstone.com/music/music-news/bob-dylan-unleashed-189723/.

Gitlin, Todd. *The Twilight of Common Dreams: Why America Is Wracked by Culture Wars* (New York: Henry Holt, 1996).

Gladnick, P. J. "WaPo Religion Blogger Attacks Sarah Palin's Religion." *Newsbusters* (September 11, 2008): http://www.newsbusters.org/blogs/p-j-gladnick/2008/09/11/wapo-religion-blogger-attacks-sarah-palins-religion.

Gleick, James. *The Information: A History, a Theory, a Flood* (New York: Vintage Books, 2011).

Goldberg, Robert Alan. *Enemies Within: The Culture of Conspiracy in Modern America* (New Haven, CT: Yale University Press, 2001).

Goldman, Shalom. "The Auspicious Timing of Glenn Beck's Zeal for Zion." *Religion Dispatches* (July 19, 2011): http://www.religiondispatches.org/archive/politics/4860/the_auspicious_timing_of_glenn_beck%E2%80%99s_zeal_for_zion_/.

Goldstein, Dana. "Two States, Eight Textbooks, Two American Stories." *New York Times* (January 12, 2020): https://www.nytimes.com/interactive/2020/01/12/us/texas-vs-california-history-textbooks.html?smid=nytcore-ios-share.

Good, Chris. "South Park Does Glenn Beck." *The Atlantic* (November 12, 2009): https://www.theatlantic.com/politics/archive/2009/11/south-park-does-glenn-beck/30090/.

Goodale, Gloria. "Glenn Beck Sticks Liberation Theology Label on Obama's Christianity." *Christian Science Monitor* (August 25, 2010): https://www.csmonitor.com/USA/Politics/The-Vote/2010/0825/Glenn-Beck-sticks-liberation-theology-label-on-Obama-s-Christianity.

Goodstein, Laurie. "Outraged by Glenn Beck's Salvo, Christians Fire Back." *New York Times* (March 12, 2010): https://www.nytimes.com/2010/03/12/us/12justice.html?searchResultPosition=9.

Goodwin, Megan P. *Abusing Religion: Literary Persecution, Sex Scandals, and American Minority Religions* (New Brunswick, NJ: Rutgers University Press, 2020).

Gorenberg, Gershom. *The End of Days: Fundamentalism and the Struggle for the Temple Mount* (New York: Oxford University Press, 2002).

Gottfried, Paul E. *Leo Strauss and the Conservative Movement in America*, reprint ed. (Cambridge: Cambridge University Press, 2013).

Gottfried, Paul E. "Not One, but Three Tea Parties." *American Conservative* (October 29, 2010): https://www.theamericanconservative.com/not-one-but-three-tea-parties/.

Gottschalk, Peter. *American Heretics: Catholics, Jews, Muslims, and the History of American Intolerance* (New York: St. Martin's Press, 2013).

Gottschalk, Peter. *Islamophobia and Anti-Muslim Sentiment: Picturing the Enemy*, 2nd ed. (Lanham, MD: Rowman & Littlefield, 2018).

Grant, Ezra. "Glenn Beck Attacks Donald Trump and the Birther Movement." *EZKool* (April 26, 2011): http://ezkool.com/2011/04/glenn-beck-attacks-donald-trump-and-the-birther-movement/.

Grant, Tobin. "Glenn Beck: 'Leave Your Church.'" *Christianity Today* (March 12, 2010): http://www.christianitytoday.com/ct/2010/marchweb-only/20\51.0.html.

Green, Donald P. and Ian Shapiro. *Pathologies of Rational Choice Theory: A Critique of Applications in Political Science* (New Haven, CT: Yale University Press, 1994).

Greenberg, David. "Dog Whistling Dixie." *Slate* (November 20, 2007): https://slate.com/news-and-politics/2007/11/what-reagan-meant-by-states-rights.html.

Griffith, Marie. "The New Evangelical Feminism of Bachmann and Palin." *Huffington Post* (July 6, 2011): https://www.huffpost.com/entry/evangelical-feminism_b_891579.

Grossman, Cathy Lynn. "Glenn Beck: Politicians Should Give Voice to God's Will." *USA Today* (August 28, 2010): http://content.usatoday.com/communities/Religion/post/2010/08/glenn-beck-god-obama-mormon/1.

Gunter, Booth. "Six Most Paranoid Fears for Obama's Second Term." *Salon* (November 4, 2012): https://www.salon.com/2012/11/04/six_most_paranoid_fears_for_obamas_second_term/.

Haberman, Maggie. "The GOP Debate: 8 Takeaways." Politico (September 8, 2011): https://www.politico.com/story/2011/09/the-gop-debate-8-takeaways-062963.

Haberman, Maggie. "Perry Back to 'Ponzi Scheme,' 'Monstrous Lie' on Social Security." Politico (August 28, 2011): https://www.politico.com/story/2011/08/perry-back-to-ponzi-scheme-monstrous-lie-on-social-security-062201.

Habermas, Jürgen. *Between Facts and Norms: Contributions to a Discourse Theory of Law and Democracy* (Cambridge, MA: MIT Press, 1996).

Habermas, Jürgen. *The Structural Transformation of the Public Sphere: An Inquiry into a Category of Bourgeois Society* (Cambridge, MA: MIT Press, 1991).

Hacker, Jacob S. *The Great Risk Shift: The New Economic Insecurity and the Decline of the American Dream*, 2nd ed. (New York: Oxford University Press, 2019).

Hafner, Katie and Matthew Lyon. *Where Wizards Stay Up Late: The Origins of the Internet* (New York: Simon & Schuster, 1998).

Hagey, Keach. "Glenn Beck Signs Off from Fox." *Politico* (June 30, 2011): www.politico.com/news/stories/0611/58175.html.

Hajnal, Zoltan, Nazita Lajevardi, and Lindsay Nielson. "Voter Identification Laws and the Suppression of Minority Votes." *Journal of Politics* 79:2 (April 2017), pp. 363–379.

Hale, Grace Elizabeth. *A Nation of Outsiders: How the White Middle Class Fell in Love with Rebellion in Postwar America* (New York: Oxford University Press, 2014).

Hall, David. *Worlds of Wonder, Days of Judgment: Popular Religious Belief in Early New England* (New York: Knopf, 1989).

Halperin, Mark and John Heilemann. *Double Down: Game Change 2012* (New York: Penguin Press, 2013).

Halperin, Terri Diane. *The Alien and Sedition Acts of 1798: Testing the Constitution* (Baltimore: Johns Hopkins University Press, 2016).

Ham, Mary Katharine. "Grand Old Tea Party: The Insurgents Meet the Insiders." *Weekly Standard* (March 1, 2010): https://www.washingtonexaminer.com/weekly-standard/grand-old-tea-party.

Hamm, Mark and Ramon Spajj. "Lone Wolf Terrorism in America: Using Knowledge of Radicalization Pathways to Forge Prevention Strategies." *National Institute of Justice Publications* (February 2015): https://www.ncjrs.gov/pdffiles1/nij/grants/248691.pdf.

Hannerz, Ulf. *Transnational Connections: Culture, People, Places* (New York: Routledge, 1996).

Hannerz, Ulf. "The World in Creolisation." *Africa* 57:4 (1987), pp. 546–559.

Harris, Matthew L. ed. *Thunder from the Right: Ezra Taft Benson in Mormonism and Politics* (Urbana: University of Illinois Press, 2019).

Harris, Michael. *The End of Absence: Reclaiming What We've Lost in a World of Constant Connection* (New York: Current Books, 2014).
Hartman, Andrew. *A War for the Soul of America: A History of the Culture Wars* (Chicago: University of Chicago Press, 2016).
Hartman, Margaret. "Bill O'Reilly Laments Left's Desire to Take Power from 'White Establishment.'" *New York Magazine* (December 21, 2016): https://nymag.com/intell igencer/2016/12/oreilly-white-establishment.html.
Harvey, David. *A Brief History of Neoliberalism* (New York: Oxford University Press, 2005).
Harvey, Paul. "American Idiot and Glenn Beck." *US Religion* (March 29, 2009): http://usr eligion.blogspot.com/2009/03/american-idiot-and-glen-beck.html.
Hatch, Nathan O. *The Democratization of American Christianity* (New Haven, CT: Yale University Press, 1989).
Havel, Václav. *Living in Truth: 22 Essays Published on the Occasion of the Award of the Erasmus Prize to Václav Havel* (London: Faber & Faber, 1990).
Hawley, George. *Making Sense of the Alt-Right* (New York: Columbia University Press, 2017).
Hawthorne, Nathaniel. *Tales and Sketches* (New York: Library of America, 1996).
Hedegaard, Erik. "Glenn Beck's Regrets." *Rolling Stone* (November 3, 2016), pp. 44–47, 56–57.
Hedges, Christopher. *American Fascists: The Christian Right and the War on America* (New York: Free Press, 2007).
Hegel, G. W. F. *Phenomenology of Spirit* (New York: Oxford University Press, 1977).
Heidegger, Martin. *The Question Concerning Technology and Other Essays* (New York: Harper Perennial, 2013).
Hertzberg, Hendrik. "Beck's Last Tapes." *New Yorker* (April 6, 2011): https://www.newyor ker.com/news/hendrik-hertzberg/becks-last-tapes.
Heyrman, Christine Leigh. *American Apostles: When Evangelicals Entered the World of Islam* (New York: Hill and Wang, 2015).
The Hill. "Obama, Congress Have Been Gun Friendly." *Real Clear Politics* (August 27, 2010): https://www.realclearpolitics.com/2010/08/27/obama_congress_have_been_ gun_friendly_240507.html.
Hinton, Timothy. "'Sentiments of the Understanding, Perceptions of the Heart': Constitutional Sentimentalism and the Authority of Morals." Unpublished paper.
Hitchens, Christopher. *God Is Not Great: How Religion Poisons Everything* (New York: Twelve Publishing, 2007).
Hitt, Jack. "Lunar-Tics." *New York Times Magazine* (February 9, 2003): https://www.nyti mes.com/2003/02/09/magazine/lunar-tics.html.
Hochschild, Arlie Russell. *Strangers in Their Own Land: Anger and Mourning on the American Right* (New York: New Press, 2016).
Hoffer, Eric. *The True Believer: Thoughts on the Nature of Mass Movements* (New York: Harper Perennial, 2010).
Hogeland, William. "Real Americans." *Boston Review* (September/October 2010): http:// bostonreview.net/hogeland-real-americans.
Holland, Joshua. "Glenn Beck's Absurd Jerusalem Rally: Why Religious Conservatives Are Obsessed with Israel." *Alternet* (May 18, 2011). Archived at https://www.greanvi llepost.com/2011/05/25/glenn-becks-absurd-jerusalem-rally-why-religious-conser vatives-are-obsessed-with-israel/.

Holmes, David L. *The Faiths of the Founding Fathers* (New York: Oxford University Press, 2006).

Holmes, T. J. "Texas Textbook Fallout." *CNN Newsroom* (May 22, 2010): http://newsroom.blogs.cnn.com/2010/05/22/textbook-fallout/.

Holton, Woody. *Unruly Americans and the Origins of the Constitution* (New York: Hill & Wang, 2008).

Honig, Bonnie. *Democracy and the Foreigner* (Princeton, NJ: Princeton University Press, 2003).

Honig, Bonnie. *Public Things: Democracy in Disrepair* (New York: Fordham University Press, 2017).

Hoover, Stewart M. and Curtis D. Coats. *Does God Make the Man? Media, Religion, and the Crisis of Masculinity* (New York: New York University Press, 2015).

Hoover, Stewart M. and Lynn Schofield Clark, eds. *Practicing Religion in the Age of Media: Explorations in Media, Religion, and Culture* (New York: Columbia University Press, 2002).

Horwitz, Tony. *Confederates in the Attic: Dispatches from the Unfinished Civil War* (New York: Vintage Books, 1999).

Hughey, Matthew W. "Show Me Your Papers! Obama's Birth and the Whiteness of Belonging." *Qualitative Sociology* 35:(June 2012), pp. 163–181.

Hughey, Matthew W. and Gregory S. Parks. *The Wrongs of the Right: Language, Race, and the Republican Party in the Age of Obama* (New York: NYU Press, 2014).

Hunt, Mary E. "Sarah Palin and the Clarence Thomas Factor." *Religion Dispatches* (June 11, 2009): http://www.religiondispatches.org/archive/politics/480/sarah_palin_and_the_clarence_thomas_factor.

Hunter, James Davison. *Culture Wars: The Struggle to Define America* (New York: Basic Books, 1992).

Hurd, Elizabeth Shakman. *Beyond Religious Freedom: The New Global Politics of Religion* (New York: Oxford University Press, 2015).

Ingersoll, Julie. "Beck's 'Dream'—Our Nightmare." *Religion Dispatches* (August 25, 2010): http://www.religiondispatches.org/archive/politics/3199/beck%E2%80%99s_%E2%80%9Cdream%E2%80%9D%E2%80%94our_nightmare.

Ingersoll, Julie. "Beck's Historian Bringing Seminar to Congressional Tea Partiers." *Religion Dispatches* (February 2, 2011): http://www.religiondispatches.org/dispatches/julieingersoll/4165/beck%E2%80%99s_historian_bringing_seminar_to_congressional_tea_partiers_.

Ingersoll, Julie. "Candidate Sharron Angle Accuses Opponent of Idolatry." *Religion Dispatches* (August 5, 2010): http://www.religiondispatches.org/dispatches/julieingersoll/3098/candidate_sharron_angle_accuses_opponent_of_idolatry.

Ingersoll, Julie. "Glenn Beck Has a Plan." *Religion Dispatches* (August 10, 2010): http://www.religiondispatches.org/dispatches/julieingersoll/3115/glenn_beck_has_a_plan.

Ingersoll, Julie. "Tea Partiers Say Slavery Not Race-Related." *Religion Dispatches* (July 15, 2010): http://www.religiondispatches.org/archive/politics/2832/tea_partiers_say_slavery_not_race-related.

Ingersoll, Julie. "Tea Party Bullies on Homosexuality: 'No Punishment Too Severe.'" *Religion Dispatches* (October 8, 2010): https://religiondispatches.org/tea-party-bullies-on-homosexuality-no-punishment-too-severe/.

Ingersoll, Julie and Sarah Posner. "Gun Ownership: 'An Obligation to God.'" *Religion Dispatches* (July 13, 2010): http://www.religiondispatches.org/archive/politics/2910/gun_ownership%3A_%E2%80%98an_obligation_to_god%E2%80%99.
Innis, Harold A. *Empire and Communications* (Lanham, MD: Rowman & Littlefield, 1994).
Irons, Peter. *God on Trial: Dispatches from America's Religious Battlefields* (New York: Viking Books, 2007).
"Is This True? Virginia Republicans Call for Armed Revolution If Obama Wins in November." *Daily Kos* (August 20, 2012): http://www.dailykos.com/story/2012/08/20/1122295/-Is-this-true-Virginia-Republicans-Call-for-Armed-Revolution-if-Obama-Wins-in-November.
Isaac, Jeffrey C. "Does Liberalism Still Have a Future?" *Los Angeles Review of Books* (November 22, 2017): https://lareviewofbooks.org/article/does-liberalism-still-have-a-future/.
Issenberg, Sasha. "Barnstorming America." *Smithsonian Magazine* (September 2018), pp. 40–51.
"It's Time to Hold Federal Judges Accountable." *Phyllis Schlafly Report*, Eagle Forum (March 1997): https://eagleforum.org/psr/1997/mar97/psrmar97.html.
Jacoby, Susan. *The Age of Unreason* (New York: Vintage Books, 2009).
Jakobsen, Janet and Ann Pellegrini, eds. *Secularisms* (Durham, NC: Duke University Press, 2008).
Jardina, Ashley. *White Identity Politics* (Cambridge: Cambridge University Press, 2019).
Jay, John, Alexander Hamilton, and James Madison, *The Federalist Papers* (Mineola, NY: Dover Books, 2014).
Jeffords, Susan. *The Remasculinization of America: Gender and the Vietnam War* (Bloomington: Indiana University Press, 1989).
Jeltsen, Melissa. "Tennessee Jumps on the Anti-Ssharia Bandwagon." *Talking Points Memo* (February 24, 2011): http://tpmmuckraker.talkingpointsmemo.com/2011/02/tennessee_state_sen_joins_effort_to_criminalize_sh.php.
Jenkins, Jack. "Sorry, Newt Gingrich: That's Not How Shariah Works." *Think Progress* (July 15, 2016): https://thinkprogress.org/sorry-newt-gingrich-thats-not-how-shariah-works-88b23d0cf353/.
Jenkins, Philip. *Decade of Nightmares: The End of the Sixties and the Making of the Eighties* (New York: Oxford University Press, 2006).
Jensen, Carol. "Sarah Palin's Religious Beliefs Too Extreme for America." *ExChristian* (September 28, 2008): http://news.exchristian.net/2008/09/sarah-palins-religious-beliefs-too.html.
Johnson, Dale L. *Social Inequality, Economic Decline, and Plutocracy: An American Crisis* (New York: Palgrave Macmillan, 2017).
Johnson, Jessica. *Biblical Porn: Affect, Labor, and Pastor Mark Driscoll's Evangelical Empire* (Durham, NC: Duke University Press, 2018).
Johnson, Kirk and Kim Severson. "In Palin's Life and Politics, Goal to Follow God's Will." *New York Times* (September 6, 2008): https://www.nytimes.com/2008/09/06/us/politics/06church.html?searchResultPosition=2.
Johnson, Sylvester A. *African-American Religions, 1500–2000: Colonialism, Democracy, and Freedom* (Cambridge: Cambridge University Press, 2015).
Johnson, Sylvester A. and Steven Weitzman, eds. *The FBI and Religion: Faith and National Security before and after 9/11* (Berkeley: University of California Press, 2017).

Jones, Caroline A., David Mather, and Rebecca Uchill, eds., *Experience: Culture, Cognition, and Common Sense* (Cambridge, MA: MIT Press, 2016).
Jones, Robert P. *The End of White Christian America* (New York: Simon & Schuster, 2017).
Jost, John T., Jack Glaser, Arie W. Kruglanski, and Frank J. Sulloway. "Political Conservatism as Motivated Social Cognition." *Psychological Bulletin* 29:3 (2003), pp. 339–375.
Joyce, Kathryn. "Can Mormon Glenn Beck Unite the Christian Right?" *Religion Dispatches* (September 21, 2010): http://www.religiondispatches.org/archive/politics/3334/can_mormon_glenn_beck_unite_the_christian_right.
Kabaservice, Geoffrey. "The Great Performance of Our Failing President." *New York Times* (June 9, 2017): https://www.nytimes.com/2017/06/09/opinion/great-performance-of-donald-trump-our-failing-president.html.
Kabaservice, Geoffrey. *Rule and Ruin: The Downfall of Moderation and the Destruction of the Republican Party, from Eisenhower to the Tea Party* (New York: Oxford University Press, 2012).
Kagan, Robert. *Dangerous Nation: America's Foreign Policy from Its Earliest Days to the Dawn of the Twentieth Century* (New York: Vintage Books, 2006).
Kahn, Paul W. "The Jurisprudence of Religion in a Secular Age: From Ornamentalism to Hobby Lobby." *Law & Ethics of Human Rights* 10:1 (May 2016), pp. 1–30.
Kant, Immanuel. *Perpetual Peace and Other Essays* (Indianapolis, IN: Hackett Classics, 1983).
Kazin, Michael. *American Dreamers: How the Left Changed a Nation* (New York: Vintage Books, 2011).
Kedrosky, Paul. "The Large Information Collider, BDTs, and Gravity Holidays on Tuesdays." In John Brockman, ed., *Is the Internet Changing the Way You Think? The Net's Impact on Our Minds and Future* (San Francisco: Harper Perennial, 2010), pp. 45–47.
Keller, Bill. "Asking Candidates Tougher Questions about Faith." *New York Times Magazine* (August 28, 2011): http://www.nytimes.com/2011/08/28/magazine/asking-candidates-tougher-questions-about-faith.html?_r=1.
Kendi, Ibram X. *Stamped from the Beginning: The Definitive History of Racist Ideas in America* (New York: Nation Books, 2016).
Kennedy, Randall. *The Persistence of the Color Line: Racial Politics and the Obama Presidency* (New York: Vintage Books, 2011).
Keyes, Scott. "Top 10 Things Rick Perry Doesn't Want You to Know about Him." *ThinkProgress* (June 10, 2011): http://thinkprogress.org/politics/2011/06/10/241830/top-10-thing-texas-gov-rick-perry/.
Kidd, Thomas. *American Christians and Islam: Evangelical Culture and Muslims from the Colonial Period to the Age of Terrorism* (Princeton, NJ: Princeton University Press, 2013).
Kidd, Thomas. "The Tea Party, Fundamentalism, and the Founding." *Patheos* (December 1, 2010): http://www.patheos.com/Resources/Additional-Resources/Tea-Party-Fundamentalism-and-the-Founding.html.
Kim, Joon K., Ernesto Sagás, and Karina Cespedes. "Genderacing Immigrant Subjects: 'Anchor Babies' and the Politics of Birthright Citizenship." *Social Identities: Journal for the Study of Race, Nation and Culture* 24:3 (2018), pp. 312–326.
Kimmel, Michael. *Angry White Men: American Masculinity at the End of an Era* (New York: Bold Type Books, 2017).

Kimmel, Michael. *Guyland: The Perilous World Where Boys Become Men* (New York: HarperCollins, 2008).
Kittler, Friedrich. *Gramophone, Film, Typewriter* (Stanford, CA: Stanford University Press, 1999).
Kitts, Margo, ed. *Martyrdom, Self-Sacrifice, and Self-Immolation: Religious Perspectives on Suicide* (New York: Oxford University Press, 2018).
Knickerbocker, Brad. "Glenn Beck Goes Home to Face—What Else?—Controversy." *Christian Science Monitor* (September 26, 2009): https://www.csmonitor.com/USA/Politics/2009/0926/glenn-beck-goes-home-to-face-what-else-controversy.
Kornacki, Steve. "Rick Perry's Descent into Birtherism." *Salon* (October 24, 2011): http://www.salon.com/2011/10/24/now_rick_perry_is_flirting_with_birtherism/.
Kotz, Pete. "Armed Conspiracy Group Will Defend Republicans at Minneapolis Trump Rally." *Minneapolis City Pages* (October 9, 2019): http://www.citypages.com/news/armed-conspiracy-group-will-defend-republicans-at-minneapolis-trump-rally/562562061.
Kreiss, Daniel, Joshua O. Barker, and Shannon Zenner. "Trump Gave Them Hope: Studying the Strangers in Their Own Land." *Political Communication* 34:3 (2017), pp. 470–478.
"Ku Klux Klan Plans Border Patrol to Help Fight Illegal Alien Problem." *New York Times* (October 18, 1977): https://www.nytimes.com/1977/10/18/archives/ku-klux-klan-plans-border-patrol-to-help-fight-illegal-alien.html.
Lambert, Frank. *The Founding Fathers and the Place of Religion in America* (Princeton, NJ: Princeton University Press, 2003).
Landler, Mark and Katie Rogers. "Trump Tells Grand Rapids Rally: 'The Russian Hoax Is Finally Dead.'" *New York Times* (March 28, 2019).
Lassiter, Matthew D. *The Silent Majority: Suburban Politics in the Sunbelt South* (Princeton, NJ: Princeton University Press, 2007).
Latour, Bruno. *Reassembling the Social: An Introduction to Actor-Network-Theory* (New York: Oxford University Press, 2007).
Lears, Jackson. *Rebirth of a Nation: The Making of Modern America, 1877–1920* (New York: HarperCollins, 2009).
Lears, Jackson. *No Place of Grace: Antimodernism and the Transformation of American Culture, 1880–1920* (Chicago: University of Chicago Press, 1994).
Lebo, Lauri. "Texas Textbook Massacre." *Religion Dispatches* (May 12, 2010): https://religiondispatches.org/texas-textbook-massacre/.
LeBon, Gustave. *The Crowd: A Study of the Popular Mind*, reprint ed. (Mineola, NY: Dover Books, 2002).
Lee, Erika. *America for Americans: A History of Xenophobia in the United States* (New York: Basic Books, 2019).
Leibovich, Mark. "Being Glenn Beck." *New York Times Magazine* (September 29, 2010): https://www.nytimes.com/2010/10/03/magazine/03beck-t.html.
LePore, Jill. *The Whites of Their Eyes: The Tea Party's Revolution and the Battle over American History* (Princeton, NJ: Princeton University Press, 2010).
Lessig, Lawrence. *They Don't Represent Us: Reclaiming Our Democracy* (New York: Dey Street Books, 2019).
Levitsky, Steven and Daniel Ziblatt. *How Democracies Die* (New York: Crown Books, 2018).
Lewis, Andrew R. *The Rights Turn in Conservative Christian Politics: How Abortion Transformed the Culture Wars* (Cambridge: Cambridge University Press, 2018).

Lienesch, Michael. *In the Beginning: Fundamentalism, the Scopes Trial, and the Making of the Antievolution Movement* (Chapel Hill: University of North Carolina Press, 2007).

Lienesch, Michael. *Redeeming America: Power, Piety, and Politics in the New Christian Right* (Chapel Hill: University of North Carolina Press, 1993).

Lilla, Mark. *The Once and Future Liberal: After Identity Politics* (New York: Harper Books, 2017).

Lilla, Mark. *The Shipwrecked Mind: On Political Reaction* (New York: New York Review of Books, 2016).

Lilla, Mark. "The Tea Party Jacobins." *New York Review of Books* (May 27, 2010): https://www.nybooks.com/articles/2010/05/27/tea-party-jacobins/.

Link, Taylor. "White Evangelicals Say Christians Face More Persecution Than Muslims: Poll." *Salon* (March 10, 2017): http://www.salon.com/2017/03/10/white-evangelicals-say-christians-face-more-persecution-than-muslims-poll/.

Lippmann, Walter. *Public Opinion* (New York: Harcourt, Brace and Company, 1922).

Lipsitz, George. *Time Passages: Collective Memory and American Popular Culture* (Minneapolis: University of Minnesota Press, 1990).

Lloyd, Mark. "Why the Left Will Never Understand the Tea Party." *Tea Party Review* 1:1 (March 2011), p. 7.

Locke, John. *Second Treatise of Government* (Indianapolis, IN: Hackett Classics, 1980).

Lofton, Kathryn. *Consuming Religion* (Chicago: University of Chicago Press, 2017).

Lofton, Kathryn. *Oprah: The Gospel of an Icon* (Berkeley: University of California Press, 2011).

Lopez, German. "Study: President Obama's Election Scared Americans into Buying More Guns." *Vox* (January 21, 2016): https://www.vox.com/2016/1/21/10801664/obama-gun-sales.

Love, Erik. *Islamophobia and Racism in America* (New York: New York University Press, 2017).

Lowry, Rich. "The Victim President." *Politico* (December 18, 2019): https://www.politico.com/news/magazine/2019/12/18/trump-impeachment-victim-087534.

Lukacs, John. *Democracy and Populism: Fear and Hatred* (New Haven, CT: Yale University Press, 2005).

Lyons, Paul. *New Left, New Right, and the Legacy of the Sixties* (Philadelphia: Temple University Press, 1996).

MacNicol, Glynnis. "Obama on Glenn Beck Rally: Folks Exercising Their Rights Exactly as They Should." *Mediaite* (August 30, 2010): https://www.mediaite.com/online/obama-on-glenn-becks-rally-folks-exercising-their-rights-exactly-as-they-should/.

Madison, James. "Federalist #10": https://www.congress.gov/resources/display/content/The+Federalist+Papers#TheFederalistPapers-10.

Mahanta, Siddhartha. "GOP's Favorite Fake Historian Spins *The New York Times*." *Mother Jones* (May 2011): https://www.motherjones.com/politics/2011/05/david-barton-new-york-times-huckabee/.

Maher, Bill. "Bill Maher Talks Glenn Beck's 'Diabetic Mall-Walkers,' Summer of Racism." *Huffington Post* (September 14, 2010): http://www.huffingtonpost.com/2010/09/14/bill_maher_glenn_beck_n_716897.html?view=print.

Mahmood, Saba. *Religious Difference in a Secular Age: A Minority Report* (Princeton, NJ: Princeton University Press, 2015).

Malin, Brenton J. *Feeling Mediated: A History of Media Technology and Emotion in America* (New York: New York University Press, 2014).

Mamdani, Mahmood. *When Victims Become Killers: Colonialism, Nativism, and the Genocide in Rwanda* (Princeton, NJ: Princeton University Press, 2002).

Mandell, Nina. "Glenn Beck Apologizes for Comparing Reform Judaism to Radical Islam." *New York Daily News* (February 24, 2011): https://www.nydailynews.com/news/national/glenn-beck-apologizes-comparing-reform-judaism-radical-islam-bad-analogy-article-1.134374.

Mandell, Nina. "Pat Robertson Slams 'Saturday Night Live' over Jesus-Tim Tebow Skit for 'Anti-Christian Bigotry.'" *New York Daily News* (December 20, 2011): https://www.nydailynews.com/entertainment/tv-movies/pat-robertson-slams-saturday-night-live-jesus-tim-tebow-skit-article-1.994366.

Mantyla, Kyle. "The Birth of the Birthers." *Right Wing Watch* (June 19, 2009): http://www.rightwingwatch.org/content/birth-birthers.

Mantyla, Kyle. "Glenn Beck's Latest Conspiracy Theory: Women's March Was George Soros, Radical Islam 'Astroturf.'" *Salon* (January 24, 2017): http://www.salon.com/2017/01/24/glenn-becks-latest-conspiracy-theory-womens-march-was-george-soros-radical-islam-astroturf_partner/.

Marcin, Tim. "Trump Voters Say Men Face More Discrimination Than Women, African-Americans or LGBT People, Poll Says." *Newsweek* (October 17, 2018): https://www.newsweek.com/men-face-more-discrimination-women-african-americans-lgbt-trump-voters-poll-1175395?utm_source=Twitter&utm_medium=Social&utm_campaign=NewsweekTwitter.

Marcus, Daniel. *Happy Days and Wonder Years: The Fifties and the Sixties in Contemporary Cultural Politics* (New Brunswick, NJ: Rutgers University Press, 2004).

Marr, Timothy. *The Cultural Roots of American Islamicism* (Cambridge: Cambridge University Press, 2006).

Martin, James. "Glenn Beck to Jesus: Drop Dead." *Huffington Post* (May 8, 2010): http://www.huffingtonpost.com/rev-james-martin-sj/glenn-beck-to-catholics-l_b_490669.html.

Marty, Martin. "David Barton's Christian America." *Christian Post* (May 10, 2011): https://divinity.uchicago.edu/sightings/articles/david-bartons-christian-america-martin-e-marty.

Marzouki, Nadia. *Islam: An American Religion* (New York: Columbia University Press, 2017).

Marzouki, Nadia, Duncan McDonnell, and Olivier Roy, eds., *Saving the People: How Populists Hijack Religion* (New York: Oxford University Press, 2016).

Massumi, Brian. *Parables for the Virtual: Movement, Affect, Sensation* (Durham, NC: Duke University Press, 2002).

Masuzawa, Tomoko. *The Invention of World Religions: Or, How European Universalism Was Preserved in the Language of Pluralism* (Chicago: University of Chicago Press, 2006).

Mathias, Christian. "A Fascist Trump Rally in Greenville." *Huffington Post* (July 18, 2019): https://www.huffpost.com/entry/fascist-trump-rally-greenville-ilhan-omar-send-her-back_n_5d30529fe4b0419fd328b270.

Mattson, Kevin. *Rebels All! A Short History of the Conservative Mind in Postwar America* (New Brunswick, NJ: Rutgers University Press, 2008).

May, Elaine Tyler. *Fortress America: How We Embraced Fear and Abandoned Democracy* (New York: Basic Books, 2017).

Mazza, Ed. "'I'd Rather Die': Glenn Beck Urges Older Americans to Work Despite Coronavirus." *Huffington Post* (March 24, 2020): https://www.huffpost.com/entry/glenn-beck-coronavirus_n_5e7ab2d6c5b620022ab30851.

Mazza, Ed. "Laura Ingraham Targets Even Legal Immigrants in Off-the-Rails Rant." *Huffington Post* (August 9, 2018): https://www.huffingtonpost.com/entry/laura-ingraham-immigration-rant_us_5b6bbfd7e4b0bdd0620646fa.

McCloud, Sean. *American Possessions: Fighting Demons in the Contemporary United States* (New York: Oxford University Press, 2015).

McClure, Kirstie M. "Difference, Diversity, and the Limits of Toleration." *Political Theory* (August 1990), pp. 361–391.

McGarvie, Mark Douglas. *Law and Religion in American History: Public Values and Private Conscience* (Cambridge: Cambridge University Press, 2016).

McGirr, Lisa. *Suburban Warriors: The Origins of the New American Right*, updated ed. (Princeton, NJ: Princeton University Press, 2015).

McLuhan, Marshall. *Understanding Media: The Extensions of Man* (Cambridge, MA: MIT Press, 1994).

McVicar, Michael. *Christian Reconstruction: R.J. Rushdoony and American Religious Conservatism* (Chapel Hill: University of North Carolina Press, 2015).

Medved, Michael. "*New York Times* Editor Bill Keller's Religious Test for Presidential Candidates." *Daily Beast* (August 30, 2011): http://www.thedailybeast.com/articles/2011/08/30/new-york-times-editor-bill-keller-s-religious-test-for-presidential-candidates.html.

Melville, Herman. *Billy Budd & Other Stories* (New York: Penguin Books, 1986).

Michaels, Walter Benn. *The Problem with Diversity: How We Learned to Love Identity and Ignore Inequality* (New York: Metropolitan Books, 2006).

Middendorf, J. William, II. *A Glorious Disaster: Barry Goldwater's Presidential Campaign and the Origins of the Conservative Movement* (New York: Basic Books, 2006).

Milbank, Dana. "Rick Perry Is No Libertarian." *Washington Post* (August 30, 2011): http://www.washingtonpost.com/opinions/rick-perry-is-no-libertarian/2011/08/30/gIQA6IsbqJ_story.html.

Milbank, Dana. *Tears of a Clown: Glenn Beck and the Tea Bagging of America* (New York: Doubleday, 2010).

Miller, James. *Can Democracy Work? A Short History of a Radical Idea, from Ancient Athens to Our World* (New York: Farrar, Straus and Giroux, 2018).

Miller, James. *Examined Lives: From Socrates to Nietzsche* (New York: Picador Books, 2012).

Miller, Laura. "The Paranoid Style of American Punditry." *Salon* (September 15, 2010): https://www.salon.com/2010/09/15/hofstadter/.

Miller-Idriss, Cynthia. *Hate in the Homeland: The New Global Far Right* (Princeton, NJ: Princeton University Press, 2020).

Mills, C. Wright. *The Power Elite*, new ed. (New York: Oxford University Press, 2000).

Mishra, Stuti. "Sarah Palin Hits Campaign Trail in Georgia, Denying Trump Lost alongside Q-Anon-Supporting Republican." *The Independent* (December 15, 2020): https://www.independent.co.uk/news/world/americas/us-election-2020/sarah-palin-trump-qanon-georgia-election-b1774085.html.

Modern, John. *Secularism in Antebellum America* (Chicago: University of Chicago Press, 2011).

Moffitt, Benjamin. *The Global Rise of Populism: Performance, Political Style, and Representation* (Stanford, CA: Stanford University Press, 2016).

Molloy, D. J. *The World of the John Birch Society: Conspiracy, Conservatism, and the Cold War* (Nashville, TN: Vanderbilt University Press, 2014).

Montgomery, Peter. "Glenn Beck's Salvation Army." *Religion Dispatches* (September 9, 2010): http://www.religiondispatches.org/archive/atheologies/3266/glenn_beck%E2%80%99s_salvation_army.

Montopoli, Brian. "ACORN Sting Lands Housing Group in Conservative Crosshairs." *CBS News* (September 16, 2009): http://www.cbsnews.com/8301-503544_162-5315 657-503544.html.

Moon, Richard. *Putting Faith in Hate: When Religion Is the Source or Target of Hate Speech* (Cambridge: Cambridge University Press, 2018).

Mooney, Chris. "The Reality Gap." *American Prospect* (July–August 2011), pp. 18–25.

Moore, R. Laurence. *Selling God: American Religion in the Marketplace of Culture* (New York: Oxford University Press, 1994).

Moore, R. Laurence. *Religious Outsiders and the Making of Americans* (New York: Oxford University Press, 1986).

Moore, Russell. "God, the Gospel, and Glenn Beck." www.russellmoore.com/2010/08/29/god-the-gospel-and-glenn-beck/.

Moran, Lee. "Glenn Beck Slammed for Comparing Trump Social Media Ban to Holocaust." *Huffington Post* (January 13, 2021): https://www.huffpost.com/entry/glenn-beck-tucker-carlson-fox-news-big-tech_n_5ffeb5e9c5b691806c4dbb57.

Morris, Meaghan. *Too Soon Too Late: History in Popular Culture* (Bloomington: Indiana University Press, 1998).

Moser, Bob. "The Crusaders: Christian Evangelicals Are Plotting to Remake America in Their Own Image." *Rolling Stone* (April 7, 2005): https://newslog.cyberjournal.org/bob-moser-the-dominionists-far-right-threat-to-u-s/.

Moser, Bob. "God Help Us." *American Prospect* (December 2011): https://prospect.org/labor/god-help-us/.

Moss, Candida. *The Myth of Persecution: How Early Christians Invented a Story of Martyrdom* (New York: Harper One, 2013).

Mouffe, Chantal. *The Democratic Paradox* (New York: Verso Books, 2009).

Moulitsas, Markos. *American Taliban: How War, Sex, Sin, and Power Bind Jihadists and the Radical Right* (Sausalito, CA: Polipoint Press, 2010).

Moyn, Samuel. *Never Enough: Human Rights in an Unequal World* (Cambridge, MA: Belknap Press of Harvard University Press, 2018).

Mueller, Jan-Werner. *What Is Populism?* (Philadelphia: University of Pennsylvania Press, 2016).

Mulholland, Thomas. "Cortical Activation during Steady and Changing Visual Stimulation." *Electroencephalography and Clinical Neurophysiology* 17:4 (November 1964), pp. 371–375.

Mullen, Lincoln A. *The Chance of Salvation: A History of Conversion in America* (Cambridge, MA: Harvard University Press, 2017).

Mullen, Mike. "Bachmann Warns Obama to Fear the Tea Party, Who Are Not All Toothless Hillbillies." *City Pages* (July 6, 2011): http://www.citypages.com/news/bachmann-warns-obama-to-fear-the-tea-party-who-are-not-all-toothless-hillbillies-6548764.

Munoz, Eduardo. "Couples Lug AR-15 Assault Rifles to Pennsylvania Church Blessing." Reuters (February 28, 2018): https://www.reuters.com/article/us-usa-guns-church/couples-lug-ar-15-assault-rifles-to-pennsylvania-church-blessing-idUSKCN1GC2V3?feedType=RSS&feedName=domesticNews&utm_medium=Social&utm_source=Twitter.

Murphy, Andrew. "Beck Plays Prophet—Politics Pervade." https://blog.oup.com/2010/09/beck-plays-prophet/.

Murphy, Tim. "Meet the White Supremacist Leading the GOP's Anti-shariah Crusade." *Mother Jones* (March 1, 2011): https://www.motherjones.com/politics/2011/03/david-yerushalmi-sharia-ban-tennessee/.

Muslim Diaspora Initiative. "Anti-Muslim Activities in the United States: Violence, Threats, and Discrimination at the Local Level." *New America*: https://www.newamerica.org/in-depth/anti-muslim-activity/.

Mutz, Diana C. "Status Threat, Not Economic Hardship Explains the 2016 Presidential Vote." *Proceedings of the National Academy of Sciences of the United States of America* (April 18, 2018): http://www.pnas.org/content/early/2018/04/18/1718155115.

Nakamura, David. "White House to Rick Perry: We Won't Respond to 'Struggling... Campaigns.'" *Washington Post* (December 9, 2011): http://www.washingtonpost.com/blogs/44/post/white-house-to-rick-perry-we-wont-respond-to-struggling--campaigns/2011/12/09/gIQATQvfiO_blog.html.

Nelson, Leah. "Farah: If Obama Re-elected 'We Will Be Hunted Down Like Dogs.'" *Southern Poverty Law Center Hatewatch* (July 9, 2012): http://www.splcenter.org/blog/2012/07/09/farah-if-obama-re-elected-we-will-be-hunted-down-like-dogs/.

"New McCarthy Era?" *The Revealer* (June 25, 2010): http://therevealer.org/archives/4326.

"The New Republic: Paladino and the Politics of Anger." *National Public Radio* (October 14, 2010): https://www.npr.org/templates/story/story.php?storyId=130559117.

Newman, Andrew. "Advice to Fake Pimp Was No Crime, Prosecutor Says." *New York Times* (March 1, 2010): https://www.nytimes.com/2010/03/02/nyregion/02acorn.html.

Newman, Todd P., Erik C. Nisbet, and Matthew C. Nisbet. "Climate Change, Cultural Cognition, and Media Effects: Worldviews Drive News Selectivity, Biased Processing, and Polarized Attitudes." *Public Understanding of Science* 27:8 (November 2018), pp. 985–1002.

Nietzsche, Friedrich. *On the Genealogy of Morals* (New York: Oxford University Press, 2009).

Nietzsche, Friedrich. *Beyond Good and Evil* (New York: Cosimo Classics, 2006).

Nietzsche, Friedrich. *Human, All Too Human: A Book for Free Spirits* (Cambridge: Cambridge University Press, 1996).

Niles, Christine L. "Epistemological Nonsense—the Secular/Religious Distinction." *Notre Dame Journal of Law, Ethics & Public Policy* 17:2 (2012), pp. 561–592.

Noble, Alan. "The Evangelical Persecution Complex." *The Atlantic* (August 14, 2014): https://www.theatlantic.com/national/archive/2014/08/the-evangelical-persecution-complex/375506/.

Norton, Anne. *Republic of Signs: Liberal Theory and American Popular Culture* (Chicago: University of Chicago Press, 1993).

Numbers, Ronald L. *The Creationists: From Scientific Creationism to Intelligent Design*, expanded ed. (Cambridge, MA: Harvard University Press, 2006).

Nutter, Warren. *Political Economy and Freedom: A Collection of Essays* (Carmel, IN: Liberty Fund Books, 1983).

Nyirkos, Tamás. *The Tyranny of the Majority: History, Concepts, Challenges* (New York: Routledge, 2018).
O'Brien, Luke. "The Making of an American Nazi." *The Atlantic* (December 2017), pp. 54–67.
O'Hara, John. *A New American Tea Party: The Counterrevolution against Bailouts, Handouts, Reckless Spending, and More Taxes* (Hoboken, NJ: John Wiley & Sons, 2010).
Ohlheiser, Abby. "Perry's Cross-Section of the Body of Christ." *The Revealer* (August 18, 2011): https://therevealer.org/perrys-cross-section-of-the-body-of-christ/.
Orlie, Melissa A. *Living Ethically, Acting Politically* (Ithaca, NY: Cornell University Press, 1997).
Ortega y Gasset, José. *The Revolt of the Masses* (New York: Norton, 1994).
Orwell, George. "Politics and the English Language." In Sonia Orwell and Ian Angos, eds., *The Collected Essays, Journalism and Letters of George Orwell*, vol. 4 (New York: Harcourt, Brace, Jovanovich, 1968), pp. 127–140.
Oulette, Mary. "Megadeth Frontman Dave Mustaine Chalks Up Obama Re-election Comments as 'Stage Fodder.'" *Metalscene* (November 17, 2012): http://metalscenenews.com/megadeth-frontman-dave-mustaine-chalks-up-obama-re-election-comments-as-stage-fodder/.
Packer, George. *The Unwinding: An Inner History of the New America* (New York: Farrar, Straus and Giroux, 2013).
Pain, Rachel. "Everyday Terrorism: Connecting Domestic Violence and Global Terrorism." *Progress in Human Geography* 38:4 (August 2014), pp. 531–550.
Palin, Sarah. *America by Heart: Reflections on Family, Faith, and Flag* (New York: HarperCollins, 2010).
Parham, Robert. "Fringe Christian Politicians Feed 'Birther' Movement." *Ethics Daily* (February 21, 2011): http://www.ethicsdaily.com/fringe-christian-politicians-feed-birther-movement-cms-17484.
Parker, Christopher S. and Matt A. Barreto. *Change They Can't Believe In: The Tea Party and Reactionary Politics in America* (Princeton, NJ: Princeton University Press, 2014).
Parker, James. "Glenn Beck in Exile." *The Atlantic* (June 2012), pp. 40–41.
Parker, James. "Why We Still Miss Jon Stewart." *The Atlantic* (March 2016), pp. 34–36.
Parker, Kunal M. *Making Foreigners: Immigration and Citizenship Law in America, 1600–2000* (Cambridge: Cambridge University Press, 2015).
Pasha-Robinson, Lucy. "White Evangelical Christians Believe They Are More Discriminated Against Than Muslims, US Poll Finds." *The Independent* (March 21, 2017): https://www.independent.co.uk/news/world/americas/white-evangelical-christians-muslims-americans-us-discriminate-racism-islamophobia-faith-a7640051.html.
Paulson, Amanda. "Texas Textbook War: 'Slavery' or 'Atlantic Triangular Trade'?" *Christian Science Monitor* (May 19, 2010): https://www.csmonitor.com/USA/Education/2010/0519/Texas-textbook-war-Slavery-or-Atlantic-triangular-trade.
Pecora, Vincent P. *Secularization and Cultural Criticism: Religion, Nation, & Modernity* (Chicago: University of Chicago Press, 2006).
Pennock, Robert T., ed. *Intelligent Design Creationism and Its Critics: Philosophical, Theological, and Scientific Perspectives* (Cambridge, MA: MIT Press, 2001).
Perlberg, Steven. "Rick Santelli Started the Tea Party with a Rant Exactly 5 Years Ago Today—Here's How He Feels Now." *Business Insider* (February 19, 2014): https://www.businessinsider.com/rick-santelli-tea-party-rant-2014-2.

Perlstein, Rick. "Exclusive: Lee Atwater's Infamous 1981 Interview on the Southern Strategy." *The Nation* (November 13, 2012): https://www.thenation.com/article/exclusive-lee-atwaters-infamous-1981-interview-southern-strategy/.

Perlstein, Rick. *The Invisible Bridge: The Fall of Nixon and the Rise of Reagan* (New York: Simon & Schuster, 2014).

Perlstein, Rick. *Nixonland: The Rise of a President and the Fracturing of America* (New York: Simon & Schuster, 2008).

Perlstein, Rick. *Reaganland: America's Right Turn, 1976–1980* (New York: Simon & Schuster, 2020).

Perrett, Connor. "Trump Threatens to Investigate and Pull Federal Funding from Schools That Teach NYT's 1619 Project on the Consequences of Slavery." *Business Insider* (September 6, 2020): https://www.businessinsider.com/trump-pull-funding-california-schools-1619-project-2020-9.

Perry, Barbara. "'White Genocide': White Supremacists and the Politics of Reproduction." In Abby L. Ferber, ed., *Home-Grown Hate: Gender and Organized Racism* (New York: Routledge, 2004), pp. 75–96.

Peters, John Durham. *Courting the Abyss: Free Speech and the Liberal Tradition* (Chicago: University of Chicago Press, 2005).

Peters, John Durham. *Speaking into the Air: A History of the Idea of Communication* (Chicago: University of Chicago Press, 2001).

Pilkington, Ed. "NRA's LaPierre Accuses Obama of Trying to Steal Gun Owners' Weapons." *The Guardian* (January 23, 2013): https://www.theguardian.com/world/2013/jan/23/nra-wayne-lapierre-obama-stealing-weapons.

Pilkington, Ed. "This Person Loves Jesus." *The Guardian* (September 6, 2008): http://www.guardian.co.uk/world/2008/sep/06/uselections2008.sarahpalin.

Popper, Karl. *The Open Society and Its Enemies*, vol. 1: *The Spell of Plato* (Princeton, NJ: Princeton University Press, 2013).

Porterfield, Amanda. *Conceived in Doubt: Religion and Politics in the New American Nation* (Chicago: University of Chicago Press, 2012).

Posner, Sarah. "Blankets, Booties, and Jesus: Spiritual War on the Uterus in Rick Perry's Texas." *Religion Dispatches* (March 19, 2012): http://www.religiondispatches.org/archive/politics/5372/blankets%2C_booties%2C_and_jesus%3A_spiritual_war_on_the_uterus_in_rick_perry%E2%80%99s_texas/.

Posner, Sarah. "Children of God." *American Prospect* (February 19, 2010): http://prospect.org/article/children-god-0.

Posner, Sarah. "Conservative Activist Says Tea Party Movement Needs 'Reverence to God.'" *Religion Dispatches* (February 19, 2010): http://www.religiondispatches.org/dispatches/sarahposner/2287/conservative_activist_says_tea_party_movement_needs_%E2%80%9Creverence_to_god%E2%80%9D.

Posner, Sarah. "Glenn Beck's Social Justice Heresies." *Religion Dispatches* (July 19, 2010): http://www.religiondispatches.org/archive/politics/2988/glenn_beck%E2%80%99s_%E2%80%98social_justice%E2%80%99_heresies.

Posner, Sarah. "The Movie the Faithful Want You to See." *Politico* (March 9, 2014): https://www.politico.com/magazine/story/2014/03/persecution-cpac-movie-the-faithful-want-you-to-see-104471.

Posner, Sarah. "The Perry v. Bachmann Primary at Liberty University." *Religion Dispatches* (July 11, 2011): http://www.religiondispatches.org/dispatches/sarahposner/4841/the_perry_v._bachmann_primary_at_liberty_unversity/.

Posner, Sarah. "Religious Right Very Much Alive in Tomorrow's Elections." *Religion Dispatches* (November 3, 2009): http://www.religiondispatches.org/dispatches/sarahposner/1970/religious_right_very_much_alive_in_tomorrow%E2%80%99s_elections.

Posner, Sarah. "Rick Perry and the New Apostolic Reformation." *Religion Dispatches* (July 19, 2011): http://www.religiondispatches.org/dispatches/sarahposner/4874/rick_perry_and_the_new_apostolic_reformation/.

Posner, Sarah. "Tea Partiers and Religious Right Court at Values Voter Summit." *Religion Dispatches* (September 24, 2009): http://www.religiondispatches.org/archive/politics/1857/tea_partiers_and_religious_right_court_at_values_voter_summit.

Posner, Sarah. "Tea Party Leader Hates United Methodist Church." *Real Clear Religion* (December 20, 2010): http://www.tngovwatch.org/2010/12/my-dream-no-more-methodist-church.

Postman, Neil. *Amusing Ourselves to Death: Public Discourse in the Age of Show Business* (New York: Penguin, 1985).

Powell, Lewis Franklin, Jr. "Attack of American Free Enterprise System." *Thirteen*: https://www.thirteen.org/wnet/supremecourt/personality/sources_document13.html.

Powers, Annette. "Reform Movement Denounces Glenn Beck's Attack on Religious Values." *Progressive Jewish Voice* (February 23, 2011): http://blog.pjvoice.com/diary/316/reform-movement-denounces-glenn-becks-attack-on-religious-values.

Purdum, Todd S. "Beck and the Beast." *Vanity Fair* (May 2012): https://archive.vanityfair.com/article/2012/5/beck-and-the-beast.

Putnam, Robert and David E. Campbell. *American Grace: How Religion Divides and Unites Us* (New York: Simon & Schuster, 2012).

Rabey, Steve. "Exploring Glenn Beck's Beliefs." *Get Religion* (October 8, 2009): http://www.getreligion.org/2009/10/exploring-glenn-beck%E2%80%99s-beliefs/.

Rabin-Havt, Ari and Media Matters. *Lies, Incorporated: The World of Post-truth Politics* (New York: Anchor Books, 2016).

Rahe, Paul A. "How to Think about the Tea Party." *Commentary* 131:2 (February 2011).

Ramsey, Ross. "Green Days." *Texas Weekly* (July 20, 2009): https://texasweekly.texastribune.org/texas-weekly/vol-26/no-28/green-days/.

Rashid, Hussein. "Texas Man Indicted for Mosque Bomb Threat." *Religion Dispatches* (June 23, 2012): http://www.religiondispatches.org/dispatches/husseinrashid/6112/texas_man_indicted_for_mosque_bomb_threat/.

Rashid, Hussein. "Tea Party Organizes Islamophobic Hate Rally." *Religion Dispatches* (March 3, 2011): http://www.religiondispatches.org/dispatches/husseinrashid/4333/tea_party_organizes_islamophobic_hate_rally.

Rauch, Jonathan. "What's Ailing American Politics?" *The Atlantic* (July–August 2016), pp. 51–63.

Rawls, John. *Political Liberalism*, expanded ed. (New York: Columbia University Press, 2005).

Rawls, John. *A Theory of Justice* (Cambridge, MA: Harvard University Press, 1971).

Reed, Ralph. *For God and Country: The Christian Case for Trump* (Washington, DC: Regnery Publishing, 2020).

Reeves, Richard. *Infamy: The Shocking Story of the Japanese American Internment in World War II* (New York: Picador Books, 2016).

Rhodes, Stewart. "Open Letter to President Trump" (December 2020): https://oathkeepers.org/2020/12/open-letter-to-president-trump-you-must-use-insurrection-act-to-stop-the-steal-and-defeat-the-coup/.

Rich, Frank. "The Rage Is Not about Health Care." *New York Times* (March 27, 2010): https://www.nytimes.com/2010/03/28/opinion/28rich.html.

Richardson, Davis. "Lindsey Graham Wants You to Know He's a 'Single White Man' Who Doesn't Forget." *The Observer* (September 28, 2018): https://observer.com/2018/09/lindsey-graham-the-single-white-male-will-not-shut-up/.

"Rick Perry's Religious Revival Sparks a Holy War." *National Public Radio* (August 5, 2011): http://www.npr.org/templates/transcript/transcript.php?storyId=138995325.

Right Wing Watch Staff. "David Barton: Propaganda Masquerading as History." *Right Wing Watch* (September 2006): http://www.pfaw.org/media-center/publications/david-barton-propaganda-masquerading-history.

Right Wing Watch Staff. "The Right Wing Playbook on Anti-Muslim Extremism." *Right Wing Watch* (July 2011): http://www.pfaw.org/rww-in-focus/the-right-wing-playbook-anti-muslim-extremism.

Right Wing Watch Staff. "Texas Textbooks: What Happened, What It Means, and What We Can Do about It." *Right Wing Watch* (June 2010): http://www.pfaw.org/rww-in-focus/texas-textbooks-what-happened-what-it-means-and-what-we-can-do-about-it.

Ringer, Robert. "Is an Obama Dictatorship in the Air?" *World Net Daily* (April 11, 2012): http://www.wnd.com/2012/04/is-an-obama-dictatorship-in-the-air/.

Riordan, Kathy. "Understanding Glenn Beck." *Salon* (August 27, 2010). Archived at http://slinkingtowardretirement.com/?p=28101.

Ritchie, Lauren. "Tea Party Should Look Closely—at Itself." *Orlando Sentinel* (February 13, 2011).

Robin, Corey. *The Reactionary Mind: Conservatism from Edmund Burke to Donald Trump*, 2nd ed. (New York: Oxford University Press, 2017).

Rockmore, Ellen Bresler. "How Texas Teaches History." *New York Times* (October 21, 2015): https://www.nytimes.com/2015/10/22/opinion/how-texas-teaches-history.html.

Rodda, Chris. "David Barton Keeps Up His Lies at Glenn Beck Event." *Huffington Post* (June 1, 2010): http://www.huffingtonpost.com/chris-rodda/david-barton-glenn-beck_b_521485.html.

Rodgers, Daniel T. *Age of Fracture* (Cambridge, MA: Harvard University Press, 2011).

Roediger, David R. *How Race Survived U.S. History: From Settlement and Slavery to the Obama Phenomenon* (New York: Verso Books, 2008).

Rogin, Michael. *Ronald Reagan, the Movie and Other Episodes in Political Demonology* (Berkeley: University of California Press, 1987).

Romano, Andrew. "America's Holy Writ: Tea Party Evangelists Claim the Constitution as Their Sacred Text. Why That's Wrong." *Newsweek* (October 17, 2010).

Rorty, Richard. *Philosophy as Cultural Politics: Philosophical Papers* (Cambridge: Cambridge University Press, 2007).

Rose, Adam. "Sarah Palin Supports Dr. Laura via Twitter: 'Don't Retreat . . . Reload!'" *Huffington Post* (August 18, 2010): http://www.huffingtonpost.com/2010/08/18/sarah-palin-supports-dr-laura_n_687148.html.

Rosenbaum, David E. "THE NATION: Buchanan and the Convention; Now, This Is the Message from Our Tormentor." *New York Times* (March 17, 1996): https://www.nyti

mes.com/1996/03/17/weekinreview/the-nation-buchanan-and-the-convention-now-this-message-from-our-tormentor.html.

Rossinow, Doug. *Visions of Progress: The Left-Liberal Tradition in America* (Philadelphia: University of Pennsylvania Press, 2009).

Rothe, Anne. *Popular Trauma Culture: Selling the Pain of Others in the Mass Media* (New Brunswick, NJ: Rutgers University Press, 2011).

Rothstein, Richard. *The Color of Law: A Forgotten History of How Our Government Segregated America* (New York: Liveright Publishing, 2017).

Rovar, Chris. "Damaging Brooklyn ACORN Sting Video Ruled 'Heavily Edited,' No Charges to Be Filed." *New York Magazine* (March 2, 2010): https://nymag.com/intelligencer/2010/03/damaging_brooklyn_acorn_sting.html.

Rucker, Philip. "Perry Casts Himself as Spiritual, Says His Life Is Shaped by Faith." *Washington Post* (September 14, 2011): http://www.washingtonpost.com/politics/perry-casts-himself-as-anti-intellectual-says-his-life-shaped-by-faith/2011/09/14/gIQAUNgASK_story.html.

Ruprecht, Louis A. "It's Not a Tea Party, Silly, It's a Rebellion." *Religion Dispatches* (June 1, 2010): http://www.religiondispatches.org/archive/politics/2652/it%E2%80%99s_not_a_tea_party%2C_silly%2C_it%E2%80%99s_a_rebellion.

Russell, Thaddeus. *A Renegade History of the United States* (New York: Free Press, 2010).

Ryan, Alan. *On Politics: A History of Political Thought: From Herodotus to the Present* (New York: Liveright Publishing, 2012).

Safi, Omid. "What Islam Says and Doesn't Say about Democracy." *New York Times* (October 4, 2012): https://www.nytimes.com/roomfordebate/2012/10/04/is-islam-an-obstacle-to-democracy/what-islam-says-and-doesnt-say-about-democracy.

Sandage, Scott. *Born Losers: A History of Failure in America* (Cambridge, MA: Harvard University Press, 2005).

Sandel, Michael. *What Money Can't Buy: The Moral Limits of Markets* (New York: Farrar, Straus and Giroux, 2013).

"Sarah Palin: Dominionist Stalking Horse." *Daily Kos* (August 29, 2008): http://www.dailykos.com/story/2008/08/29/579213/-Sarah-Palin:-Dominionist-Stalking-Horse.

Savan, Leslie. "The Beck Identity, Supremacy, and Ultimatum." *The Nation* (June 28, 2011): http://www.thenation.com/blog/161691/beck-identity-supremacy-and-ultimatum.

Schaefer, Dominic O. *Religious Affects: Animality, Evolution, Power* (Durham, NC: Duke University Press, 2015).

Schaeffer, Frank. "Franklin Graham Is Big Time Religion's 'Donald Trump.'" *Huffington Post* (April 28, 2011): https://www.huffpost.com/entry/franklin-graham-is-big-ti_b_854758.

Schaeffer, Frank. "Understanding the 'Reason' Why Fundamentalists Must Exclude Gays (and Other 'Sinners')." *Huffington Post* (May 25, 2011): https://www.huffpost.com/entry/understanding-the-reason_b_628079.

Schencker, Lisa. "Politics, Religion Draw Utahans to Glenn Beck's Holy Land Events." *Salt Lake Tribune* (August 12, 2011): https://archive.sltrib.com/article.php?id=52355250&itype=CMSID.

Scherer, Matthew. *Beyond Church and State: Democracy, Secularism, and Conversion* (Cambridge: Cambridge University Press, 2015).

Schickler, Eric. *Racial Realignment: The Transformation of American Liberalism, 1932–1965* (Princeton, NJ: Princeton University Press, 2016).

Schilling, Chelsea. "Limbaugh: 'Obama Has Yet to Prove He's a Citizen.'" *World Net Daily* (July 20, 2009): http://www.wnd.com/2009/07/104595/.

Schmitz, Matthew. "Anti-sharia Laws Are Magic." *National Review* (June 18, 2012): http://www.nationalreview.com/corner/303135/anti-sharia-laws-are-magic-matthew-schmitz.

Schneider, Nathan. *Thank You, Anarchy: Notes from the Occupy Apocalypse* (Berkeley: University of California Press, 2013).

Schor, Elana. "Rev. Graham's Tour Evokes Evangelical Support for Trump." *Associated Press* (October 7, 2019): https://apnews.com/5cfef4941efd4d23b06f7b4db8ca546a?utm_campaign=SocialFlow&utm_medium=AP&utm_source=Twitter.

Schuessler, Jennifer. "And the Worst Book of History Is . . ." *New York Times* (July 16, 2012): https://artsbeat.blogs.nytimes.com/2012/07/16/and-the-worst-book-of-history-is/.

Schultz, Kevin M. *Tri-faith America: How Catholics and Jews Held Postwar America to Its Protestant Promise* (New York: Oxford University Press, 2011).

Schwartz, Ian. "Glenn Beck Chalkboard Lesson: Chicago Marxists Are Pulling the Strings on the Attack on Our Border." *Real Clear Politics* (April 11, 2019): https://www.realclearpolitics.com/video/2019/04/11/glenn_beck_chalkboard_lesson_chicago_marxists_are_pulling_the_strings_on_the_attack_on_our_border.html.

Segura, Liliana. "Racism Is the Prime Cause for the Debunked Obama Birth Certificate Conspiracy Theory." *Alternet* (July 28, 2009): https://www.alternet.org/2009/07/racism_is_the_prime_cause_for_debunked_obama_birth_certificate_conspiracy_theory/.

Seidel, Andrew. *The Founding Myth: Why Christian Nationalism Is Un-American* (New York: Sterling Publishing, 2019).

Self, Robert O. *All in the Family: The Realignment of American Politics since the 1960s* (New York: Hill & Wang, 2013).

Shane, Scott. "In Shariah, Gingrich Sees a Mortal Threat to U.S." *New York Times* (December 22, 2011): http://www.nytimes.com/2011/12/22/us/politics/in-shariah-gingrich-sees-mortal-threat-to-us.html?hp.

Shapiro, Ian. *Political Criticism* (Berkeley: University of California Press, 1992).

Shapiro, Ian. *Politics against Domination* (Cambridge, MA: Belknap Press of Harvard University Press, 2018).

Shapiro, Ian. *The Real World of Democratic Theory* (Princeton, NJ: Princeton University Press, 2010).

Sharlet, Jeff. "Is the Tea Party Becoming a Religious Movement?" *CNN* (October 27, 2010): http://www.cnn.com/2010/OPINION/10/27/sharlet.tea.party.evangelical/.

Sharlet, Jeff. *The Family: The Secret Fundamentalism at the Heart of American Power* (New York: Harper Perennial, 2009).

Sharlet, Jeff. "Through a Glass Darkly: How the Christian Right Is Reimagining U.S. History." *Harper's* (December 2006): http://harpers.org/archive/2006/12/through-a-glass-darkly/.

Sheedy, Matt. "Trump and the Tyranny of Authenticity." *Bulletin for the Study of Religion* (November 24, 2016): http://bulletin.equinoxpub.com/2016/11/trump-and-the-tyranny-of-authenticity/.

Shenk, David. *Data Smog: Surviving the Information Glut* (New York: HarperCollins, 1997).

Shermer, Michael. *The Believing Brain: From Ghosts and Gods to Politics and Conspiracies – How We Construct Beliefs and Reinforce Them as Truths* (New York: Henry Holt, 2011).

Shields, Jon A. *The Democratic Virtues of the Christian Right* (Princeton, NJ: Princeton University Press, 2009).

Shocket, Andrew M. *Fighting over the Founders: How We Remember the American Revolution* (New York: New York University Press, 2015).

Shugerman, Emily. "Who Was Roger Ailes and Why Was He So Controversial: Five Things You Need to Know." *The Independent* (May 18, 2017): https://www.independent.co.uk/news/world/americas/roger-ailes-who-was-he-fox-news-murdoch-trump-founder-life-career-what-you-need-to-know-a7743281.html.

Shupe, Anson. "The North American Anticult Movement." In James R. Lewis and Inga B. Toellefson, eds., *The Oxford Handbook of New Religious Movements*, vol. 2 (New York: Oxford University Press, 2016), pp. 117–142.

Singh, Nikhil. *Race and America's Long War* (Berkeley: University of California Press, 2017).

Sisco, Aila. "Glenn Beck Suggests It's Americans 'Duty to Overthrow' Government If Election Is 'Stolen' by Dems." *Newsweek* (November 4, 2020): https://www.newsweek.com/glenn-beck-suggests-its-americans-duty-overthrow-government-if-election-stolen-dems-1544994.

Skocpol, Theda and Vanessa Williamson. *The Tea Party and the Remaking of American Conservatism* (New York: Oxford University Press, 2012).

Slotkin, Richard. *Gunfighter Nation: The Myth of the Frontier in Twentieth-Century America* (Norman: University of Oklahoma Press, 1998).

Smith, Christian. *Christian America? What Evangelicals Really Want* (Berkeley: University of California Press, 2000).

Smith, Christian. *American Evangelicalism: Embattled and Thriving* (Chicago: University of Chicago Press, 1998).

Somanader, Tanya. "Tennessee Bill Dubs Sharia Law 'Treasonous,' Would Punish Muslims with 15 Years in Jail." *Think Progress* (February 23, 2011): http://thinkprogress.org/politics/2011/02/23/145849/tennessee-bill-dubs-sharia-law-treasonous-would-punish-muslims-with-15-years-in-jail/.

Sorkin, Amy Davidson. "Paul Ryan's Judeo-Christian Values." *New Yorker* (November 5, 2012): https://www.newyorker.com/news/amy-davidson/paul-ryans-judeo-christian-values.

Southern Poverty Law Center. "Oath Keepers." *SPLC*: https://www.splcenter.org/fighting-hate/extremist-files/group/oath-keepers.

Specter, Arlen. "Defending the Wall: Maintaining Church/State Separation in America." *Harvard Journal of Law & Public Policy* 18:2 (Spring 1995), pp. 575–590.

Stanley-Becker, Isaac. "'We Are Q': A Deranged Conspiracy Cult Leaps from the Internet to the Crowd at Trump's 'MAGA' Tour." *Washington Post* (August 1, 2018): https://www.washingtonpost.com/news/morning-mix/wp/2018/08/01/we-are-q-a-deranged-conspiracy-cult-leaps-from-the-internet-to-the-crowd-at-trumps-maga-tour/.

Starnes, Todd. "Roger Ailes Is Our Gun-Toting, Bible-Clinging Culture War General." *Fox News* (July 14, 2016): https://www.foxnews.com/opinion/starnes-roger-ailes-is-our-gun-toting-bible-clinging-culture-war-general.

Stein, Sam. "Sen. Graham Calls Beck 'a Cynic' and Birthers 'Crazy.'" *Huffington Post* (December 1, 2009): https://www.huffpost.com/entry/sen-graham-calls-beck-a-c_n_306434.

Stein, Stephen J. *The Shaker Experience in America: A History of the United Society of Believers* (New Haven, CT: Yale University Press, 1994).

Stenner, Karen. *The Authoritarian Dynamic* (Cambridge: Cambridge University Press, 2005).

Stephens, Randall J. and Karl W. Giberson. *The Anointed: Evangelical Truth in a Secular Age* (Cambridge, MA: Belknap Harvard University Press, 2011).

Stevens-Arroyo, Anthony. "Is Glenn Beck Preaching Mormon 'Restoration' Theology?" *The Washington Post* (August 31, 2010).

Stewart, Katherine. "A Christian Nationalist Blitz." *New York Times* (May 26, 2018): https://www.nytimes.com/2018/05/26/opinion/project-blitz-christian-nationalists.html?action=click&pgtype=Homepage&clickSource=story-heading&module=opinion-c-col-top-region&region=opinion-c-col-top-region&WT.nav=opinion-c-col-top-region.

Stewart, Katherine. "Betsy DeVos and God's Plan for Schools." *New York Times* (December 13, 2016): http://www.nytimes.com/2016/12/13/opinion/betsy-devos-and-gods-plan-for-schools.html.

Stieb, Matt. "Report: Domestic Terrorism Is Still a Greater Threat Than Islamic Extremism." *NY Magazine* (March 10, 2019): https://nymag.com/intelligencer/2019/03/domestic-terror-still-greater-threat-than-islamic-extremism.html.

Stock, Catherine McNicol. *Rural Radicals: Righteous Rage in the American Grain*, new ed. (Ithaca, NY: Cornell University Press, 2017).

Stout, Jeffrey. *Blessed Are the Organized: Grassroots Democracy in America* (Princeton, NJ: Princeton University Press, 2009).

Sullivan, Amy. "Does Palin Have a Pentecostal Problem?" *Time Magazine* (October 9, 2008): http://content.time.com/time/politics/article/0,8599,1848420,00.html.

Sullivan, Daniel. "Psychology Explains How Trump Won by Making White Men Feel Like Victims." *Quartz* (November 11, 2016): http://qz.com/834713/us-election-psychology-explains-how-donald-trump-won-by-making-white-men-feel-like-victims/.

Sullivan, Kevin. "Primed to Fight the Government." *Washington Post* (May 21, 2016): http://www.washingtonpost.com/sf/national/2016/05/21/armed-with-guns-and-constitutions-the-patriot-movement-sees-america-under-threat/.

Sullivan, Winnifred Fallers. "Religion Naturalized: The New Establishment." In Courtney Bender and Pamela E. Klassen, eds., *After Pluralism: Reimagining Religious Engagement* (New York: Columbia University Press, 2010), pp. 82–97.

Sullivan, Winnifred Fallers. *The Impossibility of Religious Freedom* (Princeton, NJ: Princeton University Press, 2005).

Sullivan, Winnifred Fallers, Elizabeth Shakman Hurd, Saba Mahmood, and Peter G. Danchin, eds., *Politics of Religious Freedom* (Chicago: University of Chicago Press, 2015).

Sunstein, Cass R. *Republic.com 2.0* (Princeton, NJ: Princeton University Press, 2007).

Tanenhaus, Sam. "The Architect of the Radical Right." *The Atlantic* (July–August 2017), pp. 40–43.

Tanenhaus, Sam. "In Texas Curriculum Fight, Identity Politics Leans Right." *New York Times* (March 21, 2010): https://www.nytimes.com/2010/03/21/weekinreview/21tanenhaus.html.

Tashman, Brian. "Anti-Muslim Extremist James Lafferty Angry He Was Quoted Verbatim." *Right Wing Watch* (February 15, 2012): http://www.rightwingwatch.org/content/anti-muslim-extremist-james-lafferty-angry-he-was-quoted-verbatim.

Taylor, Charles. *The Ethics of Authenticity*, reprint ed. (Cambridge, MA: Harvard University Press, 2018).

Taylor, Charles. *Modern Social Imaginaries* (Durham, NC: Duke University Press, 2004).

Taylor, Charles. *Sources of the Self: The Making of Modern Identity* (Cambridge, MA: Harvard University Press, 1992).
Taylor, Charles. "Western Secularity." In Craig Calhoun, Mark Juergensmeyer, and Jonathan Van Antwerpen, eds., *Rethinking Secularism* (New York: Oxford University Press, 2011), pp. 31–53.
Tebbe, Nelson. *Religious Freedom in an Egalitarian Age* (Cambridge, MA: Harvard University Press, 2017).
Teles, Steven M. *The Rise of the Conservative Legal Movement: The Battle for Control of the Law* (Princeton, NJ: Princeton University Press, 2010).
Tenety, Elizabeth. "Beck Sets Religious Tone for Restoring Honor Rally." *Washington Post* (August 28, 2010). Archived at https://www.democraticunderground.com/discuss/duboard.php?az=view_all&address=389x9031372.
Tenety, Elizabeth. "Mormon Glenn Beck: Hurricane Irene and East Coast Earthquake a 'Blessing' from God." *Washington Post* (August 26, 2011). Quoted at https://thinkprogress.org/bachmann-hurricane-was-a-message-from-god-to-washington-about-spending-updated-fb997f46a606/.
Terkel, Amanda. "Racist GOP Mailing Depicts Obama Surrounded by KFC, Watermelon, and Food Stamps." *Think Progress* (October 16, 2008): https://thinkprogress.org/racist-gop-mailing-depicts-obama-surrounded-by-kfc-watermelon-and-food-stamps-bc992e34c693/.
Texas Freedom Network. "Barton on the Issues." https://tfn.org/david-barton-watch/barton-on-the-issues/.
Thompson, Robert. "Jesus Is Glenn Beck's Worst Nightmare." *Chicago Tribune* (March 16, 2010): http://newsblogs.chicagotribune.com/religion_theseeker/2010/03/rev-robert-thompson-jesus-is-glenn-becks-worst-nightmare-.html.
Thrush, Glenn. "Obama Blasts Lies, Disinformation." *Politico* (August 29, 2010): https://www.politico.com/story/2010/08/obama-blasts-lies-disinformation-041575.
Tillison, Tom. "Taking a Close Look at the Tea Party." *Red State* (February 14, 2011): https://www.redstate.com/diary/tomtflorida/2011/02/14/taking-a-close-look-at-the-tea-party/.
Times Editorial Board. "The 'Birthright Citizenship' Debate." *Los Angeles Times* (October 26, 2014): https://www.latimes.com/nation/la-ed-birthright-citizenship-20141026-story.html.
Tinker, George E. *Missionary Conquest: The Gospel and Native American Genocide* (Minneapolis: Augsburg Fortress Press, 1993).
Tobin, Jonathan S. "Backlash against Muslims? Then Why Are Their Numbers Growing?" *Commentary* (May 3, 2012): http://www.commentarymagazine.com/2012/05/03/backlash-against-muslims-then-why-are-numbers-growing/.
Townsend, Kathleen Kennedy. "Sarah Palin Is Wrong about JFK, Religion and Politics." *Washington Post* (December 7, 2010): https://live.washingtonpost.com/outlook-kathleen-kennedy-townsend.html.
Travis, Shannon. "NCAA Passes Resolution Blasting Tea Party 'Racism.'" *CNN* (July 16, 2010): http://www.cnn.com/2010/POLITICS/07/14/naacp.tea.party/index.html.
Trinko, Katrina. "NPR Exec: Tea Partiers Are 'White, Middle-America, Gun-Toting Racists.'" *National Review* (March 8, 2011): https://www.nationalreview.com/corner/npr-exec-tea-partiers-are-white-middle-america-gun-toting-racists-katrina-trinko/.
Turner, Fred. *The Democratic Surround: Multimedia and American Liberalism from World War II to the Psychedelic Sixties* (Chicago: University of Chicago Press, 2013).

Underkuffler-Freund, Laura. "The Separation of the Religious and the Secular: A Foundational Challenge to First Amendment Theory." *William and Mary Law Review* 36:3 (March 1995), pp. 837–988.

Urban, Hugh B. *New Age, Neopagan, and New Religious Movements: Alternative Spirituality in Contemporary America* (Berkeley: University of California Press, 2015).

Van der Toorn, Jojanneke et al. "A Sense of Powerlessness Fosters System Justification." *Political Psychology* (February 2015), pp. 93–110.

Vance, J. D. *Hillbilly Elegy: A Memoir of a Family and Culture in Crisis* (New York: Harper Books, 2018).

Vick, Karl. "Among His Believers: With Glenn Beck's Posse in Jerusalem." *Time Magazine* (August 25, 2011): http://content.time.com/time/world/article/0,8599,2090 466,00.html.

Wajcman, Judy. *Pressed for Time: The Acceleration of Life in Digital Capitalism* (Chicago: University of Chicago Press, 2014).

Walker, Clarence. "'We're Losing Our Country': Barack Obama, Race & the Tea Party." *Daedalus* (Winter 2011), pp. 125–130.

Walsh, Joan. "Liz Cheney Defends the Birthers." *Salon* (July 23, 2009): https://www.salon.com/2009/07/23/liz_cheney_and_birthers/.

Walzer, Michael. *Interpretation and Social Criticism* (Cambridge, MA: Harvard University Press, 1987).

Warner, Michael. *Publics and Counterpublics* (New York: Zone Books, 2005).

Warner, Michael, Jonathan VanAntwerpen, and Craig Calhoun. "Editor's Introduction." In Warner, VanAntwerpen, and Calhoun, eds., *Varieties of Secularism in a Secular Age* (Cambridge, MA: Harvard University Press, 2010), pp. 1–31.

Warren, James A. *God, War, and Providence: The Epic Struggle of Roger Williams and the Narraganset Indians against the Puritans of New England* (New York: Scribner's Books, 2018).

Washington Post Editorial Board. "An Assault on Minority Voting Continues in North Carolina." *Washington Post* (August 12, 2018): https://www.washingtonpost.com/opinions/an-assault-on-minority-voting-continues-in-north-carolina/2018/08/12/b60ea52c-9a8f-11e8-8d5e-c6c594024954_story.html?utm_term=.4af0dc49792a.

Washington Post Staff. "Identifying Far-Right Symbols That Appeared at the U.S. Capitol Riot." *Washington Post* (January 15, 2021): https://www.washingtonpost.com/nation/interactive/2021/far-right-symbols-capitol-riot/.

Watt, David Harrington. *Antifundamentalism in Modern America* (Ithaca, NY: Cornell University Press, 2017).

Webley, Kayla. "Perusing the Glenn Beck University Curriculum Guide." *Time* (July 7, 2010): https://newsfeed.time.com/2010/07/07/glenn-beck-university/.

Weigel, David. "The Dark Horse." *Slate* (January 8, 2011): www.slate.com/id/2281516/pagenum/all/#p2.

Weimer, Adrian Chastain. *Martyrs' Mirror: Persecution and Holiness in Early New England* (New York: Oxford University Press, 2014).

Weisberg, Jacob. "The Tea Party and the Tucson Tragedy." *Slate* (January 10, 2011): https://slate.com/news-and-politics/2011/01/jared-loughner-gabrielle-giffords-and-the-tea-party.html.

Weiss, Jeffrey. "Religion and Sarah Palin—Her History." *Dallas Morning News* (September 28, 2008): https://www.dallasnews.com/news/faith/2008/08/29/religion-and-sarah-palin-her-history/.

Welch, Matt. "What the Left Can Learn from the Tea Party." *Reason* 43:5 (October 2011): https://reason.com/2011/09/06/what-the-left-can-learn-from-t/.

Wenger, Tisa. *Religious Freedom: The Contested History of a Religious Ideal* (Chapel Hill: University of North Carolina Press, 2017).

West, John G. "Intelligent Design and Creationism Just Aren't the Same." *Discovery Institute* (December 1, 2002): https://www.discovery.org/a/1329/.

Wexler, Jay. *Our Non-Christian Nation: How Atheists, Satanists, Pagans, and Others Are Demanding Their Rightful Place in Public Life* (Stanford, CA: Redwood Press, 2019).

"What Is Shariah?" *Defending Religious Freedom*: http://www.defendingreligiousfreedom.com/faqst/.

"Who Is the Tea Party? There's No Short Answer." *National Public Radio* (September 15, 2010). http://www.npr.org/templates/story/story.php?storyId=129874282.

Wilder, Forrest. "Rick Perry's Army of God: Is Rick Perry God's Man for President?" *Texas Observer* (August 3, 2011): http://www.texasobserver.org/cover-story/rick-perrys-army-of-god.

Wilentz, Sean. *The Age of Reagan: A History, 1974–2008* (New York: Harper Perennial, 2009).

Wilentz, Sean. *The Politicians and the Egalitarians: The Hidden History of American Politics* (New York: Norton, 2017).

Wilentz, Sean. *The Rise of American Democracy: Jefferson to Lincoln* (Norton, 2005).

Williams, Eric. *Capitalism and Slavery* (Chapel Hill: University of North Carolina Press, 1994).

Wilson, Bruce. "A Buzzflash Interview." *Buzzflash* (September 22, 2008): http://legacy.buzzflash.com/commentary/sarah-palins-extremist-religious-beliefs-the-republic-is-at-risk.

Wilson, Bruce. "Katherine Harris, Sarah Palin Linked to Same Prayer Warfare Network." *Talk to Action* (November 2, 2008): http://www.talk2action.org/story/2008/11/2/115526/519.

Wilson, Bruce. "Palin Movement Urges 'Godly' to 'Plunder' Wealth of 'Godless.'" *Talk to Action* (November 1, 2008): http://www.talk2action.org/story/2008/11/1/14522/8804/.

Wilson, Bruce. "Palin Linked to Second Witch Hunter." *Talk to Action* (October 24, 2008): http://www.talk2action.org/story/2008/10/24/125017/31.

Wilson, Bruce. "Palin's Prayer Leader Hinted Terrorist Attack Could Make Sarah President." *Talk to Action* (November 16, 2009): http://www.talk2action.org/story/2009/11/16/172837/58.

Winters, Michael Sean. "Glenn Beck's Rally and the Banality of Goodness." *National Catholic Reporter* (August 28, 2010): https://www.ncronline.org/blogs/distinctly-catholic/glenn-becks-rally-banality-goodness.

Wolf, Z. Byron. "Trump's One Piece of Gun-Related Legislation Undid Restrictions Aimed at Mental Illness." *CNN* (February 15, 2018): https://www.cnn.com/2018/02/15/politics/trump-gun-legislation-mental-health/index.html.

Wolfe, Alan. *One Nation, after All: What Middle-Class Americans Really Think about God, Country, Family, Racism, Welfare, Immigration, Homosexuality, Work, the Right, the Left, and Each Other* (New York: Viking Books, 1998).

Wolfe, Alan. *The Politics of Petulance: America in an Age of Immaturity* (Chicago: University of Chicago Press, 2018).

Wolin, Sheldon. *Democracy Incorporated: Managed Democracy and the Specter of Inverted Totalitarianism* (Princeton, NJ: Princeton University Press, 2017).
Wong, Scott. "Matthews: Tea Party Miners Would Have Killed Each Other." *Politico* (October 14, 2010): https://www.politico.com/story/2010/10/matthews-tea-party-miners-would-have-killed-each-other-043592.
Wood, Gordon S. *The Radicalism of the American Revolution* (New York: Vintage Books, 2011).
Wood, Graeme. "His Kampf." *The Atlantic* (June 2017), pp. 40–52.
Worthen, Molly. *Apostles of Reason: The Crisis of Authority in American Evangelicalism* (New York: Oxford University Press, 2016).
Wright, Robin. "Is America Headed for a New Kind of Civil War?" *New Yorker* (August 14, 2017): https://www.newyorker.com/news/news-desk/is-america-headed-for-a-new-kind-of-civil-war.
Wyler, Grace. "Rick Perry Defends Threatening Ben Bernanke." *Business Insider* (August 16, 2011): https://www.businessinsider.com/rick-perry-defends-bernanke-threats-says-hes-just-venting-frustration-2011-8.
"Wyoming Legislation Targets Islamic, International Law." *Casper Star-Tribune* (January 20, 2011): https://billingsgazette.com/news/state-and-regional/wyoming/wyoming-legislation-targets-islamic-international-law/article_abc1a5ff-96dc-5b2e-ab34-f46d4b68f0ec.html.
Wysong, Earl, Robert Perucci, and David Wright. *The New Class Society: Goodbye American Dream?* (Lanham, MD: Rowman and Littlefield Press, 2008).
Zaitchik, Alexander. "Glenn Beck Rises Again." *Salon* (September 23, 2009): https://www.salon.com/2009/09/23/glenn_beck_three/.
Zak, Dan. "Documentary Film '2016: Obama's America' Takes Michael Moore-esque Approach." *Washington Post* (August 27, 2012): https://www.washingtonpost.com/lifestyle/style/documentary-film-2016-obamas-america-takes-michael-moore-esque-approach/2012/08/27/3ecb5198-f07e-11e1-adc6-87dfa8eff430_story.html.
Zakaria, Rafia. "The Sharia Charade." *Dissent* (September 1, 2011): https://www.dissentmagazine.org/online_articles/the-sharia-charade.
Zernike, Kate. *Boiling Mad: Inside Tea Party America* (New York: Times Books, 2010).
Zernike, Kate, Carl Hulse, and Brian Knowlton. "At Lincoln Memorial, a Call for Religious Rebirth." *New York Times* (August 29, 2010): https://www.nytimes.com/2010/08/29/us/politics/29beck.html.
Zernike, Kate and Megan Thee-Brenan. "Poll Finds Tea Party Backers Wealthier and More Educated." *New York Times* (April 15, 2010): http://www.nytimes.com/2010/04/15/us/politics/15poll.html.

# Index

*For the benefit of digital users, indexed terms that span two pages (e.g., 52–53) may, on occasion, appear on only one of those pages.*

1619 Project, 144, 159–60
1776 Project, 159–60

*Abington v. Schempp*, 169–70
abortion, 92–93, 126, 146
Adler, Renata, 51–52
Adorno, Theodor, 51–52
Ahmed, Sarah, 55–56
Ailes, Roger, 40–41
Alien and Sedition Acts, 24
alt-right, 46, 131, 134, 136–37, 139, 212–13
American Center for Law and Justice, 171–72
Ames, Bill, 149–50
anti-Catholicism, 71, 74–75
anti-politics, 9, 44, 47–48, 61, 84–85, 136, 237–38
anti-statism, 9–10, 45, 70, 93, 94, 101–2, 106, 108–9, 111, 113, 118–20, 126, 128–29, 131, 136, 198–205, 216, 217–20, 229, 230–31, 233, 237
Antifa, 15–16, 45–46, 134, 178–79
apocalyptic thought, 4, 90, 202, 210–11
Arendt, Hannah, 110–11, 162
Atwater, Lee, 31
authenticity, 63, 64, 73–74, 79–80, 82–87, 202–3
authoritarianism, 15, 52–53, 111, 136, 201–2, 206–7, 213, 231, 234, 237, 241
*Avitzur v. Avitzur*, 182

B, Cardi, 52
Bachmann, Michelle, 120–21
Balmer, Randall, 96
Bannon, Steve, 136
Barton, David, 9–10, 21, 69, 142–60
Beck, Glenn, 5–6, 9–10, 60–61, 63–87

Beecher, Henry Ward, 216
Benjamin, Walter, 141–42, 157, 160
Benson, Ezra Taft, 67
Berlant, Lauren, 83–84, 133
Bernstein, Richard J., 240
Biden, Joe, 90, 211–12
birtherism, 104, 189, 190, 195–98, 199–200, 202–3, 211
birthright, 207–8, 210–11, 213
 *See also* citizenship
Black Lives Matter, 23–24, 81–82, 133, 134, 137, 178–79, 211–12, 226
Bob Jones University, 35
*Boerne v. Flores*, 171
Boogaloo Boys, 136–37
*Braveheart*, 128–29, 133, 134, 161
Brexit, 15
Brown, Wendy, 184, 224, 237
Bryan, William Jennings, 124
Buchanan, James, 31–32
Buchanan, Pat, 24–25
Buckley, William F., 30–31
Burke, Edmund, 12
Bush, George W., 89–90, 229
Butler, Anthea, 98

Capitol insurrection, 3, 9, 93, 105–6, 108–9, 113, 133, 134–35, 137, 203, 206–7, 211–12, 241
captivity narratives, 173
Carter, Jimmy, 89–90
Castelli, Elizabeth, 171
Cheney, Liz, 195
Christian Broadcasting Network, 3, 40, 125
Christian nationalism, 2, 158–60, 163, 211–12

Christian Right, 38–39, 40, 41
Church of Jesus Christ of Latter-Day Saints (LDS), 66, 67, 68, 74–75, 77
citizenship, 2, 6, 8–10, 11–13, 16, 17–18, 19–20, 21, 26–27, 34, 36–37, 43–44, 47, 50, 52, 54, 55–57, 58, 62, 64, 65, 73, 82–83, 90, 106, 108, 109, 114–15, 125, 130–31, 133, 137, 139, 141, 145, 158, 160, 163, 181, 183, 184–88, 192–93, 207–8, 209–12, 213, 215, 216, 218–30, 231, 232–33
civic education, 155–56, 162–63, 184–85, 186, 187, 225, 226, 227, 232
civil rights movement, 16–17, 73, 124, 193
civil society, 26–27, 107, 130, 140, 226–30
Clinton, Hillary, 49, 89–90, 98, 114–15
Coates, Ta-Nehisi, 198
Colbert, Stephen, 74
Coles, Romand, 241
communism, 28–29, 32, 67, 125
conspiracy theory, 1–2, 3, 4, 29–30, 49, 54, 56–57, 59, 60–61, 63, 77, 82, 108, 158–59, 175, 177, 194–95, 196–97, 198, 200–5, 206–7, 208
constitution (United States), 26, 27–28, 67, 110–11, 119–20, 124, 130, 145, 165, 167–68, 174, 180, 185, 192, 207–8
Constitution Party, 171, 199
Coughlin, Father Charles, 70, 75
Couric, Katie, 96
Covid-19, 2, 199, 207
critical race theory, 23, 141–42
culture wars, 2, 7, 9, 17, 24–25, 37–38, 100–1, 155–56

D'Souza, Dinesh, 194
Dawkins, Richard, 18, 55, 103–4
De Landa, Manuel, 52
De Tocqueville, Alexis, 71–72
De Vos, Betsy, 158–60
*Defense of the suburbs*, 61–62, 138
Dewey, John, 110–12
Didion, Joan, 51–52
Dionysius, 25
Discovery Institute, 150–51, 158
Dobbs, Lou, 195, 198
Dominionism, 97–98, 103–4, 106, 126–27
Drake, Wiley, 195

Du Bois, W.E.B., 164
Duke, David, 209
Dyer, Mary, 25

Eco, Umberto, 157
education, 101, 141–64
Eisenhower, Dwight, 29
Eliade, Mircea, 25
Elshtain, Jean Bethke, 89–90
Emerson, Ralph Waldo, 56, 73
*Employment Division v. Smith*, 171
*Engel v. Vitale*, 169–70
Enlightenment, 6, 110–11
Epistemology of Favorites, 54, 57
Euripides, 25
evangelicals, 23, 42, 43, 91, 148
*Everson v. Board of Education*, 170

Fairness Doctrine, 53–54, 232
Falwell, Jerry, 72
federalism, 27
*Federalist Papers*, 26, 71–72, 130
feminism, 92–93
Fishkin, James, 114
Floyd, George, 23, 138
Flynn, Michael, 176–77
Force Act, 192–93
Foucault, Michel, 177
Fox News, 3, 40–41, 66, 78, 79
Foxe, John, 25–26
Framers (United States), 26–27, 31–32, 34, 70–72, 84, 94, 110, 119–20, 123–24, 130, 145, 149, 168, 169, 180
Frankfurt School, 51–52
Freedom Caucus, 3
Freud, Sigmund, 12, 191
Friedan, Betty, 13–14
Friedman, Milton, 93, 217–18
Fugitive Slave Law, 192–93
Fukuyama, Francis, 53–54

Gaffney, Frank, 175, 176, 177–78
Gates, Jr., Henry Louis, 197
Gayan, Joe, 199–200
Gibson, Mel, 128–29
Giddens, Anthony, 158
Gingrich, Newt, 39–40, 128, 147–48, 151, 176–78

Girard, René, 12
Gitlin, Todd, 13
Goldwater, Barry, 30–31, 33, 34, 119
Gotcha epistemology, 5, 97, 122
Graham, Franklin, 3
Graham, Lindsey, 44–45, 74, 208
Greene, Marjorie Taylor, 99
guns, 93–94, 126, 127, 128, 190, 198–204, 206, 209–10, 211–13

Habermas, Jürgen, 106–7, 110–11, 186
Hagee, John, 77–78
Hargis, Billy James, 29–31
Harrington, Michael, 13–14
Harris, Kamala, 212
Harris, Mark, 23
Harris, Sam, 3, 18
Havel, Václav, 86, 87
Hawthorne, Nathaniel, 57, 61
Hayek, Friedrich, 217–18
Heidegger, Martin, 83–84
Herberg, Will, 28
Heritage Foundation, 32–33
Heston, Charlton, 206
Hill, Henry, 217
historical nostalgia, 124–25, 127–28, 131, 132–33, 139, 146, 160–61
Hitchens, Christopher, 18
Hofstadter, Richard, 74, 122, 155
human rights, 13–14, 17–18, 19, 20, 113, 221, 223, 224, 225, 232, 234, 235–36, 239–40
Hunter, James Davison, 7–8, 24–25
Hutchinson, Anne, 25

Identity Evropa, 136–37, 143
identity politics, 13, 69–70, 206–7
Indian Removal Act, 24
internet, history of, 53–54
Iranian Revolution, 173
Islam, 166, 172–81, 184, 196–97, 198, 207

Jackson, Andrew, 45, 231
Jefferson, Thomas, 26
Jeffress, Robert, 153–54
Jews for Social Justice, 70
John Birch Society, 29, 67

Judeo-Christian Council for Constitutional Restoration, 171
Justice Sunday, 145, 171

Kaepernick, Colin, 1
Kavanaugh, Brett, 44–45, 183–84
Kazin, Michael, 27
Kedrosky, Paul, 59
Kendi, Ibram X., 192
Kennedy, John F., 29
Kidd, Thomas, 123, 147
Kierkegaard, Søren, 83–84
King, Larry, 195
King, Jr., Martin Luther, 193
King, Steve, 23, 208, 210
Ku Klux Klan, 193, 208–9

LaHaye, Tim, 35–36
LaPierre, Wayne, 203
Lasch, Christopher, 13
law, 165–88
Lefort, Claude, 238
legitimacy, 2, 36, 79–80, 82, 108, 109–10, 129, 139, 186–87, 202–3
Leininger, James, 101, 149
*Lemon v. Kurtzmann*, 170
Lepore, Jill, 123
Lessig, Lawrence, 114
liberal democracy, 2, 11–12, 13, 27, 70–71, 82–87, 102–3, 104–10, 184, 192–93, 215, 216–20, 223–24, 236
liberation theology, 74–75
Life as Action Movie (LAAM), 11, 15–16, 24–25, 54, 62, 76, 79, 83–84, 90, 101, 109–10, 114–15, 123–24, 126, 128, 129–30, 133, 134, 135–36, 138, 144, 148, 154, 155, 158, 160, 163, 176–77, 183, 184, 195–96, 201–2, 203–4, 206, 211–12, 216, 217, 238
Lilla, Mark, 13
Limbaugh, Rush, 40–41, 195
Lippmann, Walter, 111–12
Locke, John, 25
Long Con of Anti-politics, 12–13, 15–16, 52–53, 55, 90, 105–6, 108, 140, 158–59, 168–69, 213, 216–20, 230–31, 233
Lowe, Gail, 150
Lynn, Barry, 103

Maher, Bill, 3, 74
majoritarianism, 8, 59, 107, 116, 119, 122, 150
Manafort, Paul, 31
Manuel, David, 142
Marr, Timothy, 173
Marshall, Peter, 142
Martyrs, 5–7, 8, 9, 10, 18, 20, 21, 23, 28, 31–32, 34, 37–38, 40–41, 42, 45–46, 63, 66–67, 72–73, 81–82, 83–84, 90, 94–95, 98, 105–6, 112, 113, 127, 128, 129, 139, 141–42, 152, 159, 160–61, 169, 170, 178–79, 182–83, 186, 195–96, 202–5, 210, 211–12, 215, 218–19, 235, 241
masculinity, 44–46, 129, 137, 139
McCain, John, 91
McCarthy, Joseph, 30–31, 143
McClure, Kirstie, 181–82
*McCollum v. Board of Education*, 169–70
McLeroy, Don, 149–50, 151, 152, 153, 154
McLuhan, Marshall, 51–52
Meier, Richard, 58
Melville, Herman, 88
militarism, 44–46, 191, 231
  *See also* guns
Miller, Stephen, 177, 178–79, 212–13
Mills, C. Wright, 56
modernity, 64–65
Moore, Roy, 167
Moral Majority, 39–40
Mulholland, Thomas, 56–57

*National Review*, 30–31
National Rifle Association, 66–67, 203, 206
neoliberalism, 218–19, 232–33, 234, 235–36
New Deal, 28, 32, 75, 217–18
New Left, 44
New Right, 31, 35–36, 193
Nietzsche, Friedrich, 14, 73–74, 82–83, 84, 157, 206
Nixon, Richard, 34–35, 38
Norton, Anne, 157
Nugent, Ted, 203–4
Nutter, Warren, 31–32

Oath Keepers, 200–2, 211–12
Obama, Barack, 3, 9–10, 15, 29, 63, 65–66, 68–69, 71, 73, 90, 94, 101–3, 118, 121, 126, 130, 173–74, 175, 177, 189–92, 193–207, 210, 211–12
Occupy Wall Street, 118, 120–21, 133
O'Reilly, Bill, 198
Orlie, Melissa, 85
Orwell, George, 17–18, 220–21

Palin, Sarah, 9–10, 72–73, 88–89, 91–100, 107–8
Palmer raids, 24
Pence, Mike, 3, 5–6, 21, 55–56, 136
Pentecostalism, 91–92, 96, 97
Perry, Rick, 88–89, 100–4, 149–50
Persecution complexes, 15, 25, 102–3, 140, 143, 144, 164, 187, 191, 202–3, 220, 235
*phronesis*, 87
Pipes, Daniel, 175, 176
"Pizzagate," 49
pluralism, 16–17, 26–28, 46–47, 222
political representation, 88–89, 90, 92, 94–95, 96, 98–100, 101, 104–15
Pompeo, Mike, 136
Popper, Karl, 240
populism, 16–17, 30–31, 33, 113, 118, 119–20, 122, 126–27, 131
Postman, Neil, 52
postmodernism, 37
Powell, Lewis F., 32
progressivism, 67–68, 70–71, 77–78, 81–82
Protestant common schools, 141
Proud Boys, 45, 136–37
public participation, 117, 119, 121–25, 126, 127, 129, 130–40, 226–30, 234, 238
Puritans, 24, 25–26

QAnon, 21, 22, 29, 30, 135–36

racism, 73–74, 126, 137, 146, 164, 191–95, 206–7, 210, 211–13, 231
Rauch, Jonathan, 113
Rawls, John, 186, 240

Reagan, Ronald, 15–16, 33, 36–37, 38, 89–90, 132, 143, 175
Reed, Ralph, 3, 39–40, 103–4
Reid, Harry, 208
"religious bigotry," 8, 20
religious freedom, 19
Religious Freedom Restoration Act (RFRA), 171
*Reynolds v. United States*, 170–71
Rhodes, Stewart, 200–2, 211–12
Robertson, Pat, 39–40, 43, 171–72, 177, 178
Robison, James, 100
*Roe v. Wade*, 35, 170
Romney, Mitt, 103

Salem witch trials, 25
Sandage, Scott, 217
Sandel, Michael, 232–33
Sanders, Bernie, 114–15
Santelli, Rick, 117
Schlafly, Phyllis, 149–50, 151–52
Schlessinger, Laura, 95
Schmitt, Carl, 136
*The Secret*, 206
secularism, 64, 97, 123–24, 143, 169, 170, 182
Sekulow, Jay, 171–72
self-limiting politics, 19, 44, 125, 162, 163, 187–88, 222–25, 239–41
Shapiro, Ian, 85, 86–87, 238–39
sharia law, 9–10, 172–82
sincerity, 64, 65
Skousen, Cleon, 67, 68, 75
Smith, Christian, 18–19, 42–43
social media, 1–2, 4, 29, 38, 51–52, 53–54, 55–56, 57, 59–61, 88, 92–93, 107–8, 109, 134, 138, 210–11, 231
Southern Poverty Law Center, 201
"Southern Strategy," 31
Spencer, Richard, 136–37, 139, 212–13
Spencer, Robert, 175, 176, 178–79
Stewart, Jon, 74
Stone, Roger, 31
Strauss, Leo, 68, 217–18
Strong, Josiah, 208

Students for a Democratic Society (SDS), 33
Sullivan, Winnifred Fallers, 167, 182

Taitz, Orly, 195
Taylor, Charles, 64, 65
Tea Act, 117
Tea Party, 9–10, 60–61, 67–68, 101, 117–40
Texans for Governmental Integrity, 149
Texas Restoration Project, 101, 102
Thistlethwaite, Susan, 98
Three Percenters, 200–1
tolerance, 11–12, 135, 184, 214–15, 216, 224–25, 240
trauma, 13–14
Trilling, Lionel, 64
Trump, Donald, 2, 3, 7–8, 9, 44–45, 60–61, 68–69, 71–73, 76, 79–81, 90, 101, 104, 105–6, 112, 113–14, 121–22, 127, 137, 138, 139, 146, 159, 174–75, 178–79, 180–81, 183–84, 189–90, 198–99, 201–2, 203–4, 206–7, 208, 209, 211–12, 213, 219–20, 231, 235, 240–41
Turning Point USA, 3, 143, 159–60

United States Naturalization Law, 192

victimhood, 13–14, 34, 41, 47, 73–74, 81–82, 137
virality, 60–61
Von Mises, Ludwig, 217–18
Voting Rights Act, 192

Walker, Edwin, 29–31
Wallace, George, 31
Wallbuilders, 142, 143, 144–45
"war on Christmas," 1
"war on terror," 6, 46
Wars of Religion, 11–12
Weber, Max, 136
Welch, Robert, 29–30
Weyrich, Paul, 193
the Whirl, 4–5, 9–10, 29–30, 50–62, 76–77, 78, 83–84, 86, 87, 91, 95, 109–10, 126–27, 137–38, 153, 158, 178–79, 184, 187, 189, 193–94, 195–96, 223–24, 227, 241

Whistleblowers, 5–7, 9, 10, 18–19, 21, 33, 42–43, 55, 74–77, 79, 82, 89, 92, 96–100, 105, 112, 113, 120, 121–23, 126–27, 145, 146–49, 152, 153–55, 158, 160–61, 162–63, 179–81, 182–83, 186, 201–2, 206, 210, 215, 218–19, 229, 191–95, 199, 206–7, 210, 212–13, 231
White, Hayden, 162
White Citizens Council, 193
whiteness, 9, 44–45, 47, 72–73, 131–32, 134–35, 136, 137, 139, 191–95, 199, 206–7, 210, 212–13, 231
Williams, Roger, 25
Winthrop, John, 6, 25

xenophobia, 104, 122–23, 131–32, 202

Yerushalmi, David, 175, 176–78

Zakaria, Rafia, 182